W9-CEV-405

Families and Teachers of Individuals with Disabilities

Families and Teachers of Individuals with Disabilities

Collaborative Orientations and Responsive Practices

Dorothy J. O'Shea

Slippery Rock University of Pennsylvania

Lawrence J. O'Shea

Educational Services, Intermediate Unit 1, Coal Center, Pennsylvania

Robert Algozzine

University of North Carolina–Charlotte

Diana J. Hammitte

Georgia Southern University

BISHOP MUELLER LIBRARY
Briar Cliff University
SIOUX CITY, IA 51104

Allyn and Bacon

Boston • London • Toronto • Sydney • Tokyo • Singapore

Senior Editor: *Virginia Lanigan*
Vice President and Editor-in-Chief: *Paul A. Smith*
Series Editorial Assistant: *Jennifer Connors*
Senior Marketing Manager: *Brad Parkins*
Production Editor: *Christopher H. Rawlings*
Editorial-Production Service: *Omegatype Typography, Inc.*
Composition and Prepress Buyer: *Linda Cox*
Manufacturing Buyer: *Suzanne Lareau*
Cover Administrator: *Brian Gogolin*
Electronic Composition: *Omegatype Typography, Inc.*

Copyright © 2001 by Allyn & Bacon
A Pearson Education Company
160 Gould Street
Needham Heights, MA 02494

Internet: www.abacon.com

All rights reserved. No part of the material protected by this copyright notice may be reproduced or utilized in any form or by any means, electronic or mechanical, including photocopying, recording, or by any information storage and retrieval system, without written permission from the copyright owner.

Between the time Website information is gathered and published, some sites may have closed. Also, the transcription of URLs can result in typographical errors. The publisher would appreciate notification where these occur so that they may be corrected in subsequent editions. Thank you.

Library of Congress Cataloging-in-Publication Data

Families and teachers of individuals with disabilities: collaborative orientations and responsive practices / Dorothy J. O'Shea...[et al.].
    p. cm.
    Includes bibliographical references and index.
    ISBN 0-205-15131-0 (alk. paper)
    1. Special education teachers—United States.   2. Parent-teacher relationships—United States.   3. Family—United States.   4. Handicapped students—United States—Family relationships.   I. O'Shea, Dorothy J.

LC3969 .F34 2001
371.9—dc21

BK
$21.50

00-036182

Printed in the United States of America

10 9 8 7 6 5 4 3 2 1   05 04 03 02 01 00

43706791

In memory of our daughter and sister,
Kelly Elizabeth O'Shea,
a brief life, a profound influence

Dorothy J. O'Shea
Lawrence J. O'Shea
Lindsay J. O'Shea
Christopher L. O'Shea

To my family, growing each day—
Kate, Kathryn, Michael, Mackenzie, Mike, and Andrea

Bob Algozzine

In memory of my late parents, James and Geneva Hammitte,
and my beloved brother, Jim, who left us all too soon; and to my sister,
Pat, and my wonderful extended family (particularly the Baird
clan)—they taught me what family is all about

Diana J. Hammitte

Contents

Preface

Families and Teachers of Individuals with Disabilities highlights the ways families and teachers operate when they interact with and are responsive to each other. The text focuses on family information for novice teachers, who often require practical information on ways to understand and deal with family issues that are new and complex to them. The text's premise is that schools can better understand and support family members when new teachers possess professional knowledge of, and skills to work effectively with, students' families.

Most education texts and tertiary instruction exclude family research and practical family strategies. Teachers receive limited information on family development, professional family services, and family strategies, and little, if any, information on advice and strategies to better meet the needs of their diverse students and students' families (Wardle, 2000). Some special education texts deal with school-based collaboration services, addressing methods of helping teachers collaborate with other teachers on instructional and management issues that indirectly affect students' families (e.g., Rosenberg, O'Shea, & O'Shea, 1998). Some texts describe legislation and directions for teachers dealing with families involved in early intervention (e.g., Bailey & Wolery, 1992). Some review the planning of family goals for legal procedures (e.g., Olson & Kwiatkowski, 1992). Other texts show the professional how to understand families' needs for empowerment as seen from family members' viewpoints (Turnbull & Turnbull, 1997; Turnbull, Turnbull, Shank, & Leal, 1995; Singer & Powers, 1993).

This text, however, is written specifically for new teachers in general education and special education, and it focuses on family data that concern teachers' roles with diverse families. The rationale for the text is that most new teachers have little or no background on family research, family assessment, or effective family–teacher practices. Nonetheless, many new teachers express concern that they are unsure of their roles with family members. Our premise in writing this text is that when new teachers receive data to build their family knowledge and skill base, they have opportunities to integrate key, practical skills. As they gain knowledge, teachers begin to feel more confident in working with the families of their diverse student populations. Having a resource that shows new teachers how to recognize family needs, capitalize on family strengths and interests in education issues, and promote family–professional interactions helps them create and maintain a high level of competence and integrity in their work with the families of all students with disabilities.

Acknowledgments

We gratefully acknowledge our families for their support and patience and the contributing authors for their excellent work. Also, we appreciate the valuable feedback provided by our reviewers—Scott Sparks, Ohio University; and Vicki Stayton, Western Kentucky University. We are grateful to the editors and staff at Allyn and Bacon, especially Virginia Lanigan, Ray Short, and Jennifer Connors. These individuals kept us on task and helped us to complete our project. Finally, we would like to thank the families and teachers with whom we work. Their collaborative orientations and responsive practices, on behalf of all individuals with disabilities, have inspired us.

References

Bailey, D. B., & Wolery, M. (1992). *Teaching infants and preschoolers with disabilities* (2nd ed.). New York: Merrill.

Olson, J., & Kwiatkowski, K. (1992). *Planning family goals: A systems approach to the ISFP.* Tucson, AZ: Communication Skill Builders.

Rosenberg, M., O'Shea, L. J., & O'Shea, D. J. (1998). *Student teacher to master teacher.* Upper Saddle River, NJ: Prentice Hall/Merrill.

Singer, G. H. S., & Powers, L. E. (Eds.) (1993). *Families, disability and empowerment: Active coping skills and strategies for family interventions.* Baltimore: Paul H. Brookes.

Turnbull, A. P., & Turnbull, H. R. (1997). *Families, professionals, and exceptionality: A special partnership.* Upper Saddle River, NJ: Prentice Hall/Merrill.

Turnbull, A. P., Turnbull, H. R., Shank, M., & Leal, D. (1995). *Exceptional lives: Special education in today's schools.* Englewood Cliffs, NJ: Prentice Hall/Merrill.

Wardle, F. (2000). Children of mixed race—no longer invisible. *Educational Leadership, 57* (4), 68–72.

About the Contributors

Dorothy J. O'Shea (Ph.D., Penn State University) has worked in the special education field for over twenty-eight years. Her roles include college professor, special education teacher, public school administrator, and family liaison. Currently, she is professor of special education at Slippery Rock University of Pennsylvania. Additionally, she serves as a special education due process hearing officer in Pennsylvania. Dr. O'Shea has received both state and federal grants on the preparation and training of special educators, general educators, and school administrators. As principal investigator, her funded research has targeted teachers' inclusion training, certification of teachers and supervisors, and teachers' collaboration with diverse families of students with special needs. Dr. O'Shea's published research includes over sixty manuscripts and textbooks in the special education field. Her recent research targets teacher–family collaborations, instructional strategies, special educator standards and assessments, and legal issues in special education. She is on the editorial board of several special education journals.

Lawrence J. O'Shea (Ph.D., Penn State University) is the assistant executive director, of Intermediate Unit 1, a regional educational service agency serving the school districts, families, and students of southwestern Pennsylvania. Formerly, Dr. O'Shea was professor and chair of the Department of Exceptional Student Education, Florida Atlantic University. Additionally, he was lecturer at the University of Queensland's Schonell Special Education Research Centre in Brisbane, Australia. He served as assistant professor and associate professor in the Department of Special Education, University of Florida. Dr. O'Shea has received numerous state and federal training grants in teacher education and professional development, family collaboration, and educational technology. In addition to publishing over sixty manuscripts, he is the coauthor of *From Beginning Teacher to Master Teacher: A Practical Guide for Education of Students with Special Needs* and *Learning Disabilities: From Theory Toward Practice,* both published by Prentice-Hall.

Bob Algozzine (Ph.D., Penn State University) is professor in the Department of Educational Administration, Research, and Technology at the University of North Carolina at Charlotte. Formerly, Dr. Algozzine was on the faculty of the Department of Special Education, University of Florida. He has been a special education teacher and college professor for more than thirty years. His research interests include family collaborations, inclusion strategies, teacher preparation and development, and educational technology. In addition to having published many special education texts and journal articles, he serves on the editorial board of numerous professional journals. Currently, Dr. Algozzine is the coeditor of *Exceptional Children,* published by the Council for Exceptional Children. His recent research has been published in the *High School Journal,* the *Journal of Educational Research,* and *Teacher Education and Special Education.*

Diana J. Hammitte (Ed.D., University of Alabama) is associate professor and program coordinator of the Special Education Program, Georgia Southern University, Statesboro, Georgia. Dr. Hammitte teaches and advises at the undergraduate, master's, and education specialist levels, primarily in the areas of mild disabilities, language development, and collaboration. She is a copartner in Project SCEIs (Skilled Credentialing for Early Interventionists), a collaborative grant across the state of Georgia which is involved in training personnel for early intervention. Formerly, she served in the Department of Exceptional Student Education, Florida Atlantic University, where she taught all of the preschool special education courses. Her research interests include teacher education and professional development, early childhood special education, and families of individuals with disabilities.

The Contributors

Kate Algozzine (M.S., University of Florida) is director of tutoring and client services for ABC Tutoring and Educational Services in Charlotte, North Carolina. She has taught students with disabilities and gifts and talents in Florida and North Carolina, has been a freelance writer, and has taught college courses in English composition, gifted education, and gifted curriculum. She has published academic articles on a variety of topics, including effective teaching, improving classroom behavior, and assisting parents in monitoring medications.

David Bateman (Ph.D., University of Kansas) is a former teacher of students with learning disabilities and mental retardation. His research interests lie in special education legal and policy issues. Recently, he has published articles on preparing for due process hearings; chapters on the impact of litigation on interventions; legal issues in special education; and a book, *A Principal's Guide to Special Education,* published by the Council for Exceptional Children. Currently, he is the chair of the Department of Special Education, Shippensburg University of Pennsylvania, where he teaches course work related to learning disabilities and inclusion. He also serves as a special education due process hearing officer in Pennsylvania.

Pegi S. Davis (M.Ed., University of Cincinnati) received her master's in early childhood special education and high risk families, and she is currently working as a consultant in this area. She has considerable experience in the area of assessment in general, and in family assessment in particular. Ms. Davis's professional experience includes work as a clinical diagnostician, where she completed assessments for children with suspected developmental delays, and work as a family assessment counselor. She has taught several courses at the university level, including courses in survey of early childhood, families, and assessment. Her current research interests include at-risk families and assessment of families and children. Ms. Davis has published and presented work in the areas of families, children, and assessment.

Stephanie L. Kenney (Ed.D., Western Michigan University) is assistant professor in the Special Education Program, Georgia Southern University, Statesboro, Georgia. Dr. Kenney's primary responsibilities include instruction in teacher preparation at the initial undergraduate level and graduate instruction for master's-level students, primarily in the area of behavior disorders. Additionally, she co-coordinates and supervises student teaching for new special educators at Georgia Southern University. Her research interests include teacher and family collaboration, and portfolio assessment in teacher preparation. Her interests also include the etiologies and interventions involved when individuals display behavioral disorders.

Adrienne P. Lancaster (M.A., California University of Pennsylvania) has worked for twenty-nine years in the special education field. Her roles include special education teacher, special education supervisor, and family liaison. In her current duties as administrative assistant in the Department of Educational Services, Intermediate Unit 1, she oversees family–teacher collaboration and parent training development. Currently, she is completing her doctoral studies in the Interdisciplinary Educational Leadership Program, Duquesne University. She serves as adjunct assistant professor in the Department of Special Education, California University of Pennsylvania, where she prepares new teachers in multicultural awareness and family diversity. Her research interests include multicultural education, teachers' professional development, and family support and collaboration.

Paul L. Lancaster (M.Ed., California University of Pennsylvania) is on the faculty of the Department of Special Education, California University of Pennsylvania. Currently, he is enrolled as a doctoral student in the Higher Education Administration Program, West Virginia University. He has been involved in the special education field for over thirty-five years. His focus is on the preparation and development of new teachers in both special education and general education. His research interests include multicultural education, family diversity, behavioral support, and higher education administration.

M. J. LaMontagne (Ed.D., University of Cincinnati) is assistant professor in the Special Education Program, Georgia Southern University, Statesboro, Georgia. Currently, she teaches in the special education teacher preparation program at both the undergraduate and graduate levels. She teaches courses in language development, collaboration, and preschool endorsement. She also co-coordinates and supervises the student-teaching experience at Georgia Southern University. A primary interest in teaching for Dr. LaMontagne is in educational assessment issues in special education. Her research interests focus on early childhood special education, teacher–family collaboration, and portfolio assessment in teacher preparation. Currently, Dr. LaMontagne is involved in a state-level preparation grant related to preschool special education services in the state of Georgia.

D. Michael Malone (Ph.D., University of Georgia) is associate professor in early childhood education at the University of Cincinnati. He received his master's and doctoral degrees in child and family development from the University of Georgia, with areas of emphasis in developmental disabilities and assessment. Dr. Malone has an extensive background in interdisciplinary program development and personnel preparation. His professional background is in early childhood development and intervention, team processes, observational assessment, and interdisciplinary program development and personnel preparation. Dr. Malone has developed and taught a number of courses in early childhood education and early intervention, has directed and served on state and federal systems change grants, and has published and presented numerous works related to early childhood intervention.

Vicki A. McGinley (Ph.D., Temple University) is a faculty member in the Department of Early Childhood and Special Education at West Chester University of Pennsylvania. Dr. McGinley has extensive experience working with children with disabilities and their families through classroom teaching, administration, and consultation. Additionally, she served as a behavioral consultant in the southeastern region of Pennsylvania prior to her position at West Chester University; and she served as adjunct faculty member for Rowan University, the University of Delaware, Temple University, and Holy Family College. Her research includes the study of pragmatic communication with children with behavioral disorders. Dr. McGinley serves as a hearing officer in the states of Pennsylvania and Delaware and serves on a number of professional boards.

Sylvia Nassar-McMillan (Ph.D., University of North Carolina at Greensboro) is currently teaching in the Department of Counseling, Special Education, and Child Development at the University of North Carolina at Charlotte. She has been a counselor and college professor in public schools, community agencies, and universities in Michigan, Illinois, Tennessee, and North Carolina. Articles she has written are used in counselor education courses around the country. She has been a featured speaker at local, state, national, and international professional conferences and is widely recognized as an expert on the special needs of diverse student and client populations.

Betty M. Nelson (M.Ed., Old Dominion University) currently is on the special education faculty, of Georgia Southern University, Statesboro, Georgia. Her primary teaching responsibilities include special education policies and procedures, and collaboration with families and other professionals. In her duties at Georgia Southern University, Ms. Nelson is responsible for placement and supervision of special education practicum students. Prior to her appointment at Georgia Southern, she coordinated preschool special education services in South Georgia. Additionally, Ms. Nelson completed five years as director of a service program for people with mental retardation in Virginia.

Janet E. Riley (M.Ed., Slippery Rock University of Pennsylvania) is special education teacher, at Allegheny Intermediate Unit, Pittsburgh, Pennsylvania. Her role is initial contact and liaison for families of young children with disabilities. Ms. Riley provides diagnostic services to children and families enrolled in Allegheny Intermediate Unit's Project Dart. Project Dart is an early intervention program that assesses and places children three to five years of age in appropriate special education programs and services available within Allegheny County. Her research interests include early intervention, teacher collaboration, and families of individuals with disabilities.

Kim Stoddard (Ph.D., University of Florida) is associate professor at University of South Florida–St. Petersburg. In addition to teaching special education courses, Dr. Stoddard coordinates the student teaching experiences for beginning special educators. Her work with a school university partnership program resulted in the creation of a unique teacher education program that merges special education and general education teaching experiences and certification. Dr. Stoddard also is the principal investigator for a school–university partnership grant, focusing on improving preservice and in-service professional education practices for special and general education teachers. Her research interests include inclusive practices and the improvement of teacher education through school–university partnerships.

Greg Valcante (Ph.D., University of Florida) serves as director for the University of Florida's Center for Autism and Related Disabilities (CARD). Additionally, Dr. Valcante serves as coprincipal investigator on the Family Training Research Project, funded by the National Institutes of Health. He also serves as the project family liaison for the Autism Inclusion Project, funded by the United States Department of Education's Office of Special Education Programs. His research interests include inclusive practices, instructional strategies, autism, and family training and collaboration.

Families and Teachers of Individuals with Disabilities

Introduction to Families

Part 1 introduces new teachers to important family concepts and terminology as teachers begin their collaborative orientations and responsive practices with families. The chapters in Part 1 help new teachers to identify important family compositions, statistics, assessment issues, and effective practices. Part 1 illustrates various family household members new teachers encounter in modern schools, and issues teachers face as they work with students' families.

The authors examine teachers' work with family members initially by introducing various family research as the basis for family issues, policies, procedures, and programs. The authors highlight major research findings on pertinent family variables, including data on family definitions and characteristics, compositions, social–cultural diversity, and high risk factors.

Chapter 1: Why Learn about Students' Families?

Chapter 1 provides the rationale for new teachers' understanding of a collaborative orientation and responsive practice perspective regarding families. The chapter provides a blueprint for the text orientation in that the authors introduce teachers' professional roles with families. In keeping with a practical position, Dorothy J. O'Shea and Lawrence J. O'Shea provide key concepts for new teachers' knowledge and application of family work. These authors argue that historical thinking by professionals espousing varied family views reflects how many family programs are shaped by economical, legal, political, and social forces. Accordingly, they examine why it is necessary for teachers to understand the many economical, legal, and socictal factors explaining and helping to predict historical changes in family norms, family values, family programs, and childrearing practices.

O'Shea and O'Shea define collaborative orientations and responsive practices, making the point that family definitions and resulting characteristics from family research set the stage for professionals' views of family assessments, interventions, and practices. They introduce relevant family resources and services new teachers can use to support their understandings of and work with diverse families.

Chapter 2: Typical Families: Fact or Fiction?

Dorothy J. O'Shea and Janet E. Riley examine varied family compositions and households. These authors examine characteristics and statistics of modern families, introducing family diversity issues across households, with their resulting effects on school issues.

O'Shea and Riley identify and illustrate various perspectives on the conceptualization of "family" and resulting family characteristics. They differentiate characteristics of the concept "family," offering practical suggestions for teachers seeking to promote effective home–school partnerships. Finally, they summarize relevant family resources and services helping new teachers to understand important actions pinpointing what is known currently about the concept of family and teachers' roles.

Chapter 3: Families of Students from Diverse Backgrounds

Today, many individuals come from diverse family backgrounds and communities. Most students' homes and communities represent diverse economical or cultural settings and offer a variety of social and religious environments. Hence, all new teachers face diversity in what students bring to schools from homes and communities. Home values, family traditions, and social–cultural experiences are important considerations in teachers' effective family practices.

Dorothy J. O'Shea and Lawrence L. Lancaster address the importance of families' diversity and social–cultural influences in Chapter 3. They discuss how families' changing demographics influence images of American life. These authors discuss resulting changes in public school demographics and implications for school curricula. They further examine practical implications of families' cultural, economical, social, political, religious, and social diversity that have an impact on schools and classrooms.

These authors identify positive impacts of diversity in efforts to encourage new teachers to value and respect the richness and variety of their students' family backgrounds and communities. For example, they discuss such activities as how teachers can use social–cultural diversity to enhance school offerings. Teachers can support diverse students by integrating family traditions and customs into classroom activities. Teachers can invite family members to volunteer for school activities or to share family traditions, as a means of encouraging family input. Accordingly, in this chapter the authors identify the benefits of family diversity and vast social–cultural influences on our public schools. They end the chapter with practical suggestions, questions, family resources, and services useful to new teachers.

Chapter 4: Family Characteristics That Place Children at Risk

Authors in Chapter 4 target the statistics and characteristics of high-risk families and how teachers can help. The pertinent variables of high-risk families include those conditions that teachers, administrators, social workers, health care workers, counselors, psychologists, or other professionals fear may set the stage for school or social failure without family intervention. Thus, Stephanie L. Kenney and M. J. LaMontagne describe factors that new teachers should recognize in high-risk families (e.g., parents with limited education, families living in poverty, and so forth). They describe effects these factors may have on family functioning and children's readiness for school opportunities. They stress research and practical suggestions, analyzing those families professionals believe are likely to contain children who experience persistent school or social failure.

Chapter 5: Family Assessment

The authors in Chapter 5, Pegi S. Davis and D. Michael Malone, provide research and practice implications related to family assessment issues. These authors target family assessment variables from economical, educational, medical, psychological, and social arenas. They view various assessment devices used historically with families, summarizing the benefits and difficulties of assessing families as a heterogeneous population. The authors make the point that in order for teachers' work with families to be effective and meaningful, professionals must be willing to personalize their efforts with each unique family, and view family needs and strengths individually.

Importantly, in this chapter, the authors address controversial family assessment issues, such as the lack of appropriate family assessment instruments, and needs/strengths of families that are not necessarily measurable. They address the types and formats of assessment information teachers need to understand in dealing with local, state, and federal policies concerning family intervention programs. Finally, they summarize relevant family assessment resources and services helping teachers to understand and support important family issues.

1

Why Learn about Students' Families?

Dorothy J. O'Shea

Lawrence J. O'Shea

Chapter Objectives _____

In this chapter we will

- Describe what Chapter 1 introduces that is important to the reader
- Describe the text assumptions
- Discuss why students' families are of interest to teachers
- Introduce key concepts related to collaborative orientations and responsive practices
- Discuss strategies for collaborative orientations and responsive practices
- Provide a list of relevant resources and materials
- Summarize important chapter themes

> *Chris is the youngest family member of three children. He is the only boy in the family. He has been identified with a specific learning disability and requires special education. He is served in general education and has an Individualized Education Program (IEP). Chris's parents and teachers report that Chris initially is shy and reserved, especially outside his family members. However, once he feels comfortable, his parents and teachers find that Chris is active and responsive. He has close friends, displaying an appropriate attitude during school and home activities. His teachers say that Chris can be a class leader. However, his teachers and parents observe that Chris needs to be prodded into completing his classroom and homework assignments. When he does turn in work, it is often sloppy and disorganized, has many errors, or is incomplete. Chris's parents are working closely with his sixth-grade team of teachers to help him learn the responsibility of tackling and completing assignments. His*

parents tell his team that Chris competes often with his sisters, but seemingly wants to do well for them. While they don't always agree on similar approaches when helping Chris, his parents and teachers agree that they can help Chris most effectively when they work together to understand how Chris operates in his two most important settings: his home and his school.

All teachers, like Chris's sixth-grade team, face complex concerns, tasks, and questions as they interact with family members. This text's philosophy is to introduce new teachers to family knowledge and practical skills needed to work with students' families. The text design and organization address families of students who are at risk for or who have identified special needs, such as Chris and his family who are briefly described in the opening vignette.

Because many of these students currently receive educational services alongside their peers without special needs, we address how teachers in general education and special education work with students' families. We will be describing how teachers and families can work together to provide students the greatest possible access to the general education curriculum as a means for improving students' educational results (Office of Special Education Programs, 1999). It is our premise that awareness of families can support all new teachers' collaborative, responsive practices. Collaborating and responding together can help students, such as Chris, reap the benefits of general education curriculum access, and set the stage for continued success across the home and school.

Chapter 1 introduces the text and establishes a framework for the philosophy of working with families that we espouse in this text. This chapter provides the road map for the reader and sets the stage for an understanding of issues that have an impact on new teachers' family roles. The rationalization of why learning about students' families is important underscores the chapter's orientation to new teachers' work with families. The chapter discusses why students' families are of interest to novice teachers and examines a rationale for teachers' application of family knowledge and skills as more and more students at risk for or with identified disabilities receive services in the general education curriculum.

The text rationale emerges from major philosophical and logistical changes resulting from Public Law (P.L.) 105-17, the 1997 Individuals with Disabilities Education Act (IDEA), that established new provisions designed to improve outcomes for students with disabilities (U.S. Department of Education, 1997). These include requirements that students with disabilities be included in state- and district-wide assessments, that students' Individual Education Programs (IEPs) address issues of students' access to general education curricula, and that states establish performance goals and indicators for students with disabilities (Hehir, 1999; McLaughlin, 1999; Ysseldyke & Olsen, 1999).

Because the integration of students with disabilities in general education is inherent in the reauthorized law (Office of Special Education Programs, 1999), all teachers must be well versed in the professional knowledge, skills, and dispositions needed in the delivery of programs and services to students at risk for or with disabilities within the general curriculum, and the important work teachers do with families to ensure appropriate services. Our text provides guidelines on new teachers' work with families to meet changes in the delivery of programs and services.

We also deal with providing a framework of partnering with families. As such, the chapter presents and defines key concepts related to collaborative orientations and responsive practices. We stress information on professional organization guidelines regarding knowledge, skills, and dispositions that teachers should have for working with families. Although other organizations are important (e.g., National Association for the Education of Young Children, Association for Childhood Education International), the most influential organization in addressing new teachers' roles and responsibilities, and the needs of families with individuals at risk for and individuals with identified special needs, is the Council for Exceptional Children (CEC). Thus, we describe the most recent work advocated by CEC on teachers' roles with families (CEC, 2000). New teachers will develop and maintain healthy relationships with family members based on mutual respect for roles in achieving benefits for the individual with special needs.

Text Assumptions

The text's philosophy emphasizes the need for new teachers to learn about their students' families and to be willing partners with family members. In order to apply the text philosophy to real life, important assumptions are inherent throughout our text. These assumptions are important dispositions new teachers will possess in order to work effectively with students' families: (a) linking family issues and educational provisions, (b) understanding family–teacher issues to initiate and maintain collaborative orientations and responsive practices, (c) using family research in practical applications, (d) anticipating family member questions and professional answers, and (e) identifying and promoting family resources. Each of these is explained here and will be illustrated throughout the text.

Linking Family Issues and Educational Provisions

Family issues and educational provisions link closely: Greater resources now and in the future will be directed toward family–school services. As general education classrooms become more inclusive, strategies for providing access to the general education curriculum are vital so that students with identified problems are actively involved and progress within the curriculum in these classrooms (Hehir, 1999). Nonetheless, school professionals and students' families are important links in the success of students' opportunities in general education curricular issues. This means that school professionals cannot ignore their students' home lives as they determine with families how best to instruct students in the general education curriculum. Most students bring their family issues with them to class and take their school issues home.

Accordingly, effective family work in today's schools is done by teachers dialoguing and sharing with parents or guardians and other professionals. Because families often are the most significant influence throughout the lives of students and are in the best position to mold students' future, understanding what family issues students bring to or take from school, family perceptions of students' needs, and multiple family views shared by varied professionals is vital to all new teachers' work. New teachers increasingly must be prepared to anticipate that students will bring home issues to the classroom (and classroom issues to the home). Teachers also must work with families and with others who may not hold the same views on what the issues are or the possible solutions. New teachers can be most effective, however, when they solve educational dilemmas together with family members and other school professionals.

Understanding Family–Teacher Issues

Each chapter contains a number of specific family–teacher issues germane to the chapter content that illustrates families and school professionals. These family–teacher issues appear in boxes with the title "Collaborative Orientations and Responsive Practices." Issues in some chapters focus on the family from specific age ranges of the child. Other chapters view teachers' actions with others from cross-disciplinary perspectives. The issues relate to one or more of the following themes:

- Family members identify issues that students bring to or take from the home or school; families need school help.
- School professionals identify issues that students bring to or take from the home or school; schools need family help.
- Issues create a problem to be solved, underscoring multiple solutions from varied perspectives.

Thus, throughout the text, we embed boxes on educational issues that reflect how teachers and families collaborate and respond. Each of the boxes emphasizes important teacher and family actions:

- Teachers teaming with parents, guardians, or other family members on family issues
- Teachers teaming with other school professionals on family issues
- Parents or guardians communicating to teachers or other professionals about students' educational needs
- Teachers, other school professionals, and parents, guardians, or other family members seeking solutions to complex educational problems

Using Family Research in Practical Applications

Every text chapter shows how family research is valuable in practical applications. Some chapters rely on specific family theories or approaches to rationalize suggested practices. The text, however, takes an eclectic approach to promoting family research and theory; there is no unique family theory on which the text is based. Many theories and varied research orientations contribute to knowledge of and skills in family issues and the resulting supports, resources, and services evolving when families contain a member with special needs. However, each chapter sets the stage for practical suggestions by opening with a vignette or case study. These and other vignettes and case studies within each chapter illustrate family stories and discussions in that they support professional practices through documented research themes.

Anticipating Family Member Questions and Professional Answers

Each chapter contains a "Family Member Question" section designed to inform new teachers of on-the-spot decisions that families, classroom teachers, and other school professionals face. These represent typical questions family members might ask during school conferences. The chapters offer brief answers teachers might give in response to those questions.

Questions and answers relate to the type, level, and location of educational services required by students and important to the family.

Identifying Family Resources

Finally, each chapter provides important resources for families and school professionals. Names, addresses, and phone numbers of specific agencies and organizations can help new teachers to understand and demonstrate a supportive approach to their work with family members. When teachers seek, locate, and distribute available resources and services to concerned families about a particular issue, new teachers create with family members an underlying bond to facilitate students' opportunity for school and home success.

Why Are Students' Families of Interest to Teachers?

Over the span of the last few decades the makeup of the family has shifted greatly. Many teachers used to work primarily with students who came from traditional families—families that had both a mother and father. Today, however, teachers deal with students who come from single-parent families, extended families, residential or foster placements, and even from the streets. Learning about and partnering willingly with families can help new teachers to become more understanding of where their students come from each morning, and where or with whom students interact when they leave school.

As they learn more about their students' families, some teachers will find themselves at a disadvantage because parents or guardians are not available to help when problems occur in the classroom. Schere (1998) reported that when families live unmoored from their communities, students more than ever need significant adults to anchor them. The most significant adults, aside from the child's parents or guardians, are classroom teachers. Some teachers interpret varied parental actions as parents or guardians who are unresponsive, unavailable, or unable to work collaboratively with teachers. In a worst-case scenario, some teachers perceive that the family does not even care about the child or his or her school progress.

Given the plethora of skills that effective teachers must possess to have and develop family-teacher relationships, new teachers must learn the issue of time management very quickly when they work with parents or family members who may not be as responsive as some school professionals would like. On the other hand, some parents may report that their child's teachers are not doing all they can to support their child in the most conducive manner. Some professionals may argue that a reason why many parents do not assume more active roles in their children's education is because families say they don't have the time. The effects of moving that time burden to teachers (and other school professionals), most likely already overburdened, is one possible interpretation for inactivity by more passive teachers.

Unfortunately, teachers today face accusations of often ignoring the special concerns of—even the existence of—their students, especially multiracial and multiethnic students. Today's teachers must ensure that services they provide honor and include all of their students (Wardle, 2000). When teachers strive to work collaboratively with their students' families in honoring and including students, results are astonishing. Teachers begin to understand such influences as students' cultural and linguistic diversity. They see value and importance in students' family makeup and household arrangements. They can understand similarities and differences between single-race minority students and issues faced by students of mixed heritage. They can put into perspective the age or household expectations parents hold for their children. Teachers begin to integrate how best to support variations in beliefs, traditions, and values across cultures or homes and within society, and the effect of the relationships among their students, the students' families, and school professionals (CEC, 2000). Such integration helps to support students' access in the general education curriculum and life-long, ongoing opportunities for learning.

Hatch (1998) reported that better school safety, increased funding, and even higher student achievement performances result when teachers engage their students' families and community members to support students. Giannetti and Sagarese (1998) concurred by reporting that disinterested family members can be turned into collaborative partners with teachers. Important to new teachers' attempts to engage their students' families and turn disinterested family members into collaborative partners, are relevant factors regarding why learning about students' families is important. These include:

- Teacher efforts can influence inactive family members to be concerned about the child's schooling and to begin to assume more active roles in children's progress.
- Although parents or other family members may react negatively when they sense that inactive or overburdened teachers do not respond to family needs, new teachers will be most effective when they work to understand families and partner with them.
- Students benefit from collaborative attempts and responsive actions when there is a match between school professionals' and family efforts.

These factors underscore the importance of families to teachers and the reciprocal importance of teachers to families. Table 1.1 illustrates the factors.

Key Concepts Related to Collaborative Orientations and Responsive Practices

As illustrated by the family examples presented throughout this text, there are several key concepts important to new teachers' understanding of and their work with students' families. These concepts underscore their terms: *families, collaborative orientations, responsive practices,* and *contemporary teachers.*

Families

As detailed in Chapter 2, families represent a diverse group of students' households and living arrangements. Students come from a multitude of family settings (Giangreco,

TABLE 1.1 *Importance of Families to Teachers and Teachers to Families*

Importance of Families to Teachers	*Importance of Teachers to Families*
• Families provide teachers with personal information that may explain why certain student behaviors are occurring in the classroom.	• Teachers provide families with documented evidence of their children's progress and successes.
• Families provide background information and medical histories to teachers and to the school that may help teachers understand why a student behaves or learns in certain ways.	• Teachers can help families become more actively involved in their children's education.
• Families can reinforce directives that teachers give their students, especially on homework assignments.	• Teachers can help families determine where a student's interests lay so that appropriate long-term goals can be established.
• Families can support teachers, such as through serving as chaperones or volunteers in the classroom.	• Teachers can teach and reinforce social skills that are needed for students to be successful, contributing members of the communities in which families live.
• Families can help teachers determine students' interests so that long-term education or vocation goals can be established.	• Teachers can let families know whether their children exhibit inappropriate behaviors or academic needs in the classroom.
• Families can relay information to teachers about which types of discipline and learning strategies work best with their children.	• Teachers can locate and disseminate important educational and community data to help families stay current and knowledgeable about opportunities available for children.
• Families can help teachers find out what each student's strengths and needs are so that appropriate instructional goals are created.	• Teachers can lend a helping hand, a supportive ear, and a friendly face to all families served.

Cloninger, Dennis, & Edelman, 1994). Students have home lives entailing settings that may house the father-mother-child or children arrangement; persons related by a sharing process; descent groups (e.g., father-mother-child-grandparents); adoptive families; one-parent families (e.g., single mother with child or children, single father with child or children); remarriage families (e.g., father-mother-stepchildren); or foster families (e.g., homes for homeless children). Community factors highlight family makeup and underscore cultural, economic, ethnic, religious, and social opportunities students experience in their homes.

When new teachers understand students' backgrounds—their households, living arrangements, important family members, and the multitude of familial and community factors that define who students are and where students originate—teachers set the stage for recognizing and valuing significant individuals in students' lives.

Collaborative Orientations

Collaborative orientations imply that teachers do not operate in isolation. Teaching is about relationships among individuals. Teachers create conducive, responsive learning settings by the ways they interact with their students and by the interactions they encourage among their students and significant individuals in students' lives. Teachers supporting collaborative orientations are sensitive to family needs and strengths, while accepting home, community, and cultural norms. They teach based on what they know about their students and the learning opportunities (both within and outside of school) each student receives. Such actions encourage opportunities for learning in the general education curriculum that can be extended to students' home lives and future adult successes.

Accordingly, collaborative orientations imply that all of the students' teachers strive to understand what families expect, want, and are willing to contribute to the educational process. And, as discussed in Chapters 10 and 11 of this text, teachers who recognize, value, and act on a multitude of family perspectives with other professionals support their students' families. As mutual support increases, teachers and parents can expect that students' access to general education curricular issues will flourish, and that students will begin to generalize their successes to life beyond the classroom.

Responsive Practices

New teachers offering responsive practices recognize a relationship in what and how they teach. They realize the effects of their communication skills. They learn when to act and how to act appropriately. As effective teachers, such professionals are proactive in relationships with families. For example, by being responsive, these teachers strive actively to avoid negative stances. They seek to understand how and why families operate. They observe families. Such teachers are familiar with home or community opportunities framing the family and the family programs and services that may be available. In fact, these teachers use past knowledge of family programs and services, shaped by economical, legal, political, and social forces, to respond to school challenges and any home decisions they make with family members.

Many varied factors explain and help to predict historical changes in family norms, values, programs, and child-rearing practices. Equally important is the evolution of teachers' roles with families. New teachers operating with responsive practices make use of research and varied family theories that have been prominent throughout the past century.

The term *theories* rests on a set of assumptions that are evaluated and tested within a given context over time (O'Shea, O'Shea, & Algozzine, 1998). When they make use of relevant theories and evolving research helping to distinguish family emphases prominent during the twentieth century, new teachers can relate more readily to a general rationale for many practices associated with conceptualizing family. Additionally, as they examine various family research influencing social leaders and policy makers in the twenty-first century, new teachers may reflect on their evolving roles with family members, and fit the evolution of research and practical strategies into comprehensive and convincing accounts of the families with whom they now work.

Accordingly, the various family definitions and resulting characteristics from historical family research and theories set the stage for important family assessments, interventions, and practices. As discussed in varying reports throughout this text, teachers strive to demonstrate sensitivity to differences in family structures and backgrounds when they value and respect the social, ethnic, and cultural backgrounds of their students and the professionals working with students and families. Teachers operating in responsive practices are knowledgeable of, respect, and value varied family research shaping current family support and services.

This text provides many family views evolving from important theories on how various individuals perceive families, researchers studying family life, strategies when a family member displays school problems, and experiences families face as students age. Table 1.2 provides examples of prominent family theories. The table names the theory, prominent family themes, and examples of teachers' evolving roles with families of students with special needs. Chapters throughout the text illustrate theories in greater detail using research and practical applications.

Effective teachers, operating with responsive practices, use their knowledge of family research to work collaboratively and responsively. When confronting complex educational decisions, new teachers can help families pinpoint resources, priorities, and issues in relationship to their children's school success. Unfortunately, sometimes misinterpretation of culturally linked behaviors places diverse students and their families in conflict with expectations for social behaviors between home and school (Delgado-Rivera & Rogers-Adkinson, 1997). And, as is evident in Chapter 3, there is a historical persistence of the disproportionate representation of ethnic minority students in special education (Artiles, Aguirre-Munoz, & Abedi, 1998). Nonetheless, despite barriers to family understanding prominent in this country, teachers operating in responsive practices are knowledgeable of ways and means to remediate or extinguish negative practices. Such teachers face controversial issues and trends with contemporary teaching.

Contemporary Teachers

Contemporary teachers are those teachers who understand and confront contemporary issues and the influence teachers have on students and families. The effects of teachers' understanding of contemporary issues and their relationship to families hold enormous implications to support students' school success.

Thus, in order to make the general education curriculum come alive, effective new teachers show that they realize how teaching really is about caring and supporting. Such teachers are not afraid of changing based on students and classrooms. They demonstrate that they enjoy the process of working with parents or guardians to tackle complex decisions that influence whether a student succeeds. A big challenge in many general education classrooms housing students with disabilities, for instance, is how and when to accommodate students' specific learning or behavioral needs. An astute teacher would build into the curriculum multiple representations of information being presented. The teacher would ask family members how the family perceives the child to learn best and under what conditions. This teacher would ask parents or guardians opinions of multiple or modifiable means of expression and control. The teacher would also seek input from family members on modifiable means of motivating and engaging their child (Research Connections, 1999); that is, the teacher may not know what the family wants, but would ask questions to clarify the family's position on how family members want to promote curricular materials or homework tasks based on what they know about the child. The teacher would work with the family to design motivating projects that go hand in hand between

TABLE 1.2 *A Listing of Family Theories Indicating Family Themes and Implications for Teachers' Evolving Roles with Families of Students with Special Needs*

Family Theory	Family Themes	Implications for Teachers' Evolving Roles with Families of Students with Special Needs
Psychoanalytical Theory	Significance of parent–child relationships during the first years of life on an individual's subsequent personality functioning Personality is a physical energy system, and at various points within the system the force of energy prompts human behavior Ontogenic growth proceeds through psychosexual development in biologically determined stages Associated personality and psychosexual development	Teachers' roles did not deal directly with the whole family and did not deal directly with the family with a special needs member Those having a psychoanalytical view reiterated that family problems resulted from traumatic early childhood and unresolved conflicts of the id, ego, and superego
Behavioral Theory	Operant conditioning: increase in response frequency if followed by reward or reinforcement and less frequent if followed by punishment Classical conditioning and operant conditioning: targeted family neuroses, psychoses, mental disabilities, and conduct problems Behavior modification: applied conditioning principles in therapeutic and educational settings between parents and children	Most teachers did not deal directly with families. However, those holding learning-based approaches in family problems emphasized structuring the family environment, observational learning, and the family's social behaviors Educational programs for families evolved into parent training and parent–child behavior modification programs. Teachers started to participate in acquiring information about parent training programs
Family Development Theory	Families develop and change over time Families have developmental stages Within predictable cyclical stages, families have adjustments and transition periods	Teachers began to acquire information on life span needs across family developmental stages Many teachers' roles included recognizing that families with special needs members have additional tasks and adjustments Individual family factors helped to determine the adaptation that family members make in transitions Families with special needs members often have family stress. Teachers began to receive information on family developmental issues

(continued)

TABLE 1.2   Continued

Family Theory	Family Themes	Implications for Teachers' Evolving Roles with Families of Students with Special Needs
Family Systems Theory	Family support and self-advocacy are relevant family variables The family is an integrated system with unique characteristics, strengths, and needs Family members are interdependent	Teacher textbooks began to stress that all family members, their transitions, and their ability to cope are important (e.g., not just those of the special needs member) Teachers' roles included increasing attention focused on self-actualizing and empowering all family members
Phenomenology Theory and Ways of Knowing	Personal experiences are paramount and hold meaning in everyday life People construct their own social worlds Families hold a variety of meaning to various people	Teachers' roles included acquiring and using the knowledge that social and cultural variables affect diverse family members' identify and interactions Social and cultural variables were thought to affect interactions and individuals reactions to interactions

Source: Adapted from *Learning Disabilities: From Theory Toward Practice*, by O'Shea, L. J., O'Shea, D. J., and Algozzine, B., 1998, New York: Merrill-Prentice Hall.

classroom and home expectations. Together, the teacher and family might select quality materials that integrate effective instructional design.

Teachers offering contemporary teaching seek to understand each child's family and the roles teachers play with family members. Effective teachers integrate contemporary issues with concepts on family views and values in how, why, and what teachers can offer to students and their families. Such teachers set out to be positive with their students' families. They target students' needs, strengths, preferences, and interests by observing, asking, and working with, not separate from, families. Teachers use team building to support students' educational and psychological development from both the school and home perspective, without judging family priorities.

Contemporary teachers are aware of issues confronting students' families. Accordingly, in line with phases of general and special education reform issues, data on reshaping the provisions of students' "free appropriate public education" and students' "least restrictive" placements receive professional attention by contemporary teachers (Hart & Risley, 1995; Yell & Shriner, 1997). New teachers work with families to analyze and pinpoint placement and curricular issues that support students' inclusion. Such teachers use varied assessments, materials, and techniques to help diverse students achieve. They are proactive in supporting and managing students' academic and behavioral needs and strengths in the most appropriate setting (Epstein, Kutash, & Duchnowski, 1998; Lopez-Reyna & Bay, 1997).

However, teachers understanding families' wants and desires in decision making, planning, assessment, and service delivery view the student in the context of the whole family. That is, a contemporary teacher respects families' choices regarding their participation levels in their children's programming (Cohen & Spenciner, 1998; Falvey, 1995; Ferguson, 1995; Forman & McCormick, 1995; Franklin, 1996; Turnbull & Turnbull, 1997; Turnbull, Turnbull, Shank, & Leal, 1995).

Thus, new teachers who understand contemporary teaching are those who view each student and his or her family as important. Such teachers do everything possible in their own classrooms to individualize family services appropriate to the child and his or her significant family members. They offer students and families choices. When they set up family conferences to discuss general education access or important assessment concerns, such teachers discuss families' expectations for the students' needs. They talk about and personalize families' strengths and needs. They ask families whether they want school or community support—teachers don't impose it. Teachers seek to include families by accepting and valuing differences the families hold.

Among professionals is growing realization of the critical importance of family influence on the lives of students, especially those students with academic, behavioral, or social problems. Students demonstrating academic needs, with problems in adaptive behavior or low mental functioning, or those demonstrating problem behaviors require a special bond from teachers and family members. Teachers, like Miss Hesidence described in Box 1.1, make special efforts to learn about families of students with problem behaviors, prior to devising teaching plans. In this instance, Miss Hesidence collected important information from mothers in order to answer questions and make instructional decisions. Miss Hesidence was able to discern that parents influence their children's instructional and behavioral success—a key ingredient to making the general education curriculum come alive. As for Miss Hesidence's students, the effort pays off for all involved.

Understanding Families and Ways Teachers Can Work with Them

When teachers understand family knowledge and use their skills to support their students and families, teachers problem-solve, act, and reflect. However, attention to the various aspects of family life is somewhat new to teachers, historically engaging the attention of other professionals, (e.g., those representing the biological, social, and behavioral sciences). Additionally, because of family significance to an individual's psychological functioning, family relationships historically attracted interest among mental health professionals. Only recently have teachers been involved extensively in planning and implementing family services (e.g., implementation of P.L. 99-457 and P.L. 101-357, and more recently, the Reauthorization of the Individuals with Disabilities Education Act (IDEA) (Yell & Shriner, 1997). However, teachers who are aware of family needs, strengths, and preferences have more direct control of successful student outcomes and of their own teaching effectiveness when they directly consider and implement strategies that are collaborative and responsive.

Strategies for Collaborative Orientations and Responsive Practices. Contemporary teachers understand parent–child relationships, the significance of parent–child relationships

BOX 1.1 • *A Teacher Making a Special Effort to Learn*

Family–Teacher Issues

Miss Hesidence wanted to gather information on her special education resource room students. She planned to observe, gather, record, and interpret information to answer questions and make instructional decisions about two of her students Paul and Bob. Because both Paul and Bob have identified emotional disabilities, Miss Hesidence decided to compare their mothers' thoughts on behavioral progress with Sal and Jesse, two normally achieving students in the class. Miss Hesidence asked both sets of mothers to administer a behavioral task to their children. Miss Hesidence then compared the mothers' expectations and attributions for their sons' performance. Miss Hesidence discovered that Paul and Bob's mothers held lower performance expectations, provided more negative nonverbal responses, and attributed their sons' failure to lack of ability, more often than Sal and Jesse's mothers did. Miss Hesidence wanted to help the mothers of her students with emotional needs. She didn't want to single them out, but wanted to offer support.

Collaborative Orientations and Responsive Practices

Miss Hesidence decided to work with all classroom parents, helping them to understand their power to influence and support their children's behavioral success. She sent home biweekly notes to parents to help them understand that in order to raise performance expectations for their children, parents could help children to complete task assignments, provide structured support when needed, and increase positive responses.

Further, Miss Hesidence held monthly discussions with all parents in the class who wished to attend her informal afternoon chat sessions. Among the topics were effective parental participation in schools and ways to set home and school rules without alienating children. Miss Hesidence talked to parents directly about parental uncertainty concerning roles and responsibility for their children's behavioral failures or successes. Miss Hesidence found resources and reading materials when the parents indicated their lack of clarity about individual improvement. Within six months of initiating the monthly sessions, Miss Hesidence noted improvement in Paul and Bob's mothers' expectations and attributions for their sons' performance, and in overall behavioral improvement for Paul and Bob.

during the child's subsequent school development and functioning, and have available a barometer of family relationships. These teachers understand the home and community ecology as they embark on educational issues. Such teachers facilitate students' learning outcomes, their opportunities to succeed, and their families' school involvement by actively seeking family-member input.

Contemporary teachers understand that the most promising practice for increasing students' school performance is help at home rather than parental participation at school (Finn, 1998; Rich, 1998). However, some students do not get this opportunity for help at home. Some families rely on the support of teachers to guide their children through the educational process. Teachers who work toward understanding their students' families seek active means to keep in touch with families, the students' home lives, and community backgrounds. Brandt (1998) suggests that when teachers are out of touch with family members, school remedies to support students hinge on authenticity and listening. Teachers studying and understanding families listen first to support their students and the families. They strive to create positive relationships with family members, no matter what the family background or home conditions entail, to ensure that each student receives successful opportunities and the best education possible.

Box 1.2 illustrates a teacher who took proactive steps to understand her students' home ecology, seeking to help family members of one of her students. Mrs. Weber considered and used collaborative, responsive practices as she worked actively with the parents of a child with mental disabilities. The teacher realized the importance of the child to her parents and the child's impact on her siblings. Mrs. Weber demonstrated that she understands how the needs of all family members are important and can be supported by teachers' joint work with families.

The Council for Exceptional Children (CEC) (2000) reissued knowledge and skill statements important to teachers' family work. Table 1.3 lists important CEC common core knowledge and skills that new teachers should be able to understand and use in their work with students' families.

This CEC list of important knowledge and skills, developed to guide teachers in the twenty-first century, supports new teachers who take their family work seriously. By applying appropriate knowledge and skills to each child's family individually, new teachers have at their disposal opportunities to promote workable strategies with families and other professionals. Their strategies will help to solve educational dilemmas as teachers seek to develop relationships with parents and other family members based on mutual respect for roles in achieving benefits for students.

BOX 1.2 • *A Teacher Who Took Proactive Steps*

Family–Teacher Issues
Mrs. Weber is concerned with the impact of Terry Calhoun, a child with moderate mental disabilities, on Terry's siblings. She notes that Kathy and Lauren, Terry's older sisters, will play with other children during recess when Terry is not around. However, when Terry is nearby, the two siblings stay only with Terry and will not interact with their peers. Terry's younger brother, Karl, is very shy and rarely speaks to children or adults.

Collaborative Orientations and Responsive Practices
Mrs. Weber sets up a school conference to discuss with Terry's parents suggestions for handling sibling relationships effectively. Mrs. Weber talks to the Calhoun family about whether the parents note differences in the emotional adjustment process between Terry's older and younger siblings. Mrs. Weber also helps the Calhouns identify and explain typical sibling reactions of regression, acting out, and playing the "model child" role. As a result of the school conference session, Mrs. Weber and the Calhouns arrive at a joint consensus. They determine that there is a need for family members to be honest, find time for Kathy, Lauren, and Karl, read books to all children in the family written for siblings of children with disabilities and nondisabled children, plan family meetings to discuss concerns, help Terry's siblings deal with reactions of friends, and have their children join a sibling network.

TABLE 1.3 *Important CEC Common Core Knowledge and Skills Teachers Should Know and Use in Their Work with Families (CEC, 2000)*

Knowledge	Skills
• Factors that promote effective communication and collaboration with individuals, parents, and school and community personnel in a culturally responsive program • Typical concerns of parents of individuals with exceptional learning needs and appropriate strategies to help parents deal with these concerns • Roles of individuals with exceptionalities, parents, teachers, and other school and community personnel in planning an individualized program	• Use collaborative strategies in working with individuals with exceptional learning needs, parents, and school and community personnel in various learning environments. • Communicate and consult with individuals, parents, teachers, and other school and community personnel. • Foster respectful and beneficial relationships between families and professionals. Encourage and assist families to become active participants in the educational team. • Plan and conduct collaborative conferences with families or primary caregivers. • Engage in professional activities that may benefit individuals with exceptional learning needs, their families, and colleagues.

For instance, as they discuss the impact of general education curriculum programming, new teachers will work toward developing effective communication with family members. They will use family members' knowledge and expertise across all phases of the students' success in general education curricula. These teachers will work toward maintaining communications between families and professionals, ensuring appropriate respect for privacy and confidentiality. They will work toward extending opportunities for parent education. They will inform parents of parents' educational rights for their children. The teachers will recognize and respect family diversity. As they complete these actions, the new teachers begin to recognize that the relationship of home and community environmental conditions affects the behavior and outlook of students in schools. Creating bonds and dialoguing with their students' families will make their instructional tasks easier and more fulfilling.

Family Member Questions

Throughout the text, we provide a number of questions family members might pose to teachers during school conferences. We offer brief answers teachers might give in response to family questions. Questions often relate to the type, level, and location of educational services required by students. Following are examples.

• A question that occurs frequently is: *"Our family has problems that may be causing our child to do poorly in school. Should our child be getting special education inclusion services because of our family problems?"* Teachers may respond that the answer to this type of probing relates to the individual student's needs. All students deserve appropriate educational services based on their individual needs. However, the fact that a family has problems may have no direct impact on students' educational needs. Many students excel in school, despite a limited, supportive home situation. Likewise, inclusion services (implying a student's need for special education services within the general education classroom) should be based on sound educational decision making. The student must demonstrate that he or she meets certain eligibility requirements and demonstrates a need for special education—not whether the student's family has problems or the student is from a diverse home setting. However, the child may need special education services despite family problems. When teachers and family members can learn to listen to each other and work in sync, together, they can make the best educational decision for students. Inclusion services work best when teachers and family members together decide on appropriate services. A student's individual educational needs, not his or her home life, should be the determining factor in special services and inclusion emphases.

• *How is my child doing in each subject at school?* This is probably the most-asked question by families. Teachers should be able to access the answers to these questions quickly—if they keep frequent data on their students' progress. If a student is struggling in a certain subject, the student's family should be informed. When a student is having difficulties exhibiting appropriate behaviors, the family should be informed. Together, families and teachers can determine appropriate discipline or behavioral support strategies to help overcome these behaviors.

Collaborative orientations and responsive practices underscore the necessity of teachers' strong family support. Teachers can share strategies with family members on appropriate methods that work for individual students. It is important to ask families for their suggestions on how to make improvements in each student's progress. After all, families know more about their children than anyone else does. Such knowledge is true for families of students served in inclusion services, general content area classes, traditional special education services, and in transition services from school-based to community-based activities. When families receive early information on students' progress, they become better consumers of program practices, student learning outcomes, and eventual postschool outcomes.

• *What can I do to help my child improve?* Teachers should not be afraid to tell students' families exactly what they believe will help students succeed in school. When teachers believe families need to spend more time with their children, effective teachers tell families that very diplomatically. School leaders are struggling to find ways to make the report cards they send home more meaningful to parents. Many teachers contend that time-honored, traditional grading systems are inadequate when it comes to measuring what and how students learn in current classrooms. Often, teachers favor rating students on specific skills in a subject area or along a developmental curriculum, doing away with traditional letter grades. However, selling parents on alternative reporting can be difficult—especially when special needs students require grading adaptations. Parents who are used to report cards that simply list letter grades next to each major subject area, or in the case of elementary students, "satisfactory" or "not satisfactory" ratings, can be put off by long explanations or complex charts and rubrics.

What teachers can respond to families asking progress questions relates to the level and quality of rapport established with families. Teachers should talk to parents consistently and openly, regarding parents' support of their child's school improvement. Parents need to understand existing assessment processes and how proposed modifications or changes made for special needs students can improve progress reporting.

Accordingly, effective teachers do not want to give families negative experiences involving students' progress. Teachers operating in collaborative orientations and responsive practices help families and students. Teachers do this by asking families for input on assessment processes, reporting systems, appropriate grading modifications, and accountability measures. They work to help families understand the progress reporting, and they disseminate data on available family resources and services to all families they serve.

Family Resources and Services

There are relevant family resources and services teachers can use to support their understanding of and work with families. In each chapter of the text, we list current resources or materials that can help teachers work with families. Examples are provided here.

SERVICE ORGANIZATIONS

Accent on Information
Box 700
Bloomington, IL 61702

**Alliance for Parental Involvement
in Education**
P.O. Box 59
East Chatham, NY 12060-0059

**Center on Families, Communities,
Schools, and Children's Learning**
Johns Hopkins University
3505 N. Charles St.
Baltimore, MD 21218

Home and School Institute
MegaSkills Education Center
1500 Massachusetts Ave. N.W.
Washington, DC 20005

Summary

This chapter introduced teachers to their study of and work with students' families. The chapter provided a framework to highlight and use collaborative orientations and responsive practices. It offered a rationalization for why teachers' study of family knowledge is important. It provided an overview of teachers' roles with families, collaborative orientations, responsive practices, and contemporary teaching. Specific chapter themes relate to teachers' work with families, including

• The most significant adults, aside from the child's parents or guardians, are classroom teachers.
• Teachers understanding their students' families seek active means to keep in touch with their students' families, home lives, and community backgrounds.

- There are important reasons why teachers working closely with family members act in collaborative orientations and responsive practices.
- Families represent a diverse group of students' households and living arrangements.
- Collaborative orientations imply that teachers do not operate in isolation.
- Teachers offering responsive practices recognize a relationship between what and how they teach and economical, educational, legal, political, and social forces framing family programs and services.
- Contemporary teachers understand contemporary issues and the roles they play with families, family programs, and services.
- Research models and family theories help new teachers to understand workable practices with families and other professionals.

References

Artiles, A. J., Aguirre-Munoz, Z., & Abedi, J. (1998). Predicting placement in learning disabilities programs: Do predictors vary by ethnic group? *Exceptional Children, 64* (4), 543–559.

Brandt, R. (1998). Listen first. *Educational Leadership, 55* (8), 25–30.

Council for Exceptional Children. (2000). *What every special educator must know: The standards for the preparation and certification of special educators.* (4th ed.). Reston, VA: Author.

Cohen, L. G., & Spenciner, L. J. (1998). *Assessment of children and youth.* New York: Longman.

Delgado-Rivera, B., & Rogers-Adkinson, D. (1997). Culturally sensitive interventions: Social skills training with children and parents from culturally and linguistically diverse backgrounds. *Intervention in School and Clinic, 33* (2), 75–80.

Epstein, M. H., Kutash, K., & Duchnowski, A. (1998). *Outcomes for children and youth with emotional and behavioral disorders and their families. Programs and evaluation: Best practices.* Austin, TX: PRO ED.

Falvey, M. (1995). *Inclusive and heterogeneous education: Assessment, curriculum, and instruction.* Baltimore: Paul H. Brookes.

Ferguson, D. L. (1995). Celebrating diversity: A response. *Remedial and Special Education, 16* (4), 199–202.

Finn, J. D. (1998). Parental engagement that makes a difference. *Educational Leadership, 55* (8), 20–24.

Forman, E. A., & McCormick, D. E. (1995). Discourse Analysis: A sociocultural perspective. *Remedial and Special Eduction, 16* (3), 150–158.

Franklin, C. (1996). Learning to teach qualitative research: Reflections of a quantitative researcher, In M. B. Sussman & J. K. Gilgun (Eds.), *The methods and methodologies of qualitative family research* (pp. 49–68). New York: Hayworth Press, Inc.

Giangreco, M. F., Cloninger, C. J., Dennis, R. E., & Edelman, S. W. (1994). Problem-solving methods. In J. S. Thousand, R. Villa, & A. Nevin (Eds.). *Creativity and collaborative learning: A practical guide to empowering students and teachers* (pp. 321–346). Baltimore, MD: Paul H. Brookes.

Giannetti, C. C., & Sagarese, M. M. (1998). Turning parents from critics to allies. *Educational Leadership, 55* (8), 40–42.

Hart, B., & Risley, T. R. (1995). *Meaningful differences in the everyday experiences of young American children.* Baltimore, MD: Paul H. Brookes.

Hatch, T. (1998). How community action contributes to achievement. *Educational Leadership, 55* (8), 16–19.

Hehir, T. (1999). The changing roles of special education leadership in the next millennium: Thoughts and reflections. *Journal of Special Education Leadership, 12* (1), 3–8.

Lopez-Reyna, N. A., & Bay, M. (1997). Enriching assessment: Using varied assessments for diverse learners. *Teaching Exceptional Children, 29* (4), 33–37.

McLaughlin, M. J. (1999). Access to the general education curriculum: Paperwork and procedures or redefining "special education." *Journal of Special Education Leadership, 12* (1), 9–14.

Office of Special Education Programs. (1999). *To assure the free appropriate public education of all children with disabilities: Twentieth annual report to Congress on the implementation of the Individuals with Disabilities Education Act.* Washington, DC: Author.

O'Shea, L. J., O'Shea, D. J., & Algozzine, B. (1998). *Learning disabilities: From theory toward practice.* New York: Merrill-Prentice Hall.

Rich, D. (1998). What parents want from teachers. *Educational Leadership, 55* (8), 37–39.

Research Connections in Special Education. (1999). *Universal design: Ensuring access to the general education curriculum.* U.S. Office of Special Education Programs. Washington, DC: Author.

Schere, M. (1998). The shelter of each other: A conversation with Mary Pipher. *Educational Leadership, 55* (8), 6–11.

Turnbull, A. P., & Turnbull, H. R. (1997). *Families, professionals, and exceptionality. A special partnership.* Upper Saddle River, NJ: Prentice Hall/ Merrill.

Turnbull, A. P., Turnbull, H. R., Shank, M., & Leal, D. (1995). *Exceptional lives: Special education in today's schools.* Englewood Cliffs, NJ: Prentice Hall/Merrill.

U.S. Department of Education. (1994). *Calculations based on information from the 1994 Condition of Education, the 1993 Digest of Education Statistics and the 1993 Statistical Abstract of the United States.* Washington, DC: Author.

U.S. Department of Education. (1997). *Nineteenth annual report to Congress on the implementation of the Individuals with Disabilities Education Act.* Washington, DC: Author.

Wardle, F. (2000). Children of mixed race—no longer invisible. *Educational Leadership, 57* (4), 68–72.

Yell, M., & Shriner, J. G. (1997). The IDEA Amendments of 1997: Implications for special and general education teachers, administrators, and teacher trainers. *Focus on Exceptional Children, 30* (1), 1–19.

Ysseldyke, J., & Olsen, K. (1999). Putting alternate assessments into practice: What to measure and possible sources of data. *Exceptional Children, 65* (2), 175–185.

2

Typical Families: Fact or Fiction?

Dorothy J. O'Shea

Janet E. Riley

Chapter Objectives _____

In this chapter we will

- Discuss teachers' relationships with families
- Discuss what we know about family needs
- Describe statistics and characteristics of family compositions and living arrangements
- Examine important family issues that teachers face with families
- Provide examples of family life
- Offer practical suggestions for teachers working with family members in schools, classrooms, homes, or communities
- List relevant family resources and services that teachers can use to support their understandings of and work with families
- Summarize important chapter themes

> *There are twenty-four hours in a day and 365 days in a calendar year. Mary spends approximately 14 percent of her daily life in school. Mary learns to read and write in school. She learns to spell and calculate. She learns how to expand her socialization skills. However, the other 86 percent represents time Mary spends with her family. Mary has a "typical" family in that she has a mother, father, and three brothers. Mary lives in a large urban community, but lives close to her mother's parents and her father's brothers and children. Mary's mother and father both work and her family has a limited, but steady, income to pay the monthly bills on time.*
>
> *Mary learns about relationships in her home. In her supportive home, she learns to love and be loved by her mother, father, siblings, grandparents, aunts, uncles, and cousins. Mary learns to be dependent on and independent from her*

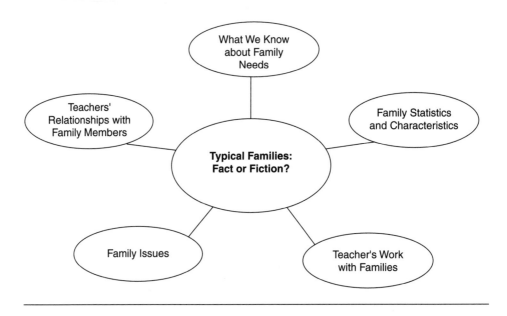

family members. Mary's family members are her first teachers. As primary care-givers, they have the greatest influence on Mary throughout her life.

This chapter examines the nature of American families. The chapter identifies family compositions, characteristics, statistics, and facts. Information on the current state of families with children under eighteen years of age includes data on family issues affecting family life. The chapter identifies important family variables comprising the current state of families with children under age eighteen years of age. *Family variables* include such factors as family size; whether family members work, parents' income, marital status and educational status; where families live and community location; and families' beliefs, traditions, and backgrounds.

Family life invariably affects what Mary and other children bring to and take from their school experiences. This chapter's underlying focus is to examine children's backgrounds and experiences affecting family life, introduce teachers' roles with parents or other primary caregivers, and identify major elements of effective home–school partnerships.

Teachers' Relationships with Family Members

Teachers' relationships with family members, such as with Mary's parents and siblings, are vitally important in effective home–school partnerships. Teachers are at the forefront in helping children and their family members to feel positive about school life and educational opportunities. However, while many families express strong feelings of support for the schools their children actually attend (70 percent of all public school parents give their children's school a grade of A or B), there is a strong feeling of disconnection with public education in general (Elam, Lowell, & Gallup, 1994). Aside from reports of the public education system as a convenient scapegoat for social ills or political failures (Reid, 1997; Katisiyannis & Maag, 1998), many family members report that family interests are not fully taken into account by teachers or other school personnel. At times, some parents find that school personnel talk down to parents or speak in educational jargon they do not understand. Some parents report that school personnel ignore their social or cultural influences in deciding what works best for their children (Elam, Rose, & Gallup, 1996; U.S. Department of Education, 1997). Ironically, family members often are more educated than teachers, especially in matters pertaining to their own children (Turnbull & Turnbull, 1997; Singer & Powers, 1993).

Teachers' training and preservice experiences with family members may link to their in-service success with their students' family members. Knight and Wadsworth (1998) examined the practices of universities and colleges throughout the United States with regard to the inclusion of family issues courses in their teacher preparation programs. These authors reported that the need to train teachers in effective communication/consultation skills, to foster constructive relationships, and to engage in responsive collaboration with parents on planning education programs is a high priority in the reported programs. Cultural and environmental influences on learner characteristics, knowledge of family diversity and dynamics relative to developing instruction, and involvement of family in assessment and as members of the educational team reflected the lowest levels of concerns by the study participants. These authors argued that the reluctance of some experienced teachers to form partnerships and embrace family inclusion with teachers appears to be due, in large part, to teachers' insecurity and uncertainty. They suggested that preparing teachers to work with families is a key component in underscoring families as partners in education.

Davern (1999) found that teachers' attitudes toward parents' goals and ideas, parents' perceptions of teachers' attitudes toward the child, and parents' perspectives on personal qualities and characteristics (e.g., teachers' honesty and openness, accessibility, showing friendliness, and willingness to ally with parents) are key ingredients in effective family–teacher relationships. Many parents believe that teachers' attitudes toward them and their child make a difference in successful home–school interactions, especially when students participate in the general education curriculum. Partnering with parents—in which teachers work toward developing program principles in relation to family goals, learning about the history of families of children in their programs, and knowing and interacting with families—is seen as vital to supporting parental roles in the educational community.

However, the use of families as *partners in education* is one of the greatest natural resources in home–school partnerships, but untapped in many schools. Some family members express feelings of incompetence in the task of educating the child or in working with teachers. Some teachers give the impression that they consider family issues relatively unimportant when planning on what to include in school curricula, or on how to teach children. Or, school professionals may give an overt or inadvertent impression that family involvement is not welcome in school activities—especially as children age. Approximately three-quarters of American parents report high or moderate involvement in schools when their children are eight to ten years old; however, only 50 percent of parents report such involvement by the time their children reach age sixteen. Parents who want to be more involved often meet some resistance, because many schools have long accepted their absence, and may passively or actively discourage parental participation (Turnbull & Turnbull, 1997; Turnbull, Turnbull, Shank, & Leal, 1995; U.S. Department of Education, 1996).

On the other hand, a majority of teachers express concerns that parents, as primary caregivers, need to be more engaged in the education of their children. Active parent involvement in their children's education positively affects students' school achievement, increased attendance, participation in school activities, decreased school drop-out rates, supportive school climates, and greater parental satisfaction with school and teacher effectiveness (Shore, 1995). Active school involvement by Mary's parents may help her to feel more successful in school, achieve more, attend more regularly, and feel better about her school and teachers' effectiveness. Clearly, parent involvement holds positive benefits for children, families, and school personnel. Active family involvement with teachers and parents working together can strengthen the structure of home–school partnerships.

Black (1998) identified six types of family involvement in school-related activities. These include the following:

• *Effective parenting:* Effective parenting provides home conditions that support school learning and provides for each student's essential needs of shelter, food, and safety. Mary's parents provide a supportive home in a clean apartment. It is a safe setting. Mary regularly receives meals and clothing.

• *Two-way communication between teachers and family members:* Teachers and family members who demonstrate two-way communication respond to report cards, newsletters, phone calls, face to face interactions, and so forth. Mary's parents attend school conferences. They write to and receive notes from Mary's teachers regarding her school progress. They review progress reports and report cards with Mary's teachers.

• *Volunteer service:* Family members provide unpaid services to schools, such as monitoring hallways or recess activities; organizing food drives, book fairs, parties, and assemblies; and tutoring students under teachers' directives. Mary's mother assists at school book fairs once a year. She volunteers to buy gift wrapping paper during the annual holiday sale. She saves store coupons, donating her coupons to the school fund for future computer purchases for Mary's peers.

• *Support via home learning:* Family members encouraging learning at home engage in such activities as visiting libraries or museums with their children, providing homework assistance after school or at night, and supplying home computer or technology opportunities. Both Mary's mother and father regularly check Mary's homework. Mary visits the library once a month with her father and siblings.

• *Decision-making efforts by family members and school personnel:* Activities include parents on site-based management committees and organizations where parents work with teachers and administrators on school policies, issues, and management. Mary's parents volunteer to be on the school advisory council. They do not attend regular meetings, but complete written school surveys on issues such as report card modifications, changes in the health curriculum, and direction for school playground purchases.

• *Collaboration efforts:* Family–teacher activities include collaborating with the community, which links family members to schools and teachers to the community's resources and services. Mary's parents attend all school picnics with Mary and Mary's teachers. They also attend school concerts, plays, and holiday activities.

Teachers encourage the type of parent involvement important to their students and families served in the local area. However, in the recent past, some parents took on the challenge of being overly active with their children's schools. Administrators and teachers were finding it increasingly difficult to maintain order and get their jobs done. There was such a trend toward active parent involvement that administrators and teachers began voicing concerns on how to keep "parent involvement" from turning into "parent interference." Investigators began discussing whether it may be important for schools to build both "bridges and buffers" for parent involvement. Bridges are necessary so parents can help their children succeed in school (e.g., offering parent newsletters, seeking parental assistance during class activities), but buffers need to be in place to protect teachers and administrators so they can do their jobs—exercise their professional judgment and expertise—without parent interference. Buffers include such activities as limiting parent involvement hours in school, or structuring the number of family chaperones during schoolwide activities (Black, 1998).

Because school and home partnerships may suffer, due to misinterpreting parents' needs for involvement or a lack of trust among significant individuals in the child's life, school personnel increasingly must make every effort to communicate with family members straightforwardly. Teachers would benefit by including important family members in educational decisions affecting the students' school opportunities and by seeking parental input into all educational decisions. Mary's teachers are successful with Mary's family because they actively include Mary's parents in educational decisions. Her school personnel seek parental input into all of Mary's educational opportunities.

However, some teachers, families, and students are not as lucky as Mary, her teachers, and family. Many students do not have the same school or family opportunities as Mary. Teachers cannot judge what is the best family. They can deal with the only family the child has and work to improve the partnership between child, family, and school. When families believe that their children's teachers understand and value family needs, families are more likely to react positively to teachers and home–school partnerships. Box 2.1 illustrates the case of Keysha and her mother. Keysha's teachers understand that they must work very hard to partner with Keysha's mother and to support Keysha's mother's school efforts.

In order to help Keysha, her teachers must work toward developing activities in relation to Keysha's mothers' goals. They must seek information on Keysha's family. Teachers must get to know and interact with Keysha's family. However, Keysha's teachers realize that they must work with her mother to get Keysha into a consistent school attendance pattern. Attendance is their number one issue. Gaining her mother's support will aid in long-term benefits for Keysha. Her teachers realize that they must work toward understanding Keysha's family needs.

BOX 2.1

Family–Teacher Issues

Keysha Haverton, a slim child with a noted respiratory problem, is eight years old. Keysha has three younger siblings and lives at home with her mother. She is in third grade at North Saxton Elementary. (North Saxton is in a suburb of Glover, PA.) Keysha's school attitude and behavior are appropriate, as noted by her classroom teacher, Mr. Grant. However, Mr. Grant and Mrs. Main, the learning support teacher, are concerned. Keysha has missed eleven school days. (There are still four months of school left.) Keysha is beginning to experience many problems in word comprehension skills, especially in the area of understanding implicit meaning from her third-grade reader. Mr. Grant reports that she has adequate skills in third-grade basic vocabulary and phonetic analysis. However, he worries that Keysha is beginning to fall behind in comprehending more complex third-grade tasks (especially in reading for details and in sequencing story events). Her language arts and penmanship skills are not up to the other children's in the class. Also, Keysha is falling behind others in her mathematics skills, especially in word-problem solving.

Collaborative Orientations and Responsive Practices

Mr. Grant immediately calls in Mrs. Haverton to discuss Keysha's problems. Mr. Grant and Mrs. Main would like to identify with Mrs. Haverton why Keysha is missing so much school. The teachers tell Mrs. Haverton up front that they are concerned with Keysha's academic achievement, especially in reading and mathematics. Mr. Grant realizes that in order to help Keysha succeed, he must elicit the support of Mrs. Haverton. Mr. Grant begins by asking Mrs. Haverton to discuss when Keysha goes to bed, when she gets up for school, and how she gets to school. Mr. Grant and Mrs. Main both agree that a discussion on Mrs. Haverton's homework policy with Keysha, the books available in her home, and the amount of time Mrs. Haverton believes it takes Keysha to complete assignments is better suited for another conference. The immediate concern is to get Keysha to school on a consistent basis.

What We Know about Family Needs

The past few decades provided many sources of information on family needs. For instance, many families need recognition by school professionals of what families are and are not. Generally, a *family* comprises two or more individuals who live together and are related to one another by blood or marriage. Included are *husband/wife households* (with or without children present) and *single-parent households* (usually the mother and always with children present, such as in Keysha's family). A *household* is one or more people who may or may not be related but who maintain a separate living unit. Households include husband/wife and other family compositions, but also include individuals living alone or with roommates (Brunner, 1998; Bureau of the Census, 1997; O'Shea, O'Shea, & Algozzine, 1998).

There is debate concerning a definitive answer of what families entail. For example, Popenoe (1993) accepted that there may be a single adult heading the household, but a family requires the presence of a dependent child or adult. Varied family researchers (Doherty, Boss,

LaRossa, Schumm, & Steinmetz, 1993; Smith, 1995; Sprey, 1990) argued that there is no single definition of family that embodies all the particulars known about how and where individuals live. Rather, there are multiple definitions formulated from varied theoretical perspectives shaping observations and expectations of family life. Accordingly, rather than debating how to define families, it may be more helpful to discern what families are not.

A "typical family" is a misnomer in American society. There is no one type or group that represents "the family." American families exemplify individuals with a multitude of characteristics, statistics, and important demographics. Modern American families, such as Mary and Keysha's families, represent diversity in composition and living arrangements.

Teachers will encounter families with many or few family members. Housing and community opportunities will vary. Families represent all walks of life, from indigent families without homes, to those families with multiple residences. Family members may or may not hold educational degrees. Primary languages will vary. Families may practice daily religious traditions, or may hold little or no religious affiliations.

Teachers' recognition of complex variables that define the state of families with children under eighteen years of age is vital in supporting their students and families, and in building effective home–school partnerships. Table 2.1 summarizes information on family needs and teacher actions.

Understanding the State of Families with Children under Eighteen Years of Age

Teachers' understanding of the state of families with children under eighteen years of age sets the stage in how professionals approach families, school conferences, and home or school involvement. For instance, in an early study by Wertheimer (1989), parents were asked to respond to a series of interviews on interactions with school professionals. During the course of the interviews, parents were to indicate how they felt professionals could be helpful and what they considered unhelpful. Positive experiences reported by parents included having family needs, backgrounds, and expertise as parents acknowledged; really being listened to; having access to professionals who have the right skills for the job; having their difficulties as parents really understood; and having a professional the parent can trust. Negative experiences reported by parents included being asked to do fund-raising, when what is needed is active support for the child, parent, or other family members; professionals who look down on families; professionals who do not keep their promises to help; and professionals who are in contact with a parent's family, but not with each other. Even by today's standards, families want and respond to teacher understanding of their family's uniqueness and needs (Knight & Wadsworth, 1998; Davern, 1999).

School Effectiveness and Teacher Understanding

Reports on school effectiveness verify the importance of teacher understanding regarding students' families. Studies show that school practices to encourage parents to participate in

TABLE 2.1 *Information on Family Needs*

Families Require	Teacher Actions
Recognition by professionals of what families are and are not	• Accepts and Values That There Is No "Typical Family" in American Society: Families Are Diverse • Includes in School Planning Indicators of Families' and Student's Needs, Interests, and Preferences
Understanding by professionals of the state of families with children under 18 years of age	• Accepts and Values That Families Are Complex: Varied Family Types and Compositions Entail Students' Households, Living Arrangements, and Community Settings
Specific professional action that engages families actively in home–school partnerships	• Works With Families, Students, and Other Professionals Toward a Common Goal of Students' Educational Success • Approaches Families, School Conferences, and Home or School Involvement Positively • Promotes Supportive School Practices to Encourage Parent Participation in Children's Education: Acknowledges Families' Contributions in Decisions • Validates Others' Insights and Expertise by Demonstrating Mutual Regard, Respect, Empathy, Openness, Congruence, and Team Decisions • When Differences Arise, Faces Conflicts and Works to Resolve Them Rather Than Avoid or Let Conflicts Escalate • Uses Open Communication Methods Often, Such as Letters Home, Shared Reports, Face to Face Contacts, and Home Visits • Schedules Time to Discuss Program Issues, Student Progress, Parent Options, Community Representative Input, or Other Issues
Support for effective family functioning	• Values and Respects Family Members' Views on Family Functioning • Provides Information in a Variety of Forms (e.g., Books, Materials) to Help Students, Families, Siblings, and Other Professionals Function More Effectively • Shares Resources and Information with Families on Changing Needs and Behaviors Across Children's Ages • Demonstrates Awareness of Relevant Local, State, and Federal Laws Having an Impact on Students, Families, and Teachers
Professionals who recognize and respond skillfully to family customs, traditions, and rituals	• Provides Information to Students on Family Customs, Traditions, and Rituals • Seeks Students' and Families' Choices, Needs in Integration and Inclusions, and Independence and Interdependence • Shares Information Such as Family Traditions and Customs • Demonstrates Respect for Cultural Ethnic Differences • Links Instructional Goals and Objectives across Home and School Settings

Families Require	*Teacher Actions*
	• Plans Curricular Offerings with Input to Family and Cultural Expectations Provided by Parents and Family Members
	• Meets with Families, Students, and Significant Professionals Often, as Part of Best Practices
	• Uses Flexible Planning and Recognition of Programming Variables in Families' Values, Goals, and Experiences

their children's education often are more important in effective home–school partnerships than family characteristics like parental education, family size, marital status, socioeconomic level, or student grade level in determining whether parents get involved (Bennett, DeLuca, & Bruns, 1997; Dauber & Epstein, 1993). At the same time, school personnel need to make a concerted effort to help low-income families become involved, because these family members often wait for an approach from teachers. Such families may also have increasing difficulty in helping children with their academics, as children advance in age and in grade (Lee & Croninger, 1994). However, researchers have long held that children from low-income families who are at risk of failing or falling behind, can succeed academically and socially when their parents are provided with home–school support and teacher encouragement (Radin, 1969, 1972; Bronfenbrenner 1974; Scott & Davis, 1979).

More recent reports suggest that teachers and other school-based professionals can do much to engage families actively. And by engaging families, teachers become proficient in understanding their students and their family's needs and uniqueness. When professionals make efforts to encourage families, home–school partnerships increase in many ways (Shore, 1995; U.S. Department of Education, 1996). For instance, teachers can play a vital role, ensuring that parents are welcome in the school building. As appropriate, teachers can give parents or other family members substantive roles in various aspects of school planning, including curriculum and instruction. Experienced teachers and administrators can offer the faculty professional development that is designed to foster family awareness and involvement. In cases where parents are not the most, or only, influential adults in a student's life, teachers may reach out to other people who are potential sources of support, such as older siblings or grandparents. When teachers engage family members in such constructive activities, effective teachers are building the cornerstones of effective home–school partnerships. Effective teachers model collaborative orientations and responsive practices. Ruth's teachers and family, in Box 2.2, demonstrate collaborative responsiveness.

Effective Family Functioning

Engaging families actively, as Ruth's teachers did, and understanding how each family operates underscores teachers' work. However, although most children attend school in the

BOX 2.2

Family–Teacher Issues

Ruth's medical history is unremarkable. Mr. Renes reported that his late wife's pregnancy and labor were of normal length. Birth was natural. Ruth's developmental milestones, also, were within normal limits. However, Ruth had early reports of speech and language difficulties. Currently, Ruth receives the assistance of a speech therapist, Mr. Monrey, at least twice a week for articulation problems. Additionally, during Ruth's first five years, her father indicated that Ruth was prone to mild temper tantrums. It was at this time that his wife, Heather, passed away. However, because Ruth never spoke much or asked about her mother, Mr. Renes believed that Heather's demise and absence from the home did not affect Ruth a great deal.

Father and daughter currently live in a large, western-California community with Mr. Renes' sister. Ruth is in fifth grade. Mrs. Capucchi, Ruth's current teacher, reports that on the latest group ability tests, Ruth scored in the high average range. However, since second grade, Mrs. Capucchi finds that there have been many academic problems noted in Ruth's cumulative file, including speech and interaction difficulties. Past teachers seem to confirm many problem behavior occurrences during instruction in Ruth's "weak subjects." Ruth's teachers have concluded that most of her problems seem to center on Ruth's willingness to cooperate, her language skills, and her articulation problems. Ruth's current teachers have noted that Ruth seems to get frustrated when peers tease her about her speech difficulties. Mr. Renes states that Ruth has few friends and is becoming less responsive at home.

Collaborative Orientations and Responsive Practices

Mr. Renes indicates that he wants help now, before Ruth enters the middle school years. He says he wants school professionals to give him some direction in helping Ruth to make and keep friends, and to learn how to adjust to her speech difficulties. While he recognizes that his sister is helping to raise Ruth, Mr. Renes believes he needs added help from teachers to develop Ruth's social areas.

Mrs. Capucchi and Mr. Monrey indicate that the first step is to get Ruth a comprehensive language assessment. They want Mr. Renes's permission to refer Ruth to Dr. Bell, the school psychologist. Further, they indicate that Mr. Renes might consider contacting the Sutton Mental Health Clinic, pointing out that Ruth needs comprehensive behavioral and emotional assessments that can help them to plan a more effective school program. Mr. Renes signs all the permission forms, indicating that he is willing to do anything to help his little girl.

---

morning and are home with caretakers in the afternoon, there is no norm in a typical day at home for all students. Some children go home to empty housing, as their parents work. Some children split their household living routines across separated family structures, and some children interact with multiple generations under the same roof. There are, however, reports concerning how effective families operate. Building a family and raising children are life's most important opportunities and difficult challenges. Effective family functioning requires basic elements that all successful and enduring institutions share: (a) a legal system, (b) resources, and (c) strong traditions based on shared values (Eyre & Eyre, 1994).

To operationalize what an effective family does highlights the necessity of fair, consistent discipline based on family rules and limits; a way of allocating resources for children to earn, save, and spend money; and a sharing process based on family traditions and values. Accordingly, effective family functioning entails a process in which family members can build communication, trust, and togetherness.

What researchers studying families find is that family effectiveness transcends economical, educational, ethnic, religious, and social parameters. Effective families spend time together. Family members report that they are comfortable with each other. While members may involve themselves in work or community activities, effective families look after and take care of each other. Members achieve a level of understanding and bonding that cannot be erased over time or during separations. Ineffective family members, in turn, may be apathetic toward each other. In times of family crises, they are not there for each other. Communication is lacking and a general lack of support is pervasive in daily interactions (Eyre & Eyre, 1994; Turnbull & Turnbull, 1997; Singer & Powers, 1993).

Recent research supports what parents and teachers have long held: that the quality of family functioning, particularly relationships with parents, has a dramatic impact in school, especially in students' later school years. The quality of family functioning may either enhance or impede educational development, especially as children age. For instance, high-school-age youth report that they intensively want a supportive family, characterized by both warmth and firm discipline. In a survey of teens from all ethnic and economic backgrounds, young people expressed the lack of parental attention and guidance when they believed they need it most: for making decisions about their future, forming adult values, and taking on the challenges of adult roles (Shore, 1995).

The quality of family functioning maintains increasing importance as students age. Additionally, most young people report that they need family traditions—the family customs, rituals, belief systems, and history—that bond members (Eyre & Erye, 1994). Family traditions are positive habits and experiences that are both anticipated and remembered. Every family has some traditions, whether they are aware of them or not. Family traditions based on food, clothing, shared holidays, or family vacations, for instance, offer opportunities to create memories, share love, and build strong bonds between family members.

Tradition often plays a role in passing on to younger generations long-held family customs, household rituals, or ancestral beliefs. However, as many teachers and parents recognize, family functioning is also a result of indirect and direct influences that caregivers have with their children. For instance, parents indirectly influence family functioning by the quality of the interpersonal relationships they establish with their children. These influences generally take the form of (a) the quality of an attachment relationship between children and parents, and (b) the family's approach to the children's socialization. Teachers may encounter a number of family members who approach family interactions by how parents involved themselves in their own family operations.

Accordingly, children's social development and how they approach school interactions depend on their relationships with their families and their home opportunities. (For example, although her teachers can help Ruth's successful social development, how well Ruth succeeds with school age peers depends, to a large degree, on Ruth's relationship with her father and aunt.) Such factors as the child's development of social skills as an infant or toddler and relationships with family members during the preschool or elementary years, influence the child's social consequences in later school years. Equally influential is the caregivers' approach to discipline. The degree to which parents maintain expectations for their children's behavior, attempt to control the outcome of their children's development, and the caregivers' responsiveness (i.e., acceptance or rejection of children by caregivers) influences the styles of care children experience (Krantz, 1994). Teachers may confront family members with varied caregiving styles, such as those identified in Table 2.2. Recognizing the caregiver style children receive from significant individuals in their home life helps teachers to understand relevant factors related to family needs.

Family tradition and caregiver styles are prominent in the family compositions and living arrangements that comprise most students' living arrangements. However, there are family compositions and living arrangements more prominent than others in modern families. These include the nuclear family, extended family, stepfamily, single-parent family, foster families, and homeless children. Table 2.3 summarizes family compositions and living arrangements.

Nuclear Families

The nuclear family usually takes a form in which a biological mother and biological father live in the same household with the children. Parents live, work, and bond with each other and their offspring. Mary's family represents the nuclear family.

A nuclear family might seem like the ideal environment for children's development and learning. With both parents living in the home, children have opportunities to receive both mother's and father's attention. However, such family arrangements are becoming

TABLE 2.2   Caregiving Styles

Limit Setters

- Caregivers set strict limits and standards on children's behavior.
- The household functions on a strict code of rules.
- Children challenging the caregivers' authority receive moderate to severe punishment.

Avoiders

- Caregivers avoid setting boundaries.
- Caregivers exert little to no control over children's behaviors.
- Caregivers avoid making demands for compliance on their children in terms of bedtime, mealtime, household chores, and so forth.

Tolerant Seekers

- Caregivers have rules and exceptions.
- Caregivers allow children some say in household rules and regulations.
- Both children and caregivers express their perspectives on daily functioning.
- Both children and caregivers are responsive to each others' needs.

Uninvolvers

- Caregivers are emotionally distant.
- Caregivers minimize the time and effort afforded to child care.

TABLE 2.3 *Common Family Compositions and Living Arrangements*

- **Nuclear Family:** A family in which a biological mother and biological father live in the same household with the children
- **Extended Family:** Another relative or close friend living in the same house permanently
- **Stepfamily:** Two parents in home, but only one is biological
- **Single-Parent Family:** One biological parent raising children alone
- **Foster Parent/Homeless Children:** Not the natural parents, paid by the government to care for children until a permanent arrangement can be made

---

less common. For instance, between 1980 and 1990, households made up of married couples and children increased only slightly in number, while other types of households increased dramatically. Vital statistics for the United States revealed that in 1996 there were 8.8 marriages per 1,000 and 4.3 divorces per 1,000. In 1997, only 7 of 10 children lived with 2 parents (Brunner, 1998; Bureau of the Census, 1997).

A nuclear family can assume various household arrangements, each of which poses confounding issues for parents, children, and teachers. For example, the nuclear family might include Bob and Debbie, two young, working parents. In order for both parents to meet daily career opportunities, the family might have to rely on day care arrangements for their children: Conor, age six and Patrick, age six months. Arrangements might include before- and after-school day care. Or, the family may have to depend on grandparents or other family members in order to get to work. Stressors, including time constraints, transportation problems, and coordinating multiple family schedules can wreck havoc on these parents, children, grandparents, and daycare workers alike.

Or, the nuclear family arrangement might include one stay-at-home parent (Bob) and one working parent (Debbie). One parent (Debbie) may travel extensively, due to work constraints. Such a family arrangement might entail a hectic home situation with one parent (Bob) assuming a majority of parenting duties. There might be a lack of consistency and routine in daily interactions, when the working parent (Debbie) arrives from or leaves for another work trip.

In the case of Jerry and Terry's family, both of these teenage parents work to support their infant child, Sean. However, the two incomes are barely enough for basic family survival. This family of three cannot afford to own a home. Jerry and Terry's meager income goes toward rent, utilities, food, and clothing. Jerry and Terry must both split Sean's parenting duties, finding time to interact with Sean between their tedious work schedules.

While the nuclear family may offer opportunities for influences by both parents, implications for school personnel are many. Such implications might include the possibility that many nuclear families, such as Debbie and Bob's or Jerry and Terry's family, have no time to be active in school. These two-worker families are likely to have some financial resources, but less time than demographically similar one-worker families (O'Shea et al., 1998). Teachers' perspective of nuclear families' involvement may, thus, depend on differences in parents' time allotted to homework tasks, in leisure activities among family members, and in the choice and direction parents want in their child's educational program and their educational involvement. Because family members may be assuming basic home functioning tasks, such as shopping, cooking, cleaning, child care, and so forth, teachers' priorities (e.g., homework, volunteer work, parent–teacher groups) may take a back seat to the family's home survival needs. Teachers in effective home–school partnerships recognize and respect families' needs and priorities.

Extended Family

An *extended family* is one in which another relative or close friend resides in the same house permanently (Popenoe, 1993). Grandparents or aunts and uncles are common residers. Reasons for the increase of such relatives as grandparents living in modern family households relate to economic and social issues. For example, there are fewer affordable habitation options for the elderly. Many older adults may face a lack of health insurance, while undergoing increasing health problems as they age. What were once independent adults, now increasingly may become more dependent on their adult children for basic housing, transportation, clothing, and food needs. In turn, many working parents may use their own parents as extended daycare workers for their parents' grandchildren. Turner (1987) examined culturally specific values among African Americans, reporting on many black families' dependence on family rather than on social agencies for assistance in child care and support. Extended family members provide support and care. Nonetheless, negative dependence issues and stressors may be at the forefront of extended family life for many individuals.

Important issues for teachers to consider concern the stressors these family members may experience. These issues include the following:

• Ill parents/grandparents living in the home can create direct or indirect consequences on the family and the parent's marriage. When others move into the household, the living arrangements can take away from family time together—hours that might have been spent by parents and children together.

• Generation issues may arise over parenting style, household organization, management control, or finances. Such control issues may set the stage for older parents' disagreements with sons-in-law, daughters, and so forth.

• Increased attention to elderly parents and school-age children may translate into little or no private parent time. Such stressors may have an enormous effect on the level and type of bonding parents can achieve with their own children, as they cope with the demands of caring for their elderly parents. Little or no attention and time may be afforded to school involvement, as parents try to juggle family members and maintain an effective marriage.

There are many benefits afforded to families in extended families, but extended living arrangements may mean that parents have less time, personal energy, and financial resources to devote to their children and themselves. For example, in Suzy and Tom Ling's family, having Tom's elderly mother and father live with the couple and their four children provides many opportunities for the younger generation to learn about the Ling's family history, traditions, and customs. The grandparents can share child care arrangements with Suzy and Tom. However, potential stress on Suzy, Tom, their children, and Tom's parents centers on maintaining adequate living arrangements for eight people, keeping all family members busy, having household organization and a family living style appropriate to every household member, and finding time alone to maintain productive and conducive relationships.

The Ling family and children can receive support from caring teachers who recognize the benefits, and trials and tribulations, afforded in extended family arrangements. Teachers' understanding is vital in recognizing the impact of the family structure, the economic and social issues operating within the family dynamics, and the time/lack of time issues that may arise when school activities or conference needs surface.

Stepfamilies

Stepfamilies are on the increase and are becoming more and more common in American households. Nearly one out of three Americans is now a stepparent, a stepchild, a stepsibling, or some other member of a stepfamily (Larson, 1992; Some Facts about Stepfamilies, 1998). More than half of Americans today have been, are now, or will eventually be in one or more step situations during their lives. Of the 72.5 percent of children under eighteen living in two-parent families, 20.8 percent live in stepfamilies (two-thirds of the children in stepfamilies are stepchildren; 6.4 percent are half-siblings); 2.1 percent are in "other remarried families" (children born to the current union). In 1990, 72.5 percent of children under eighteen were living with two parents (including step- and adoptive parents), 24.7 percent were living with one parent, and 2.7 percent were living with neither parent. In 1970 these same figures were 85.2 percent, 11.9 percent, and 2.9 percent (Bureau of the Census, 1997; Some Facts about Stepfamilies, 1994).

Although many stepfamilies thrive, important issues for teachers that such stepfamily arrangements pose can include family dynamic complications. Discussion of these complications might arise during school-based conferences. The following examples represent some of these issues:

• Stepsiblings may have to face other children living in their households—those that are not biological brothers or sisters.

• Stepchildren may have to adjust to moving between biological parents on weeknights or weekends, with different household rules, regulations, and organizational systems. Homework rules and attention may differ across households.

• Many stepchildren may have a hard time dealing with issues of stepparent, friend, or adult in charge. Often, an adult in charge may not be clear to many stepchildren. All adults influence the parenting style, behavioral management or reward system in the home, and behavioral support children experience. The loyalties children anticipate, and the discipline style of biological parent versus stepparent, may be a major obstacle for many stepchildren.

• A divorce or widow situation may make a difference in others' acceptance. For instance, some children may face a sense of abandonment or competition as their parent devotes more time and energy to the new boyfriend, girlfriend, or spouse. Children may be forced to give up hope that custodial parents will reconcile.

- Children may face a higher risk of emotional and behavioral problems and may be less likely to have developed resiliency in stressful home life situations complicated by not really understanding where or with whom they live.

- Families often confront myriad lifestyle adjustments and challenges, especially as the ties between stepparents and children may conflict.

For example, in thirteen-year-old Cindy Martin's case (Box 2.3), her mother, Tina, married Bill Nicoll, who was already the father to two teenage girls, Beth (fourteen) and Linda (sixteen). Cindy's adjustment in this new stepfamily arrangement includes rearranging her time spent with her mother, her new stepfamily, and her biological father, Joe. Additionally, Cindy faces readjusting to new living quarters on a biweekly custody agreement. Cindy must adjust to and bond with her new, already established family of Bill, Beth, and Linda. Cindy experiences loyalties and bonds to her mother, Tina, and her father, Joe. Having Mrs. Jones, her teacher, available to share family concerns and discuss school or home adjustment issues can help make Cindy's home life and school transitions proceed more smoothly. Because Mrs. Jones actively supports effective home–school partnerships with all significant family members in Cindy's life, Cindy, her mother, her new stepfamily, and her father can all share and receive Mrs. Jones' support.

BOX 2.3

Family–Teacher Issues
Cindy resides with her natural mother and stepfather, Mr. and Mrs. Nicoll, and two stepsisters. Mr. Nicoll is self-employed outside the home setting, while Mrs. Nicoll is a homemaker. Cindy's father, Joe Martin, lives in a town about 20 miles away. Both her natural parents and stepfather say that Cindy exhibits an intense curiosity about everything and she also teaches herself through reading. Mrs. Jones, her teacher, characterizes Cindy as a voracious reader. Mrs. Jones reports that Cindy is an outgoing child who seems to learn quickly, is respectful, friendly, honest, and sensitive. Cindy has expressed an interest in reading novels. Cindy informed Mrs. Jones that she enjoys cooking, swimming, and camping. Her favorite school activities are drawing, computers, writing, and reading.

Collaborative Orientations and Responsive Practices
Mrs. Jones would like to work with Mr. and Mrs. Nicoll, and Mr. Martin, on securing enrichment services for Cindy. Mrs. Jones indicates that she would like to refer Cindy for individual testing to determine whether Cindy's needs are best met in her current school situation. Until Cindy can be tested individually in about six weeks, however, Mrs. Jones tells Cindy's parents and stepfather that she will provide Cindy enrichment novels for homework. She encourages Mr. and Mrs. Nicoll to send in books as well, and to speak to Cindy about her novels as often as possible. She wants Mr. Martin to spend homework time with Cindy as well, listening to Cindy retell excerpts from her favorite novels. With all of Cindy's family members' cooperation and participation, Mrs. Jones' school conferences proceed very smoothly. Cindy's homework can be enhanced by her family members' cooperation, not distracted by Cindy's living arrangements.

As in most stepfamily arrangements, home and school conferences are complicated, but can be workable. Complex family interactions may arise. Astute teachers can continue to work toward effective home–school partnerships, no matter how many households are relevant in the child's life.

Single-Parent Families

A single-parent family often consists of one biological parent raising the children alone. Single-parent families may originate after the parents' divorce, death of a parent, or from out-of-wedlock unions. Among first births to women 15 to 34 years old in the 1985–1989 period, 29 percent were born out of wedlock, up from 13 percent in the 1960–1964 period. Out-of-wedlock childbearing increased sharply in the past generation for all women. Among first births to women ages 15 to 34 years old during the 1980s, 29 percent were born out of wedlock. Out-of-wedlock childbearing also increased sharply during the recent past. For example, a child in a single-parent living arrangement in 1995 was nearly as likely to be living with a parent who had never been married (35 percent) as with a parent who was divorced (38 percent). Another 23 percent of these children lived with a parent who was separated or living apart from his or her spouse for some other reason, and 4 percent of them lived with a widowed parent (Bureau of the Census, 1997).

Ethnic and cultural backgrounds often correlate with the number of single-parent families. For example, white children are less likely to be living with one parent than are African American children or children of Hispanic origin. The proportions living with one parent in 1995 were 21 percent for white children, 56 percent for African American children, and 33 percent for Hispanic children (Brunner, 1998).

The following scenarios may be relevant to teachers working with families in single-parent households. For example, these scenarios are common:

• Primarily, one biological parent raises the children. The other (biological) parent may be deceased, divorced from the primary caregiver, or completely out of the picture and not involved in the child's life.

• Primarily, one biological parent raises the children. However, the other biological parent may be involved on alternate weekends.

• Primarily, one biological parent raises the children. The other biological parent may be involved a few times a year for extended periods (e.g., summer vacations, holidays).

• Split custody by both biological parents may represent the legal agreement and child's living arrangements. For example, the child may spend half of the year living with each biological parent in two separate households, but within the same school or community.

Such family compositions can be complicated. Many may hold dire consequences for children and families. For instance, the child may be used as a pawn between openly sparring parents, or the children may be forced to make unreasonable and hard choices in living arrangements. Such children may be forced to side with one parent over the other on custody, housing, or financial issues. The emotional tensions between parents may influence a high stress level in already vulnerable children; many of these children may be suffering emotional distress from the divorce or loss of parent due to death. Finally, sensitive children, either willingly or inadvertently, may be taking on the roles and responsibilities of caregiver to the remaining parent. Or, such children may be forced to assume adult roles in place of the absent parent.

Teachers can play vital roles in helping children adjust to home and school and in supporting families. Teachers can be available, listen to students when they have needs, refer the family to appropriate support agencies, and seek to understand the implications of the child's home and family life on school success.

Foster Parents and Homeless Children

Some children receive the support of foster parents. Foster parents are temporary parents assigned to look after the well-being of the child. Although not the natural parents, individuals assuming the foster parent role receive funding, often paid by the government, to care for the children. Parenting responsibilities usually occur until a permanent arrangement can be made for the child or children involved.

Many foster children are homeless children. As such, these children may receive services of the McKinney Homeless Assistance Act (Pennsylvania Department of Education, 1994). This Act, P.L. 100-77, was passed by Congress in 1987 to aid homeless persons. A section of the Act addresses the educational needs of homeless children and youth. This law was amended by P.L. 101-645, Education of Homeless Children and Youth, Homeless Assistance Amendments of 1990 Act. The McKinney Act's education provision applies to all homeless children and youth, who are guaranteed a free and appropriate public education. Homeless children and youth include those living with or without their parents in a shelter (e.g., temporary family shelter, domestic violence shelter, runaway shelter), transitional housing in foster homes, hotel or motel, campground, cars, or on the street. Also included are those children and youth temporarily living with relatives or friends (with or without their parents) because they do not have a fixed, regular, safe, and adequate residence (Pennsylvania Department of Education, 1994).

Important to teachers are educational decisions and the school options foster and homeless students have. In many states, school decisions are implemented through the cooperative efforts of respective chief school administrators. Teachers work with other school professionals, community and social workers, foster parents, and if appropriate, students to determine educational decisions. In all cases, school personnel consider the biological parents', foster parents', or legal guardians' requests regarding the children's school selections. Effective partnerships require collaboration and responsive practices with regards to minimizing home and school disruptions for the children, and working to maintain the highest possible degree of continuity in educational services for homeless students.

The new Individuals with Disabilities Education Act (IDEA) regulations provide some important clarifications involving children with foster parents. The new regulations specifically add foster parents to the category of parent. However, some strict conditions must be met first. For example, the natural parents' authority to make educational decisions must first be extinguished. This condition sets the stage for foster parents to act as informed advocates for the child by ensuring that a sufficient history exists between the child and foster parents and that there is not a legally competing natural parent (Annino, 1999).

Relevant themes that teachers may face during school conferences can relate to the following issues.

- *Many foster placements or home shelter situations may be on a short-term basis.* As such, many children placed in temporary homes often face anxiety and stress as they anticipate leaving the home or school environment at any time. Teachers may discuss with foster parents or other legal guardians ways to decrease children's anxiety and stress. Teachers and foster parents can discuss ways of helping children to find comfort in school services and community opportunities.

- *Living arrangements with foster parents or other legal guardians may vary.* Often, teachers and school personnel are unaware or uninformed of the guidance, structure, support, love, and attention the child receives in the home environment. Ascertaining specifics of the living arrangements with foster parents or legal guardians can help teachers to link school and home strategies more effectively. Home visits can support teachers' actions.

- *Children often move between various foster families or other temporary housing arrangements over short periods of time.* As such, parental styles vary. Many children face a variety of rules and consequences concerning homework, amount of television, free time, and so forth. Teachers can help to support children by noting what works with individual children and disseminating this information to appropriate adults during school and home conferences.

- *Biological parents, foster parents, legal guardians, and children often face tremendous stress in parenting required by the individual children.* Many adults assigned to foster or homeless children are capable of giving emotional and physical care, while considering the background and individuality of each child. However, some adults are not capable of providing such amenities. Foster children may suffer enormous and complex consequences as a result. By being aware of stressors, and working with the child's caregivers to support the child and family, teachers can be the bridge that holds children together.

- *Some foster or homeless children's caregivers in some living arrangements may accept an "only a substitute parent" philosophy.* Again, consequences to vulnerable children may be enormous. Teachers' sensitivity to such arrangements can help.

- *Many foster parents or legal guardians must be open to others' ideas of parenting, and are not totally in charge of the children.* Many arrangements are under the direction and supervision of a family case manager or a social worker. Such an arrangement may cause conflicts for adults and children alike. Teachers' support can lessen effects on the child and family.

- *Some foster children may experience a limited sense of belonging to anyone.* Many may express to teachers or school personnel that they feel abandoned and alone. Many have no siblings, or are separated from siblings and relatives.

Teachers' roles and responsibilities with children in such living arrangements are vast. Teachers will help to oversee proper educational decisions made on behalf of these children. Some teachers may be involved in children's attention to school attire, transportation, meal arrangements, after-school care, and medical attention, as in the case of Ann, a fourteen-year-old child (Box 2.4). Ann has been moved from foster home to foster home. Attention to collaborative practices underscores the necessity of responsive practices as Ann's teachers work with representatives of the legal, social, and educational systems on Ann's behalf. Her teachers can help Ann's current foster family to provide the love, support, guidance, and structure that can help Ann to survive and succeed in school settings.

Teachers' Work with Families

Understanding and responding to data on living arrangements, and understanding children's unique home situations, promote successful educational practices. Successful home-school partnerships are built when teachers recognize the strength and needs of each child, the family, and the living arrangements. Teachers encourage collaboration with family members, setting the stage for responsive practices, when teachers respond to roles and responsibilities supporting families and children. As teachers recognize and value what families offer, respond positively to individuals, and use cooperative, sharing ideas on behalf of their students, teachers are building effective home-school partnerships. Teachers build bonds based on their work with families in classrooms and schools (Stainbeck & Stainbeck, 1996; Stainbeck, Stainbeck, & Stefanich, 1996).

Today's decreased family size, varied living arrangements, economics and resources, family stressors, and the difficulties in maintaining family ties may increase the impor-

BOX 2.4

Family–Teacher Issues
Ann Loren is extremely light sensitive and squints when attempting close work during reading class. Her teacher, Mrs. Foley, wants to refer Ann for screening to the school nurse, Mrs. Jamal. Mrs. Foley suspects visual problems in Ann, especially as Mrs. Harris, Ann's foster mother, has expressed concerns about Ann's difficulty in completing written homework assignments and in seeing the television clearly.

Collaborative Orientations and Responsive Practices
Mrs. Foley telephones her concerns to Ann's foster mother, Mrs. Harris. Mrs. Jamal also contacts Mrs. Harris. Mrs. Harris, Mrs. Foley, and Mrs. Jamal jointly decide that Ann can profit from a visit to Vision Hospital. After Ann receives an in-depth eye exam at Vision Hospital, Mrs. Harris arranges for Ann's new glasses. Ann's difficulties in completing written homework assignments disappear when she wears her new glasses. Concurrently, Mrs. Foley moves Ann's seat away from the window so that unnecessary light does not hamper Ann's reading attempts. Ann no longer squints when attempting close work during reading class and her foster mother is pleased that Ann can see more clearly.

tance of schools, friendship, neighborhoods, and organizations as social support systems and personal ties (O'Shea et al., 1998). As teachers gain information on children's unique family experiences and living arrangements, teachers are in better positions to offer realistic educational decisions. Teachers can take advantage of their leadership and modeling roles by working productively with family members in home–school partnerships.

Teachers can work with family members by helping all families feel welcome. Teachers can show family members how to improve learning at home; such teachers are likely to have more support from caregivers and motivated students (Bempechat, 1992; Epstein, 1991a). For partnerships to work, there must be mutual trust and respect, an ongoing exchange of information, agreement on goals and strategies, and a sharing of rights and responsibilities. Some effective school-to-home partnerships have established pledges or contracts—written agreements among students, parents, and school staff to work together to increase learning. Teachers work well with caregivers when they help parents to feel like full partners. But many teachers say that although they would like to work more with families, they simply do not have enough time in the day. They need to be given the time and training to work with families (U.S. Department of Education, 1994). In fact, family training and strategies to work with family members are core to new imperatives sanctioned by the reauthorization of IDEA. Yell and Shriner (1997) reported how Congress viewed the reauthorization process as an opportunity to strengthen and improve the IDEA by strengthening the role of parents; giving increased attention to racial, ethnic, and linguistic diversity to prevent inappropriate identification and mislabeling for special education; and encouraging parents and teachers to work out educational differences using nonadversarial means. Thus, there are federal incentives to support teachers' work with families. Accordingly, teacher training programs can include general information on the benefits of and barriers to parental involvement, information on awareness of different family backgrounds and lifestyles, techniques for improving two-way communication between home and school, information on ways to involve parents in helping their children learn in school and outside of school, and ways that schools can help meet families' social, educational, and social service needs.

Effective home–school partnerships may be helped through the use of technology to link parents to the classroom. Computer networking, audiotapes, and videotapes can be used as alternatives to written communication for many parents. These are especially helpful in reaching families who do not read or do not have the time for more active school participation. Such technology may be the wave of the future to reach family members during alternative school conferences in the home, at work, or during off-peak school hours.

Table 2.4 provides suggestions for teachers to incorporate family involvement into class and school activities. Incorporation of these ideas may make the work between school and home easier. In the long run, effective home–school partnerships can flourish.

Family Member Questions

A school conference question that frequently occurs concerns the role of single-parent families and school involvement. Scenarios such as the following may be common: *Will anyone understand my needs as the parent doing all for my child? How can I be involved in school activities when I have such little home time with my child?*

TABLE 2.4 *Suggestions for Teachers to Incorporate Family Involvement into Class and School Activities*

- Consider varied family compositions and living arrangements that differ from the teacher's personal experiences.
- Empathize with students and family members to understand what they may be experiencing and act according to their needs instead of personal needs.
- Value individual families, cultures, and their uniqueness instead of trying to categorize and stereotype families.
- Consider that all children will not suffer from abuse or divorce situations in the same way. For example, all foster parents do not parent their children the same way. Consider the entire picture and all of the issues, before acting.
- Take time each morning to speak with students. Communicate regularly with family members.
- Allow options when communicating with families. Use a variety of contacts, including phone, face to face, notebook, or home visits. Determine the school professional with whom the family members may feel most comfortable: the teacher, counselor, principal, or other school professional.
- Demonstrate a genuine interest in what is happening on the home front and communicate with both households when there is a joint custody arrangement. Don't assume the information from school is reaching both parents.
- Be considerate of home arrangement facts when assigning homework. There may be no one at home to help with projects or difficult assignments that would need adult supervision. There may not be anyone checking to see whether homework is complete or done correctly.
- Plan alternative conference times in addition to school hour conferences: Think convenience for the families instead of teachers only. Hold conferences frequently. Seek to be helpful to everyone involved (teacher, student, and parents). Avoid talking over or under parents' heads: Avoid educational jargon.
- Make every conference meaningful and productive. Include the student in some of the conferences: Begin and end every conference, conversation, meeting, with a positive fact or work sample.
- Invite families into the classroom as much as possible. Value any and all contributions or suggestions family members make. Incorporate into the lessons family issues that can be helpful. Assume families are not teaching these skills at home. Use lessons to incorporate family customs, rituals, and traditions.
- Value the diversity of all students and their family compositions. Even though a family composition may seem unstructured or confusing, there are lessons and a contribution they can make to the class. Set up programs that benefit all students and all types of households.
- Get educated about the families of the students. Know what is going on at home. Find out more about each students' family and living arrangements.

Solutions to such questions are complex. Because single parenting has been on the rise in the 1990s, and with a predicted trend continuing in the future (Brunner, 1998), it is helpful for teachers to get specific information on ways the children and parent both can profit from educational and home support. Relevant single-parenting issues that parents may discuss with teachers during conferences may require teachers' knowledge of and skills in issues such as (a) the parents' and children's life beyond divorce or widowhood, including new relationships, dating, and sex; (b) the children surviving home stressors associated with divorce and the impact on their school functioning; (c) available media, pamphlets, electronic, or audio-video resources on informing the children and other relatives about divorce or the death of a parent; (d) strategies to control separation shock for the single parent and the children, while minimizing effects on the children's school adjustment and achievement; (e) parenting the children alone, with realistic family involvement in school functions; (f) helping the children cope with separation, loneliness, and rejection from the missing parent or from peers or other adults; (g) dealing with custody and visitation dilemmas, as the primary caretaker or as the parent without custody; and (h) using grandparents or neighbors as a resource and support system (Dodson, 1987).

Teachers can emphasize that although tasks may increase in number and duration when raising children without the other parent present, child-raising skills required by a single parent (or other alternative family structures) are essentially the same as those required by parents in an intact family. That is, teachers can help to clarify important actions parents should take: (a) establish family authority, (b) set up positive reward systems for the children, (c) create order and structure in the family, (d) stay physically and mentally fit as a parent with close attention to self-needs, and (e) establish personal and family goals for children and parents (Dodson, 1987). Teachers can be an important resource and support system for parents facing childrearing alone. Effective home–school partnerships are possible when teachers deal with issues in the child's life.

Family Resources and Services

This section lists relevant resources and services for family members. Teachers may share resources during school conferences, or provide written notice to family members periodically concerning the names, addresses, telephone numbers, contacts, and target concerns of each reference listed.

GENERAL RESOURCES

National Parent Information Network
ERIC Clearinghouse on Elementary
and Early Childhood Education
University of Illinois
805 W. Pennsylvania Ave.
Urbana, IL 61801-4897
(800) 583-4135

Parents as Teachers National Center
10176 Corporate Square Drive, Suite 230
St. Louis, MO 63132
(314) 432-4330

INTERNET SITES

**"Family Involvement in Children's
Education: Successful Local Approaches"**
U.S. Department of Education
www.ed.gov/pubs/FamInvolve

**"National Standards for Parent/
Family Involvement Programs"**
National PTA
www.pta.org/programs/pfistand.html

"Parental rights: An Infobrief Synopsis"
Education Issues
Association for Supervision and Curriculum
Development
www.ascd.org/issue/par.html

Summary

This chapter's purpose was to examine the nature of American families. The chapter identified the variety of family compositions, characteristics, statistics, and facts that comprise American families. Information on the current state of families with children under eighteen years of age included data on family issues affecting family life. The chapter examined children's backgrounds and experiences affecting family life. Various family arrangements received attention, including the nuclear family, extended family, stepfamily, single-parent family, and foster families/homeless children. Specific chapter themes relate to effective home–school partnerships and teachers' roles with parents or other primary caregivers, including:

- Families are the child's first teachers and primary caregivers. Parents and other family members have the greatest influence on their children.
- The use of families as partners in education is one of the greatest natural resources in home–school partnerships, but is untapped in many schools.
- Teachers' understanding of the state of families with children under eighteen years of age sets the stage in how professionals approach families, school conferences, and home or school involvement.
- Family effectiveness transcends economical, educational, ethnic, religious, and social parameters.
- A supportive way for all school professionals to demonstrate understanding of family needs is to be up-to-date on family statistics and characteristics that represent students' backgrounds and households.
- American families include nuclear families, extended families, stepfamilies, single-parent families, and foster families/homeless children.
- Successful home–school partnerships are built when teachers recognize the strength and needs of each child and his or her living arrangements.

References

Annino, P. G. (1999). The new IDEA regulations: The next step in improving the quality of special education. *Mental & Physical Disability Law Reporter, 23* (3), 439–442.

Bempechat, J. (1992). *Fostering high achievement in African American children: Home, school, and public policy influences.* New York: Columbia University.

Bennett, T., Deluca, D., & Bruns, D. (1997). Putting inclusion into practice: Perspectives of teachers and parents. *Exceptional Children, 64* (1), 115–131.

Black, S. (1998). Parent support. *The American School Board Journal, 185* (4), 50–52.

Bronfenbrenner, U. (1974). Is early intervention effective? A report on longitudinal evaluations of preschool program (Vol. 2). Washington, D.C.: Department of Health, Education & Welfare.

Brunner, B. (1998). *Information please almanac.* Boston, MA.: Information Please LLC.

Bureau of the Census. (1997). How we're changing: Demographic state of the nation: 1996. *Current Population Reports, Special Studies Series.* Washington, DC: U.S. Department of Commerce.

Davern, L. (1999). Parents' perspectives on personnel attitudes and characteristics in inclusive school settings: Implications for teacher preparation programs. *Teacher Education and Special Education, 22* (3), 165–182.

Dodson, F. (1987). *How to single parent.* New York: Harper & Row.

Doherty, W. J., Boss, P. G., LaRossa, R., Schumm, W. R., & Steinmetz, S. K. (1993). Family theories and methods: A contextual approach. In P. G. Boss, W. Doherty, R. LaRossa, W. R., Schumm, & S. K. Steinmetz (Eds.). *Sourcebook of family theories and methods* (pp. 3–30). New York: Plenum Press.

Elam, S., Lowell, C. R., & Gallup, A. M. (1994). The 26th annual Phi Delta Kappa/Gallup poll of the public's attitude toward the public schools. *Phi Delta Kappan, 72,* 116–120.

Elam, S. M., Rose, L. C., & Gallup, A. M. (1996). The 28th annual Phi Delta Kappa/Gallup poll of the public's attitude toward the public schools. *Phi Delta Kappan, 78,* 41–59.

Epstein. J. L. (1991). Paths to partnerships: What we can learn from federal, state, district, and school initiatives. *Phi Delta Kappan 72* (5), 344–349.

Eyre, L., & Eyre, R. (1994). *Three steps to a strong family.* New York: Simon & Schuster.

Katsiyannis, A., & Maag, J. W. (1998). Disciplining students with disabilities: Issues and considerations for implementing IDEA '97. *Behavioral Disorders, 23* (4), 276–289.

Knight, D., & Wadsworth, D. (1998). A national survey of special education teacher preparation programs regarding their inclusion of family focused components of the CEC Common Core of Knowledge and Skills. *Teacher Education and Special Education, 21* (3), 214–226.

Krantz, M. (1994). *Child development: Risk and opportunity.* Belmont CA: Wadsworth Publishing Company.

Larson, J. (1992). Understanding step families. *American Demographics, 14,* 360.

Lee, V. E., & Croninger, R. G. (1994). The relative importance of home and school in the development of literacy skills for middle-grade students. *American Journal of Education, 102* (3), 286–329.

O'Shea, L. J., O'Shea, D. J., Algozzine, B. (1998). *Learning disabilities: From theory toward practice.* New York: Merrill-Prentice Hall.

Pennsylvania Department of Education. (1994). *Education of Homeless Children and Youth Program.* Harrisburg, PA: Author.

Popenoe, D. (1993). American family decline, 1960–1990: A review and appraisal. *Journal of Marriage and the Family, 55,* 527–541.

Public Law 101-645. (1990). *Education of Homeless Children and Youth, Homeless Assistance Amendments of 1990 Act.* Washington, DC: U.S. Department of Education.

Radin, N. (1969). The impact of a kindergarten home counseling program. *Exceptional Children, 3,* 18–26.

Radin, N. (1972). Three degrees of maternal involvement in a pre-school program. Impact of mothers and children. *Child Development, 4,* 355–364.

Reid, R. (1997). Reforming educational reform. *Journal of Behavioral Education, 7,* 1–12.

Scott, R., & Davis, A. (1979). Preschool Education and Busing: Do we have our priorities straight? Paper presented at the National Urban Education Association, New York.

Shore, R. (1995). *The current state of high school reform.* New York: Carnegie Corporation.

Singer, G. H. S., & Powers, L. E. (Eds.) (1993). *Families, disability and empowerment: Active coping skills and strategies for family interventions.* Baltimore: Paul H. Brookes.

Smith, S. (1995). Family theory and multicultural family studies. In B. B. Ingoldsby & S. Smith (Eds.). *Families in multicultural perspective* (pp. 1–29). New York: The Guilford Press.

Some Facts about Stepfamilies (1998). www.stepfam.org/facts.htm.

Sprey, J. (1990). Theoretical practice in family studies. In J. Sprey (Ed.). *Fashioning family theory* (pp. 9–33). Newbury Park, CA: Sage.

Stainbeck, S., & Stainbeck, W. (1996). *Inclusion: A guide for educators.* Baltimore: Paul H. Brookes.

Stainbeck, W., Stainbeck, S., & Stefanich, G. (1996). Learning together in inclusive classrooms. What about the curriculum? *Exceptional Children, 28* (3), 4–19.

Talbert-Johnson, C. (1998). Why so many African-American children in special ed? *School Business Affairs, 64* (4), 30–35.

Turnbull, A. P., & Turnbull, H. R. (1997). *Families, professionals, and exceptionality: A special partnership.* Upper Saddle River, NJ: Prentice Hall/ Merrill.

Turnbull, A. P., Turnbull, H. R., Shank, M., & Leal, D. (1995). *Exceptional lives: Special education in today's schools.* Englewood Cliffs, NJ: Prentice Hall/ Merrill.

Turner, A. (1987). *Multicultural considerations: Working with families of developmentally disabled and high-risk children. The black perspective.* Paper presented at the conference of the National Center for Clinical Infant Programs, "Vulnerable Infants, Stressed Families: Challenges for Research and Practice," Los Angeles, CA.

U.S. Department of Education. (1994). *Calculations based on information from the 1994 Condition of Education, the 1993 Digest of Education Statistics and the 1993 Statistical Abstract of the United States.* Author.

U.S. Department of Education. (1996). *The condition of education.* Washington, DC: National Center for Education Statistics: Author.

U.S. Department of Education. (1997). *Nineteenth annual report to Congress on the implementation of the Individuals with Disabilities Education Act.* Washington, DC: Author.

Wagner, M. (1991). *Drop outs with disabilities: What do we know? What can we do?* Menlo Park: SRI International.

Wertheimer, A. (1989). *Self-advocacy and parents. The impact of self-advocacy on the parents of young people with disabilities.* London: Further Education Unit.

Yell, M., & Shriner, J. G. (1997). The IDEA Amendments of 1997: Implications for special and general education teachers, administrators, and teacher trainers. *Focus on Exceptional Children, 30* (1), 1–19.

3

Families of Students from Diverse Backgrounds

Dorothy J. O'Shea

Paul L. Lancaster

Chapter Objectives _____

In this chapter we will

- Describe what *diversity* is
- Identify what we know about understanding family diversity
- Describe family diversity statistics
- Describe what new teachers can do to begin their work in recognizing and accepting family diversity
- Illustrate use of specific actions that show how teachers can value family diversity
- Examine how teachers can help diverse students and their families to feel a part of the school community
- Identify culturally responsive teaching using family input
- Pose family member questions and answers that may arise during school-based conferences
- List resources for families of students from diverse backgrounds
- Summarize important chapter themes

> *As the daughter of an Irish Catholic father and an African American Jewish mother, eighteen-year-old LaToya Mulligan grew up understanding the effects of diversity between her parents' backgrounds right in her own home. She remembers going to Sunday mass with her parents to celebrate her Catholic heritage. She also remembers celebrating Kwanzaa and the feeling of contentment she felt when she and her family wore traditional African garb to celebrate. On school assembly day, she remembers the joy in presenting to her classmates the family videos that reflected her father's fancy for Jewish food and her mother's love of Celtic music and African art.*

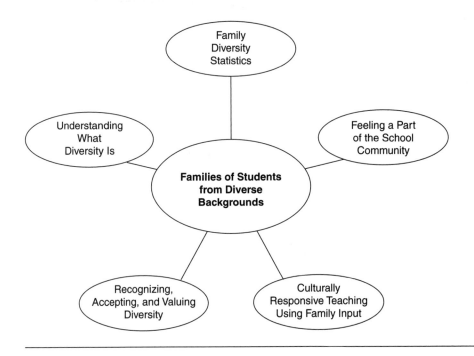

LaToya is ready to begin college in the fall and plans on becoming a scientist. LaToya has two sisters and a brother. Each of her siblings also is succeeding very well academically and behaviorally. LaToya talks about her family's diversity with ease. She believes that the reason she and her siblings have done so well is due to her parents' hard work in creating an accepting family atmosphere. While her father, Philip, and her mother, Iris, never had a great deal of money, LaToya believes that her parents provided their children with so much more: a model of parenting and family life that LaToya wants to emulate when she marries; a striving for continual self-improvement, no matter what life's circumstances entail; a love of reading to help in her continuing education; and the desire to travel to far-off places in order to experience the world.

LaToya also credits her teachers with influencing her positively. LaToya remembers that Miss Parker, her biology teacher, helped LaToya to grow in her love of animals and her knowledge of science. LaToya thinks of Mr. Sullivan, her learning support teacher, as a model of tenacity and persistence. LaToya did not enjoy rewriting her English compositions two and three times, but now she senses accomplishment in writing skills fostered by Mr. Sullivan. LaToya credits Mrs. Harrison, her choral teacher, with expanding LaToya's love of music and her creative expression. LaToya further believes that Mrs. Harrison's influence helped LaToya to want to do more to support the community. When she is finished with college, LaToya vows that she will return to start a health care practice in her urban neighborhood, near the high school from which she graduated.

Why are LaToya's beliefs and actions so important? LaToya's story reflects the growing recognition of diversity and the positive ramifications that evolve when diversity is nurtured by teachers and families. LaToya's story also reflects the need for increased multicultural understanding and education in American society so that other parents and teachers can replicate what LaToya and her siblings received.

What Is Diversity?

Diversity is the condition of being different from others. It entails having differences. As a person develops from infant to adult, that individual is constantly changing. Noted differences may be minimal initially. As the individual matures, however, those differences often magnify. Because we all have differences that are valued by society to varying degrees, the issue of diversity casts important influences in students' school experiences and opportunities for success.

One can hardly pick up any newspaper, magazine, or textbook without facing diversity implications and influences. Teachers examining public schools find diverse compositions of their student bodies. They find diverse compositions of their administrators, faculties, and staffs. They find that diversity underscores the curricula provided to students, notably in assessment and programming options from preschool to graduation standards and requirements. As they examine instructional goals or objectives, teachers also consider whether students' diverse needs and strengths are met in local schools. Diversity may highlight the level and type of financial support a school district receives. However, many typically associate a discussion on diversity with students' family backgrounds and origins.

As discussed in Chapter 2, researchers cannot agree on what "families" entail. For example, Turnbull, Turnbull, Shank, and Leal (1995) describe what is perceived to be family, indicating that professionals often view a student's family as consisting of a mother and father. In fact, however, teachers typically communicate with mothers and expect them, not fathers, to attend school meetings. Accordingly "family" is operationalized as "mothers" only. Fuligni (1997) reported that a dominant American Caucasian definition of family often focuses on an intact, nuclear family. However, a common household arrangement in many diverse families is an extended family model, as described in Chapter 2. Thus, African American families universally rely on a wide network of kin and community, as they describe their own families. In Italian families, a family can encompass a strong, tightly knit group of three or four generations (which also includes godparents and old friends). Many Chinese families cite ancestors and descendants from their family perspective (Bennett, 1995a; 1995b).

LaToya's nuclear family members and her teachers capitalized on LaToya's cultural and religious diversity in helping her to achieve a sense of self and a pride in her family and community. In LaToya's case, her teachers and family members worked together to focus on strengths in LaToya's culture, ethnicity, religion, and race. Diversity issues affecting other students relate to such factors as age, disability, gender, language, personality, or sexuality. The intersection of issues (e.g., race and ethnicity, language and religion, gender and sexual orientation, generation and age, and so forth), operate within each individual, cross-cut, and come out differently in every person (Cortes, 1999).

Similar to LaToya's experiences, today's teachers must work with family members to examine students' differences and how these differences have an impact on students' opportunities for success. Caring teachers examine the home and school setting and what is made available, or denied, to diverse students. Such teachers support their students' uniqueness, understanding that diverse American families represent vast backgrounds. A family's background, notably its culture, has a major impact on, and undeniably influences the behavior of its members. Each culture has a set of values and beliefs that guides the members of that culture in social interactions (Lewis & Doorlag, 1995; Nieto, 1996).

What may be accepted in one culture as appropriate or desirable, may not be the desired goal in another. For instance, some South American and Australian cultures encourage listeners in conversations to glance away from, not toward, speakers holding more authoritarian status (e.g., religious or community authority figures). When working with students from these communities, teachers need to respect the values these students have been taught for authority figures and to understand that the resulting behaviors displayed may be signs of respect. Rather than trying to change students, teachers work toward understanding how their backgrounds influence their behaviors and value systems (and are reflected in the beliefs family members hold about the family's role in the education of their children) (Hayes, 1994).

Unfortunately, students from diverse backgrounds historically received such descriptors as over-compliant, timid, indecisive, and lacking leadership (Leung, 1990), resulting in many people considering these students to be socially incompetent in a broader social context (Cartledge & Milburn, 1995). Some teachers may overlook the fact that many of these behaviors are expected and rewarded in students' home settings or cultural environments. The rapid demographic changes in the United States pose a challenge to all teachers. Teachers must be sensitive to the needs of students and families from varied diverse backgrounds. Misinterpretation of culturally linked behaviors places diverse students and their families in conflict with expectations for social behaviors between home and school (Delgado-Rivera & Rogers-Adkinson, 1997).

The challenge for new teachers is to use diversity knowledge constructively to support students, not destructively, subtly, or stereotypically. In order to understand their students and the influences of students' backgrounds, teachers begin by understanding family diversity.

What We Know about Understanding Family Diversity

Astute teachers are observant. They observe to make sense of potential needs or strengths implied by their students' diversity. They seek to understand how and why students are unique. Teachers do not focus on differences alone. They look for commonalities that all people share, trying to make sense of prior learning opportunities and future experiences.

Teachers aware of each students' uniqueness consider the importance of significant people with whom students interact. Thus, students' family members, peers, community friends, and religious associates, all help to shape the student into whom he or she is or will become. However, teachers cannot just passively state acceptance of family diversity. Teachers operating with collaborative orientations and responsive practices understand the strength that family diversity implies. A goal must be to demonstrate the value of family diversity and ways to teach tolerance and value sharing in the classroom.

Such is not an easy task. For instance, Noel (2000) reported on a number of teachers who stood alone because they insisted on a more inclusive curriculum or called for increased cultural sensitivity among students and staff at their school. Reflective teachers often work with family members to confront the biased comments of younger children when defending the rights of a student with a disability. Other teachers elicit the help of family members to determine best how to build confidence in students who receive biased comments because they happen to be the only African American or Jewish or Latino classroom member. However, even in the face of difficult situations, when teachers elicit the support of students' family members, they can use the family's insights to get students to engage in self-examination, questioning, and learning from negative experiences.

What Families Expect

Most families expect that when their students attend school in this multicultural society, teachers will be there to facilitate students' acquisition of the academic, behavioral, and social skills necessary to function and succeed in school. Most families want their child to graduate from high school and be prepared to function successfully in adult life. In order to help students and families reach these goals, many teachers try to understand the impact of family beliefs, customs, and traditions within our diverse society.

New teachers' work with diverse family members will be crucial as teachers increase students' access to the general education curricula. For instance, many students with disabilities will face negative experiences requiring teachers and family members to face issues, solve problems, and share strategies together. As teachers demonstrate understanding of diversity, they show communication, acceptance of differences, and commitment to students and families—key ingredients in having successes of the general education curriculum generalize to students' success in adult life. Acceptance, communication, and commitment extend to opportunities for the value of diversity to spread across students, families, places, and events.

Increases in collaborative orientations and responsive practices occur when teachers work with diverse families as the teacher in Box 3.1 did. In this case, Mrs. Martinez actively sought to develop stronger home–school relationships with her student's family by holding team meetings at a time and place conducive for the family. Mrs. Martinez demonstrated responsive practices when she tried to convince other school personnel of the need to understand the family's attendance during school meetings and their real concern for their child's progress. Mrs. Martinez worked to gather important data on her student's background before making conclusions about the student or his family.

Family Diversity Statistics

Students, such as those in Mrs. Martinez's class, come from diverse family backgrounds. Diverse families represent their family bonds, culture, community, ethnicity, kinship, traditions, or religion. Diversity represents the changing demographics of American society.

BOX 3.1

Family–Teacher Issues

Mrs. Martinez has four third-grade students who had been identified as "at risk" by former teachers. The children range in age from 8 to 9.5 years old. Half of the children are Hispanic, from homes where Spanish is the dominant language. Last month, Mrs. Martinez made home visits to discuss the children's school progress with the families. Mrs. Martinez noted in her anecdotal records some important information for the school's multidisciplinary evaluation team. First, Mrs. Martinez noted that discrepancies existed between parents' and former teachers' perceptions of the four third graders. Further, information was often not solicited from parents by former teachers. In the case of Romulas, one of the four students from a stepfamily home which had ten family members, Romulas's former teachers' perceptions were given higher priority than Romulas's parents' perceptions in making decisions about the child's school options. Mrs. Martinez was concerned when Romulas's mother indicated that information was sometimes withheld from her by school officials. Romulas's mother indicated that while other parents seemed to accept the judgments of school officials and set aside their own doubts, Romulas's mother wanted to speak up on her son's behalf.

Collaborative Orientations and Responsive Practices

Mrs. Martinez arranged immediately for the school's multidisciplinary evaluation team to consider important cultural information that was not previously included in each of the four students' files. In the case of Romulas and the other three students, Mrs. Martinez insisted that parent input and cultural data must be considered in their formal and informal discussions. Mrs. Martinez indicated that she could begin working with the other fourth grade teachers to develop stronger home–school relationships with her students' families. She would begin by holding Romulas's team meetings at a time and place conducive for Romulas's family—who had no transportation to school. Among her other suggestions were the importance of teachers' understandings of parent involvement in schools. Mrs. Martinez suggested that because families often cannot attend school meetings when school personnel choose the time, doesn't mean that the families are not concerned about their child's progress. Mrs. Martinez suggested that the teachers and administrators start brainstorming with families on how to develop wider community partnerships.

Changing Demographics

One way of understanding students' families is recognizing the continuing, changing demographics of the United States, and the substantive diversity in school-age populations. America's profile is rapidly changing. Shaw (1999) reported that in 1998 there were 69.9 million children in the United States, .3 million more than in 1997. These numbers demonstrate that the demand for schools is likely to increase. Racial and ethnic diversity continues to climb dramatically in the United States. In 1998, 65 percent of U.S. children were white, non-Hispanic; 15 percent were African American, non-Hispanic; and 15 percent were Hispanic. These figures are expected to increase as the year 2020 approaches.

In the year 2000, however, one out of every three Americans was of African American, Hispanic, Asian American, or Native American heritage (Bureau of the Census,

1997). Diversity analyses in public schools indicate continued increases in births of nonwhite, non-Anglo students (up from 16 percent in the 1970s to 36 percent in 1984, with a continuing rise in the 1990s) (Bauwens & Hourcade, 1995; Research and Policy Committee of the Committee for Economic Development, 1987). The issue of whether students from diverse backgrounds and cultures receive full educational opportunity is important in understanding the types, level, and location of services students receive. Some professionals contend that students from diverse backgrounds and their families face dire consequences as students enter public schools.

Overrepresentation Issues

There are major philosophical and logistical changes resulting from P.L. 105-17, the 1997 Individuals with Disabilities Education Act (IDEA) '97, which established new provisions designed to improve outcomes for students with disabilities (U.S. Department of Education, 1997). As discussed in Chapter 1 of this text, such changes include requirements that students with disabilities be included in state- and district-wide assessments, that students' Individual Education Programs (IEPs) address issues of students' access to general education curricula, and that states establish performance goals and indicators for students with disabilities (Hehir, 1999; McLaughlin, 1999; Ysseldyke & Olsen, 1999). Current teachers must work with family members to determine how diverse students, especially those with disabilities, can be included in state- and district-wide assessments. Together, teachers and family members must address students' IEPs and access to general education curricula. Teachers and family members must work productively in helping states to implement students' performance goals and indicators.

IDEA also underscores diversity issues important to teachers and families of students from culturally and language diverse backgrounds. These included the following points:

- The federal government must be responsive to the growing needs of an increasingly diverse society.
- More equitable resource allocation is essential to provide an equal educational opportunity for all students.
- Serious recruitment efforts are necessary to attract professionals from minority backgrounds into the teaching profession: Students with cultural and language diversity require teachers, role models, and personnel to address the changing demographics of their special education needs.
- Students from the upper middle-class social strata are placed disproportionately in higher academic tracks; students from the low-income social strata are placed disproportionately in lower academic tracks.
- Even when students demonstrate no differences in ability, academic tracks continue to reflect race, gender, language, and class differences.

Although a controversial topic, researchers contend that more diverse students are at risk for school and social difficulties than other students. For example, more minority students continue to be served in special education than would be expected based on minorities represented in the general school population. Thus, students with specific learning disabilities (SLDs) compose the largest category of students in special education classrooms. The SLD category appears to be favored nationally when diagnosing minority students, particularly students from Hispanic backgrounds (Artiles, Aguirre-Munoz, & Abedi, 1998; O'Shea, O'Shea, & Algozzine, 1998).

The number of students with a variety of cultural backgrounds and limited English proficiency placed in special education programs is growing at a disproportionate rate. Reasons for the placement trend relate to (a) inability of culturally and linguistically diverse students to perform to teacher expectations for correct academic performance and classroom behavioral standards; (b) inappropriate labels, due to poor assessment and evaluation scores which may result from their cultural and linguistic diversity; and (c) professional expectations and assessment instruments that generally reflect a bias toward the cultural expectations of the majority, white, Anglo-American population in this country (Artiles, Aguirre-Munoz, & Abedi, 1998; Helge, 1991; Jacobs, 1991; MacMillan & Reschly, 1998).

Nonetheless, controversy continues over the issue of overrepresentation in special education. Artiles, Aguirre-Munoz, and Abedi (1998) commented on overrepresentation for children with SLD, explaining that problems centered on professional practices; problematic identification and placement practices; conceptual vagueness and variability in identification and eligibility criteria; and social deviance variables (e.g., school suspension and corporal punishment).

MacMillan and Reschly (1998), however, suggested that socioeconomic status, rather than ethnicity, is the primary risk factor for children encountering severe and persistent academic problems in public schools. Their report on overrepresentation involved linking information on the ethnicity of the child to the categorical membership of that child in high-incidence disability categories. Based on their surveys conducted in 1978, 1986, and 1990, they found an increase in the total percent of children from White, African American, and Hispanic groups served in the combined three program categories of SLD, mild mental retardation (MMR), and serious emotional disturbance (SED). These researchers concluded that the increase in percentages for all three ethnic groups is primarily attributable to the increase in the percentage of each ethnic group classified as SLD. Nonetheless, the percentage of Hispanic students served in individual and combined categories is substantially lower than the percentages of African American and White students in both the 1986 and the 1990 surveys. They suggested that Hispanic students are not overrepresented in these categories at the national level. Further, they contended that the African American–White difference for all three categories combined, gradually diminished from 1978 to 1990. This trend was also evident in African American–White differences in MMR over the same period; however, MMR continued to be the category in which African American–White differences were most pronounced. It accounted for nearly all of the overrepresentation found for the combined categories. Finally, they reported that the dramatic increase over the years in the percentage of each ethnic group served in SLD appeared to be of comparable magnitude for all three ethnic groups. Accordingly, MacMillan and Reschly argued that the attitudes held by many toward categories, such as MMR and SED, are both stronger and more negative when overrepresentation is evident because such evidence might reinforce negative portrayals and stereotypes of minority groups.

Talbert-Johnson (1998) argued that the total percentage of minority students placed in special education should be plus or minus 10 percent of the minority students found in the overall population. Students from African American backgrounds and poor families are two to three times more likely to be identified by their teachers as having mental retardation than their White counterparts. Analyses of demographic differences between secondary school youth with disabilities and the general population of youth revealed that 24.2 percent of youth identified with disabilities were African American, compared to 14.0 percent of the general population of youth (SRI International, 1993).

However the overrepresentation factor plays out, many diverse students fare worse than traditional students in statistical comparisons of "at risk" factors for academic and/or social failure. As discussed in Chapter 4, students from poor families who are illiterate face the possibility of dropping out from school. The school dropout rate is 68 percent higher for minorities than for whites. More than 50 percent of minority students in large cities drop out of school (Helge 1991; Campbell, 1996; Talbert-Johnson, 1998). Wagner's (1991) findings were that students with high absenteeism and those failing school classes do not often develop social bonds with schools, or identify their classes as relevant.

No matter how the statistics reported from various advocates and agencies play out, the topics of overrepresentation and at-risk factors continue to raise considerable professional attention. Overrepresentation of minority students in special education services requires close scrutiny by teachers and family members. Although there is controversy over whether students from minority backgrounds are indeed overrepresented or at risk for school failures due to their ethnicity or other factors (such as poverty), it is clear that teachers and family members must work together to support students. Working together can encourage teachers and family members to model for students ways of recognizing, accepting, and valuing individual strengths and needs of all diverse people.

What Can New Teachers Do to Begin Their Work in Recognizing and Accepting Diversity?

There are specific actions new teachers can take as they begin their important work in recognizing and accepting diversity. Teachers' work with family members can begin by examining personal beliefs about minority groups when referring students for special education services. Teachers can work with family members to determine whether the student has a need for special education or can be supported by other educational means.

When interacting with diverse families, teachers can reflect on their own cultural expectations to identify possible incongruences. Appropriate educational decisions for students and families demonstrate respect for cultural behaviors, while assisting in the development of skills to function successfully in the mainstream culture (Delgado-Rivera & Rogers-Adkinson, 1997; Harry, 1994). Thus, teachers can examine self-biases when setting up classroom observations and strategies meant to change students' behaviors. By working toward students' access in the general education curricula, teachers can work with family members so that all students have opportunities to survive and succeed.

Teachers also can strive for quality education that not only meets the standards of excellence, but also satisfies those concerned with equity in education. Unfortunately, because disproportionately large numbers of students from lower socioeconomic systems often receive assignments to low-ability groups in their early school years (Gollnick & Chinn, 1998), teachers must consciously review their expectations for students and their behavior toward students' families. Teachers can self-examine and work actively to ensure that discrimination does not exist. Working toward collaborative orientations and responsive practices means resolving to build trust and support, over time, through sincere efforts of all involved.

Another important consideration is teachers' need to gather information on where their students live. Delpit conducted extensive research in Alaska, New Guinea, and in historically African American universities, concluding: "If I want to learn how best to teach students who may be different from me, then I must seek the advice of adults—teachers and parents—who are from the same culture as my students" (Delpit, 1995, p. 102). This means that new teachers must come to know the community and understand cultural norms and values that are important to family members. Teachers can familiarize themselves with the communities in which they teach by spending time there, getting to know families, and finding out what parents or guardians want for their children. Teachers can ask questions about how teachers can help (Grant & Sleeter, 1998).

Thus, an important strategy to demonstrate that new teachers recognize and accept diversity is to participate in community events. This helps teachers to develop a range of teaching strategies that are congruent with students' home cultures (Neuman, Hagedorn, Celano, & Daly, 1995). Too often, teachers are at a disadvantage because they do not live, or have never lived, in the community in which their students live. The only parents with whom some teachers interact are those who are able to attend parent–teacher meetings, or who have scheduled school conferences. In many cases, teachers have not been in their students' homes, nor have they been active participants in community activities. To make classrooms conducive for family interactions with school personnel, teachers can learn about their students' cultures and traditions, and participate in important community events (Gollnick & Chinn, 1998).

The increasing numbers of students from culturally and language diverse backgrounds served in general education in the public schools create a corresponding need for well-prepared teachers who can communicate with students within the context of their cultures and native languages (Talbert-Johnson, 1998). Teachers familiarize themselves with the communities in which they teach by spending time there, getting to know the community, and finding out what families want for their children. Family members increase support of their children's learning at home through concrete suggestions, which they seek from teachers whom they believe care about them and their children. When teachers are known in the community, families may be more open to communicating and reciprocating.

Many school professionals have different viewpoints than those of their students' parents. Tiegerman-Farber and Radziewicz (1998) described administrators' views of parents. Administrators indicated that the system cannot make decisions in a vacuum. As mentioned previously in this text, some parents demonstrate that they are apathetic and do not show up for meetings or for school events. Parent apathy suggests that parents must take a look at themselves and "show up" for their students. Parents, on the other hand, complain that administrators, like teachers, treat them like "naughty little students" (Tiegerman-Farber & Radziewicz, 1998 p. 108).

However, teachers working with collaborative orientations and responsive practices recognize and accept that family members must be an integral factor in important decision making. Familiarity with parents' views of their children's school behaviors and social difficulties becomes necessary to understand how to support family members productively and to educate students effectively.

As they observe and interact within the community, many teachers find that most families, from all socioeconomic, ethnic, cultural, and religious walks of life, want their children to receive the best education possible. Being able to determine what "the best education possible" means to students' families is an important step in individualizing instruction. As in LaToya's case, teachers can often rely on students' families and friends for support of individual goals and realistic expectations to guide students productively.

Thus, teachers become familiar with their students' families and communities by personalizing the knowledge of those families and in working within the school to increase family involvement. This might mean that teachers capitalize on families' diverse backgrounds by integrating classroom lessons and units with what they know about students' backgrounds. Increases in collaborative orientations and responsive practices occur when teachers act professionally, as do the teachers in Box 3.2. In this case, teachers in the Benson

BOX 3.2

Family–Teacher Issues
Teachers in the Benson School District decided that in this school year they would start off by targeting strategies to encourage multicultural educational opportunities to children in their district. The teachers reacted to a local newspaper report that suggested Benson has a higher than state average of students and their families facing transience, homelessness, and lack of community involvement. During their faculty meeting in August, the teachers noted that although many Benson students come from poor homes, they usually have strong attendance by parents during community recognition day. These teachers decided to highlight their community diversity as a teaching theme in courses taught during the month of November.

Collaborative Orientations and Responsive Practices
Benson School District teachers decided to elicit the support of their local community groups when they highlighted November as community diversity month. Professionals agreed to focus on "community and family diversity" themes in the presentation of social studies, language, and reading classes. Among the activities Benson District teachers and their parent volunteer groups decided to focus on were (1) securing from the library high-interest-level readers dealing with ways to help children sense pride in cultural and religious heritage, (2) fighting stereotypes by asking students to write language compositions on ways to ignore or eliminate hurtful comments from others, (3) forming cultural food and costume day in all classrooms, (4) setting up banners schoolwide proclaiming diversity pride day, and (5) staging "social issues tolerance" day. Teachers and parent volunteers decided that they would disseminate joint information and continue to meet after November on effective strategies that help local children want to do well.

School District decided that they would elicit family members' help by targeting strategies to encourage multicultural awareness and parent involvement opportunities in their district.

Specific Actions That Show How New Teachers Value Diversity

There are specific actions teachers can take to show that they value family diversity. The following points summarize how new teachers first recognize and accept and then demonstrate active valuing of their students' family diversity:

• Teachers seek to be sensitive to the diversity of students' homes and communities by becoming familiar with family backgrounds and communities.

• Teachers plan events in students' homes and communities to involve family members.

• Teachers use responsible decision making that links planning and programming implementation to family needs.

• Teachers work to reduce negative expectations that may exist for families.

• Teachers work toward the goal of considering and using others' viewpoints—even when viewpoints differ from their own.

• Teachers become aware of parents' and guardians' needs for involvement. Teachers do not make unrealistic demands on family commitment to time and involvement.

• Teachers support the diverse families, seeking family input on how best to serve students in the general education curricula.

By generalizing the skills starting in recognizing and accepting family diversity, and in extending these skills across people, place, and time, teachers set the stage for valuing family diversity. Box 3.3 illustrates a teacher who actively worked toward helping a diverse family work together to support their child. The teacher demonstrated collaboration with the school counselor and parents to help the student's family members realize that they need to spend increased time alone with the child on a continuing basis. The teacher set the stage for her long-term commitment of valuing family diversity.

Part of Miss Washington's role in helping Chantal's family members was to send home written material that was clear, concise, and easily readable to ensure that parents or other caregivers had access to important educational information. Important notices must be in the family's primary language and reading levels. (Miss Washington's newsletters for parents actually included a glossary of terms and icons to help Chantal's family understand school efforts.) Also, teachers can change the traditional image of contacting diverse families only when a student is in trouble, or when the school needs help with a bake sale. By reporting to families continually on their childrens' needs, strengths, and progress, and by making phone contacts and home visits, teachers show that they value their students and families.

Miss Washington also can reduce distrust and cultural barriers between Chantal's families and school personnel by arranging contacts in neutral settings. These might include

BOX 3.3

Family–Teacher Issues

Chantal is now ten years old and is in Miss Washington's fourth-grade class. Chantal is biracial. His mother is Asian American and his father is African American. Chantal lives with his mother and stepfather, who is Asian. Chantal is very polite, usually remembering to say please and thank you to the crossing guard and to the school staff he meets on the way. Further, Chantal seems to have friends. He eats in the school cafeteria with Sammy and Bud, his next door neighbors. Chantal plays the goalie position on the community soccer team and he sings in the church choir. His mother and stepfather, Mr. and Mrs. Scott, report that Chantal gets along fine with his younger stepsister, Mariah. Chantal also reportedly gets along with his half-brother, Seth, on his paternal side. Chantal visits Seth and his father every other weekend, and on holidays. Although he doesn't have his own bedroom in Seth's house, Chantal says he likes sleeping on the top bunk bed there.

Mr. and Mrs. Scott report that they want to have more meetings with Chantal's current teacher, Miss Washington. The parents report that Chantal tries to do his homework each night but is frustrated because he is being teased by some students. Chantal says that some of the older students have been taking his book bag lately and calling him names. The parents have concerns that Chantal's attention for school is starting to wane. Concurring, Miss Washington reports that Chantal is beginning to get further and further behind in his homework completion. Further, class time is problematic. Chantal seems to get distracted easily by outside stimuli, especially when he hears the older students in the hallway. Miss Washington notes that Chantal will stare out the window. Constantly, she must remind him to follow along with class events. She questioned him on why he was not attending, asking him whether the older students bothered him. Chantal reported that he can handle the older students. However, he was concerned because no one from his two families came to either his community soccer game or heard him sing solo in the church choir. Chantal said that he doesn't know where his real home is or where he belongs.

Collaborative Orientations and Responsive Practices

Miss Washington called in Chantal's parents on both sides to try to discern how and when the family provides individual attention to Chantal. With the help of the school counselor, Miss Washington was able to help Chantal's families realize that they need to spend some time alone with him and on a continuing basis. Even if the time allotted is only ten minutes, Miss Washington pointed out that Chantal needs their recognition, attention, and support. She reiterated that his families can help Chantal to focus during the day more readily. When Chantal reported that his father and stepfather each agreed to take biweekly turns to observe his soccer games, Chantal's attention in class and his homework completion showed improved progress.

---

using resource centers, offering informal learning sessions, conducting home visits by family liaison personnel, or holding meetings off school grounds. Because the first contact a parent has with his or her child's school is often negative, some districts make sure that the first contact with diverse parents is a positive one (U.S. Department of Education, 1996).

However, some family members from diverse backgrounds have not always come forth and volunteered to become major players in their child's education. The reason for the lack of involvement may be multifaceted. For example, some diverse family members report that they do not always feel welcome in schools, in part because many schools reflect the dominant culture and language, rather than those of the parents (Gollnick & Chinn, 1998). A possible solution to this situation might be for teachers to make an active effort to engage parents in informal school activities. School-sponsored clubs, sport events, cook-outs, and fairs can be ice-breakers. A true collaboration requires that family members and teachers are partners in the teaching–learning process. When they receive reciprocity from others, families and teachers learn to respect, value, and accept others. However, starting informally may be the key to initiating reciprocal actions.

Helping Diverse Students and Their Families to Feel a Part of the School Community

Shore (1995) offered relevant directions for contemporary teachers that can help diverse students and their families to feel a part of the school community. These include the following ideas that support new teachers' efforts:

• Stress participatory management and leadership at the school level, and ensure that parents have a voice in decision making.

• Make schools flatter organizations, so that they can become less bureaucratic and more communal.

• Be connected to students and families. Assume the role of adults who can become students' and families' main contact for guidance and support and can serve as their consistent advocates.

• Use mixed-ability grouping in all classes, including mathematics and science.

• Stress instructional strategies, including cooperative learning, that challenge students to work and learn together.

• Use alternative assessment practices, such as portfolio assessments, that are shared with families. Reduce reliance on multiple choice tests and encourage extended writing assignments. Monitor individual students' progress in achieving goals on a regular basis.

• Collaborate and share with students' families, including the provision of opportunities for families and teachers to work and learn together, so that they can begin to understand each other's cultures, expectations, and views.

Supporting Diverse Families in School Events

New teachers can demonstrate respect for differences by looking for and using family strengths when planning school events. For example, part of teachers' roles in supporting diverse families is to help students learn about and respect the varied family traditions that are important in the local school and school community (Lewis & Doorlag, 1995).

Teachers who understand and respond skillfully to their students' needs and family traditions invite family members to share their customs and traditions. Teachers can have students research other students' family traditions, habits, and customs. Teachers can integrate family customs and rituals into the school's academic and social curricula. They can spend class time to clarify family traditions with students. They can discuss ways that family members can strengthen good family traditions, throw out the counterproductive ones, and add new traditions that families want or think could be helpful.

Teachers can identify and give recognition to effective family functioning through traditions in family music, art, language, food, travel, or dress. By doing so, teachers can create and maintain a high level of competence and integrity in their work with families. As in LaToya's case, her teachers worked hard to allow LaToya to present to her classmates family videos that reflected her father's preference for ethnic food and her mother's love of music and art. LaToya's teachers demonstrated that they are aware of, accept, and value diversity by building up trust and commitment to important memories in LaToya's life. Table 3.1 offers tips that may help to ensure new teachers' support as they demonstrate their commitment to valuing diversity.

Culturally Responsive Teaching Using Family Input

Teaching students from multicultural backgrounds requires affirmative and direct steps to ensure that the value of diversity integrates across curricula. Teachers need to seek input from students' family members to find out family views on relevant curricular issues. A first step is to determine the microcultures that exist in the school or community. Although communities are not always rich in ethnic diversity, they all have cultural diversity. With a current emphasis on the value of family diversity, multicultural teaching that supports culturally responsive practices brings students' diverse family backgrounds from the margin to the center of curricula (Bennett, 1995; Gollnick & Chinn, 1998; Noel, 2000).

By establishing classroom cultural goals that reflect social and interpersonal aspects of classroom interaction, teachers can concentrate on students' increased self-esteem, friendship building, effective communication, personal achievement, leadership, and peer facilitation (Tiegerman-Farber & Radziewicz, 1998). Teachers can work with families to translate the values of multiculturalism from communities, schools, and classrooms to support the valuing of each student's diversity (Nieto, 1996).

Wlodkowski & Ginsberg (1995b) suggested a framework for culturally responsive teaching that new teachers can use when they plan with family members how best to bring cultural diversity and input alive in the classroom. These researchers contend that there is no one teaching strategy that will engage all learners. The key element to effective teaching with students from diverse backgrounds is to help students relate lesson content to their own backgrounds and family experiences. Accordingly, conditions necessary for culturally responsive teaching include the following practices (Wlodkowski & Ginsberg, 1995a):

- *Establish inclusion:* Teachers should emphasize the human purpose of what is being learned and its relationship to the students' experiences. Such teachers share the ownership of knowing with all students. Teachers encourage collaboration and cooperation, while students assume a hopeful view of all people and their capacity to change.

TABLE 3.1   *Tips That May Help to Ensure New Teachers' Support in Valuing Diversity*

- Teachers can learn as much as they can about their students' diverse families by talking with parents and other staff, reading books, attending in-service sessions, and viewing films on diversity.
- Family structures, values, and childrearing practices vary greatly. Teachers can use cultural differences as strengths rather than working at cross-purposes.
- Instead of lumping all groups together, effective teachers recognize that many differences exist within groups of Hispanics, Whites, African Americans, or Asian individuals. Lessons reflect this philosophy.
- Each country, each region, and most importantly, each individual has unique ways of interpreting individual cultural experiences. Teachers recognizing the uniqueness of interpretation experiences plan lessons accordingly.
- Effective teachers actively seek to weed out the stereotypes and prejudices that have been acquired through the teachers' own cultural roots. They try to approach people individually and openly in all home–school encounters.
- Teachers can support families' cultural pluralism by recognizing students' contemporary cultures, cultural pride, and identity.
- Teachers can discuss the negative effects of prejudice and discrimination during lessons.
- Planning ways to include families of linguistically/culturally diverse students in classroom activities can recognize students' use of their native language, while encouraging family members to participate in school activities.
- Teachers can plan how to involve minority parents formally and informally in their children's education by asking families how and when they want to be involved.
- Adjusting instructional approaches and activities to accommodate cultural backgrounds can help teachers to adjust cultural differences and bring schools and families together.
- Teachers can capitalize on celebrations and special traditions. They can familiarize themselves with different cultural, language-based, and religious practices, such as fasting or holiday celebrations, that might affect students' school attendance and participation. They can learn to correctly pronounce students' names in the proper order and how to address students' parents.
- Effective teachers realize the importance of never feeling that they have to apologize for their own culture or ethnicity. As human beings, they recognize that all people have something special to contribute.
- Teachers seek actively to learn about family differences and are sensitive to unique differences. They seek opportunities for students to share information about their home life during social studies, geography, and other classes.

   • *Treat all students equitably:* Teachers constantly review how they treat all students. They invite students to point out behaviors or practices that discriminate.

   • *Develop positive attitudes:* Teachers relate teaching and learning activities to students' background experiences or previous knowledge. Teachers encourage students to make choices in content and assessment methods based on students' experiences, values, needs, and strengths.

• *Enhance meaning:* Teachers provide challenging learning experiences involving higher-order thinking and critical inquiry. They address relevant, real-world issues in an action-oriented manner. Further, teachers encourage discussion of relevant experiences. Rather than avoiding students' family diversity, for example, teachers incorporate family traditions into classroom dialogue.

• *Rely on competence:* Teachers connect the assessment process to the students' world, frames of references, and values. By so doing, teachers recognize home and community backgrounds. Teachers include multiple ways to represent knowledge and skills and allow for attainment of outcomes at different points in time. Teachers encourage self-assessment.

Teachers and school administrators have a responsibility to be aware of and capitalize on students' differences. Positive and accepting relationships among teachers, family members, and students become established when teachers respond to and value their students' family diversity. Knowledge of family roles, expectations, and patterns of behavior within various microcultures furnish invaluable insights (Banks, 1993; Fuligni, 1997; Seymour, Champion, & Jackson, 1995). Table 3.2 offers tips for teachers, useful for various practices across cultures and languages.

Family Member Questions

Questions may arise during school-based conferences. Questions and answers may help to support teachers' work with their diverse student's families.

The first question relates to the issue of whether there are culture-specific values concerning diverse families with a child with disabilities. *Do diverse families react differently when a child with a disability enters the family?* The usefulness of family members' support in reaching students with disabilities from minority families demonstrates insights into culture-specific values. For example, Turner (1987) examined cultural values among African American families from low socioeconomic households. Families were to comment on values that influence responses to a disabled or high-risk child within the family. One identified value related to the extended family and the dependence on family, rather than on social agencies, for assistance in child care and support. A second identified cultural value, the overall openness of African American families in expressing their feelings, especially to other family members, was thought to account for limited use by African American families of schools' counseling services and support groups. A third value, the general attitude toward and expectations for children with disabilities, was seen as causing difficulties because many African American families stress a highly personal style for their children, rather than one emphasizing exploration of objects and the physical environment, as many intervention programs stress. Finally, the daily support that religion provides for many African American families was seen as a primary support value to help families cope when a child with a disability enters their family structure.

A second important question provides further insight into whether a relationship exists between cultural background and families' attitudes toward educational programming for a child with a disability. *Is there a strong correlation between families' diversity and school programming emphases?* Rivers (1990) examined whether relationships exist

TABLE 3.2   *Tips for Teachers Interested in Various Practices across Cultures and Languages*

- *Anglo-American*

Free expression of opinions are common.

Family members are generally considered equal: individuality prevails.

Hand shaking is a common form of greeting.

Establishment of eye contact is considered important.

Social distance is important—an individual's space must be respected.

Punctuality is considered a positive attribute.

The mother is often the individual most directly involved in the educational process of the child.

Informality may be the standard for family–teacher meetings.

Many individuals are goal-oriented and believe that they have control over their environment.

Directness/openness/honesty are highly valued.

- *African Americans*

Kinship and extended family are important.

Authoritarian childrearing practices are often usual.

Often believe it is disrespectful to be familiar (e.g., call an individual by his or her first name before being given permission).

Often demonstrate a religious, spiritual orientation to life.

Often exhibit a great respect for the elderly and their role in the family.

Most do not appreciate ethnic jokes about any group.

Often attach great importance to nonverbal behaviors.

Maternal grandmothers may exhibit strong influence on child-rearing practices.

- *Hispanic Americans*

Extended families are common.

Overt respect for elders is often expected.

Have a collective rather than individual orientation.

Foster interdependence among family members.

May work best in cooperative rather than competitive situations.

Often have a spiritual/magical belief system.

Tend towards a patriarchal society (e.g., often considered inappropriate to address the wife before the husband if both are present).

May react negatively to impatience or hurrying.

- *Asian Americans*

Many regard the individual as secondary to the family.

Family patterns tend to be hierarchical, with parents making decisions for their children.

Many believe in family solidarity and continued dependence on family.

Many believe in self-denial, self-discipline, and contemplation.

Often greet family members in order of age, with males before females.

Generally consider direct physical contact inappropriate public behavior (e.g., hand shaking, hugging, kissing, slapping on the back, and so forth).

May be fatalistic in viewpoint of life.

May believe that waving arms, pointing, or beckoning with an index finger are signs of contempt.

Are generally modest, self-effacing.

Often avoid prolonged gazing or direct eye contact with strangers and at formal meetings.

May believe that the head is the most sacred part of the body and should not be touched.

• *Native Americans*

Family and cultural patterns include respect for elders, spiritual beliefs, and symbolism.

Generally, the group may be viewed as more important than the individual.

May believe that certain toys, animals, and so forth may be bad luck or bring evil to the child.

In some tribes, grandparents, not parents, have the primary parental role.

Some students with special needs may not be disciplined at home as it may be felt that they have suffered enough.

May involve numerous extended family members and other tribe members in conferencing.

Many are likely to be introverted and avoid criticism of others.

Many appreciate sincere attempts to learn about their culture through asking questions, observing, and so forth.

References

Bennett, C. I. (1995). *Comprehensive multi-cultural education: Theory and practice.* 3rd. ed. Boston: Allyn and Bacon.

Duarte, E. M., & Smith, S. (2000). *Foundational perspectives in multicultural education.* New York: Longman.

Lynch, E. W., & Hanson, M. J. (1992). *Developing cross-cultural competence: A guide for working with young children and their families.* Baltimore, MD: Paul H. Brookes.

Thomas, D. D. (1993). Minorities in North America: African-American families. In J. L. Paul & R. J. Simeonsson (Eds.). *Children with special needs: Family, culture, and society.* Orlando FL: Harcourt, Brace, & Jovanovich.

Note: It is important to note that every individual has a culture, and we are all a product of that cultural heritage. Although it is impossible to assume that an individual from any given culture will display certain characteristics, there are some characteristics that are found in many individuals from a given culture.

between cultural background (e.g., White, Hispanic, or African American) and families' attitudes toward educational programming. Rivers was able to identify program quality indicators including factors linking diversity and views on integration, data-based instruction, individuals' functioning, professional practices, and staff development. This researcher contended that the generally positive attitudes of parents toward functional programming for their children provided social validation for the best-practice literature base in the field of severe disabilities. Parental satisfaction with educational programs correlated highly with objective measures of program effectiveness. Among the differences between cultural groups were the finding that many African American parents felt more strongly that students with disabilities should not be prepared for the same types of living situations as nondisabled adults. Parents of sons were more positive about the curriculum than parents of daughters. Results supported individual family centered intervention programs, the development of parent awareness of "best practices"; and the maintenance of control of services with the family.

Harry (1990) examined attitudes among Puerto Rican-American parents toward the processes of assessment, placement, and instruction of students with disabilities. Findings included the following: (1) These families attached significantly different cultural meanings to classification terms (some carrying moral implications), (2) parents had their own theories explaining their children's difficulties, and (3) inadequate communication efforts by school administrators were compounded by language difficulties and a reliance on written communication between school and family.

What the research cited implies is that diverse families represent various levels of acceptance, commitment, rejection, feelings of responsibility, and knowledge of educational needs for their children with disabilities. Teachers can support diverse families when they recognize factors in reactions to the experience of having a child with a disability. These factors are the disability and its characteristics, the characteristics of the family, and the balance of individual problems and resources to cope (Hayes, 1994).

The nature and degree of severity of the disability may influence the impact on the diverse family. Some families may rally around the child; others may rely on relatives, friends or agencies to help. Family size, form (e.g., nuclear, single-parent, and so forth), and cultural or ethnic traditions can also influence the impact of life events within the family. Some families may try to find the meaning of having a child with problems by seeking support offered from the community or school. Other families may seek support from counseling or religious affiliations.

The effects of the disability will vary depending on each family's resources to cope. Families with a wide variety of resources may not need outside support to the same degree as less fortunate families. Families with strong family bonds and traditions may have enough resources, through church and community, to cope individually or with minimal school interventions.

However, for those families requiring more directed support, new teachers can offer critical help. Teachers can do the following:

• Teachers can respond as a liaison when parents receive initial information on the child's disability. Teachers can be families' sources of important educational, legal, and social procedures and practices.

• Teachers can be the key support when the family first comes into contact with a service delivery system. Teachers can be advocates as families work across public schools or community agencies.

• Teachers can act as vital information sources when families make transitions across schools, programs, or habitations. Teachers can be the link to smooth transitions.

• Teachers can act as referral agents when the parents realize that they are too old, or do not have necessary resources and coping skills, to care for their child. Teachers can offer lists of organizations, addresses, telephone numbers, faxes, e-mails, and contact names for targeted life needs of families and their member with a disability.

What this research strongly implies is the necessity of professional understanding regarding the backgrounds, beliefs, needs, resources, and values of students' families. New teachers must understand the barriers faced by and supports valued by students' families. New teachers must demonstrate supportive actions in understanding what diverse families want and expect when dealing with a family member with a disability. Table 3.3 lists examples of teachers' supportive actions.

TABLE 3.3 *Teachers' Supportive Actions*

- Observe to make sense of potential needs or strengths implied by students' differences
- Seek to understand how and why students differ
- Look for commonalties that all students share
- Try to make sense of prior learning opportunities and future experiences available to students
- Show acceptance of differences, communication, and commitment to students and families
- Work actively with families
- Communicate on appropriate interventions
- Promote effective family–teacher team building
- Address ethical and professional issues
- Gather information on where students live
- Are familiar with families' cultural norms and community expectations
- Familiarize themselves with the communities
- Seek to understand the importance of linguisitic and religious diversity
- Understand how to support and address students' contemporary issues
- Send home written material that is clear, concise, and easily readable
- Consider family's primary language and reading levels
- Report to families continually on their children's needs, strengths, and progress
- Make phone contacts and home visits
- Arrange contacts in neutral settings
- Use resource centers
- Engage parents in informal school activities
- Review expectations for students and their behavior toward students' families

- Work actively to ensure that discrimination does not exist
- Participate in community events
- Learn about their students' cultures and traditions
- Get to know parents and find out what parents want for their children
- Help diverse students and their families feel a part of the school community
- Recognize that family members must be an integral factor in important decision making
- Consider viewpoints that differ from your own
- Look for and use family strengths
- Reflect on own cultural expectations to identify possible incongruences
- Invite family members to share customs and traditions
- Have students research own traditions, habits, and customs, or others' family traditions
- Integrate family customs and rituals into academic and social curricula
- Spend class time to clarify family traditions with students
- Discuss ways that family members can strengthen good family traditions
- Identify and give recognition to effective family functioning
- Work toward building up trust and commitment with diverse families
- Use culturally responsive teaching practices

Family Resources and Services

The following resources and services may help teachers in their work with diverse families. The resources and services target minority family groups and resource organizations.

MINORITY FAMILY GROUPS AND RESOURCE ORGANIZATIONS

COFFO, Inc.
P.O. Box 900368
305 South Flagler Avenue
Homestead, FL 33030
(305) 246-0357 or (305) 245-1052
Fax: (305) 246-2445

COFFO supports migrant farm workers, particularly those who are Hispanic.

Creating Opportunities for Parent Empowerment (COPE)
300 I Street, NE, Suite 112
Washington, DC 20002
1-800-515-2673 (National) or
(202) 543-6482
(202) 543-6682 (Fax)
e-mail: Cope@erols.com

COPE assists diverse populations.

**Federation for Students
with Special Needs**
95 Berkeley Street, Suite 104
Boston, MA 02116
(617) 482-2915
Fax: (617) 695-2939
e-mail: fesninfo@fesn.org

The federation provides technical assistance for grassroots consortia.

**Inter-Island Parent Coalition
for Change**
4008 Estate Diamond
P.O. Box 4402
Christianstead, St. Croix
U.S. V.I. 00822
(809) 773-3494 or (809) 778-2275

The coalition assists families of African descent.

**Island Parents Educational Support
and Training Center (IPEST)**
Martha's Vineyard
P.O. Box 4081
Vineyard Haven, MA 02568
(508) 693-8612
Fax: (508) 693-7717 (Attention IPEST)

IPEST assists diverse populations.

Loving Your Disabled Child (LYDC)
4715 Crenshaw Boulevard
Los Angeles, CA 90043
Contact: Theresa Cooper
(213) 299-2925 or (310) 676-3527
Fax: (213) 299-4373
e-mail: lydc@pacbell.net

LYDC assists African American families primarily, but also assists other minorities.

Marilyn Ruiz
332 W. Alverez Ave.
Clewiston, FL 33440
(941) 983-4417
Fax: (941) 983-3479

Ms. Ruiz works closely with Parent Empowerment Project.

Oglala Sioux Tribe (OST)
Public Safety Commission
Box 300
Pine Ridge, SD 57770
(605) 867-1314
Fax: (605) 867-5832

OST works with Native Americans.

Parent Empowerment Project
4255 Fifth Avenue SW
Naples, FL 34119
(941) 455-4567
e-mail: Marianne@naples.net

Project staff works primarily with Hispanic migrant workers and their families.

Parents of Watts (POW)
10828 Lou Dillon Avenue
Los Angeles, CA 90059
(213) 566-7556
Fax: (213) 569-3982

POW works with inner-city African American families.

Parent Power
1118 S.142nd Street
Tacoma, WA 98444
(206) 531-2022
Fax: (206) 531-2002
e-mail: Ylink@aol.com

Parent power staff assists Asian families.

Pyramid Parent Training Project
3132 Napoleon Avenue
New Orleans, LA 70125
(504) 895-5970
Fax: (504)899-573
e-mail: Dmarkey404@aol.com

Project staff assists African American families.

Special Kids, Inc. (SKI)
P.O. Box 61628
Houston, TX 77208
(713) 643-9576 or (713) 250-5469
Fax: (713) 643-6291
e-mail: SpecKids@aol.com

SKI assists parents of children with special needs.

United We Stand (UWS)
c/o Francis of Paola Preschool
201 Conselyea Street
Brooklyn, NY 11206
(718) 782-1462
Fax: (718) 782-8044
e-mail: uwsofny@aol.com

UWS aides African American, Hispanic, and Puerto Rican families.

Urban Parents Becoming Effective Advocates Through Training (UPBEATT)
9950 Fielding
Detroit, MI 48228
(313) 837-1343
Fax: (313) 837-0358
e-mail: Upbeatt@aol.com

UPBEATT assists urban families.

Summary

Family diversity issues are major educational issues. New teachers operating with collaborative orientations and responsive practices must be aware of the intricate interrelationship of these issues and how each, ultimately, has an impact on teachers' work with students. Traditionally, many diverse students and their families did not feel welcome in public schools. Often, they felt excluded. However, many current classroom undertakings emphasize all students' inclusion (e.g., inclusion of students with diverse abilities in the classroom, inclusion of the concept of multiculturalism into schools and curricula).

New teachers must actively strive to understand families. Teachers cannot afford to view the school and community as a place to work, and forget their students or families at the day's conclusion. When families believe that their diversity is understood, valued, and respected, families respond, in tandem, with supportive teachers. Families and teachers, together, operate with collaborative orientations and responsive practices. Families and teachers ensure that students have opportunities to survive and succeed.

This chapter's purpose was to examine the diversity of American families. We examined diversity statistics. Embedded throughout the chapter were specific themes related to teachers' roles with diverse families. These included the following:

- Diversity is the condition of being different from others. Diversity entails having differences.
- All teachers encounter students and their families from diverse backgrounds.
- One way of dealing with students' families is recognizing the continuing, changing demographics of the United States, and the substantive diversity in school-age populations.
- Diverse students face tremendous risks.
- With such increases in a diverse population added to the historic tendency to identify and place a disproportionate number of students from diverse populations in special education, teachers and other school professionals can expect a concurrent rise in the number of diverse families and students receiving their attention.
- Because diverse students with special needs now are receiving more services in general education classes, there is increased understanding required of every school professional working with families and students.
- There are specific actions that teachers can take to support culturally responsive teaching and their work with diverse families.

References

Artiles, A. J., Aguirre-Munoz, Z., & Abedi, J. (1998). Predicting placement in learning disabilities programs: Do predictors vary by ethnic group? *Exceptional Children, 64* (4), 543–559.

Banks, J. A. (1993). Multicultural education: Historical development, dimensions, and practice. In L. Darling Hammond (Ed.), *Review of research in education, Vol. 19*. Washington, DC: American Educational Research Association.

Bauwens, J., & Hourcade, J. J. (1995). *Cooperative teaching: Rebuilding the school for all students*. Austin, TX: Pro-Ed.

Bennett, C. I. (1995a). *Multicultural education: Comprehensive theory and practice*. Boston: Allyn and Bacon.

Bennett, C. I. (1995b). *Comprehensive multi-cultural education: Theory and practice*. 3rd. ed. Boston: Allyn and Bacon.

Bureau of the Census (1997). How we're changing: Demographic state of the nation: 1996. *Current Population Reports, Special Studies Series*. Washington, DC: U.S. Department of Commerce.

Campbell, D. E. (1996). *Choosing democracy: A practical guide to multicultural education*. Englewood Cliffs, NJ: Prentice Hall.

Cartledge, G., & Milburn, J. F. (Eds.). (1995). *Teaching social skills to children and youth*. Boston: Allyn & Bacon.

Cortes, C. (1999). Searching for patterns. *Teaching Tolerance, 16*, 10–15.

Delgado-Rivera, B., & Rogers-Adkinson, D. (1997). Culturally sensitive interventions: Social skills training with children and parents from culturally and linguistically diverse backgrounds. *Intervention in School and Clinic, 33* (2), 75–80.

Delpit, L. (1995). *Other people's students: cultural conflict in the classroom.* New York: New York Press.

Fuligni, A. J. (1997). The academic achievement of adolescents from immigrant families: The role of family background, attitudes, and behavior. *Child Development, 68,* 351–363.

Gollnick, D. M, & Chinn, P. C. (1998). *Multicultural education in a pluralistic society.* New York: Merrill/ Prentice Hall.

Grant, C. A., & Sleeter, C. E. (1998). *Turning on learning.* New York: Prentice Hall.

Harry, B. (1990). *I know what it says, but I don't know what it means: An ethnographic study of the views of Puerto Rican parents.* Paper presented at the annual conference of the American Educational Research Association, Boston, MA.

Harry, B. (1994). Behavioral disorders in the context of families. In R. L. Peterson & S. Ishii-Jordan (Eds.). *Multicultural issues in the education of students with behavioral disorders* (pp. 149–161). Cambridge, MA: Brookline Books.

Hayes, A. (1994). Families and disabilities. In A. Ashman & J. Elkins (Eds.). *Educating children with special needs* (pp. 37–69). New York: Prentice Hall.

Hehir, T. (1999). The changing roles of special education leadership in the next millennium: Thoughts and reflections. *Journal of Special Education Leadership 12* (1), 3–8.

Helge, D. (1991). *Rural, exceptional, at risk.* Reston, VA: Council for Exceptional Children.

Individuals with Disabilities Education Act Amendments of 1997, Public Law 105-17, 20 U.S.C. Chapter 33, Section 1415 et seq. (EDLAW, 1997).

Jacobs, L. (1991). Assessment concerns: A study of cultural differences, teacher concepts, and inappropriate labeling. *Teacher Education and Special Education 14* (1), 43–48.

Leung, E. K. (1990). Early risks: Transition from culturally linguistically diverse homes to formal schooling. *Journal of Educational Issues of Language Minority Students, 7,* 35–51.

Lewis, R. B., & Doorlag, D. H. (1995). *Teaching special students in the mainstream.* New York: Merrill/ Prentice Hall.

Macmilian, D. L., & Reschly, D. J. (1998). Overrepresentation of minority students: The case for greater specificity or reconsideration of the variables examined. *Journal of Special Education, 32* (1), 15–24.

Mclaughlin, M. J. (1999). Access to the general education curriculum: Paperwork and procedures or redefining "special education." *Journal of Special Education Leadership 12* (1), 9–14.

Nieto, S. (1996). *Affirming diversity: The sociopolitical context of multicultural education* (2nd ed.). New York: Longman.

Neuman, S. B., Hagedorn, T., Celano, D., & Daly, P. (1995). Toward a collaborative African-American community. *American Educational Research Journal, 32* (4), 801–827.

Noel, J. (2000). *Developing multicultural educators.* New York: Longman.

Orozco, L. (Ed.) (1998). *Educating diverse populations.* Columbus, OH: Course-wise Publications.

O'Shea, L. J., O'Shea, D. J., & Algozzine, B. (1998). Learning disabilities: From theory toward practice. New York: Merrill/Prentice Hall.

Research and Policy Committee of the Committee for Economic Development (1987). *Children in need: Investment strategies for the educationally disadvantaged.* New York: Committee for Economic Development.

Rivers, E. (1990). *The relationship between cultural background and parental perceptions of functional educational programming for students with severe handicaps.* Paper presented at the annual meeting of the Midsouth Educational Research Association, New Orleans, LA.

Shaw, D. (1999). The at-risk student: A closer look. *Curriculum Adminstrator, 35* (9), 30–31.

Seymour, H., Champion, T., & Jackson, J. (1995). The language of African American learners: Effective assessment and instruction programming for children with special needs. In B. Ford, F. Obiakor, & J. Patton (Eds.). Effective education of African American learners: New Perspectives (pp. 89–122). Austin, TX: Pro-Ed.

Shore, R. (1995). *The current state of high school reform.* New York: Carnegie Corporation.

SRI International. (1993). *Action seminar. The transition experiences of young people with disabilities: Implications for policy and programs. Briefing materials.* Menlo Park, CA: SRI International.

Talbert-Johnson, C. (1998). Why so many African-American students in special ed? *School Business Affairs, 64* (4), 30–35.

Tiegerman-Farber, E., & Radziewiez, C. (1998). *Collaborative decision making: The pathway to inclusion.* Upper Saddle River, NJ: Merrill/Prentice Hall.

Turnbull, A. P., Turnbull, H. R., Shank, M., & Leal, D. (1995). *Exceptional lives: Special education in today's schools.* Englewood Cliffs, NJ: Prentice Hall/ Merrill.

Turner, A. (1987). *Multicultural considerations: Working with families of developmentally disabled and high-risk children. The African-American perspective.* Paper presented at the conference of the National Center for Clinical Infant Programs, "Vulnerable Infants, Stressed Families: Challenges for Research and Practice," Los Angeles, CA.

U.S. Department of Education. (1996). *The condition of education.* Washington, DC: National Center for Education Statistics: Author.

U.S. Department of Education. (1997). *Nineteenth annual report to Congress on the implementation of the Individuals with Disabilities Education Act.* Washington, DC: U.S. Department of Education.

Wagner, M. (1991). *Drop outs with disabilities: What do we know? What can we do?* Menlo Park, CA: SRI International.

Wlodkowski, R. J., & Ginsberg, M. B. (1995a). *Diversity and motivation: Culturally responsive teaching.* San Francisco: Jossey-Bass.

Wlodkowski, R. J., & Ginsberg, M. B. (1995b). A framework for culturally responsive teaching. *Educational Leadership, 3,* 17–21.

Ysseldyke, J., & Olsen, K. (1999). Putting alternate assessments into practice: What to measure and possible sources of data. *Exceptional Children, 65* (2), 175–185.

Family Characteristics That Place Children at Risk

Stephanie L. Kenney

M. J. LaMontagne

Chapter Objectives

In this chapter we will

- Describe the family characteristics that place children at risk for developmental and learning problems across the life span
- Examine the research related to family risk characteristics that influence children's development across the lifespan
- Explore family roles and structures that may place children's development at risk
- Consider implications for supporting families with risk characteristics during their children's educational life span
- Discuss classroom, school, and community inclusion and related collaborative models that support children from families with risk characteristics
- Provide useful resources for families with risk characteristics
- Summarize important chapter themes

> *Marty is from a poor family and lives in western Idaho. Her family of nine lives in a substandard housing unit on the outskirts of a rural town. It is rumored that Marty's mother and father use drugs and have done so since before Marty's birth. Her mother was 14 years old when Marty was born. Marty's teachers are worried that Marty's background places her at risk for school failure.*

Family factors that place children at risk for developmental and learning problems in both their current and future educational environments are as varied as the individual children and families they characterize. These risk factors span a continuum and appear to have a foundation in family poverty. Children, youth, adolescents, and adults are variously affected by these family risk factors, with the intensity of impact modified by individual child resiliency

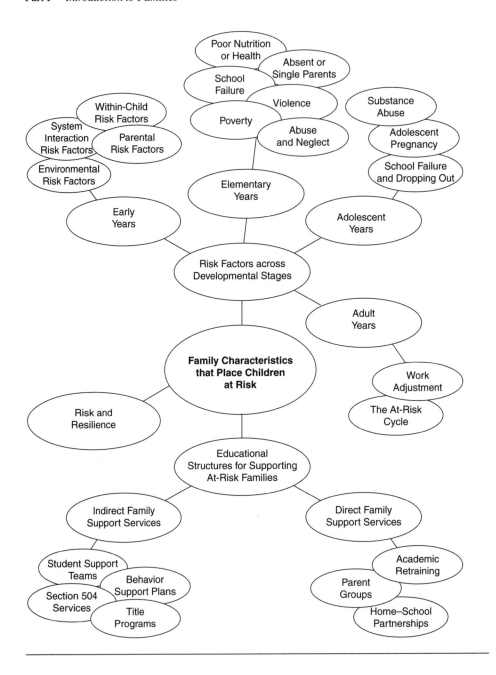

traits. Intervention and support programs are designed to address the risk factors experienced by both families and children. This chapter discusses the multiple interaction of family risk characteristics and describes interventions and support systems.

Changing family demographics have created a set of factors that may influence the developmental progress of children over their life spans. Societal concerns such as substance abuse, child poverty, family violence, prenatal health care issues, homelessness, family structures, and family instability are continuous threads that undermine the fabric of providing appropriate educational services to children and youth (Children's Defense Fund, 1999; Hanson & Carta, 1996). The Children's Defense Fund (1998; 1999) has reported a forward momentum in addressing many concerns related to the welfare of children in America. The trend in births to teenage mothers has slowly but consistently continued to decrease over the last six years. Unfortunately, poverty remains a significant environmental factor with one in five children living in poverty and one in eleven children living at less than half the poverty level (Children's Defense Fund, 1999). These statistics have earned children the label of the poorest population in the United States (Children's Defense Fund, 1998). Children currently exist in a context in which:

- Twelve children are killed daily by gunfire
- 1 million teenagers become pregnant on an annual basis
- 22.4 percent of live births are to mothers who have not completed high school
- One-third of homeless Americans comprise families with children
- It is estimated that almost 3 million children are abused or neglected annually
- 520,000 children are in foster care placements
- For 1995 between 1/3 and 1/2 of children exposed to domestic violence were direct victims, with as many as 87 percent witnessing the abuse
- A 1998 survey of the United States identified substance abuse and poverty/economic status as the top two problems of families reported to child protective service agencies with cases of maltreatment
- According to 1997 statistics, at least half of foster care placements for children were partially due to parental substance abuse (Children's Defense Fund, 1998; 1999)

For education to be successful, new teachers must be able to acknowledge the diverse characteristics that families bring to the educational experience. We know that unique family factors extend beyond traditional cultural, linguistic, and regional differences and into risk factors which may influence the development of the child within the family context. These developmental influences have the potential to affect the educational progress of a student. It is necessary to understand the risk characteristics and to address the child and academic outcomes that these factors produce. Within this same conceptual framework, as depicted by the advanced organizer presented at the beginning of this chapter, the interrelatedness of the risk factors determines impact, intervention, and outcomes. For one child and family certain risk factors may interact with others to create a more destructive outcome than in a second family with similar risk factors.

Take a few minutes to read the case scenario in Box 4.1, which depicts an interaction between a family and a teacher. As you read this chapter keep the Perez family in mind, and try to relate the ideas presented in the chapter to them.

Family Characteristics That Place Children at Risk across Developmental Stages

Families in today's society exist along a continuum. As discussed in Chapter 2, there is no single definition of what constitutes a "good" or a "bad" family situation. As Kauffman

BOX 4.1

Family–Teacher Issues

Mrs. Henry, a seventh-grade special education teacher, is interviewing Mrs. Perez to get a social history of her son, Jeorge, before he enrolls in their rural middle school. As Mrs. Henry talks with Mrs. Perez, she learns many interesting facts. Mrs. Perez's son, Jeorge, was born two months premature and remained hospitalized for six weeks due to medical complications. Mrs. Perez reported that as a teenage mother, she was quite unprepared for the birth of her medically fragile son. To try and help him, Mrs. Perez quit working and stayed at home with her son. Her husband tried to take on other jobs to help with the medical bills. When Jeorge was two, a lady started coming to their home to teach Jeorge to learn. Mrs. Perez loved to watch her son with his teacher because it seemed like he was okay when he did things with her. Jeorge has always been sickly, and even to this day, she worries that his ongoing health problems will prevent him from attending school. She finds it difficult to get consistent quality health care due to lack of insurance and the migratory nature of her job as an onion picker. When Mrs. Henry asks Mrs. Perez about Jeorge's early school experiences, she indicates that Jeorge has had a difficult time understanding what teachers and other students say to him in school since they mostly talk in Spanish at home. Mrs. Perez tells Mrs. Henry that Jeorge had a really good teacher at the school in Texas, but the picking season ended after six weeks and they had to move north to get work. When asked, Mrs. Perez recalls that Jeorge has been to four or five schools in the United States and Mexico since first grade. At the end of the interview Mrs. Henry asks Mrs. Perez what she would like Jeorge to accomplish this year at school and Mrs. Perez says, "I just want him to learn to read and write and make some friends."

Collaborative Orientations and Responsive Practices

Recognizing the importance of a family's context in the education of a child, Mrs. Henry carefully documented the many family risk factors and family strengths described by Mrs. Perez. Mrs. Henry worked with Mrs. Perez to identify risk factors that were of the greatest concern to Mrs. Perez. In addition, family strengths were discussed and ways in which these strengths could help address family concerns. Together they decided on a path of action to manage these concerns and to support Jeorge in his new seventh-grade classroom. Mrs. Henry and Mrs. Perez agreed to meet again in six weeks to discuss Jeorge's educational progress and any new concerns that Jeorge's family might have.

(1997) has pointed out, the inherent resiliency of children enables some of them to survive family circumstances that society and teachers perceive to have negative influences on academic and developmental growth. However, years of research suggest that certain family characteristics and conditions do place children at risk for developmental learning problems. These risk factors can be categorized as environmental, parental, within-child, and system interaction risk factors. Although any particular category of risk factor may be more or less apparent during a specific life stage (e.g., infant/toddler, preschool, elementary, secondary), it is important to remember that these risk factors can and do exist across a life span.

Risk and Resilience

Although research has helped us clearly identify family factors that may place children at risk, we cannot confidently predict outcomes for individual children within the same family environments for the following reasons. First, environmental influences affect each child uniquely. Plomin (1989) reminds us that rather than operating on a family-by-family basis, environmental influences operate on a child-by-child basis. Second, because family environmental factors influence each child uniquely, a stressful family experience may serve to strengthen the survival instinct of one sibling while leaving another sibling weakened and vulnerable (Ratter, 1990). Further, whether or not a particular life experience impacts negatively on a child depends not only on the presence of risk factors, but on how the child copes, and the degree and patterns of exposure to the particular life experience (Kauffman, 1997). Lorsbach and Frymier (1992), in comparing the impact of five at-risk factors on a group of students with learning disabilities and a group of nondisabled students, found that the influence of certain risk factors varied in individuals by grade. For example, family instability seemed to have a greater impact on tenth graders as compared to fourth graders. This finding clearly supports the idea that negative family life experiences have differential risk impact on children, depending on the interaction of other factors co-occurring at that time. For the purposes of this discussion, it is important to recognize that while numerous risk factors may reside in a family, it is impossible to predict their impact on any individual child, making it absolutely essential that teachers look carefully at the progress and needs of the individual whole child within the at-risk family environment.

The Early Years

Environmental Risk Factors. Environmental risk factors have been described in early childhood special education literature as elements found in children's physical environment or within their early life experiences that jeopardize their physical or developmental health (Hanson, 1996; Bowe, 1995). Many young children are born with their physical and developmental structures intact and are for all intents and purposes ready to learn and grow within their environment. Unfortunately for some children, the environments in which they are born have certain characteristics that can impede their developmental progress. These environmental characteristics range from economic influences to nonstimulating environments which impact the infant/toddler's acquisition of cognitive, social, linguistic, and motoric concepts.

Poverty is a critical issue for young children in America and affects children across the country from all ethnic groups (Children's Defense Fund, 1998; 1999). The 1997 Census Bureau data portrays a discouraging state: 36.8 percent of Hispanic children, 37.2 percent of African American children, 20.2 percent of Asian and Pacific Islander children, and 16 percent of Euro American children live in poverty (Children's Defense Fund, 1999). Children born into conditions of poverty have been identified as being at greater risk for developmental concerns (Huston, 1991; Kaplan-Sanoff, Parker, & Zuckerman, 1991; Bowman, 1992, Hanson & Carta; 1996). Current data indicate that one in four children are born into poverty (Children's Defense Fund, 1999) and literature tells us that children who live in poverty are more likely to become sick and receive inadequate health care. When young children experience chronic infections they become passive and irritable (Bowman, 1992). Continually sick toddlers are less interested in exploring their environments and are less able to understand environmental feedback and information, resulting in interruptions in cognitive, social, and affective development. It has been suggested that chronic health problems associated with poverty could potentially account for up to 30 percent of the variance between the cognitive development of poor and middle-class children (Research Bulletin, 1989). The Children's

Defense Fund (1999) stated that recent research has indicated that the longer young children (infants through preschoolers) live in poverty, the more likely these children are to exhibit anxiety, depression, and antisocial behavior in later years.

Families who live at or below the poverty level may live in substandard housing which poses environmental hazards for the young child's well-being. We know that lead toxins in paint, asbestos housing materials, or environmental contaminants found in pesticides that are ingested by curious infants or toddlers are significant health hazards which can have serious effects on the developmental status of the young child (Crain & Bennett, 1996). Accidents resulting in head injuries can have a lifetime impact on development and learning. Children living in unsafe environments are at a much higher risk of postnatal dangers which can alter their typical developmental course.

Another aspect of poverty is the existence of family stress which may result in neglect or abuse of the young child (Huston, 1991; Kaplan-Sanoff, Parker, & Zuckerman, 1991; Hanson & Carta; 1995). Bowman (1992) describes families in poverty as victims of intensified typical life stresses. Financial strain, inadequate community resources and supports, and psychological impoverishment all serve to deplete parents' physical and emotional energies (Bowman, 1992; Hanson & Carta, 1996). It is important that teachers recognize that worrying about having enough money to buy food and pay rent in addition to struggling to find and pay for adequate child care distracts adults from responsive and responsible child caregiving. Though not by choice, the day-to-day struggle of trying to meet basic needs can prevent the most loving parent from demonstrating positive, nurturing, and affectionate parenting skills. Family stress may manifest itself in angry tones and a lack of concern for others with an unraveling of basic coping skills (Bowman, 1992; Osofsky & Jackson, 1994). Infants and toddlers need consistent and responsive caregivers and a predictable and trusting environment so that they may experience a healthy developmental progression. These same infants and toddlers whose parents are grappling with financial, emotional, and physical strains are at significant risk for neglect and abuse (Bowman, 1992; Hanson & Carta, 1995). If the family stressors associated with living in poverty continue beyond the preschool years learning and academic achievement of school-aged children are negatively impacted (Hanson & Carta, 1996).

Safety is a nationwide concern in the communities of America. Children are exposed on a daily basis to acts of violence (Osofsky, 1994; Hanson & Carta, 1996; Children's Defense Fund, 1998). A survey in Boston indicated that one in ten children under six years old attending a health clinic had witnessed a violent act with half of the violent acts occurring within their home environment (Groves, Zuckerman, Marans, & Cohen, 1993). In 1990 it was estimated that at least 3.3 million children annually witnessed parental abuse (Jaffe, Wolfe, & Wilson, 1990). It is not surprising that children who witness violence question the trustworthiness and dependability of relationships, which affects their own self-concept and social/emotional development (Osofsky, 1994). Boys who watch parental fighting tend to be more aggressive, while girls observing the same domestic violence are more withdrawn (Osofsky, 1994). Toddlers may exhibit post-traumatic stress disorders characterized by eating and sleeping disruptions, anxiousness and fearfulness, and problems with attending and relating to others (Drell, Siegel, & Gaensbauer, 1993).

In 1996 approximately one million children were confirmed victims of abuse and neglect (Children's Defense Fund, 1999). Sadly, we know that inner-city children have reported their expectation of dying during their teen years due to violence in their communities (Osofsky, 1994). Clearly, we see a picture of our society in which violence has become an unnerving part of children's lives, affecting their school performance, social skills, ability to focus attention, emotional self, and future existence (Osofsky, 1994).

Also associated with poverty and environmental conditions are a child's early learning experiences. We know that in an environment full of nurturing caregiving and rich learning experiences a young child will thrive and develop. However, in an environment that is violent, stressful, and physically and emotionally unstable, that same child will not be able to gain access to the quality and quantity of learning opportunities that support growth. Young children need to explore, experience, engage, experiment, and play with materials, objects, and people in their environment. From these interactions and manipulations, children form concepts about themselves and their world and from these concepts emerge cognitive, language, social/emotional, and motor development. Without developmentally appropriate materials and caregiver interactions, young children develop inadequate concepts or fail to master specific skills on which more complex skills are based. Because early learning experiences set the stage for future learning (Hanson, 1996; Bowe, 1995), deficient learning opportunities in the preschool years may result in academic problems during school years.

Schorr and Schorr (1988) made a statement over a decade ago that is a succinct synthesis of the impact of poverty on young children: "Persistent and concentrated poverty virtually guarantees the presence of a vast collection of risk factors and their continuing destructive impact over time" (p. 30). Multiple risk factors associated with poverty have a substantial and long-lasting impact on children's development (Sameroff, Seifer, Barocas, Zax, & Greenspan, 1987; Hanson & Carta, 1996; Children's Defense Fund, 1998). When working with children it is essential to remember that the constellation of environmental risk factors that place children at risk for current and future developmental and learning problems do not exist in isolation. Rather, they are a series of interrelated factors which are devastating in their longevity and challenging to ameliorate.

Parental Risk Factors.   Included within the parameters of environmental risk factors are certain parental characteristics which may place a child's development at risk. One parental risk factor that has been studied and researched is the parenting capabilities of adults with mental retardation. When a child is born to parents who have mental retardation there exists the concern that these parents will not be able to adequately care for their infant across the life span. Some research has suggested that children of parents with mental retardation have lower mean IQs (Feldman & Walton-Allen, 1997) while other studies have reported no difference in IQ distribution for children of parents with mental retardation when compared to the general population (Tymchuk, Andron, & Unger, 1987; Tymchuk, 1990a). An issue of common agreement relates to parenting skills. Parents with mental retardation may neglect their child due to insufficient preparation for parenting (Tymchuk, 1990b; Espe-Sherwindt & Crable, 1993). Parents with mental retardation appear to have problems with decision making and problem solving in relation to childrearing (Feldman & Walton-Allen, 1997; Tymchuk, Yokota, & Rahbar 1990; Budd & Greenspan, 1984). As caregivers, these parents may not provide responsive and reinforcing feedback to their infants during interactions (Tymchuk & Andron, 1992; Feldman, Sparks, & Case, 1993).

Fortunately, research tells us that parent education and training have strong long-term benefits for both the parents with mental retardation and their children (Tymchuk, 1990b; Espe-Sherwindt & Crable, 1993; Feldman & Walton-Allen, 1997). With appropriate supports, children of parents with mental retardation can be successful in their adolescent and adult lives (O'Neil, 1985; Espe-Sherwindt & Crable, 1993).

Another parental risk factor is related to parental use of drugs during pregnancy. Although data do not currently exist that specifically detail the incidence of drug use by pregnant women, it is acknowledged that one in eight pregnant women uses alcohol, tobacco, or drugs prior to giving birth (Children's Defense Fund, 1999). In 1990 an estimated 4.8 million women of childbearing age during a given month used illegal drugs, 30.5 million women used alcohol, and 17.4 million women used nicotine (Khalsa & Gfroerer, 1991). We see in these overwhelming statistics the presence of a real threat to the prenatal development of an infant. Further, research has indicated that children who are exposed prenatally to alcohol typically have growth deficiencies, facial anomalies, lower performance on intelligence and achievement scales, and potential motor coordination problems (Conry, 1990; Streissguth, Barr, & Sampson, 1990). Intrauterine exposure to cocaine may result in prematurity, small head circumference, intrauterine growth retardation and congentital malformations, and a review of research and literature summarized cocaine-exposed babies as being excitable with demonstrated difficulties in visual and auditory orientation skills (Singer, Garber, & Kliegman, 1991). These infants are not easily consolable and have poor state regulation, abnormal reflexes, and impaired habituation. These infant characteristics can affect infant–caregiver interactions which in turn affect the infant's developmental progress, which is directly associated with academic learning outcomes. Studies related to maternal use of marijuana have yielded little relationship between intrauterine exposure and long-term effects of this drug use on children's development (Shriver & Piersel, 1994). Data have supported the impact of prenatal exposure to drugs on the development of young children. It is important to understand that intrauterine growth and development is the beginning foundation for all later development. Maternal ingestion of toxic substances that can impede and alter that development will only serve to place a child at risk for future developmental and learning success.

In 1996, 505,000 infants were born to teenage mothers (Children's Defense Fund, 1998). The Children's Defense Fund (1998) listed four key indicators associated with teenage mothers: early school failure, early behavioral problems, family dysfunction, and poverty. The greater the number of these factors present by the time a young girl is in eighth grade, the more likely she is to give birth prior to turning twenty years of age. Data suggest that an estimated 78 percent of adolescent girls engage in sexual intercourse by age twenty, and approximately 1.1 million girls ages fifteen through nineteen become pregnant each year, of which 84 percent are unplanned pregnancies (Children's Defense Fund, 1998; 1999). Poverty is a reality for young mothers who have dropped out of school. The Children's Defense Fund *1998 Yearbook* reported that almost two-thirds of teenage mothers did not finish their high school education. The combination of lack of economic stability due to inadequate job skills and inadequate parenting skills related to education and supports places the teenage mother and her child at significant risk. In this situation the mother is at risk for stressors associated with poverty and the child for social, physical, and cognitive problems (Smith, 1997; Hanson & Carta, 1995). Babies born to teenage mothers have additional health risks which may impact later development. These babies have a higher incidence of low birthweight (birthweight less than 5 lbs. 8 oz.), which may jeopardize their physical and cognitive development (Children's Defense Fund, 1998). Research has revealed that preschool children born to teenage mothers demonstrate cognitive delays which continue throughout their life spans and they display higher levels of impulsive and aggressive behaviors (Children's Defense Fund, 1998). Older children experience higher rates of school failure and delinquency. The long-term effects of teenage births can be traced back to the teenage mother's own social and physical immaturity and deficits in parenting, nurturing, and caring for an infant.

Another less obvious risk factor is parental stress. It is widely known that stress can produce physiological symptoms that may cause a person to feel ill. Indeed, some research suggests that parents of children with special needs have a higher level of stress than parents who do not have such children (Beckman, 1991). This stress seems to be due to extra caregiving responsibilities common to parents of at-risk children and children with disabilities. In some cases this stress may cause a sense of helplessness, frustration, and even depression in parents. This vicious cycle continues as caregivers who are not feeling well experience greater parenting stress when dealing with challenging caregiving responsibilities. This stress, in turn, often directly affects the quality of care given to such children. We know that a child who lives with a parent who is depressed is at higher risk for becoming depressed than a child who does not live with such a parent (Kaslow & Rehm, 1991; Stark et al., 1995). In another example of the reciprocal effects of the child–parent relationship, research suggests that children who have conduct disorders are at risk from an early age, particularly because they are infants with difficult temperaments and have parents who do not have the ability to nurture such children and cope with the stress of having a difficult child (Campbell, 1995; Kazdin, 1991). The outcome is that children who experience inconsistent or no parental expectations are more likely to exhibit behavior problems at school (Hanson & Carta, 1996).

Within-Child Risk Factors.   As families anticipate the birth of a child, their minds and hearts may focus on dreams and hopes for their newborn son or daughter. With the birth of a child with biological concerns (e.g., prematurity, small for gestational age, birth complications, medically fragile status) comes the reality of neonatal intensive care units (NICUs) and emotional, physical, and financial strains on a family unit. These within-child characteristics have the potential to affect the infant's developmental status over a lifetime and to influence the family's relationship with the infant.

As a result of prematurity (birth prior to thirty-seven weeks' gestation) the infant is born without complete physical maturation and, depending on the gestational time of birth, the infant may experience a variety of developmental problems such as blindness, hearing impairments, motor deficits, expressive or receptive language problems, intellectual deficits, and learning or behavior problems (Gorski & VandenBerg, 1996). Small for gestational age (SGA) is a condition in which the infant may be born full term, but is underweight for gestational age. Maternal drug use, smoking, or systemic infection are known to be causal factors in SGA infants (Williams & Howard, 1993; Blackman, 1990). Caregivers have tended to describe these babies as being intense and very active, with problems in social exchanges. These behavioral characteristics can influence the caregiver–infant interactions, thus impacting the social/emotional and language development of the baby, as well as the emotional relationship between the parent and infant.

An additional set of within-child risk factors is related to complications during and immediately following the birth process. These perinatal factors are associated with a higher risk of cerebral palsy (fifteen times greater), neonatal seizures, multiple apneic episodes (cessation of breathing for more than twenty seconds), and feeding difficulties which result in tube feeding of the infant (Nelson & Ellenberg, 1981; Gorski & VandenBerg, 1996). Babies with chronic lung disease have prolonged hospitalization and daily exposure to strange hospital stimuli that may interrupt developmental sequences, behavioral patterns, and relationships with family members. Early experiences help to define the patterns for later learning and growth. Newborn infants whose early life experiences are in a neonatal intensive care unit, are faced with high-tech, low-human interactions which can directly affect their ability to confidently and successfully explore their environment and interact with caregivers.

System Interaction Risk Factors.   School communities are created and exist as microcosms of the larger majority culture they serve. As families from minority cultures send their children to public schools, they may discover differences between their cultural background and patterns which place their children at risk particularly for academic problems. For example, the U.S. Department of Education (1995) reported that within a group of minority students, numbers of students with limited English proficiency are growing rapidly. The U.S. Department of Education estimated that in 1990 there were approximately 1.9 million students with limited English proficiency, with slightly more than three-fourths of these students speaking Spanish. A disproportionate number of these students have been identified as having disabilities (Baca & Almonza, 1991), supporting the notion that this group is at high risk. While this phenomenon may be partially due to the language barrier, the mobile nature of migrant families creates instability in learning environments and opportunities for their children. In addition, the changing demographics of American society represent an increase in linguistically different cultures relocating in the United States. Laotian, Vietnamese, and Hmong families are a few examples of immigrants with limited English proficiency. Entering into American schools is a direct challenge for children from foreign countries. The inability to speak and understand the English language used in American schools places these children at additional risk for school failure.

Elementary Years

Many of the risk factors that manifest themselves or influence children during the preschool years continue to impact children during their elementary school years. Unless existing risk factors are ameliorated, they are very much a part of that child as he or she comes to school. For example, a study that followed children from birth who were exposed to drugs prenatally found that certain speech and language deficits, particularly in semantic and pragmatic skills areas, persisted in the years beyond age six (Rivers & Hedrick, 1998). Further, some of these children reportedly had global learning disabilities as well as attention deficits, distractibility, and low self-esteem. Although any such deleterious impact on a child's health or behavior depends on a complex interaction of many risk factors, this study clearly points to long-term effects of certain early risk factors on the overall development and capabilities of children and supports the importance of continually monitoring children who have experienced early risk factors as they progress through school and at home.

It is important to consider that children respond differentially to the same risk factor as they pass through the various developmental stages of their lives. For example, Lorsbach and Frymier (1992) reported that fourth graders who are at-risk, regardless of the presence of a disability, experienced a greater degree of academic failure than did comparison groups of seventh- and tenth-grade students. To determine the nature of the influence of a risk factor on a child or family, teachers should evaluate each factor on the following dimensions: (1) intensity of the risk factor (how much), (2) its duration (how long), (3) its degree (how often), (4) the developmental stage (when), (5) presence of co-existing risk factors, and (6) current support resources. Understanding the characteristics of a child's and family's risk factors will help us determine if, how, and when we should intervene and with what supports. Remembering that no risk factor operates in isolation from other family factors, several family risk factors that often affect children particularly during their elementary school years are discussed in the following sections.

Poverty. Poverty has a continuing impact on children and families during the school years. According to Knitzer and Aber (1995), poverty may be the most critical problem undermining families today. We know that more families of students in special education have annual household incomes below $25,000 than do families of students in general education (U.S. Department of Education, 1995). One subgroup of families in poverty are homeless families. We know that among the devastating effects that homelessness has on children are problems with health, peer interactions, transitions, academics, and school attendance. School-age children living on the street or in shelters live a transient lifestyle that is not conducive to consistent school attendance. Even if homeless children are able to attend school, the unsettled nature of their home life makes settling in and concentrating on learning tasks very difficult, if not impossible. Teachers can assist homeless families and other families in poverty by facilitating their connecting with community agencies that can help them meet their basic needs. According to Maslow and others, it is only after these basic needs are met that our students will be able to begin to focus on learning in our classrooms. Many believe that poverty and its associated social problems are issues our society must address aggressively if we hope to reduce family stress and its effects on our nation's children (Knitzer & Aber, 1995).

School Failure. It is when such basic needs as those just described are not met that students have difficulty achieving in our classrooms. In fact, school failure is linked to several family and family-related factors. Table 4.1 shows a wide range of risk factors for school failure and dropout.

For a variety of reasons, children may begin their school careers ill-equipped to succeed academically or socially. Once this cycle of school-related failure begins, the child is often caught in a self-perpetuating cycle of school failure that continues until school personnel intervene or the student is old enough to stop attending school. In Table 4.1 the "Within-student factors" category indicates several factors that often have their roots in the

TABLE 4.1 *Risk Factors for School Failure and Dropout*

Demographic Predictors	*Within-Student Factors*
Low socioeconomic status	Academic failure
Minority status, especially African American or Latino American	Grade retention, being two or more years behind grade level
More likely to live in the South	External locus of control for academics
Greater risk in urban population than in rural population	Delinquency
	Disciplinary problems in school
Family Predictors	Truancy or poor attendance record in elementary school
Single-parent family	
Large family	Pregnancy
Parent dropped out of school	
Parent in jail	

Source: Adapted from Simeonsson, R. J. (1998). *Risk, resilience and prevention: Promoting the well-being of all children.* Baltimore, MD: Paul H. Brookes.

elementary school experience (e.g., grade retention, disciplinary problems, and truancy or poor attendance) place a student at later risk for further school failure or dropping out. This is a clear example of the importance of prevention programs which address children and youth at risk for school-related problems. Currently the United States does not have a congruous national program or policies addressing the national epidemic of our nation's children who are at risk for school failure. The few programs in existence generally offer primary prevention in the form of compensatory or remedial education for children at risk due to such demographic factors as low SES or minority status. Such programs include Head Start and Title programs which offer secondary-level prevention. These programs include the Job Training Partnership Act, which provides education and training to youth in school and dropouts, and Job Corps, which provides work for youths from sixteen to twenty-four years of age.

Poor Nutrition/Health.   Table 4.2 provides a descriptive list of childhood health problems. Notice that the factors presented in this table again support the idea that risk factors often co-exist and persist across developmental stages. Indeed, attitudes and behavior patterns of diet, physical activity, and tobacco use are examples of risk factors that may begin in childhood, continue in adolescence, and persist into adulthood if no intervention takes place (Simeonsson & Gray, 1994).

Abuse and Neglect.   Abuse and neglect consist of physical or mental injury, sexual abuse or exploitation, negligent treatment, or maltreatment that harms or threatens a child's health or welfare (Turnbull, Buchele-Ash, & Mitchell, 1994). *Maltreatment,* the term most often used by practitioners and researchers, refers to physical, emotional, and sexual abuse and neglect and includes specific types of improper treatment. *Abuse* is usually nonacci-

TABLE 4.2   *Child Health Problems*

• One in ten infants living in the United States has no routine source of health care; approximately ten of every 1,000 babies born in the United States each year die before they reach their first birthday; the mortality rate is higher for black infants, who die at twice the rate of white infants.

• 2,685 babies a day are born into poverty.

• Several threats to children's health are associated with low socioeconomic status; mental retardation, learning disorders, emotional and behavior problems, and vision and speech impairments all appear to be more prevalent among children living in poverty.

• Risk factors for chronic disease in later years have their roots in youthful behavior. One in three twelfth graders smokes regularly. Three-fourths of high school seniors who smoke had their first cigarette by ninth grade and one-fourth smoked their first cigarette by sixth grade. The average first use of alcohol and marijuana is at age thirteen, while 26 percent of fourth graders and 40 percent of sixth graders reported their peers had tried alcoholic beverages and one in five eighth graders reports being drunk within the past year.

Sources: Adapted from Children's Defense Fund, (1998, 1999) *The state of America's children yearbook.* Washington, DC: Author.

dental and intentional infliction of pain, including physical acts that result in injury, sexual molestation/exploitation, and emotional abuse. The term *neglect,* on the other hand, usually refers to a failure to provide a child with basic needs such as food, shelter, and education (Turnbull, Buchele-Ash, & Mitchell, 1994).

One of the ways caregiver stress is vented is through child abuse. For example, severe economic hardship is known to be associated with abusive or neglectful parenting and children's maladaptive behavior (Achenbach et al., 1991). Maltreatment of children may result in long-term and serious emotional, cognitive, and physical problems (Cicetti & Toth, 1995). Among the stressors that have contributed to the recent increase in child abuse are (1) economic stress caused by poverty, (2) unemployment and related work concerns, (3) substance abuse, and (4) improvements or changes in reporting (Huntington, Lima, & Zipper, 1994). Other common factors are a history of family violence, the presence of a premature or ill infant, history of abuse, a single-parent situation, maternal age, separation of mother and child for more than twenty-four hours at the time of birth, and characteristics of the child (Browne and Saqi, 1988; Campbell, 1995). Additionally, children with disabilities seem to be at greater risk for abuse by family members and other caregivers than are other children (National Center on Child Abuse and Neglect, 1993). It is important to consider that because the previously mentioned risk factors interact, resulting in a multiplicative impact on families, the ability of the family to cope with the resulting stress is a key determinant of the level of impact such risk factors will have on a family (Ayoub, Willett, & Robinson, 1992).

Violence.   The Children's Defense Fund (1999) reported that 4,643 infants, children, and teens died as a result of gunfire in 1996. Of these 4,643 children and youth, two-thirds died as victims and one-third died as a result of suicide. In 1995, 28 percent of American students acknowledged the presence of street gangs at their schools (Children's Defense Fund, 1999). The epidemic of violence that affects children, youth, and adults is of particular concern because it reflects the vicious cycle that occurs when many preventable risk factors are not addressed. Of great concern is the fact that intentional injury and homicide are witnessed and perpetrated by our children and youth at a staggering rate. Not surprisingly, for children and youth who view or experience violence daily in the media and in their neighborhoods, schools, and homes, the greatest risk factor is antisocial behavior leading eventually to violent behaviors (Buka & Earls, 1993). Indeed, students who are already at risk due to other family factors are at greater risk of being involved in or at least negatively influenced by neighborhood, school, or home violence (Achenbach et al., 1991). Social learning theorists point out that children learn aggressive responses by observation. From analysis of aggression in youth, social learning researchers have found the following information about environmental conditions that foster aggressive behavior:

- Viewing televised aggression increases aggressive behavior.
- Deviant peer groups or street gangs maintain aggressive behavior by modeling and reinforcing aggression.
- Families of aggressive children are characterized by high rates of aggression among family members.
- Aggression begets aggression. When one person acts aggressively toward another, the affronted person is more likely to react aggressively.

Absent Parents or Single Parents.   Today more than 50 percent of all children born in the United States are born into single-parent homes. The majority of single parents with custody are women, but about 15 percent of all children are being raised by single fathers because of divorce, widowing, and adoption (Seligman, 1992). Research on the negative impact of single parenting remains equivocal; however, characteristics common in single-parent homes, such as absent parents, do present a risk factor for children (Radke-Yarrow, 1990). Lack of structure and supervision places children at risk for their physical health and safety as well as their emotional security (Patterson, Reid, & Dishion 1992; Zins et al., 1994). Absenteeism can be involuntary when economic risks force parents to choose employment over family. In such situations parents may face the dilemma of trading one risk factor (poverty) for another (lack of supervision) and encountering a no-win situation. Likewise, lack of parental involvement in their child's education often is a product of involuntary absenteeism.

The National PTA (1992) asked local PTA presidents to outline the problems they experienced in getting parents involved with school activities. The major reasons families cited included:

- *Time*—Single and working parents have difficulty finding time to get to meetings, conferences, and school functions.
- *Intimidation*—Some parents feel intimidated by principals, counselors, and teachers.
- *Don't understand the system*—Parents do not understand how the general and special education systems work.

- *Child care*—Parents often have other children at home, and they feel discouraged in bringing their children to school events.
- *Language*—English-as-a-second-language parents may have problems understanding the printed materials or speeches at meetings.
- *Cultural differences*—Manners and courtesies are different in different cultures. One can, unintentionally offend or embarrass parents from different cultures. Also, religious holidays can cause conflicts.
- *Transportation*—Some parents lack transportation to attend meetings, conferences, and other school events.
- *Not welcomed*—Parents sometimes feel they are not welcomed in the school. Professionals do not make them feel comfortable. (Adapted from National PTA. (1992). *For our children: Parents and families in education.* (Results of the National Parent Involvement Summit, April, 1992, Chicago: Author.)

Whatever the reason for lack of family involvement, research nevertheless has clearly indicated that children perform better academically and socially if their parents are actively involved in their education (Henderson, 1988; White, Taylor, & Moss, 1992). Sadly, a family's lack of participation in their child's education has a cumulative effect, showing its greatest impact through middle school and high school, if a student remains in school into his or her adolescent years (Kroth & Edge, 1997).

Adolescent Years

Generally, if a family is uninvolved in its child's school experiences, it is also uninvolved in the child's life outside of the school setting. This lack of involvement often sends ongoing, powerful messages to adolescents that they and their school are not valued by their family, causing them to reach out to other sources to find acceptance. The cumulative effects of this lack of involvement combined with the many risk factors already discussed place the adolescent uniquely at risk for experiencing school failure, dropping out, adolescent pregnancy, sexually transmitted diseases, drug use, and association with delinquent peers (Carnahan, 1997; Ekstrom, Goertz, Pollack, & Rock, 1986; Kauffman, 1997). Many of the family factors that place young children at risk continue to influence children into their adolescent years. However, there are certain factors that seem to play a stronger role during adolescence as these young adults look beyond their family for support and identity.

School Failure and Dropping Out. In 1997 the high school dropout rate for students from different ethnic backgrounds was 38.2 percent for Hispanic students, 13.1 percent for African American students, and 7.1 percent for Euro American students. While they may have experienced some combination of family risk factors, the one characteristic that youth who drop out of school seem to have in common is a lack of vision regarding the role of education in their present and future lives (Carnahan, 1997). As previously discussed, often these youth have begun to fail early in their school careers, many by grade three. In a culture and time when high school completion rates are at an all-time high and the job market for unskilled labor positions is steadily declining, our society's loss is enormous. We know that school dropouts will be more likely to commit crimes and become increasingly reliant on public assistance while not contributing to the tax base (Johnston, 1987). This is a bleak picture which our society must begin to address preventively, beginning with the belief that all children from a very early age must have equal opportunity to an appropriate education.

Adolescent Pregnancy.   In recent years it has become clear that adolescent pregnancy and childbearing are significant contributors to poverty. In addition to risking poverty, the trend since the 1960s of earlier and earlier sexual activity has placed our adolescent girls at risk for such problems as unwanted pregnancies and sexually transmitted diseases, including acquired immunodeficiency syndrome (AIDS). Another serious consequence of adolescent pregnancy identified through research is that in adolescent pregnancy both the mother and child are at risk for compromised development due to a number of factors. Risk factors for the adolescent mother include economic problems, physical problems, and social/emotional problems. Risk factors for the child are closely connected to problems the mother experiences as an adolescent mother and include physical, emotional, and intellectual or school problems (Smith, 1997). As these problems manifest themselves in the child, we can clearly see a vicious cycle of risk which, if not prevented, perpetuates itself generation after generation.

Substance Abuse.   Of the families who have been referred to child protective agencies, 40 to 80 percent have identified alcohol or drug abuse problems. In our earlier discussion we learned that prenatal drug exposure may have devastating effects on the exposed child's development. The effects of drug exposure are complicated by the fact that the mother and the environment that she provides for the child are often compromised by her ongoing drug habit, robbing the child of the nurturing that is so necessary for healthy childhood development. For a more in-depth discussion of prenatal drug use, the reader is referred to the resource list provided at the end of this chapter.

Drugs such as marijuana, tobacco, and cocaine carry with them a host of substance-specific consequences for the child before and after birth. However, the results of drug use by school-age children, often beginning in the elementary years, may have equally devastating outcomes. It is well known that early use of alcohol and tobacco, as well as many other toxic substances, correlates with family problems, low socioeconomic status, and school failure. Substance abuse has multiple causes and multiple related risk factors. Family factors known to increase risk include:

- Poor and inconsistent parental discipline
- Lack of emotional bonding of family members
- Socialization to deviant family members or peer groups
- Community conditions of joblessness and hopelessness related to the lack of socioeconomic opportunity, crowding, and violence

Finally, depression often results from alcohol and other substance abuse and directly affects school performance. Depressed delinquents more often have a substance abuse disorder than do those who are not depressed (Riggs et al., 1995).

Caretakers or teachers are most likely to observe the first signs that a child has transitioned from experimentation to intensified use of alcohol or other toxic substances. Changes will occur in social behavior and academic performance at the point of this transition. Kauffman (1997) outlines seven possible symptoms of drug involvement:

1. Change in school or work attendance or performance
2. Alteration of personal appearance
3. Mood swings or attitude changes
4. Withdrawal from responsibilities/family contacts
5. Association with drug-using peers
6. Unusual patterns of behavior
7. Defensive attitude concerning drugs

Although prevention is preferable to intervention, a wide range of programs are available to assist youth with substance abuse problems. Alternatives include the traditional twelve-step programs such as Alcoholics Anonymous, group therapy, family therapy (either single families or groups of families), cognitive-behavior modification, and psychopharmacological treatment. Family involvement and programs that are consistent with cultural traditions are thought to be critical features of prevention and intervention efforts (Bukstein, 1995; Ross, 1994).

Association with Delinquent Peers.   There is unequivocal evidence that antisocial youngsters tend to gravitate toward their deviant peers (Patterson, Reid, & Dishion, 1992). These relationships are extremely significant for their social/emotional development during middle school and high school years. It is there that they find acceptance and some degree of relief from their feelings of failure which the home and school environments may have fostered. Unfortunately, central to these relationships are the antisocial behaviors and delinquent activities that are generally the focus of our society's disenfranchised youth. Studies of delinquents and their families generally reveal that delinquents have experienced low levels of family affection, high levels of family conflict, frequent use of ineffective parental discipline, and parental models of antisocial behavior (Goldstein, 1991).

Adult Years

The move into adulthood carries with it the responsibility of meeting one's own needs in the areas of affection, self-esteem, economics, daily care, socialization, recreation, and education (Turnbull, Summers, & Brotherson, 1984). One of the major tasks of this period is work and community adjustment. With this transition young adults are expected to be self-sufficient and self-determined, displaying all signs of autonomy or "being one's own person" (Ferguson & Ferguson, 1993). In addition to becoming autonomous, the young adult is expected to develop community connectedness, which is achieved through affiliation as a good citizen and participant in the community. Finally, the young adult is expected to continue growing and developing as a person throughout his or her adult years. These expectations present a monumental task for all young adults. However, these challenging tasks of adulthood may seem almost insurmountable for those individuals who bring with them the risk baggage of their youth, such as poverty, childhood abuse, academic failure, substance abuse, teenage motherhood, and disconnectedness from family and community. It is here that we clearly see the self-perpetuating vicious cycle of the at-risk family, and it appears that the only variable that can break this cycle is outside intervention. Recent legislation that places strong emphasis on the transition of welfare mothers into the work force is an example of governmental attempts to intervene and reverse the negative cycle of poverty and dependency which so often disempowers young adults and their new families (Zaslow & Emig, 1997).

Educational Structures for Supporting Families with Risk Factors

Currently there is a combination of direct and indirect support services available to at-risk families that are important to new teachers. Direct support services are offered directly to parents and indirect support services are offered to the children of at-risk families in the school setting.

Direct Family Support Services

Direct family support services provide specific supports to individuals and families as they try to circumvent the results of risk factors. These family support services are often supported by educational, human resources, and health agencies and are geared to focus on specific outcomes such as increased parenting skills, family involvement in children's education, and academic remediation for parents.

Parent Groups.   Parent support groups may be associated with public schools or community, regional, and national organizations. The underlying goals of such groups usually include the following: Help parents overcome isolation, provide support for each other, learn skills, and develop insights about their children and themselves (Carter & Harvey, 1996).

Home–School Partnerships.   Historically, family–teacher interactions have centered around parent–teacher organizations. The primary focus of these organizations has been parents supporting schools in ways that would indirectly benefit their children (e.g., fundraisers for school play equipment). At-risk families are much less likely to be involved in PTO groups because of lack of time, resources and, in some cases, interest (Epstein, 1995). Epstein (1995) describes a model of parent involvement which is presented in Table 4.3.

Academic Retraining Opportunities.   Schools have organized efforts to retrain parents in skills areas that will enable them to help their children with school work at home. A program developed in Richmond, Vermont (Whiteford, 1998) involved a series of seven, hourlong workshops designed to deepen parents' conceptual knowledge and relational understanding of the mathematics their children would encounter during the elementary school years. At the end of each workshop parents were given a "Math at Home" handout which provided ideas for applying what parents had learned to helping their children with math

TABLE 4.3 *Epstein's Framework of Six Types of Involvement*

Type 1: Parenting	Help all families establish home environments to support children as students
Type 2: Communicating	Design effective forms of school-to-home and home-to-school communications about school programs and children's progress
Type 3: Volunteering	Recruit and organize parent help and support
Type 4: Learning at Home	Provide information and ideas to families about how to help students at home with homework and other curriculum-related activities, decisions, and planning
Type 5: Decision Making	Include parents in school decisions, developing parent leaders and representatives
Type 6: Collaborating with Community	Identify and integrate resources and services from the community to strengthen school programs, family practices, and student learning and development.

Source: Adapted from Epstein, J. L. (1995). "School/Family/Community Partnerships: Caring for the Children We Share." *Phi Delta Kappan, 76* (9), 704.

assignments at home. Whiteford reported that as a result of their workshops parents felt more confident helping their children.

Indirect Family Support Services

Student Support Teams (SST).   These teams, often called *prereferral teams,* are made up of a variety of professionals, often including general and special educators, school principals, parents, and school psychologists. The purpose of these teams is to support general education teachers in developing strategies for teaching at-risk learners (Chalfant, Pysch, & Moultrie, 1979; Gerber & Semmel, 1984). Limited research indicates that SSTs cut down on the number of referrals to special education and members and administrators report that the teams are effective (Schram et al., 1984).

Positive Behavior Support Plans.   The 1997 reauthorization of the Individuals with Disabilities Education Act (IDEA) mandated that schools, with input from parents, complete functional behavioral assessments and design behavior intervention plans (i.e., positive behavior support plans) for students whose behavior interferes with their learning (Katsiyannis, & Maag, 1998; Office of Special Education and Rehabilitative Services, 1997).

Title I Programs.   The Elementary and Secondary Education Act (ESEA), established in 1965 and reauthorized by Improving America's Schools Act of 1994 (IASA), authorized most federal elementary and secondary education programs, including the Title I program, to provide compensatory education to educationally disadvantaged students (Stedman,

1994). Schools identified as Title I schools may receive funding which enables them to provide intensive instruction in reading and mathematics.

Title II Programs.   Title II programs focus on youth and adults who are at risk for failure in securing and maintaining employment. These programs provide education and training to youth in school and to those students who have chosen to drop out of school. Such programs include The Job Training Partnership Act (TJTP) of 1982 and the School-to-Work Opportunities Act. These programs have the potential to interrupt the vicious cycle of poverty that so many at-risk families face.

Section 504 Services.   Section 504 of the Vocational Rehabilitation Act of 1973 was the earliest significant civil rights legislation to expressly prohibit discrimination against any individual who (a) has a physical or mental impairment which substantially limits one or more major life activities, (b) has a record of such impairment, or (c) is regarded as having such an impairment. Parents may use this legislation, if their child does not receive special education services, to request special services in the regular education program if appropriate under Section 504 guidelines.

Community Supports

In addition to the specific educational strategies used to support at-risk families and students, there are many community programs available to provide parallel prevention and intervention services. Examples of these programs include after-school programs (e.g., Big Brothers/Big Sisters, Project DARE, Head Start, and Early Head Start).

Family Member Questions _____

New teachers will face the following questions as they interact with families that place children at risk.

• *How can I help my child at home?* Teachers will want to explain to the parents some of the learning strategies that have been successful at school. It is important that teachers not expect parents to be "home-bound teachers." All students need down time from school-work to play and have fun. Give parents one or two suggestions on how to help their child with a specific assignment and be sure to recognize (e.g., note home, telephone call) their efforts when the child brings in a completed homework assignment.

• *My kid is going wild after school while I'm at work. What can I do?* Teachers should keep a list of after-school programs with identified contact people, costs, and locations to assist in answering this question. Don't make the mistake of just handing out the after-school program list. Instead, ask the parents about their child's interests and try to narrow the list down to a couple of suggested programs. One method of staying current with existing community programs is to get on the mailing lists of local parks and recreation agencies, libraries, volunteer organizations (e.g., Habitat for Humanity), social service agencies (e.g., United Way, Red Cross, Big Brothers/Big Sisters), and community agencies (e.g., police department, Boys/Girls Club of America).

- *I don't have any money for eyeglasses (or braces, or adaptive communication equipment or the class field trip or a child's winter coat). How can I buy that when I can't afford food?* Again, having a resource list of groups that will sponsor a child (e.g., Lion's Club, Rotary Club, College Fraternity or Sorority) is very valuable. Tell the parents that these people are part of organizations whose goal is to help others. Ask the parents if it would be all right for you to contact the organization and ask for a sponsorship. Accept the parents response…positive or negative.

- *I can't believe it, but my daughter has taken up smoking. Got any ideas on how to make her quit?* Teachers can have brochures and handouts from the American Cancer Society available for parents to share with their child. In addition, this is a nice opportunity to implement a lesson on smoking and health concerns. Teachers should support parents as they try to keep their children from smoking, but teachers cannot accept the responsibility for making the child quit.

- *I think my son is smoking marijuana, but I don't know if I should search his room? What do you think?* In this instance, the teacher should tell the parents that now would be a good time to bring in another person, the school counselor, to help discuss this matter. The teacher can tell the parents that they're not sure what to do, so having a professional who has more training in this area would help them make the right choice. Telling parents to invade a child's privacy is not within the teacher's instructional role. It is important to address the issue and provide support to the parents as they talk to more trained individuals to make a decision regarding whether to search their son's room for illegal drugs.

Family Resources and Services

The following family resources and services may be helpful.

MODEL PROGRAMS

High Scope Foundation
600 N. River Street
Ypsilanti, MI 48198

National Center for Clinical Infant Programs
733 15th Street, N.W., Suite 912
Washington, DC 20001

INTERNET SITES

www.eparent.com
www.national.perinatal.org
www.peds.umn.edu/center (chronic illness)
www.acch.org (Association for the Care of
Children's Health)
www.notes.org (Fetal Alcohol Syndrome)
www.sunsite.unc.edu/asha (AIDS)
www.edcnac.org (AIDS)

PUBLICATIONS

Boyd, F. N., Steiner, G. L., & Boland, M. G. (Eds.) (1995). *Children, families, and HIV/AIDS: Psycho-social and therapeutic issues.* New York: Guilford Press.

Byron, E., & Katz, G. (Eds.) (1991). *HIV prevention and AIDS education: Resources for special educators.* Reston, VA: Council for Exceptional Children.

Donnelly, A. H. C. (1991). What we have learned about prevention: What we should do about it. *Child Abuse and Neglect, 15,* 99–106.

Leone, P. (1991). *Alcohol and other drugs: Use, abuse and disabilities.* Reston, VA: Council for Exceptional Children.

McGowan, B. G. (1990). Family-based services and public policy: Context and implications. In J. K. Whittaker, J. Kinney, E. M. Tracy, & C. Booth (Eds.). *Reaching high-risk families: Intensive family preservation in human services* (pp. 65–87). Hawthorne, NY: Aldine Degruyter.

Summary

Family factors that place children at risk for current and future learning problems do not exist in a vacuum. It is the interaction between factors, the duration and intensity of factors, as well as the number of factors present in a family system that determine longitudinal effects on the child. Integral in this risk equation is the notion of resiliency and the child's innate ability to cope with risk factors known to have detrimental effects on learning. Although many risk factors such as poverty continue to be a challenge in terms of prevention, national, regional, community, and local school programs do exist which take a proactive approach to the amelioration of a variety of risk factors. It is important for new teachers to recognize the source of family risk factors and the resources for addressing the needs of students at risk for school failure.

References

Achenbach, T. M., Howell, C. T., Quay, H. C., & Conners, C. K. (1991). National survey of problems and competencies among four- to sixteen-year-olds. *Monographs of the Society for Research in Child Development, 56* (3), Serial No. 25.

Ayoub, C. C., Willett, J. B., & Robinson, D. S. (1992). Families at risk of child maltreatment: Entry-level characteristics and growth in family functioning during treatment. *Child Abuse and Neglect, 16,* 495–511.

Baca, L. M., & Almonza, E. (1991). *Language, minority students and disabilities.* Reston, VA: Council for Exceptional Children.

Beckman, P. J. (1991). Comparison of mothers' and fathers' perceptions of the effect of young children with and without disabilities. *American Journal of Mental Retardation, 95* (5), 585–595.

Blackman, J. A. (1990). Low birth weight. In J. A. Blackman (Ed.). *Medical aspects of developmental disabilities in children birth to three* (2nd ed., pp. 181–184). Rockville, MD: Aspen.

Bowe, F. (1995). *Birth to five: Early childhood special education.* Albany, NY: Delmar.

Bowman, B. T. (1992). Who is at risk for what and why. *Journal of Early Intervention, 16* (2), 101–108.

Browne, K., & Saqi, S. (1988). Approaches to screening for child abuse and neglect, In K. Browne, C. Davies, & P. Stratton (Eds.). *Early prediction and prevention of child abuse* (pp. 57–85). Chichester: John Wiley & Sons.

Budd, K., & Greenspan, S. (1984). Mentally retarded mothers. In E. Blechman (Ed.). *Behavior modification with women* (pp. 477–506). New York: Guilford Press.

Buka, S., & Earls, F. (1993). Early determinants of delinquency and violence. *Health Affairs, 12* (4), 45–64.

Bukstein, O. G. (1995). *Adolescent substance abuse: Assessment, prevention, and treatment.* New York: Wiley.

Campbell, S. B. (1995). Behavior problems in preschool children: A review of recent research. *Journal of Child Psychology & Psychiatry, 13,* 113–149.

Carnahan, S. (1997). Preventing school failure and dropout. In R. J. Simeonsson (Ed.). *Risk, resilience and prevention: Promoting the well-being of all children* (pp. 103–123). Baltimore, MD: Paul H. Brookes.

Carter, N., & Harvey, C. (1996). Gaining perspective on parenting groups. *Zero to Three, 16* (6), 1–8.

Chalfant, J. C., Pysch, M. V., & Moultrie, R. (1979). Teacher assistance teams: A model for within-building problem solving. *Learning Disability Quarterly, 2,* 85–96.

Children's Defense Fund. (1998). *The state of America's children yearbook.* Washington, DC: Author.

Children's Defense Fund. (1999). *The state of America's children yearbook.* Washington, DC: Author.

Cicchetti, D., & Toth, S. L. (1995). A developmental psychopathology perspective on child abuse and neglect. *Journal of the American Academy of Child and Adolescent Psychiatry, 34,* 541–565.

Conry, J. (1990). Neuropsychological deficits in fetal alcohol syndrome and fetal alcohol effects. *Alcoholism: Clinical and Experimental Research, 14,* 650–655.

Crain, L. S., & Bennett, B. (1996). Prenatal causes of atypical infant development. In M. J. Hanson (Ed.). *Atypical infant development* (pp. 47–83). Austin, TX: ProEd.

Drell, M., Siegel, C., & Gaensbauer, T. (1993). Post-traumatic stress disorder. In C. H. Zeanah (Ed.). *Handbook of Infant Mental Health* (pp. 291–304). New York: Guildford Press.

Ekstrom, R. B., Goertz, M. E., Pollack, J. M., & Rock, D. A. (1986). Who drops out of high school and why? Findings from a national study. *Teachers College Record, 87* (3), 356–373.

Epstein, J. L. (1995). School/family/community partnerships: Caring for the children we share. *Phi Delta Kappan, 76* (9), 701–712.

Espe-Sherwindt, M. & Crable, S. (1993). Parents with mental retardation: Moving beyond the myths. *Topics in Early Childhood Special Education, 13* (2), 154–174.

Feldman, M. A., Sparks, B., & Case, L. (1993). Effectiveness of home-based early intervention on the language development of children of mothers with mental retardation. *Research in Developmental Disabilities, 14,* 387–408.

Feldman, M. A., & Walton-Allen, N. (1997). Effects of maternal mental retardation and poverty on intellectual, academic, and behavioral status of school-age children. *American Journal on Mental Retardation, 101* (4), pp. 352–364.

Ferguson, P. M., & Ferguson, D. L. (1993). The promise of adulthood. In M. Snell (Ed.). *Instruction of persons with severe disabilities* (4th ed.) (p. 59). Englewood Cliffs, NJ: Merrill/Prentice Hall.

Gerber, M. M., & Semmel, M. I. (1984). Teacher as imperfect test: Reconceptualizing the referral process. *Educational Psychologist, 19,* 137–148.

Goldstein, A. P. (1991). *Delinquent gangs: A psychological perspective.* Champaign, IL: Research Press.

Gorski, P. A., & VandenBerg, K. A. (1996). Infants born at risk. In M. Hanson (Ed.). *Atypical infant development* (pp. 85–114). Austin, TX: ProEd.

Groves, B., Zuckerman, B., Marans, S., & Cohen, D. (1993). Silent victims: children who witness violence. *Journal of the American Medical Association, 269,* 262–264.

Hanson, M. J. (1996). Early transactions: The developmental context for infants whose development is atypical. In M. J. Hanson (Ed.). *Atypical infant development* (pp. 3–16). Austin, TX: ProEd.

Hanson, M. J., & Carta, J. J. (1996). Addressing the challenges of families with multiple risks. *Exceptional Children 62* (3), 201–212.

Henderson, A. T. (1988). Parents are a school's best friends. *Phi Delta Kappan, 70* (2), 148–153.

Huntington, G. S., Lima, L., & Zipper, I. N. (1994). Child abuse: A prevention agenda. In R. J. Simeonsson (Ed.). *Risk, resilience and prevention: Promoting the well-being of all children* (pp. 169–182). Baltimore, MD: Paul H. Brookes.

Huston, A. C. (Ed.) (1991). *Children in poverty: Child developmental and public policy.* Cambridge: Cambridge University Press.

Jaffe, P., Wolfe, D., & Wilson, S. (1990). *Children of battered women.* Newbury Park, CA: Sage Press.

Johnston, W. B. (1987). *Workforce 2000: Work and workers for the 21st century* (Report No. HI-3796-RR). Indianapolis, IN: Hudson Institute. (ERIC Document Reproduction Service No. ED 290-887).

Kaplan-Sanoff, M., Parker, S., & Zuckerman, B. (1991). Poverty and early childhood development: What do we know, and what should we do? *Infants and Young Children, 4* (1), 68–76.

Kaslow, N.J., & Rehm, L. P. (1991). Childhood depression. In T. R. Kratochwill & R. J. Morris (Eds.). *The practice of child therapy* (2nd ed., pp. 43–75). New York: Pergamon.

Katsiyannis, A., & Maag, J. W. (1998). Disciplining students with disabilities: Issues and considerations for implementing IDEA '97. *Behavioral Disorders, 23* (4), 276–289.

Kauffman, J. M. (1997). *Characteristics of emotional and behavioral disorders of children and youth* (6th ed.). New York: Merrill.

Kazdin, A. E. (1991). Aggressive behavior and conduct disorders. In T. R. Kratochwill & R. J. Morris (Eds.). *The practice of child therapy* (2nd ed., pp. 174–221). New York: Pergamon.

Khalsa, J. H., & Gfroerer, J. (1991). Epidemiology and health consequences of drug abuse among pregnant women. *Seminars in Perinatology, 15,* 265–270.

Knitzer, J., & Aber, J. L. (1995). Young children in poverty: Facing the facts. *American Journal of Orthopsychiatry, 65,* 174–176.

Kroth, R. L., & Edge, D. (1997). *Strategies for communicating with parents and families of exceptional children.* Denver, CO: Love Publishing.

Lorsbach, T. C., & Frymier, J. (1992). A comparison of learning disabled and nondisabled students on five at-risk factors. *Learning Disability Research and Practice, 7,* 137–141.

National Center on Child Abuse and Neglect. (1993). *A report on the maltreatment of children with disabilities* (Report No. 20-10030). Washington, DC: U.S. Department of Health and Human Services.

National PTA. (1992). *For our children: Parents and families in education* (Results of the National Parent Involvement Summit, April 1992). Chicago: Author.

Nelson, K. B., & Ellenberg, J. H. (1981). Apgar scores as predictors of chronic neurologic disability. *Pediatrics, 68,* 36–44.

Office of Special Education and Rehabilitative Services. (1997). *Changes in Part B of the Individuals with Disabilities Education Act, as required by the Individuals with Disabilities Education Act amendments of 1997.* Washington, DC: U.S. Department of Education.

O'Neill, A. M. (1985). Normal and bright children of mentally retarded parents: The Huck Finn syndrome. *Child Psychiatry and Human Development, 15,* 255–268.

Osofsky, J. D. (1994). Introduction. In J. D. Osofsky & E. Fenichel (Eds.). *Caring for infants and toddlers in violent environments: Hurt, healing, and hope* (pp. 3–6). Arlington, VA: Zero to Three.

Osofsky, J. D., & Jackson, B. R. (1994). Parenting in violent environments. In J. D. Osofsky & E. Fenichel (Eds.). *Caring for infants and toddlers in violent environments: Hurt, healing and hope* (pp. 8–12). Arlington, VA: Zero to Three.

Patterson, G. R., Reid, J. B., & Dishion, T. J. (1992). *Antisocial Boys.* Eugene, OR: Castalia.

Plomin, R. (1989). Environment and genes: Determinants of behavior. *American Psychologist, 44,* 105–111.

Radke-Yarrow, M. (1990). Family environments of depressed and well parents and their children: Issues of research methods. In G. R. Patterson (Ed.). *Depression and aggression in family interaction* (pp. 169–184). Hillsday, NJ: Erlbaum.

Ratter, M. (1990). Psychosocial resilience and protective mechanisms. In J. Rolf, A. S. Mastern, D. Cicchetti, K. H. Nuechterlein, & S. Weintraub (Eds.). *Risk and protective factors in the development of psychopathology* (pp. 81–214). Cambridge, MA: Cambridge University Press.

Research Bulletin (1989). Cambridge, MA: Center for Health and Human Resources Policy, John F. Kennedy School of Government, Harvard University.

Riggs, P. D., Baker, S., Mikulich, S. K., Young, S., & Crowley, T. J. (1995). Depression in substance-dependent delinquents. *Journal of the American Academy of Child and Adolescent Psychiatry, 34,* 764–771.

Rivers, K. Y., & Hedrick, D. L. (1998). A follow-up study of language and behavioral concerns of children prenatally exposed to drugs. *Infant-Toddler Intervention, 8* (1), 29–51.

Ross, G. R. (1994). *Treating adolescent substance abuse: Understanding the fundamental elements.* Boston: Allyn & Bacon.

Sameroff, A. J., Seifer, R., Barocas, B., Zax, M., & Greenspan, S. (1987). IQ scores of 4-year-old children: Social-environmental risk factors. *Pediatrics, 79* (3), 343–350.

Schorr, E., & Schorr, D. (1988). *Within our reach: Breaking the cycle of disadvantage.* NY: Anchor Press/Doubleday.

Schram, L., Semmel, M. I., Gerber, M. M., Bruce, M. M., Lopez, M. M., Reyna, N., & Allen, D. (1984). *Problem solving teams in California.* Unpublished manuscript, University of California at Santa Barbara.

Seligmann, J. (1992). It's not like Mr. Mom. *Newsweek, 120* (24), 70–73.

Shriver, M., & Piersel, W. (1994). The long-term effects of intrauterine drug exposure: Review of recent research and implications for early childhood special education. *Topics in Early Childhood Special Education, 14,* 161–183.

Simeonsson, H. W., & Gray, J. N. (1994). Healthy children: Primary prevention of disease. In R. J. Simeonsson (Ed.). *Risk, resilience and prevention: Promoting the well-being of all children* (pp. 77–102). Baltimore, MD: Paul H. Brookes.

Singer, L. T., Garber, R., & Kliegmen, R. (1991). Neurobehavioral sequelae of fetal cocaine exposure. *Journal of Pediatrics, 119,* 667–672.

Smith, T. M. (1997). Adolescent pregnancy. In R. J. Simeonsson (Ed.). *Risk, resilience and prevention: Promoting the well-being of all children* (pp. 125–149). Baltimore, MD: Paul H. Brookes.

Stark, K. D., Ostrander, R., Jurowski, C. A., Swearer, S., & Bowen, B. (1995). Affective and mood disorders. In M. Hersen and R. T. Ammerman (Eds.). *Advanced abnormal child psychology* (pp. 253–282). Hillsdale, NJ: Erlbaum.

Stedman, J. B. (1994). *Improving American's Schools Act: An overview of P.L. 103-382.* CRS Report for Congress. Report No. EA026543. Washington, D.C.: Library of Congress, Congressional Research Service. (ERIC Document Reproduction No. ED 379792).

Streissguth, A. P., Barr, H. M., & Sampson, P. D. (1990). Moderate prenatal alcohol exposure: Effects on child IQ and learning problems at 7½ years. *Alcoholism: Clinical and Experimental Research, 14,* 662–669.

Turnbull, H. R., Buchele-Ash, A., & Mitchell, L. (1994). *Abuse and neglect of children with disabilities: A policy analysis prepared for the National Symposium on Abuse and Neglect of Children with Disabilities.* Lawrence: University of Kansas, Beach Center on Families and Disability.

Turnbull, A. P., Summers, J. A., & Brotherson, M. J. (1984). *Working with families with disabled members: A family systems approach.* Lawrence: University of Kansas, University Affiliated Facility.

Tymchuk, A. J. (1990a). Parents with mental retardation: A national strategy. *Journal of Disability Policy Studies, 1* (4), 43–55.

Tymchuk, A. J. (1990b). *Parents with mental retardation: A national strategy.* Concept paper developed for the President's Committee on Mental Retardation. Los Angeles, CA.

Tymchuk, A. J., & Andron, L. (1992). Project parenting: Child interactional training with mothers who are mentally handicapped. *Mental Handicap Research, 5,* 4–32.

Tymchuk, A. J., Andron, L., & Unger, O. (1987). Parents with mental handicaps and adequate child care—A review. *Mental Handicaps, 15,* 49–54.

Tymchuk, A. J., Yokota, A., & Rahbar, B. (1990). Decision-making abilities of mothers with mental retardation. *Research in Developmental Disabilities, 11,* 97–109.

U.S. Department of Education. (1995). *The community action toolkit.* Washington, DC: Author.

White, K. R., Taylor, M. J., & Moss, V. D. (1992). Does research support claims about the benefits of involving parents in early intervention programs? *Review of Educational Research, 62* (1), 91–125.

Whiteford, T. (1998). Math for moms and dads. *Educational Leadership, 55* (8), 64–66.

Williams, B. F., & Howard, V. (1993). Children exposed to cocaine: Characteristics and implications for research and intervention. *Journal of Early Intervention, 17* (1), 61–72.

Zaslow, J. M., & Emig, C. A. (1997). When low-income mothers go to work: Implications for children. *The future of children: Welfare to work, 7* (1), 10–23.

Zins, J. E., Garcia, V. F., Tuchfarber, B. S., Clark, K. M., & Laurence, S. C. (1994). Preventing injury in children and adolescents. In R. J. Simeonsson (Ed.). *Risk, resilience and prevention: Promoting the well-being of all children* (pp. 183–201). Baltimore, MD: Paul H. Brookes.

Family Assessment

Pegi S. Davis

D. Michael Malone

Chapter Objectives

This chapter will explore family assessment, a key component in any work with children and their families. In this chapter we will

- Describe the history of the process of family assessment
- Explain the rationale for teachers' study of family assessment
- Describe family theories and their relationship to family assessment
- Describe appropriate procedures for family assessment
- Discuss the outcomes of family assessment
- Describe the influences of various disciplines on family assessment
- Discuss implications for inclusion and collaborative practices
- Provide assessment tools that are appropriate for different needs and concerns
- Furnish practical suggestions to teachers on family assessment
- Provide a list of relevant resources and materials
- Summarize important chapter themes

As my three children went through school, the experience for each of them was very different. My first child had no problems and seemed to breeze through school without any involvement from me at all. In fact, most times I was not really sure what was going on at school. My second child had some problems in kindergarten and first grade. The school gave him some tests and told me he had ADD and some learning disabilities. They told me what they could do and what I needed to do to make him more successful. I really tried but it was hard on the whole family for me to spend so much time with him and sometimes I just let it go. My last child was, except for being a girl, very much like my second son. She had some problems in kindergarten, but the teacher asked me what worked at home and we got her doing O.K. Then in first grade she had more

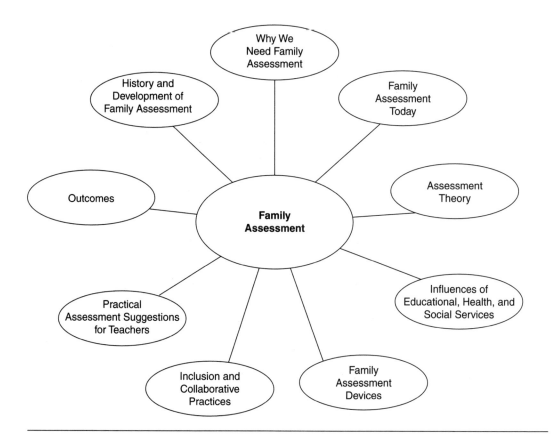

problems. That teacher asked me to come to a meeting with some other people and we all talked about what to do. We decided to give her some tests and they asked me to help. I completed some questions on our family and how she does things at home, like eat and play. Then I watched her in class for a few days and talked to the teacher and the special education teacher after school. They gave her some tests, too. Then we all met to watch her in some regular activities. When we met again they wanted to know what I found out and then we all decided how to help her learn. You know, it has been so much easier for her and for the whole family. We all help and no one complains about me spending so much time with her. My sons join in her "homework" time and I think it's helping all of them. Now I've gotten more involved in their classes and what they are doing in school. The boys are doing better too. This is how it should always be for families with children in school (Davis, 1996).

In this chapter we will be exploring issues related to family assessment, a key component in new teachers' work with families. Family assessment may be part of an assessment for an individual or performed for the family as a whole. However, whether the primary purpose of the assessment is for an individual or the whole family, working with the family is critical to success for two reasons. First, parents/guardians have the right to participate—it is the law. Second, it helps families develop feelings of empowerment, and satisfaction with the assessment and with the ultimate intervention.

Similar to the development of work with families in other areas, the evolution of family assessment has shifted from the professional-directed procedure to the family-centered and family-directed process in effect today. Assessment now looks past deficits and toward the family's strengths, needs, and goals. Both assessment instruments and procedures have evolved as a result of this change in philosophy. This move toward family-centered and family-directed practice developed from the infusion of family systems into the various disciplines that serve families. The acceptance of the family systems theory in the medical, social service, and education disciplines, especially in early childhood education, has led to the current model for family assessment.

History and Development of Family Assessment

Whether an assessment was for the purpose of serving an individual or the family as a whole, family assessment has historically been part of a process focused on deficits. Assessments were conducted for the purpose of identification and remediation of deficits. Deficits and current functioning levels dominated all intervention planning, from assessment through service delivery. The findings were used to determine eligibility for specialized services, appropriate intervention goals and objectives, and appropriate intervention settings.

Assessments were conducted by highly trained professionals in formal, clinical settings. The instruments were usually standardized. Administration of the assessment instruments was formal, with set procedures that could not be violated without affecting the validity of the instruments. The feeling of professionals as they performed assessments, planned intervention, and delivered services was "I am the educated one, so obviously I have all the answers. I will tell you what is wrong and I will then fix it." Unfortunately, this was often communicated to the family. This chapter case study is an example of this mode of assessment.

Why was assessment conducted in this manner? Primarily, knowledgeable professionals were taught that they were responsible for the assessment. As knowledgeable professionals, they knew these formalized methods required a controlled setting to achieve the "normed" (tested/measured average of a group) results of standardized testing. This meant the assessment could provide a numerical answer that could be compared to similar people and used to define the disorder or difficulties of the individual or family. This promoted labeling, necessary for eligibility and placement decisions (Bailey & Wolery, 1992). However, these formal procedures did not always achieve the outcomes desired. When family members were excluded and not valued, the knowledge gained by assessors was limited, often omitting important information, which meant the results often did not address the needs for the individual's or family's success. In addition, the goals established from the assessment could be nonfunctional (Bailey & Wolery, 1992) or not supported by family members.

Characteristics of Ecological, Family-Centered Assessment

Over the course of the past two decades we have seen significant philosophical changes regarding children and families, both nationwide and throughout multiple disciplines. As the theory of family systems has become more prevalent, assessment in general, and more specifically family assessment, has changed. Less formal instruments are accepted as part of an assessment, usually with more relaxed procedures and in more natural settings. Even more important, families are valued and respected by service providers. From this, family involvement in assessment procedures became common and professionals began to realize the importance and necessity of family participation. As these professionals began to acknowledge the importance of assessing the contexts (the individual, family, relatives, friends, and environments) within which people function, they adopted a systems view of human development (Grotevant & Carlson, 1989). The acceptance of various systems models within the different disciplines (e.g., Sameroff, 1983: transactional model; Bronfenbrenner, 1979: model of human ecology; and von Bertalanffy, 1968: general systems model) promoted the importance of family influence on all outcomes.

The theoretical base for ecological, family-centered assessment as discussed here is from the family systems and ecological theories of development by Bronfenbrenner (1970). He states that people do not develop within a vacuum. They grow, develop, and learn from their family and social environments, whether or not these environments nurture and support them. People learn through interactions with other people about cultural heritage, social mores, attitudes toward learning, and beliefs and values. The interrelationships of the people within this environment guide future relationships. All of the conditions within this environment, as well as the external influences that act on it, become important elements in the successful development of individuals within the family. This includes school, community services, church, and recreational activities. Families hold the unique position of being ultimately responsible for the individual.

Each person within the family system has his or her own strengths and needs. Each family has an existing history and culture which includes interpersonal interactions. Ecological family assessment evaluates the interrelationships between an individual and family members, other people, the systems in which each person operates, and includes the environment within each system. Family systems are constantly changed by the many influences on families, including service delivery and intervention (see Figure 5.1).

Ecological, family-centered assessment must be nondiscriminatory, respecting family culture and values. It must include parents as assessment team members to assure that critical information from the home environment is included, and that intervention targets areas of importance to the family. This must go beyond supplying background information. Parents should have the opportunity to assess the individual, especially in relation to the family environment. Families participate in several roles: Observer, team member, advocate, advisor, service provider, and individuals.

Ecological, family-centered assessment must take place in multiple, natural settings with the involvement of a variety of people engaged in typical activities. As the family system operates within and with a variety of other settings, family assessments address elements within these multiple environments.

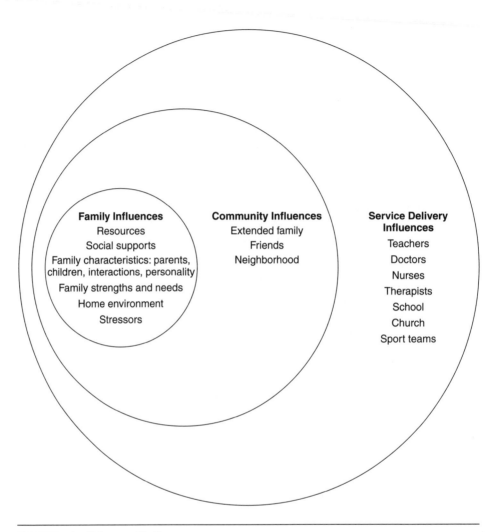

Family Influences
Resources
Social supports
Family characteristics: parents,
children, interactions, personality
Family strengths and needs
Home environment
Stressors

Community Influences
Extended family
Friends
Neighborhood

**Service Delivery
Influences**
Teachers
Doctors
Nurses
Therapists
School
Church
Sport teams

FIGURE 5.1   *Spheres of Influence*

In the move from single-discipline, individual-based assessment with its standardized testing, professionals have learned to accept and value the contribution families make from their own rich experiences. The awareness of the family's resources, priorities, and concerns can help us to more effectively assess, support, and promote positive outcomes. Epstein (1989) identified five types of parental involvement: Parenting, communication, volunteering, learning at home, and representing others. The resources, priorities, and concerns of families can be described within these five categories.

• *Parenting:* From the assessment of family resources, priorities, and concerns can be identified so that the home environment is safe and supportive according to the family's needs.

- *Communication:* The assessment can determine the family's communication strengths and preferred method of communication.

- *Volunteering:* Families have resources that may be utilized in the classroom for observation and decision making for their children, as well as seeing that priorities are addressed.

- *Learning at home:* As a part of the assessment team, the family's resources, priorities, and concerns are identified and made part of the overall intervention and appropriate materials and support can be provided to the family.

- *Representing others:* Families may serve as resources to each other as they provide support to other families. When assessment is a new concern for families, those who have been through the process offer support so that resources, priorities, and concerns are identified correctly.

Fundamental Assumptions of Assessment

The development of family assessment and the need to evaluate multiple levels of family structure and functioning (systems) support Hawkins' (1979) fundamental assumptions of assessment. These include the idea that assessment is a process and not a single test to determine an outcome. His assumptions, still important to new teachers, include

- Assessment does not occur in a vacuum; it involves various ingredients (e.g., child characteristics, parent characteristics, family patterns), sources (e.g., child, mother, father, teacher), and contexts (home, school, community, sociohistoric).
- Assessment is ongoing; it is not a static, one time event.
- Assessment leads to program planning. Program planning leads to program implementation. Program implementation leads to program monitoring, evaluation, and revision.

So it can be seen that assessment is part of a broader process that can include, but is more than, measurement, testing, and evaluation.

Legal Developments That Support Family Assessment

Several federal programs mandate family involvement in children's education. We will look at two of the most important. Head Start, which began in 1965, is foremost in its efforts to involve families. The Handicapped Children's Early Education Program (HCEEP), in 1968, began to provide grants to encourage original programming in early intervention. Participation of parents was required. Research from HCEEP programs provided the proof needed that family involvement has a positive impact on children's education.

Family advocacy for educational rights for their children brought about the Education for All Handicapped Children Act, P.L. 94-142. Passed in 1975, P.L. 94-142 established the process for assessing children to determine eligibility for special education services. This law applied to all school-age children. It was amended by P.L. 99-457 in 1986, which had two sections important to this discussion: Part B and Part H. Part B mandated that a free and appropriate education should be extended to children with disabilities from three to five years of age. This included the regulations for parent participation in assessment of preschool children. Parental concerns and priorities from the assessment must be included in any IEP or IFSP developed. Under Part H, states were given incentives to provide services to young children with special needs from birth to three years of age. Consequently, Part H establishes the regulations for assessing infants and toddlers. In 1991 the Education for All Handicapped Children Act was reauthorized as P.L. 102-119 and renamed the Individuals with Disabilities Education Act (now known as IDEA). Included in this law are two key regulations. Assessments are to be parent directed and language was changed from "strengths and needs," to "resources, priorities, and concerns." The most recent reauthorization (P.L. 105-117) changed Part H to Part C and continues the standard of family participation. These laws have encouraged and advanced the shift from single-discipline, child-centered services to interdisciplinary, family-centered service delivery.

Why We Need Family Assessment

One of the primary reasons for all assessments continues to be the determination of service eligibility. This means that assessment continues to focus on identification and remediation of disabilities. With the focus on family-centered support and services, there may come a time when this is less emphasized, but for now eligibility is still important.

Assessment has historically been used to determine appropriate intervention goals and objectives as well as an appropriate setting for intervention by determining the needs of both the individual and family. It provides the opportunity to consider the level of parent–child interaction, family functioning, and parenting skills. However, this should not be the primary focus for a family assessment and is not where we want to begin. It is more important to identify the strengths, abilities, and priorities of the family and individual.

Through a family assessment, we are also able to determine what parents expect from the assessment (Bailey & Wolery, 1992) and the later intervention. Family assessment often begins with a family interview or inventory of needs in which the family strengths, priorities, resources (financial and social), and concerns are determined (see Figure 5.2 for suggested questions on a family needs assessment). Insufficient resources may so overwhelm the family that there is not enough time or energy to accomplish intervention goals (Turnbull & Turnbull, 1990). Family involvement is critical in needs and priority identification for both individuals and the family as a whole. It is of utmost importance that the services provided match the identified needs and priorities of the family. New teachers may never understand why a family does not follow through with agreed on interventions unless family needs and priorities are determined. When the individual's strengths are not the focus of assessments, intervention will be developed for deficit remediation instead of the development of strengths (Bailey & Wolery, 1992). When families do not feel like part of the decision making process and valued by professionals they may object to the recommendations and neglect or disregard professional opinions (Bailey & Wolery, 1992; Berheimer & Keogh, 1995).

There are two additional reasons for conducting family assessments. First, is to determine the family's level of satisfaction with the intervention plan. Second, we need to determine the effectiveness of interventions and services provided to individuals and families. Families provide the most important information in these two assessment needs. Families may choose to direct the assessment or to be part of the collaborative assessment team. In any case, they are equal partners in this process.

FIGURE 5.2 *Suggested Questions for the Family Needs Interview*

- Tell me about your child.
- What concerns you and what makes you happy about your child?
- Describe what happens at home, when you shop, at a friend's home.
- What does your child like to do? not like to do?
- When is your child most happy?
- Describe some things that are difficult for your child.
- Tell me more about (anything you need more details about).
- Tell me about your family. Who lives in the home? What are they like? Describe their interests and skills.
- Who helps you when you need support or time off—family, friends, agencies?
- Who helps your family?
- How has all of this affected the parents, siblings, other family members?
- What do you want for your child? What are your concerns?

- What are your goals for your child? for your family?
- How can we help you and your family achieve these goals?
- What are you doing now for your child? How is it working?
- If it is not working, what can be done differently?
- What information do you need?
- What services and support does your family need, including your child?
- What do you think we should do?
- Who else have you discussed these issues with? what other agencies?
- What are you doing now to get what you want?
- What services are you receiving?
- Are you happy with what you received from them?
- What should we do first? next?

Look for evidence of stressors affecting the family, which may include

- Parents working
- Single parent
- Divorce
- Remarriage and stepfamilies
- Teen parents
- Homeless parents

- Poverty
- Violence
- Abuse
- Neglect
- Substance abuse
- Education level

Collaborative Family Assessment

New teachers' collaboration with families is essential for many reasons. Family members not only have the right to participate in the process, but have valuable information and insights to share. They provide information about family members that no one else has or can obtain without family support. Equally important, individuals affect and are affected by the families with whom they live. In comparison to agency-based services, which can be relatively brief in duration, families represent a continuous influence in the lives of children. Similarly, children affect their families throughout their lifetimes. We cannot truly determine the family's level of satisfaction with the assessment and intervention plan without their input.

In collaboration with the family, teachers can select the appropriate intervention goals and objectives for the individual and family. A collaborative family assessment allows families and professionals to develop a cooperative partnership.

Collaboration acknowledges the rights of family members to participate, the importance of family empowerment, and the need for family satisfaction with the assessment and ultimate intervention. The strengths and needs of each family member affect the growth and development of the whole family (Bailey, Buysse, Edmondson, & Smith, 1992; Beckman & Bristol, 1991; Beckman, Robinson, Rosenberg, & Filer, 1994; Dunst, Trivette, & Deal, 1988; McBride, Brotherson, Joanning, Whiddon, & Demmitt, 1993). The call from professionals today is for family involvement in the assessment process (Bailey, McWilliam, Winton, & Simeonsson, 1992; Crais, 1993). Families are viewed as capable and valuable instead of deficient and problematic. Intervention drawn from family assessment is designed around family strengths (Berheimer & Keogh, 1995).

Today, new teachers work with the family to determine needs, strengths, and wishes of everyone involved. This requires collaboration and responsive practices. If families participate in the assessment, they will have greater understanding of the full process, be able to identify the areas of service with which they are satisfied as well as those with which they are unhappy, and determine the effectiveness of interventions and services provided to individuals and families. Thus, it is critical that teachers work to assess children and families as integrated systems.

Models of Collaboration

There are four models of collaboration seen in work with families. The first model is the multidisciplinary assessment. In this model, professionals from various disciplines conduct individual assessments with minimal interactions between or among the professionals. Individual reports and recommendations are then provided for the family and service delivery personnel (McLean, Bailey, & Wolery, 1996). Family participation in this model would usually be as an observer and recipient of information.

In the opening case study, the assessment process for the second child utilized the multidisciplinary method. "Experts" assessed her son and informed her of the problem and how the school would solve it. They wrote out directions of activities for her to complete at home. However, the intervention at home was intrusive on the family so the mother did not follow through with it. The mother was only a recipient of information.

A more collaborative model is the interdisciplinary assessment. Here, professionals from multiple disciplines assess the individual separately but collaborate afterward. This allows for enhanced interactions among assessment professionals, who look to each other for key information. A collaborative plan for services can be then developed among team members. Collaboration can occur during and between assessments as well as during the collaborative team meeting (McLean, Bailey, & Wolery, 1996). Families may participate in this model as a team member, as well as observer and information recipient.

An example of the interdisciplinary model can be seen in Evan's case study, Box 5.1. Evan's family participated as a team member, information provider, and recipient of information. They were happy with their assessment experience.

Transdisciplinary assessment is the third model. Professionals from multiple disciplines collaborate during a single session to assess the individual and design a plan for services. All the professionals and the family assess and interact with the child and among themselves during the observation. Services are often provided by one or two of the professionals who participated in the collaborative assessment and represent the primary areas of need for the individual (McLean, Bailey, & Wolery, 1996). This model involves role relinquishment and cross-disciplinary training. Both advantages (interaction and collaboration) and disadvantages (possible lack of expertise in service delivery) can occur in this model. Family participation, however, happens at multiple levels within the assessment process.

An example of the transdiscipinary model can be seen in the opening case study with the third child, a daughter. Although the team members did some assessments individually, they also collaborated at a single assessment to assure they saw the same behaviors in the same setting. The family, as part of the team, was present at the individual assessments as well as the collaborative assessment. The team met after the final assessment to discuss diagnosis and plan the intervention. Everyone was very happy with the outcomes and

BOX 5.1

Family–Teacher Issues

Evan was a four-year-old boy with developmental delays. He was seen by a group of professionals in a diagnostic clinic. During the two weeks of assessment, clinical diagnosticians met or talked often among themselves and with the family. After all of the assessments were completed, the team, including the family, met to discuss a diagnosis and treatment plan.

Collaborative Orientations and Responsive Practices

The team, led by the family's priorities, agreed on an intervention that would be implemented at home and in his preschool. The intervention consisted of two sessions of fifteen minute social skills training per day. The team also decided that although Evan was old enough to start kindergarten in the fall, he would wait another year. The decision to wait on Evan's initiation of kindergarten was at this mother's urging.

BOX 5.2

Family–Teacher Issues
Jayna was a five-year-old girl. The full assessment team, including her parents, met for a single assessment. Because many of her problems involved language difficulties, the speech pathologist interacted directly with Jayna for the assessment. Other team members took notes and completed their own portions of the assessment at this time.

Collaborative Orientations and Responsive Practices
The next day the team met to discuss what they had seen. They decided on a diagnosis and planned a home-based intervention according to the family's desires and priorities. Jayna's mother wanted to be part of her language interventions. The team agreed, and decided to meet again before school started in the fall.

---

follow-through at home was much better. Family participation occurred throughout the assessment process.

The final model in collaborative assessment is arena assessment, often discussed in relation to the transdisciplinary model. For this model the professional with expertise in the individual's or family's primary areas of need takes the lead while professionals from other disciplines observe the assessment and record their findings. An advantage here is that all the professionals observe the individual at the same time, without multiple people interacting with the individual at once. The members of the team conduct their assessments in the same setting, under the same conditions, while observing the same activities. Family members can easily become part of the assessment process at all levels.

Jayna's case study is a good example of the arena model, Box 5.2. The family was very happy with Jayna's assessment experience. They were fully involved in all aspects of the assessment.

Regardless of the model selected, parents or primary caregivers must be accepted and valued as a critical part of the assessment team. This is important and beneficial to all team members.

Outcomes of Family Assessment

One challenge that teachers must face is that of measuring outcomes. The foremost challenge is in determining from whom to get information. Given the nature of families, does the perception of one member represent that of the entire family? If not, is that information sufficient? Does the information provided by various members of the family add to the assessment information gathered? Can a true family-wise measure of functioning be obtained? Some information (e.g., family demographics) can be accurately addressed by accessing a single family member. However, other outcome information, such as the experience of stressors, is more individually oriented and necessitates the gathering of information from various individuals. The complexity of assessing family outcomes requires that the professional develop effective interview and active listening skills (see Figure 5.3 for examples of effective interview skills and Figure 5.4 for details on active listening skills). As a framework for assessing family outcomes, Bailey et al. (1998) propose a set of questions related to family perceptions and impacts to think about when conducting a family interview (see Figure 5.5).

The outcomes of family assessment can be in four areas. First, outcomes related to an individual may include traditional IEP goals as well as goals that represent the preferences of the family. Family outcomes related to the individual are the second type of outcomes of family assessment. These outcomes are similar to those related to the individual in that they address specific individual outcomes. However, they emphasize changes for the individual that affect the family in a positive manner. These may include safety issues and support for a peaceful atmosphere in the home. The third type, individual outcomes related to the family, include those outcomes that address family needs related to the individual, including support and respite for all family members, as well as needed resources. The last type of outcomes from family assessment are those related specifically to the family. These outcomes are concentrated on specific family needs that may include spousal difficulties, substance abuse, and basic needs that may affect family functioning such as poverty, housing, food, or clothing (Beckman & Bristol, 1991). Family involvement in a collaborative assessment may bring benefits in other areas, such as changes in family and child attitudes about school and learning, fewer behavior difficulties at school, and a stronger, more positive relationship between family members, as well as with the professionals (Epstein, 1987; Greenberg, 1989).

Training

Although the need for family-centered assessment and practice has been stressed for some time, the teachers were not prepared to adopt the family emphasis required in PL 99-457. Indeed, the legal mandate for a family-centered assessment approach, including the Individualized Family Service Plan (IFSP) in Part H, forced professionals to recognize a need for training teachers in family studies and issues. The family-centered components of IDEA exceed the training and competencies of most professionals who are currently working to support children. Reflecting the emphasis seen in practice, personnel preparation programs have traditionally focused on building child competencies. However, professionals are now being asked to collaborate with entire families. In one survey of early intervention personnel (Bailey, Palsha, & Simeonsson, 1991), respondents indicated only a moderate level of perceived competence in working with families. These same personnel rated their skills in working with families significantly lower than their skills in working with children, probably due to a lack of training in working with families. The 1989 Carolina Policy Studies program national survey indicated that states were slow in implementing the family portions of PL 99-457. Since that initial report, great strides have been made toward improving the system of teacher training in higher education, which strengthens skills in family services. However, there is still great need for training in family assessment.

New teachers need to learn how to collaborate with other service providers as well as with families. They need to learn to respect family's rights to a central role in assessment and decision making. Every family has its own set of talents, strengths, priorities, and goals,

FIGURE 5.3 *Suggestions for Effective Interview Skills*

I. **Setting up the Interview**
- Be positive when arranging the first meeting.
- Establish harmony and understanding.
- Be sensitive to and prioritize the family's schedule.

II. **Introductory Phase of the Interview**
- Begin with a friendly greeting.
- Share important details.
  - Time that will be needed
  - Format that will be used
  - Confidentiality issues
- Structure the physical environment for interaction; limit interruptions, reduce distractions, and accommodate young children (if present).

III. **Interview Phase**
- Be open, honest, show empathy, and use no professional jargon.
- Acknowledge the parents' competence and expertise with their child.
- Encourage active participation (encourage parents to ask questions).
- Practice active listening and the art of silence. Solicit family input.
  - Restate and summarize key points to check understanding
  - Translate emotions of others into words
- Communicate positively at all times.
- Allow the family to tell their own story.
- Show respect for the family story.
- Avoid patronizing responses, unsolicited advice, premature solutions, too many questions, cliches, and unsupported empathy (e.g., "I know how you feel").
- Use relaxed body language.
- Identify concerns in a straightforward, sensitive manner.
- Identify unresolved concerns and issues.
- Gather information sensitively and efficiently.
- Provide reassurance and normalize problems.
- Maintain an awareness of time considerations.
- If necessary, schedule another meeting.

IV. **Summary and Closure Phase**
- Summarize issues addressed (resources, priorities, needs, concerns).
- Ask family members if your summary is accurate and if there is anything that was not covered that they (the family) believe should be covered.
- Express positive and realistic expectations for change honestly.
- Acknowledge the time, effort, and contribution the family has made.
- Ask if they have any thoughts, concerns, or questions about the interview.
  - If necessary, schedule additional meetings.

FIGURE 5.4 *Active Listening Skills*

Reflecting
- Repeat word for word what the other person said
  - The speaker knows that you heard what was said
  - Both parties have the same understanding of what was said

Paraphrase
- Restate key information in the listener's words
  - The speaker knows that you heard what was said
  - Both parties have the same understanding of what was said

Clarifying Questions
- Ask questions to get the speaker to elaborate on what was said
  - Clarifies what was meant
  - Clarifies why and what the speaker is talking about

Drawing out Questions
- Ask questions that allow the speaker to expand on what was said
  - Other conditions that may affect the what and why of what was said
  - Basic feelings of the speaker

Nonverbal Communication
- Notice posture, expressions, gestures, eye contact, and voice quality for an idea of what the speaker is feeling

which should influence and direct the assessment as well as service planning and delivery (Powell, Batsche, Ferro, Fox, & Dunlap, 1997). These collaborative skills must be part of teacher training.

Following is a list of abilities new teachers will need to learn:

- Collaboration and consultation skills
- Cultural competence
- Multidisciplinary roles
- Strategies based on research-proven best practices

Influences of Educational, Health, and Social Services on Family Assessment

Family functioning has been viewed through a variety of theories and disciplines, including medicine, education, social work, psychology, and anthropology (Grotevant & Carlson, 1989). Historically, professionals interested in child health and well-being have considered the focus of assessment and treatment to be on the individual. As noted earlier,

FIGURE 5.5 *Questions for Family Perceptions and Impact on Families*

Family Perceptions—Does the family

- See the process as appropriate in making a difference in their child's life?
- See the process as appropriate in making a difference in their family's life?
- Have a positive view of professionals and the service system?

Impact on the Family—Will/did the process

- Enable the family to help their child grow and learn?
- Enhance the family's perceived ability to work with professionals and advocate for services?
- Assist the family in building a strong support system?
- Help enhance an optimistic view of the future?
- Enhance the family's perceived quality of life?

Source: Adapted from "Family Outcomes in Early Intervention: A Framework for Program Evaluation and Efficacy Research," by Bailey, D. B., McWilliam, R. A., Aytch-Darkes, L., Hebbeler, K., Simeonsson, R. J., Spiker, D., and Wagner, M., 1998, *Exceptional Children, 64,* pp. 313–328.

emphasis has shifted to the family as occupying paramount importance. The ecological, family systems philosophy guides service delivery and states that in order to effectively address the needs of an individual, new teachers must consider the various systems in which the individual lives, works, and plays, including family and social contexts. One of the fundamental principles of systems theory is that interaction and involvement with one person or component of the system influences the other people and components within the system. Therefore, professionals must include in family assessment all involved people and components of the system if we are to make informed decisions that will benefit the whole family.

This trend toward an ecological, family systems approach supports the idea that for services to benefit the individual as well as the family, teachers must also promote family strengths. The promotion of family strengths ultimately enhances all outcomes (Guralnick, 1997).

The disciplines identified in Figure 5.6, along with many others, have influenced the process of family assessment. Each person educated in a particular discipline brings to the assessment process individual and disciplinary perspectives. Individual views are influenced by a variety of personal, educational, and professional experiences. Disciplinary influences are based on the traditional approach to practice that has evolved within both the discipline at large and at the particular training programs.

Assessment teams should be comprised of individuals representing a range of disciplines and experiences relevant to the needs of the child and family. The old quote, "The whole is greater than the sum of its parts," is applicable as the team develops its own personality. The team's personality is a function of the group's diversity, created by the members' experience and disciplinary differences. This "personality" and interaction then influence team members' attitudes and perceptions about the team process, performance, and outcomes. In other words, team development and functioning may not be entirely a function of discipline affiliation and personal experience, but may include influences from diversity in group interaction. Thus, family assessment and practice can be viewed as a

FIGURE 5.6 *Specific Influences from Various Disciplines*

Social Work

- Social systems as a theory for work with families (Chess & Norlin, 1991)
- Subsystems within the family system: marital, parental, sibling, and individual. Each subsystem affects the others (Andreae, 1996; Durst, Wedemeyer, & Zurcher, 1985; Furr, 1997)
- Ecological theory (environmental influences) included in family systems philosophy
- Environmental influences important in work with families (Anderson, 1988; Fisher & Karger, 1997)
- Empowerment theory, helping families control situations (Fisher & Karger, 1997).

Psychology

- Systems theory suggests that the difficulty may lie outside the individual (Bor, Legg, & Scher, 1996)

Nursing

- Nursing utilizes social and family systems in family health medicine (Caudle, 1996; Scherwen, Scoloveno & Weingarten, 1995)
- Duvall describes eight family stages; each stage has its own family tasks (Bor, Legg, & Scher, 1996):
  1. Beginning: married with no children
  2. Childbearing: children up to 30 months
  3. Preschool: children up to 6 years
  4. School age: children up to 13 years
  5. Teenage: children up to 20 years
  6. Launching: time when children are leaving home
  7. Middle: no children up to retirement
  8. Aging: retirement period up to death of both parents
- Developmental theories describe individual developmental stages

Occupational Therapy (AOTA, 1991)

- Family systems theory in work with families
- Family ecology describes interaction with systems outside family
- Family life cycles characterize stages of family life

Education

- Family systems theory of Bronfenbrenner (1979)
- Developmental theory (e.g., Piaget and Erickson) describes individual development
- Development and use of the Individual Educational Plan (IEP) and the Individualized Family Service Plan (IFSP)

process guided by an interdisciplinary team composed of family members, their representatives, and agents from a variety of disciplines, including teachers, special educators, clinical therapists, psychologists, social workers, nurses, family therapists, doctors, and other medical specialists.

Practical Suggestions for New Teachers

Professionals must recognize and communicate that assessment is a process, not a product. To this end, teachers must (a) strive to hear and respect the family's viewpoint; (b) work to address family goals in the home, school, and community; (c) accept and support family emphases on social concerns; (d) look for areas of agreement; (e) concentrate on the individual's and family's strengths; (f) express individual viewpoints in an honest, sensitive, and straightforward manner; (g) let families see respect and value of their opinions through actions and language; (h) seek out available resources in which the family may be interested, and make this information available to the family; and (i) remain flexible, committed, and collaborative. Finally, the family must sense that teachers accept, respect, and value them, their culture, and their lifestyle.

When teachers begin the assessment process, or take part in assessment with other professionals, it is necessary to look at multiple settings to achieve and complete an assessment of the behaviors and abilities of the individual and family, such as home, school, and community. In all locations the physical layout will be noted. Then observations of parenting practices and interactions among family members may be recorded. It might be beneficial to draw the layouts. In the classroom and around the school, interactions with peers and adults, the individual's attention and participation with academic activities, and the ability of the individual to move and function in the building will be recorded.

Community observations may include similar information at locations such as the family church, a recreational group, or with primary caregivers while running errands and shopping. While observing in each setting, teachers must note cultural and social influences and any difficulties that may arise as a result of these differences (Berheimer & Keogh, 1995; Trivette, Deal, & Dunst, 1986). Finally, perceptions of people who utilize these settings should be recorded.

With the active participation of family members, these observations can be made with little or no interference in normal activities. Family members may conduct some of the observations. A grandparent or close family friend may observe in the home. A parent, relative, or family friend may conduct the observation in the community. With the support of the family, instructional assistants, and area specialists, the classroom and school observations may be completed with little disruption of the daily school schedule. (See Figure 5.7 for an example of a simple observation form that is easy to complete.)

A survey of family needs interview will begin to advance family independence, advocacy, strengths, and empowerment. Guidelines for conducting interviews with parents, adapted from Bruder (1989), Glasser (1975), and Slater, Martinez, & Habersang (1989), are found in Figure 5.3. Some possible questions are proposed for the assessment of family needs in Figure 5.2.

Similar to historical views on intervention, the majority of research has concentrated on needs and deficits (Berheimer & Keogh, 1995). Although these are necessary considerations during an assessment, it is important that teachers begin the assessment with strengths and priorities.

From the interview it will be possible to decide, with the family, what additional instruments and tools will be used to complete the assessment. It is appropriate to use multiple assessment tools and procedures, as well as multiple settings. The assessment will be individ-

FIGURE 5.7 *Observation Form*

Date	Location Description	People Present	Behavior Occurring

ualized for specific individual and family strengths and needs. Just as an intervention is individualized, assessment instruments and procedures should be specifically designed for family and individual strengths and needs instead of relying on a traditional standardized battery of instruments with standardized procedures (Bailey & Wolery, 1992). This information will then be used to collaboratively set family and individual goals in a cooperative planning session between professionals of various disciplines and family members.

Parents, and often siblings, can provide valuable information about unique behaviors and abilities derived from extended observations of the children in a variety of settings (Bagnato, Neisworth, & Munson, 1989; Diamond & Squires, 1993). Further, seeking family input promotes both participation in the assessment process and a partnership between the family and professional (Diamond & Squires, 1993). Such outcomes may help to validate the assessment and intervention process for family members, and therefore, influence the success of intervention efforts (Bailey & Wolery, 1989; Guralnick, 1997).

The final components of any assessment include a satisfaction evaluation for the individual and family, and an assessment of the actual services provided to determine if goals and services are appropriate and successful.

It is critical that parents be given information in a face-to-face meeting before any formal decision making meeting takes place. Parents should have the opportunity to review, discuss, and seek clarification on any information. It is important to listen to parents' needs and aspirations for their child prior to making recommendations or decisions. There should be no surprises during the decision making phase.

Formal and informal processes to discuss and resolve disagreements and to promote communication and collaboration between parents and professionals should be established (Bruder, 1989). These approaches clearly place family members in the powerful role of providing information and generating alternative solutions. In this role, the family's status on the assessment team changes from passive information recipient and provider of signatures to that of active, invaluable team member.

All teacher strategies for family collaboration should be grounded in ecological, family systems with a family-centered attitude if they are to be effective in practice. New teachers must also understand that all interactions with family members represent opportunities to build rapport and informally gather information.

Specific suggestions might include:

- Welcome all children and their families into the classroom. This creates a positive attitude when assessments become necessary.
- Establish a collaborative partnership with the parents of the individual.
- Create collaborative working relationships with other service providers.
- Include support personnel (therapists, social workers, etc.) in your collaborative assessment teams.
- Always think of families first and demonstrate this attitude to families, service providers, and other people involved in assessment.
- Become knowledgeable of the assessment instruments required by the agency/school/district. Describe their purpose to the families.
- Become familiar with family interview structure.

Family Assessment Devices

Family assessment devices may include a variety of instrument types, processes, and actual tools. The family assessment should start with an interview that begins with individual strengths, goals, and resources. Although teachers may not collect the data, family assessment includes a history of the pregnancy, child development, and the child's likes, dislikes, needs, and strengths. It should contain questions about the home environment, including family stability and parenting practices. Family needs, availability of resources, and their utilization should be addressed. Other family assessment devices may include self-reports, which address issues similar to those in a family interview, and checklists, which look at a specific listing of skills and developmental needs. There are also parent-completed assessment devices that address individual needs and strengths. The following is not intended to be an exhaustive list but rather examples of some of the types of assessments available. See the section on resources for more information.

Some specific family assessment devices that teachers may see in reports include:

• *The Family Adaptability and Cohesion Evaluation Scales* (FACES I, II, or III) is completed by parents or in an interview setting. It addresses family interactions.

• *The Family Environment Scale* (Consulting Psychologists Press, Inc.) determines family perceptions of the family system. May be completed by parents and child or in an interview setting with each.

• *Maternal Behavior Rating Scale* (Mahoney, 1992) Family Child Learning Center, 143 Northwest Avenue, Building A, Talmadge Ohio, 44278; (216) 633-2055. This is a global rating scale designed to assess parent–child interaction. Variables measured include enjoyment, sensitivity to child's interest, responsivity, effectiveness, achievement orientation, pace, acceptance, and directiveness. Items are rated on a five-point Likert scale.

• *Parent as a Teacher Inventory* (Strom, 1995) published by Scholastic testing Service, Inc., Bensenville, Illinois 60106. The Parent as a Teacher Inventory is designed to assess parent expectations related to five areas: creativity, frustration, control, play, and teaching/learning. Items are rated using a four-point Likert scale and are intended to help parents recognize their positive qualities and identify areas for personal growth.

There are many other instruments available for a variety of assessment purposes. Any may become part of a family assessment. Importantly, most family assessment begins with a family interview. Each family interview begins with questions about family strengths, goals, and resources. (See additional instruments in Figure 5.8.)

FIGURE 5.8 *Additional Instruments*

• **Behavior Checklists**
  (1) Child Behavior Checklist (CBCL) (Achenbach) completed by caregivers (e.g., parents or teachers) in any setting
  (2) Behavior Emotional Rating Scale (BERS) a strengths-focused checklist completed by parents

• **Development Checklists**
  (1) Hawaii Early Learning Profile (HELP for infants or preschoolers) (Vort Corporation) completed by parents or in an interview setting
  (2) Minnesota Infant Development Inventory (birth to 15 months) (Ireton & Thwing) completed by parents to measure parent perceptions
  (3) Child Development Inventory (1 to 5 years) (Ireton) completed by parents to measure parents perceptions and understanding of the child's development

• **Parent–Child Interaction Scales**
  (1) Teaching Skills Inventory (Rosenberg & Robinson, 1985) (North Dakota Department of Education) completed by professional observer. Measures five dimensions of mother–child interaction: maternal directiveness, maternal responsivity, maternal sensitivity, positive feedback, and child interest. Each dimension is rated on a global 7-point Likert scale.

Family Member Questions

During an assessment, family members will ask questions that may be difficult for new teachers to answer. The question most frequently heard by many assessment team members is related to the diagnosis. The parent may ask, *What is the problem/diagnosis?* or *What is wrong with my child?* This question can also be more specific, such as, *Do you think this is autism (or retardation)?* Although this is a difficult question to answer, it is important to remember that the parents are under tremendous stress.

• Teachers may explain that as this is the information-gathering stage of the assessment, it is too early to decide on any diagnosis. However, teachers need to let them know when that discussion will begin and that the team will want to include their viewpoints in any decisions.

• Teachers may want to ask why they are asking or thinking that. Maybe a relative or friend has suggested this child looks just like a child they know with the same diagnosis. Understanding why they ask this question can lead teachers to an appropriate response.

• If the parent really pushes for a response, teachers will need to say, "I simply cannot give you an answer at this time. It is just too early."

The second most frequent question is related to concerns about the child's capability and future competence. Teachers may be asked, *What will she be able to do? Will he go to college?* or *Will she be able to play sports?* A response to this question will rely somewhat on the age of the individual.

• For a preschooler, the most straightforward response would be, "All children develop at different rates and at this early age it is too soon to put any limitation on your child."

• For an older child, teachers want to remind the family that this is the information gathering stage and the question will be discussed when the team meets to investigate diagnosis and intervention options. It may also be appropriate to ask the family what they would like to work toward as a goal for the individual.

Another question may be, *How will all of this affect our home?* While teachers are concerned with the best outcomes for the individual, the family probably has additional priorities that they must address. The assessment session may not be an appropriate time to address these issues, but teachers can let the family know that they will be happy to discuss it at a later date.

• To be sensitive to their concerns, teachers may want to set an appointment for this discussion before they go further with the assessment.

• On the other hand, if the assessment process began with a family interview, this may have been addressed at that time. In the interview teachers will be able to discover family priorities, needs, and concerns. If this is the case, the teacher can remind the family that he or she talked about this earlier and will be responding to these concerns at the team diagnosis meeting.

The final question teachers may hear is, *What is the purpose of the assessment? What will it tell me?* Most likely this question will come near the end of the assessment process as the entire team, including family members, is beginning to understand the individual and think about what the assessment may reveal.

• Teachers can explain that everyone can make more informed decisions, understand the available options better, and plan for the intervention and future education/work with a complete, reliable assessment.

• Using appropriate assessment devices, the family will better understand what service providers may be able to offer them or their child. Professionals will get a better understanding of the family's needs, values, culture, and strengths. Effective assessment addresses specific strengths and needs, and gives a better understanding of the strengths, needs, and wishes of the family and the child.

Family Resources and Services

These resources and services can assist new teachers in disseminating assessment data to families.

Family Assessment: A Guide to Methods and Measures (1989)
By Harold Grotevant and Cindy Carlson
Published by The Guilford Press

A comprehensive listing of family-oriented assessment tools including abstracts. Organized by observational measures (family interaction coding schemes and rating scales of family functioning) and self-report measures (whole-family functioning, family stress and coping, parent–child relationships).

Family Assessment in Early Intervention (1988)
By Don Bailey and Rune Simeonsson (Eds.)
Published by Merrill

Textbook addressing practical topics in family-centered assessment.

Transdisciplinary Play-Based Assessment: A Functional Approach to Working with Young Children (1993)
By Toni W. Linder
Published by Paul H. Brookes

Book that addresses a structured, play-based assessment in which multiple disciplines and family members can participate.

Supporting and Strengthening Families: Methods, Strategies and Practices (1994)
By Carl Dunst, Carol Trivette, and Angela Deal
Published by Brookline Books

Textbook addressing practical topics in supporting families, including family-centered assessment.

Enabling and Empowering Families: Principles and Guidelines for Practice (1988)
By Carl Dunst, Carol Trivette, and Angela Deal
Published by Brookline Books

Appendices A–F include a variety of assessment measures (needs, social support, family functioning style, family support, family strengths). The measures can be purchased separately.

Assessing Young Children **(1988)**
By Elizabeth Danielson, Evelyn Lynch, Anne Moyano, Bonnie Johnson, and Ann Bettenburg
Published by NAYSE Publications

Provides information on parent involvement, systematic observational procedures, and assessment reports.

Young Adult Institute
460 West 34th Street
New York, NY 10001
(212) 563-7474

YAI markets a variety of videotapes on developmental disabilities, a number of which are relevant to working with families (e.g., "Working with Families: What Professionals Need to Know").

Child Development Resources
P.O. Box 280
Norge, VA 23127-0280
(804) 566-3300

Child Development Resources markets a variety of videotapes on developmental disabilities, a number of which are relevant to working with families (e.g., "A Family-Centered Team Process for Assessment").

Child Development Media, Inc.
5632 Van Nuys Blvd., Suite 286
Van Nuys, CA 91401
(818) 994-0933
Internet site: www.childdevmedia.com

Child Development Media, Inc. markets a variety of videotapes on developmental disabilities, a number of which are relevant to working with families (e.g., "Family Focused Interview," "The Ages & Stages Questionnaires," "First Years Together: Involving Parents in Infant Assessment," "Listening to Families Series by the American Association of Marriage and Family Therapy, Family and the IFSP Process," "Parents as Partners").

National Information Center for Children and Youth with Disabilities (NICHCY)
P.O. Box 1492
Washington, D.C. 20013-1492
(800) 999-5599
(703) 893-8614 (TDD)

Fact sheets on various topics related to developmental disabilities.

Summary

This chapter addressed family assessment. Family assessment can mean family participation in individual assessment or assessment of the family. The main ideas addressed in this chapter include:

- Family assessment was developed out of family systems theory.
- Systems theory is found in many different disciplines, including social work, health, psychology, and occupational therapy.
- Family assessment is mandated (required by law) for assessing children with disabilities.
- Family assessments must be directed by the family.
- Typical outcomes of family assessment were identified.
- Practical strategies for teachers were described.
- Common questions families may ask were reviewed.
- A list of possible resources for teachers involved in family assessment was provided.

References

Anderson, J. (1988). *Foundations of Social Work Practice.* New York: Springer Publishing Company.

Andreae, D. (1996). Systems theory and social work treatment. In F. J. Turner (Ed.). *Social work treatment: Interlocking theoretical approaches* (pp. 601–616). New York: Free Press.

AOTA. (1991). *Guidelines for curriculum content in pediatrics (Section II, Family Issues).* Washington, DC: Commission on Education.

Bailey, D. B., Buysse, V., Edmondson, R., & Smith, T. (1992). Creating family-centered services in early intervention: Perceptions of professionals in four states. *Exceptional Children, 58,* 298–309.

Bailey, D., McWilliam, P., Winton, P., & Simeonsson, R. (1992). *Implementing family-centered services in early intervention: A team-based model for change.* Cambridge, MA: Brookline Books.

Bailey, D. B., McWilliam, R. A., Aytch-Darkes, L., Hebbeler, K., Simeonsson, R. J., Spiker, D., & Wagner, M. (1998). Family outcomes in early intervention: A framework for program evaluation and efficacy research. *Exceptional Children, 64,* 313–328.

Bailey, D. B., Palsha, S. A., & Huntington, G. S. (1990). Preservice preparation of special educators to serve infants with handicaps and their families: Current status and training needs. *Journal of Early Intervention, 14,* 43–54.

Bailey, D. B., Palsha, S. A., & Simeonsson, R. J. (1991). Professional skills, concerns, and perceived importance of work with families in early intervention. *Exceptional Children, 52,* 156–165.

Bailey, D. B., & Wolery, M. (1992). *Teaching infants and preschoolers with disabilities.* Englewood Cliffs, NJ: Merrill/Prentice Hall.

Bailey, D. B. & Wollery, M. (1989). *Assessing infants and preschoolers with handicaps.* Columbus, OH: Merrill.

Bagnato, S. J., Neisworth, S. J., & Manson, S. M. (1989). *Linking developmental assessment and early intervention: Curriculum-based prescriptions.* Rockville, MD: Aspen.

Beckman, P. J., & Bristol, M. M. (1991). Issues in developing the IFSP: A framework for establishing family outcomes. *Topics in Early Childhood Special Education, 11* (3), 19–31.

Beckman, P. J., Robinson, C. C., Rosenberg, S., & Filer, J. (1994). Family involvement in early intervention: The evolution of family-centered services. In L. J. Johnson, R. J. Gallagher, M. J. LaMontagne, J. B. Jordan, J. J. Gallagher, P. L. Hutinger, & M. B. Karnes (Eds.). *Meeting early intervention challenges: Issues from birth to three* (2nd ed.) (pp. 13–41). Baltimore: Paul H. Brookes.

Berheimer, L. P., & Keogh, B. K. (1995). Weaving interventions into the fabric of everyday life: An approach to family assessment. *Topics in Early Childhood Special Education. 15,* 415–433.

Bertalanffy, L. von. (1968). *General systems theory.* New York: Braziller.

Bor, R., Legg, C., & Scher, I. (1996). The systems paradigm. In R. Woolfe & W. Dryden (Eds.). *Handbook of Counseling Psychology* (pp. 240–257). London: Sage Publications.

Bronfenbrenner, U. (1979). *The ecology of human development.* Cambridge, MA: Harvard University Press.

Bruder, M. B. (1989). What professionals can do to facilitate partnerships with parents. *Early Childhood Update, 5* (2) 4–11.

Caudle, P. (1996). Care of the family client. In M. J. Clark. *Nursing in the community (2nd ed.)* (pp. 365–387). Stamford, Ct: Appleton & Lange.

Chess, W. A., & Norlin, J. M. (1991). *Human behavior and the social environment: A social systems model (2nd ed).* Boston: Allyn & Bacon.

Crais, E. (1993). Families and professionals as collaborators in assessment. *Topics in Language Disorders, 14* (1), 29–40.

Diamond, K. E., & Squires, J. (1993). The role of parent report in the screening and assessment of young children. *Journal of Early Intervention, 17* (2), 107–115.

Dunst, C. J., Trivette, C. M., & Deal, A. G. (1988). *Enabling and empowering families: Principles and guidelines for practice.* Cambridge, MA: Brookline Books.

Durst, P. L., Wedemeyer, N. V., & Zurcher, L. A. (1985). Parenting partnerships after divorce: Implications for practice. *Social Work, 30,* 423–428.

Epstein, J. (1987). Parent involvement: What research says to administrators. *Education in Urban Society, 19* (2), 119–136.

Epstein, J. (1989). Building parent teacher partnerships in inner city schools. *The Family Resource Coalition Report, 8 (2).*

Fisher, R. & Karger, H. J. (1997). *Social work and community in a private world: Getting out in public.* New York: Longman.

Furr, L. A. (1997). *Exploring human behavior and the social environment.* Boston: Allyn & Bacon.

Glasser, W. (1975). *The identity society.* New York: Harper & Row.

Greenberg, P. (1989). Parents as partners in young children's development and education: A new American fad? Why does it matter? *Young Children, 44* (4), 61–75.

Grotevant, H. D., & Carlson, C. I. (1989). *Family assessment: A guide to methods and measures.* New York, NY: The Guilford Press.

Guralnick, M. J. (1997). *The effectiveness of early intervention.* Baltimore, MD: Paul H. Brookes.

Hawkins, F. P. (1979). The eye of the beholder. *Outlook, 32,* 10–33.

McBride, S. L., Brotherson, M. J., Joanning, H., Whiddon, D., & Demmitt, A. (1993). Implementation of family-centered services: Perceptions of families and professionals. *Journal of Early Intervention, 17,* 414–430.

McLean, M., Bailey, D. B., & Wolery, M. (1996). *Assessing infants and preschoolers with special needs.* Columbus-OH: Merrill-Prentice Hall.

Powell, D. S., Batsche, C. J., Ferro, J., Fox, L., & Dunlap, G. (1997). A strength-based approach in support of multiple-risk families: Principles and issues. *Topics in Early Childhood Special Education, 17* (1), 1–26.

Sameroff, A. J. (1983). Developmental systems: Contexts and evolution. In W. Kessen (Ed.). *Handbook of child psychology: Vol. I. History, theories, and methods* (pp. 238–294). New York: Wiley.

Sherwen, L. N., Scoloveno, M. A., & Weingarten, C. T. (1995). *Nursing care of the childbearing family (2nd ed.).* Norwalk, Connecticut: Appleton & Lange.

Slater, M., Martinez, M., & Habersang, R. (1989). Normalized family resources: A model for professionals. In G. H. S. Singer & L. K. Irvin (Eds.). *Support for caregiving families.* Baltimore, Maryland: Paul H. Brookes.

Trivette, C. M., Deal, A., & Dunst, C. J. (1986). Family needs, sources of support, and professional roles: Critical elements of family systems assessment and intervention. *Diagnostique, 11,* 246–267.

Turnbull, A. P., & Turnbull, H. R. (1990). *Families, professionals, and exceptionality: A special partnership.* Columbus, OH: Merrill Publishing.

Part II

Families across the Years

Authors in Part 2 stress information to new teachers on specific roles teachers play with family members and other school-based or community-based professionals. Each author stresses that teachers play different roles and assume multiple responsibilities when interacting with families who have children with special needs at various chronological ages. Authors target essential understandings and skills that teachers require when interacting with families of individuals in various services: early childhood special education services, elementary age services, middle and high school services, and adult programs.

In order to help teachers understand the families with whom they interact, authors tackle chronologically important data and implications for teachers' inclusion and collaboration practices in schools and classrooms. They describe for teachers the characteristics of the individual with special needs during specific chronological time frames. Each identifies teachers' roles or responsibilities in understanding and responding to the various issues during the chronological age span.

Chapter 6: Families of Children in Early Childhood Special Education

Diana J. Hammitte and Betty M. Nelson address needs and issues of families with very young children. Because teachers of young children face different issues, concerns, tasks, and questions as they interact with family members and other school or community professionals, these authors provide data on chronologically relevant implications for inclusion and collaborative practices in the home, school, or community. They include parental reactions to the initial diagnosis of the child's disability, services available to families of young children, and empowerment strategies among families and professionals.

Chapter 7: Families of Children in Elementary Age Services

Kim Stoddard and Greg Valcante address issues new teachers of elementary aged students may encounter in their work with their students' families. These authors' specific focus is to discuss the power of a family partnership for children during the elementary years. Accordingly, they describe family characteristics and statistics, and implications for inclusion and collaborative school practices. Further, they offer practical home or community suggestions, questions family members may ask elementary teachers during school-based conferences, and relevant family resources and services for teachers' use in dealing with these chronological issues. The authors provide many case studies to reflect their main points.

Chapter 8: Working with Families of Adolescents

Kate Algozzine, Dorothy J. O'Shea, and Bob Algozzine examine various family issues when teens enter the adolescent years. These authors provide specific research and practical strategies that can help teachers in middle schools work effectively with family members. Among their issues are transitions adolescents face as they approach adulthood and the varied challenges faced by parents. Working effectively with families of children in their teens involves helping families to understand and adjust to the changes they will observe during this time frame in their child's life.

Chapter 9: Families of Adult Individuals with Disabilities

Adults with special needs face the many challenges that all humans face as they age. However, David Bateman examines why aging is one of the most confusing and often most stressful periods for individuals with disabilities as well as their families. He describes important facts about adults with disabilities, major challenges that adults with disabilities and their families encounter, roles of the nondisabled siblings, and important transition issues for adults with disabilities.

6

Families of Children in Early Childhood Special Education

Diana J. Hammitte

Betty M. Nelson

Chapter Objectives _____

In this chapter we will

- Identify parental responses to the diagnosis of their child's disability, including a discussion of the stages of grief and equilibrium/disequilibrium theories
- Discuss legislative requirements for family-centered services
- Identify service delivery models for young children with disabilities and their families and the degree to which the models affect families
- Discuss implications for inclusion and collaborative practices in schools and classrooms in early childhood special education
- Discuss family systems theory and the effects of family functioning and family subsystems on interactions with professionals
- Identify specific areas in which families and professionals may develop collaborative partnerships
- Identify resources and services available to families of young children with disabilities
- Summarize important chapter themes

> *It is 5 o'clock in the morning. The sounds of the last "Push, Donna!" continue to echo in Donna's head, filling the sudden silence in the room. Donna begins to feel panicky as the doctor, nurses, and even Jim, her husband, whisper among themselves. "What's wrong with my baby?" she finally manages to utter. "Well, Donna," her doctor begins, "I'm sorry to tell you that your little girl has been born with some birth defects." "Let me see her!" Donna cries. A nurse lays the bundled up child on Donna's chest, and with Jim looking on Donna begins to inspect her first child. What she sees is the top of the head of*

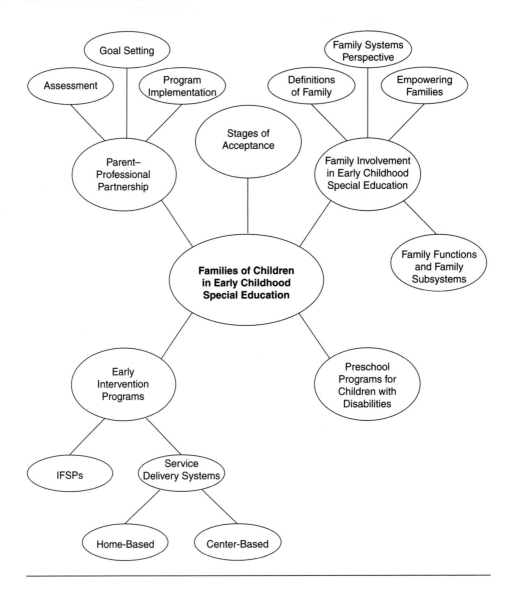

a 7 pound, 3 ounce baby girl with lots of dark curly hair. As she looks into her baby's face, however, she discovers a severely cleft lip and palate. A heart-wrenching sob escapes from Donna's throat as she thinks, "Oh, God, what will I do now?"

Twenty-four hours after Tyrone was delivered, Dr. Smith approached the room of Shauna, his mother, to deliver what he knew to be shattering news. "Shauna, I'm sorry to tell you that Tyrone has been diagnosed with Down syn-

drome." Shauna, an unmarried mother, is alone in the room, shocked and pan-icked. "What does this mean?" she thinks to herself as the tears begin to drop.

At twelve months, Anne was finally diagnosed with cytomegalovirus (CMV). Nancy and Chris, her parents, had continually sought answers to why she was not sitting up, why it was so difficult to get her to eat, and why she was not babbling or even reacting to sounds. She was the third child in the family and the other two children had achieved these skills well before this age. After nu-merous tests, and visits to a variety of doctors, her parents were told that as a result of the diagnosed CMV, Anne would never walk, was deaf and blind, and would have limited cognitive abilities. Nancy and Chris could only ask: "Where do we go for help? How can we interact with this child?"

Three-year-old Samuel is still not initiating or, in fact, participating in conver-sation. Everyone tells his parents that it is common for boys to begin talking later than girls, and not to worry, he'll catch up! But they know better. Some-thing is wrong with their youngest son. Speech is not the only area in which he doesn't seem to match his peers, or the development of their two older chil-dren. He doesn't pay attention to the wonderful toys they have provided and, in fact, often sits just staring into space, sometimes moving his right index finger in a circular motion. Late at night, his mother and father talk quietly, wonder-ing "What is wrong with Samuel? What should we do?"

Any textbook dealing with working with families of individuals with disabilities would be incomplete unless it included a chapter on working with families of children in early child-hood special education. Perhaps at no other time are we more likely, as professionals, to work with families than during the early child development years. The mandates of legis-lation clearly require extensive involvement of families with young children in develop-ment of programs, transitions, and curricula, as well as requiring families to work with their children themselves.

This chapter will address issues specific to early childhood special education, includ-ing parental reactions to the diagnosis of their child's disability, services available to chil-dren with disabilities and their families, and a review of family systems theory as it relates to working with parents of young children with disabilities. Empowering families to assume leadership roles is addressed, and some practical interactions between parents and professionals are described.

All of these families have something in common. They are dealing with their first awareness of atypical development in their children, often experiencing feelings ranging from denial to panic to shock. What they do not have in common is the time frame in which they became aware of their child's disability. Interestingly enough, time frame has little to do with parental reaction to this distressing news. Most times they still go through the same process of achieving acceptance of their child. It is important, however, to take a look at reactions across the time span with regard to the effect of educational services on the families of children with disabilities.

Most families experience overwhelming joy, generally mixed with feelings of anxiety, at the impending birth of a new child. Thoughts of caring for this new baby, achieving the necessary bonding for development, and planning for the child's future are all integrated with the anticipation of seeing this child who was so long awaited. Parents whose children are born with disabilities experience the same feelings; however, they may have the added difficulty of facing possible medical care situations, making health care decisions, and accepting additional responsibilities for child care and child development. They have added a life to their family that will likely necessitate major role changes beyond those experienced by families of children without disabilities. These changes may include accepting the continued involvement of a variety of professionals to address their child's unique needs, initial dependency on such professionals, and developing skills necessary to ensure the health of their child (e.g., tube feeding, catheterization). As the child progresses through infancy and toddlerhood, the family may find that their need for professional support has declined, or may face additional responsibilities as the preschool years approach.

Although today's families more often than not make use of daycare or preschool facilities, seeing your child off to preschool for the first time can be a traumatic experience. For the family of a child with disabilities who has been receiving family-centered early intervention services, the change to child-centered preschool can be a difficult one. On the one hand, they are somewhat aware of the educational system in place in their community, may have received training in parenting skills, and worked closely with a professional team. On the other hand, without the support of the professionals they are accustomed to, they may feel like they are starting over as they face the slow development of their child or medical crises. In reality, the transition process is traversed in a variety of ways, depending on the individuals involved. Some parents express satisfaction with the process and excitement at the prospect of their child's integration into the public school system. Other parents express considerable anxiety and fear of the unknown.

Those parents whose children are diagnosed with a disability for the first time during the preschool years often experience shock and major changes in their family life. Perhaps they noticed that something was not quite as it should be, but they were unprepared for the distressing news they have received. While they are trying to take in the news they are also expected to learn to provide for their child's special needs and even to participate in the preschool program that will serve their child. Learning about the presence of a disability at this time is likely to be just as difficult to adjust to as learning about it at birth is.

Regardless of when a child is diagnosed with a disability, parents are faced with dealing with an adjustment to their lives and the lives of other family members. Several theories have been espoused in attempts to explain how parents react and adjust to the presence of a child with a disability within the family. However, as indicated by Allen & Affleck (1985), parents demonstrate a variety of reactions upon learning of their child's disability. Parents have indicated that the equilibrium they had previously experienced within their family context has been disrupted by the presence of a child with a disability, causing feelings of disequilibrium. Such feelings remain in place until parents and families have completely accepted and adjusted to the child's presence. Unfortunately, however, some parents may always remain uncomfortable with their child, thereby remaining in a state of disequilibrium. While some families may be faced with these outcomes, others have indicated that strengthening of their lives or their marriage has occurred as a result of having a child with a disability (Bradley, Knoll, & Agosta, 1992). Nevertheless, many parents go through a grief process. Some parents may feel they have unexpectedly been confronted with the loss of the child they expected to have, and their hopes and expectations may not be appropriate for the child they birthed. As a result of such feelings, many parents proceed through several common stages, ranging from shock and disbelief in what has occurred to acceptance and control of the situation.

Stages of Acceptance

Not all parents respond to the diagnosis of their child's disability in the same manner, but it is important to note that research has identified a series of common steps or stages experienced by many parents. Dr. Elizabeth Kubler-Ross (1969) initially identified these stages, commonly called stages of grief, while conducting research with cancer patients. The stages are identified as shock, disbelief, and denial; anger and resentment; bargaining; depression and discouragement; and, finally, acceptance. Table 6.1 provides the behavioral characteristics at each stage and discusses the support that professionals can give to assist families as they move through the stages.

Howard, Williams, Port, and Lepper (1997) indicated that passage through the stages of grief is cyclical rather than sequential in nature. Parents report moving in and out of stages throughout their life, depending on what is occurring within the context of the family system at any given time. According to Turnbull and Turnbull (1997), a variety of factors are involved in determining when or how parents will reach the acceptance stage. The area and degree of disability, the unique characteristics of the family (e.g., size, cultural background), and the strength of the family subsystems (e.g., marital partner, siblings) may all impact greatly on the parents ability to reach acceptance.

The Kubler-Ross cycle, currently referred to as *stage theory response,* can be very useful to both parents and professionals. Parents can use the system to describe what they are feeling, which can be helpful in their interactions with other parents of children with disabilities who have been through the same stages. Professionals may use their knowledge about stage theory response to assist them in identifying and accepting the emotions and behaviors they see in the parents they are working with. However, Howard, et al. (1997) indicate that "when it is used to label parents or to associate a pathology with a particular stage, stage theory response is badly misused. Perhaps most important, it is necessary to realize that passage through grief, like any other life passage, is not a sign of dysfunction but of normalcy" (p. 319). Several parents and professionals have disagreed with the use of this paradigm to explain parental behaviors, and have indicated that many parents do not go through the process of grief at all (Lerner, Lowenthal, & Egan, 1998). Revisions to the stage model have been proposed by a number of professionals in response to such disagreement (e.g., Anderegg, Vergason, & Smith, 1992; Berry and Zimmerman, 1983). A review of literature presented by Blacher (1984) indicated that families experience a wide range of responses to the diagnosis of their child's disability. Feelings ranging from detachment to bewilderment to guilt were reported.

TABLE 6.1   *Characteristics of Grief Stages and Suggestions for Professional Support*

Stage/Characteristics	Professional Support
Shock, Disbelief, and Denial	
• May experience feelings of guilt or shame • May try to deny the presence of the disability • May shop for more acceptable medical diagnoses • May completely refuse to accept the diagnosis or provide the necessary supports	• Listen with acceptance • Encourage families to express emotions • Assure families that these feelings are normal • Find strengths concerning the child to share with the family (we all have them!) • When the family is ready, direct them to needed resources and services
Anger and Resentment	
• May show anger to individuals who are trying to help—spouse, professionals, family • May resent friends who have children who are developing typically • May try to argue with professionals about the accuracy of their diagnosis	• Practice reflective listening • Encourage families to express/vent anger and resentment • Do not argue with the family—they "feel" what they feel • Do not become defensive if verbally attacked
Bargaining	
• May accept the belief that if they do what they are told, the disability with disappear • May bargain with God—"I'll do this if you take this away"	• Practice active listening • Show support • Don't force your viewpoint on the parents • Avoid criticism
Depression and Discouragement	
• May begin to accept reality and grieve over the loss of the child they expected • May be unable to look at the child's potential, but see only the child's deficits	• Practice active and reflective listening • Suggest resources such as parent support groups • If depression appears chronic, discuss counseling options • Continue to discuss child's strengths
Acceptance	
• May begin to see the strengths of the child instead of focusing on needs • May begin to assume a proactive stance of working to make a difference in their child's life	• Continue to listen • Praise progress • Continue to accentuate strengths of the child • Begin process of relinquishing case management role to the family • Support the family's empowerment

Regardless of whether the Kubler-Ross stages of grief responses or other responses are given to the diagnosis of disability, one common thread is certain. Parents are faced with the reality of caring for a child who may require the development of skills and changes to the family's normal routines that can be overwhelming. Parents are expected to master the strategies required to care for their child with a disability, while at the same time they are often expected to surrender that care to the dictates of professionals. This can present an enormous challenge to parents, regardless of the degree of acceptance they have achieved. Fortunately for today's parents, early intervention programs have been developed across the nation that provide family-centered services that include a developmental curriculum for use with the child with a disability and also provide support and training for the family.

Donna and Jim, the parents identified in our first scenario, like many parents, progressed through the stages of grief. Unable to deny the presence of the birth defects, the shock and dismay evidenced by her parents at Andrea's birth was soon followed by anger as the question "Why has this happened to us?" began to form in both Donna's and Jim's minds. Donna began to find herself dreading visits to the grocery, or family gatherings, particularly those in which her young nieces and nephews would be present. The presence of Andrea's facial anomalies in the same room with normally developing children brought resentment to Donna.

Donna and Jim began taking Andrea from one doctor to another, shopping for the one who could make Andrea look like the other children. Doctors cautioned that although surgery was possible, it would be a long, slow process for Andrea. The first surgery occurred when Andrea was twelve months old. When Donna realized how involved the process would be and how much pain Andrea appeared to suffer, she began to bargain with God. "If you will make her look 'normal,' I'll…." When this failed to happen, Donna became despondent and severely depressed while Jim began to withdraw from the family.

At this point a friend recommended that Donna contact the local early intervention program to see if they could provide assistance in working with Andrea in speech development while she was undergoing her surgeries. Fortunately for Donna and Jim, they were assigned a caring, well-trained service coordinator who understood the grief process they were going through. She began to visit with the family in their home and, in addition to working with Andrea on oral language development, spent a significant amount of her time addressing the needs of both Donna and Jim as they struggled to deal with the issues before them. The service coordinator worked to focus Donna and Jim's attention on the positive, unique characteristics of Andrea, who was becoming a warm, friendly child with well-developed motor abilities. When, six months after beginning early intervention services, Andrea loudly and clearly identified Jim as "Daddy," the prior feelings experienced by both Jim and Donna faded, and a true acceptance of Andrea as their daughter, regardless of her physical characteristics, occurred.

Two years and four operations later, Andrea is now an active, fun-loving three-year-old. True, she still has some articulation difficulties and continues to receive speech therapy twice a week in her daycare setting. However, except for some minor scarring she looks a great deal like the other children in her family and neighborhood.

Shauna, on the other hand, although initially shocked, did not appear to go through any of the remaining stages of grief, but arrived early at acceptance. A single mother, she nevertheless was surrounded by caring family members who took Tyrone into the fold and refused to consider the presence of Down syndrome as a deficit. As her mother often told Shauna, "Tyrone is just a child. He has his own ways of doing things, and he looks a little different, but he's my grandbaby and I love him!"

The early, successful acceptance evidenced by Shauna may be a result of the early, strong support she received. Shortly after the doctor gave Shauna Tyrone's diagnosis, a woman who was also the mother of a child with Down syndrome visited her. After describing all the wonderful things her child had learned to do, the mother suggested Shauna might want to enroll Tyrone in an early intervention program to get started on achieving development skills. At six weeks of age, Tyrone was a welcome addition to the local center-based early intervention program. Shauna had to work outside of the home to provide for Tyrone and herself; however, her mother began to participate in the center-based program and was helpful in ensuring that Tyrone progressed through developmental stages.

Tyrone is now six years old, has been through both early intervention services and an integrated early childhood special education program. He is very outgoing and friendly, and is obviously well-loved and cared for by his family. This year he was enrolled in a general education kindergarten where he is involved in actively learning new skills. His grandmother continues to visit him at school, and can always be counted on if cupcakes or cookies are needed.

Early Intervention Programs

In 1986, P.L. 99-457, an amendment to P.L. 94-142 (the Education for All Handicapped Children Act [EHA]), was passed which mandated services for preschool children (ages three through five) with disabilities. The law further provided incentive monies to states that sought to provide services to infants and toddlers with disabilities. Table 6.2 provides an overview of the legislation leading up to and including legislation addressing the provision of services to infants and toddlers at risk for or with disabilities.

The most recent reauthorization of the Individuals with Disabilities Education Act (IDEA, P.L. 101-476) has strengthened the role of the parent in the provision of services to infants and toddlers with disabilities. Part C of the reauthorized IDEA (P.L. 105-17), continues to provide financial assistance to states to make services available to infants and toddlers with disabilities and their families. According to the U.S. Department of Education (1995, 1996), in addition to facilitating development of infants and toddlers to minimize the possible effects of their disability, a major purpose of Part C of IDEA includes the enhancement of the capacity of families to meet the special needs of their infants and toddlers with disabilities. Family-centered or family-focused intervention continues to be the basis for the delivery of early intervention services. Professionals no longer focus only on facilitating the development of the child, but on providing families with the support and services they need to allow them to be involved in the educational development of their child with a disability. The early intervention component of IDEA provides a requirement for

TABLE 6.2 *History of Legislation Affecting the Development of Special Education*

1965	P.L. 89-10 Elementary and Secondary Education Act (ESEA)	South to provide equal educational opportunities to children who were economically disadvantaged.
1965	Project Head Start	Established programs from children 4 years of age from economically disadvantaged homes
1966	P.L. 89-313 Amendment to ESEA	Provided incentive monies through grants to universities and state institutions to provide services to children with disabilities
1966	P.L. 89-750 Handicapped Children's Early Education Act	Provided funding for the development of experimental and model programs for serving young children with disabilities
1972	P.L. 92-424 Head Start	Required head start programs to reserve 10% of their total number of placements for children with disabilities
1974	P.L. 93-380 Amendment to ESEA	Signaled commitment for federal support of education for children with disabilities, and provided funds for teacher training
1975	P.L. 94-142 Education for All Handicapped Children Act (EHA)	Landmark legislation that provided for free appropriate public education for all children with disabilities from 5 through 18 years of age; identified categories for services and made provision for related services
1983	P.L. 98-199 Amendments to EHA	Provided funding for research and demonstration projects in early childhood special education and early intervention and provided for parent training centers
1986	P.L. 99-457 Amendments to EHA	Provided for public education of preschoolers (ages 3 through 5) with disabilities and provided incentive monies for states to establish programs to serve infants and toddlers with disabilities and their families; also extended services from 18 to 21 years of age
1990	P.L. 101-476 Individuals with Disabilities Education Act (IDEA)	Reauthorized EHA and added the mandate for transition services and assistive technology; also added disability categories and additional related services
1991	P.L. 102-119 Early Childhood Amendments to IDEA	Changed the language in IDEA with regard to eligibility and related services and allowed for use of either IEPs or IFSPs for preschoolers; also addressed LRE and funding issues
1997	P.L. 105-17 Reauthorized Individuals with Disabilities Education Act	Reauthorizes and updates IDEA to include Part C (formerly Part H), Infants and Toddlers with Disabilities; also changes preschool programs to include strengthened family involvement

the development of Individual Family Service Plans (IFSPs) which focus on assisting families in the provision of services to their child with a disability.

Individual Family Service Plans

The IFSP is intended to provide a guide for the provision of appropriate services and support to infants and toddlers and their families. (See Figure 6.1 for a representation of the process of determining eligibility and developing an IFSP.) This document serves as a legal agreement between the families and the service providers, as does the Individual Education Program (IEP) for children beyond age three. However, it does provide for a more holistic approach to intervention. Components of an IFSP are:

• A description of the child's current developmental characteristics in several domains including communication, social/emotional, cognition, and physical, all based on results of a multidisciplinary assessment.

• A statement of the family's strengths and areas of need, should they decide to include it, as the strengths and needs relate to their child's development.

• A clear listing of the major goals set for the child and family, with clear criteria for achievement, a time line for achievement, and evaluation procedures to measure achievement of the goals.

• A statement of the specific services that are to be provided to meet the identified goals for the child and family. This statement should include the location, duration, frequency, and method of delivery of services. Information about payment arrangements and about additional services for which no payment will be received may also be included.

• Dates for the beginning of services and the anticipated duration of services must be included.

• The name of the individual serving as service coordinator. This individual is responsible for assuring that services are provided according to legal requirements and should provide support for the family's seeking and obtaining additional services if and when they become necessary. It should be noted that parents may serve as the service coordinator for their child.

• A transition plan for the child that will ensure smooth transfer to preschool once the child reaches age three.

Of major importance in the successful delivery of the services identified in an IFSP is the development of appropriate goals and objectives. Notari-Syverson and Shuster (1995) identified five criteria that are necessary for objectives to be developed that address real-life needs. They must be skills that are:

1. *Functional*—Will the skill that is being taught need to be learned for the child to meet the demands of the environments in which he or she interacts?
2. *Generalizable*—Will the skill be used in a variety of situations and environments?

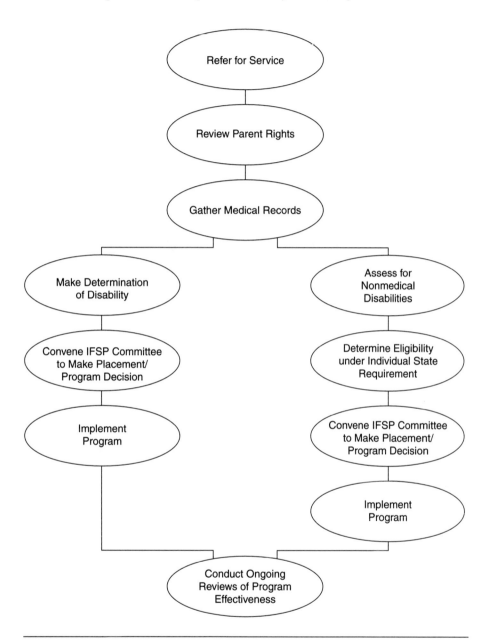

FIGURE 6.1 *The IFSP Process*

Source: Adapted from *Planning Family Goals: A System Approach to the IFSP.* Copyright © 1992 by Communication Skill Builders, a division of the Psychological Corporation.

3. *Natural*—Will the skill be one that can be used daily in the classroom, home, or integrated settings?
4. *Measurable*—Can the skill be seen, heard, counted, or measured?
5. *Sequential*—Do the skills become increasingly more complex, building on skills previously learned?

An additional major component of successful intervention planning is determination of where services are to be provided. Two major formats have been used in the provision of services: home-based and center-based programs.

Service Delivery Systems

Home-Based Early Intervention.   As indicated previously, it is important for very young children to learn skills that are appropriate to their natural environment. Home-based early intervention services may afford the opportunity for learning in a more natural environment. Most often such services are designed to fit into the schedule of the parents, which is important in this day in which both parents are often in the work force. In this model, a variety of service providers ranging from medical professionals (e.g., occupational therapists, physical therapists, nurses) to early intervention specialists (generally individuals trained in special education methodology) provide intervention for the child and family within the confines of the home. When interventions in the home include working with parents, parents are more likely to develop skills in using everyday situations to stimulate learning (Gestwicki, 1996). Gestwicki indicates that "all home-based programs assume that parents are the most important teachers of their children during the early years, and the skills they are taught have a long-term impact on all children in a family" (p. 244–245). In fact, home-based interventions tend to build stronger bonds between the parent and child because of the increased opportunities for interaction that are not available in center-based programs (Lerner, Lowenthal, & Egan, 1998). Additionally, research has shown that parents involved in home-based services develop more positive relationships with the professionals with whom they work and are more likely to follow through on recommended activities as identified in the IFSP (Hanson & Lynch, 1995). It would appear that a cyclical relationship exists. Positive interactions with professionals would lead to an increase in parental comfort level in working with their child. In turn, this increased comfort level would lead to strengthening of the parent–child bonds which would strengthen parent–professional relationships.

There are individuals who are not as strongly supportive of home-based services. Lerner, Lowenthal, and Egan (1998) indicate that a possible disadvantage of home-based services is the level of stress that may be placed on the parent who must become the primary service provider. The parent may have difficulty separating the role of primary service provider from the role of nurturing parent.

In the case of Nancy and Chris, after accessing home-based early intervention services for a year, they elected to remove Anne from early intervention services within the home because they were beginning to think of her as a broken object that needed fixing. Anne required several large pieces of equipment for physical therapy, and adaptive equipment for feeding. Almost all interactions between the parents and Anne were therapeutic in nature. Finally, Nancy reported that she was no longer enjoying Anne as her "child" and although the decision was a difficult one, she felt that interacting with her as a "child" first was most important at this point in time. Instead of implementing "work-based" therapy with Anne, Nancy began using the skills she had learned in the year of early intervention services to play with Anne. One year later, Nancy reports that Anne has progressed, is babbling, holding her head up, eating solid food, and, best of all, has become an integral part of their family. In this family's situation, the ability to forego the requirements of weekly intervention and use learned skills in an approach that allowed Anne's parents to consider her childhood first, worked well to provide Anne with the intervention she needed. Nancy and Chris have indicated that now that Anne has turned three, they will be placing her in a preschool program for children with disabilities on a part-time basis. They have discovered that there are additional supports Anne now needs that they are unable to provide. Although all of Anne's family benefited from the year in which services were not provided, it is important to remember that each family and each child with a disability has unique needs and strengths. A decision such as the one made by Anne's parents may not be appropriate for other families.

One additional possible disadvantage of home-based early intervention is the lack of adequate opportunities for young children to interact with their peers. In fact, this lack was a major factor in leading Nancy and Chris to the decision to place Anne in a center-based program.

Center-Based Early Intervention.   While the majority of professionals appear to support the use of the more natural home environment for the provision of early intervention services, more and more frequently, home-based services may not meet the needs of parents. In fact, based on the Children's Defense Fund (1998), fully two-thirds of mothers of young children are in the work force outside of the home, and every day approximately 6 million infants and toddlers are in child care settings. Although the exact figures of children with disabilities in child care are not available, it is likely to mirror the prevalence figure of children with disabilities served in special education across the nation, which is 7.7 percent of the general school-age population (U.S. Department of Education, 1998). Many of these children will be receiving early intervention services in specially designed center-based programs. Services at such programs are generally focused on facilitating the development of the child in all domains of development.

Currently, the trend in the development of center-based programs is the establishment of inclusive centers (e.g., Early Head Start programs or private day care facilities) in which children with disabilities are integrated with children without disabilities (Fox, Hanline, Vail, & Galant, 1994). The benefits of such programming include:

- The opportunity for children to develop more appropriate social skills through interactions with their normally developing peers (Lamorey & Bricker, 1993)
- The opportunity for families of children with disabilities to become a part of the community together with families of children without disabilities (Dunst, Trivette, & Deal, 1994)
- The opportunity for typically developing preschool children and their families to learn about and to accept individuals with disabilities (Peck, Carlson, & Helmstetter, 1992)

Once again, it is important to remember that each child and family present individual characteristics, strengths, and needs, and the service delivery model selected for early intervention should be appropriate to addressing individuality.

Preschool Programs for Children with Disabilities

The 1997 Reauthorization of IDEA reaffirmed the requirement for states to provide free, appropriate public education and related services to all eligible children with disabilities from age three through five under Part B. Unlike early intervention services, states do not have the option to withhold services to this population if they are to continue to receive federal monies for special education. They do have the option to develop preschool programming to fit the needs of the individual state. Such programming differences may include the amount of time spent in preschool and the degree to which parents are involved in service delivery.

Part B predominantly provides for facilitation of developmental learning with preschool children with disabilities. However, recent Reauthorization to IDEA strengthened the family involvement component of Part B. According to Lerner, Lowenthal, and Egan (1998), P.L. 102-119 in 1991 allowed individuals involved in program development for children with disabilities ages three through five to use either IEPs or IFSPs to determine program services. Inclusion of family goals in programming as part of an IFSP, when requested, could facilitate development of parenting skills necessary to deal with the possible effects of a disability on family functioning. IDEA reauthorizations strengthened the decision making role of the parents beyond that of IEP/IFSP development. Under the 1997 reauthorization parents are to be notified of all meetings to discuss eligibility of their child for special education services, and have the right to mediation before their child can be denied, placed, or terminated from a special education service. If mediation is unsuccessful, parents and the school both have the right to a due process hearing to resolve the issue.

The majority of programs for preschool children with disabilities are delivered in center-based settings. These center-based settings can encompass special schools, preschool classrooms within the public school setting, private preschool programs, hospitals, commercial daycare centers, as well as home care centers. Home-based services may be an option, depending on the placement needs of the child as determined in the IEP meeting. However, such home-based services are generally reserved for those children who are considered to be medically fragile. Center-based services in integrated settings provide numerous opportunities for development in social, cognitive, motor, communication, and self-help domains for preschool children.

Professionals continue to promote the use of inclusionary programs for preschool children with disabilities, citing the more natural, less restrictive environment as the most appropriate placement for all children. Professionals in both early childhood special education and early childhood education have evidenced strong similarities in the ways in which educational experiences for young children with disabilities and those without disabilities are designed and have placed emphasis on the development of a shared vision for early childhood programming. To explore these similarities, the professional memberships of both the Division for Early Childhood (DEC) of the Council for Exceptional Children and the National Association for Education of Young Children (NAEYC) have been working together to determine issues and characteristics common to both populations. (See Figure 6.2 for a reprint of the 1998 DEC position statement regarding services for young children with special needs and their families.)

Some fundamental differences do appear to be evident, however, that must be overcome if inclusionary programming is to work for all children. According to Johnson and Carr (1996), early childhood educators and early childhood special educators have not reached agreement with regard to whether programs should be child centered or family centered. They further indicated that although both groups of educators appear to agree in principle with the importance of parental involvement, early childhood special educators have been the group to continue to emphasize family-centered programs. Parents accessing services for their child with a disability may find that inclusionary programs, while addressing the specific needs of the child, may not meet the needs of the family.

A case in point is that of Samuel, identified earlier in this chapter. Although his parents believed something might be wrong, they did not search for a diagnosis until Samuel reached the age of three. No longer able to accept the platitudes of their family and friends, Samuel's parents decided to take him to a child development specialist for an evaluation. The local university provided this service to concerned parents at a low cost, and staffed a fully integrated private child development center with trained, qualified personnel, including a school psychologist who conducted diagnostic assessments.

After the psychologist conducted an assessment battery with Samuel and collected observational and background data, the parents were called in for a conference. Without preamble, the school psychologist told them that she would like to place Samuel in their class for three-year-olds and work with him to overcome the deficits of the mild mental retardation and autistic tendencies she had discovered. Stunned by hearing this diagnosis for the first time, the parents didn't know what to do, so agreed to the placement. An IEP was developed at a follow-up conference the following week with little input from the parents, and Samuel began attending the center-based program three mornings each week.

Samuel's first day at the center-based program was a traumatic experience for his mother. This was to be the first time she had left Samuel for an extended period of time. She asked the classroom teacher if she might stay for the first day and, added that, as she did not work outside the home, she would like to be involved in the provision of services to her child. The classroom teacher told her that the program did not believe that parental involvement within the classroom was appropriate. Their philosophy was one in which the services they provided were to focus on the child and assist him or her to become an integral member of society. They did not address family issues or family involvement. Again, believing that what they had suggested was best, Samuel's mother accepted the judgment of the center-based teacher and left Samuel at the program, despite her feelings of misgivings.

A month passed, and although Samuel appeared to be making some progress in development, his parents continued to feel left out of this major part of his life. Feelings of anxiety about their placement decision began to develop and they began to question the appropriateness of the integrated placement for Samuel. In addition, they began to argue between themselves over disciplinary actions and many other issues. Finally, acting on the suggestion of a friend, they decided to check on the services offered by a regional program for children with autism.

***Position on Services for Children
Birth to Age Eight with Special Needs
and Their Families
Adopted: December, 1993
Revised: July 21, 1998
Division for Early Childhood, Council for Exceptional Children***

DEC strongly supports and encourages the identification and delivery of comprehensive and coordinated supports and services to children with special needs and their families as early as possible, in accordance with the priorities of their families. Young children with special needs are those between birth and age eight who have disabilities, developmental delays, are at-risk for future developmental problems, or who are gifted and talented.

This position is based on the following beliefs: (1) all young children are valued and full participants in their families, communities and schools; (2) high quality early intervention can help ensure that all young children reach their full developmental potential and attain functional skills in the areas of communication, mobility, social competence, cognition and self care; and, (3) families benefit from consistent and supportive partnerships and collaborations with service providers such as early childhood special educators, early childhood educators, related service personnel, child care providers and others who provide supports and services to their children. This position is derived from: the professional literature, which provides ample research evidence for the efficacy of early intervention for young children with special needs and their families; parental leadership and collaborations across the country; and federal, state, and provincial policies that encourage and support early intervention and early childhood special education services.

DEC proposes that all young children with special needs are entitled to early intervention services that reflect recommended practices as presented in the literature and the DEC Recommended Practices (1993). These practices emphasize the individualized nature of service delivery as determined collaboratively by families and professionals through the Individualized Family Service Plan (IFSP) or Individualized Education Program (IEP) process. This process guarantees each child a comprehensive assessment to identify individual strengths and needs; appropriate intervention at the intensity and scope warranted by the child's eti-

ology and developmental profile, research and best practice related to these variables, and family preference. Further, the IFSP or IEP process should monitor child progress to assure service modifications as needed.

All children in need of early intervention or early childhood special education should be able to attain basic skills in the areas of communication, mobility, cognition, social competence and self care through the delivery of individualized and comprehensive supports and services.

DEC recognizes that the family is the constant in the life of a child and the purpose of early intervention is to enhance the capacity of the family to facilitate their child's development. Children aged birth to eight spend most of their time with their family or other care givers. Early intervention and early childhood special education services should be designed in response to the concerns and priorities of each family as related to the development of their child, and service delivery should reflect a respect for each family's uniqueness and family system. Service providers should respond to families within the cultural context of both family and community. Similarly, culturally competent community based service systems should be designed to support the participation of children representing the full range of diversity; diversity not only of ethnicity, economics, language and culture, but of ability, as well.

DEC supports the rights of all children, regardless of their diverse abilities, to participate actively in natural environments within their community. A natural environment is one in which a child would spend time if he or she did not have special needs. Family-centered and community based care means that service providers not only provide support for children, but they provide support to families and those in the community as well. Service providers should be able to facilitate parent-to-parent connections and link young children and their families to community-based natural sup-

FIGURE 6.2 Continued

ports such as babysitters, play groups and libraries. Instead of providing direct supports and services only to young children and their families, service providers should also serve as consultants, coordinators, advocates, facilitators, and team members with community providers.

DEC believes that there is a particular need to develop personnel standards that support the practice of serving all young children in natural and inclusive early childhood setting. While acknowledging that related service personnel, early interventionists, and early childhood special educators will require training within their particular disciplines, we believe that there is a common core of knowledge that all such professionals should possess. In addition, early childhood educators should also possess a core of knowledge about serving children with special needs.

Certification standards should be developed to ensure not only that service providers possess the high degree of specialization that their discipline requires, but also to guarantee that service providers from all disciplines possess the common core of knowledge and skills they need in order to work with young children with special needs in inclusive settings.

DEC is aware of the complex needs of young children with special needs and their families. It is highly unlikely that any individual professional or agency will be able to address all of the needs of children and families. A coordinated and collaborative approach is needed to ensure the availability of comprehensive supports and services by families. The delivery of coordinated supports and services requires a commitment to a common framework of operation guided by a philosophical foundation of collaboration. In many instances, this means the design of new service structures and models of personnel deployment across a variety of disciplines. It also requires that personnel have the requisite knowledge and skills to work with individuals from other professional disciplines and engage in collaborative efforts. Within programs, this means collaborative teamwork skills in assessment and intervention.

Across programs, this means collaborative abilities to coordinate and integrate services. DEC believes that policy makers, institutions of higher education, professional organizations and other sources of technical assistance, and local service delivery systems share responsibility for ensuring that services from a variety of disciplines are available and are delivered in a collaborative and integrated manner.

DEC believes that the complex needs of families are best met when every family has access to a service coordinator who becomes a partner with them as they seek appropriate supports and services for themselves and their child. In some cases this coordination role is best met by the family themselves. The coordinator's role is to support families in identifying and obtaining the supports and services (both formal and informal) they want. The service coordinator, to the extent that each family desires, can assist all family members in obtaining the skills needed during the early childhood years and beyond. As with other service providers, there is a need for a sufficient number of skilled service coordinators who are able to deliver culturally competent services. We believe that members of each and all disciplines share with families a responsibility for advocacy on behalf of children with special needs. However, service coordinators have a special responsibility to identify and eliminate gaps in the service system, thus developing a model of service integration for individual families, as well as the service delivery system in general.

DEC believes that great strides continue to be made toward meeting the needs of infants and young children with special needs and their families. While appreciating and honoring the effort resulting in these gains, we also recognize that many children and families remain unserved or under served, and that ensuring that services and supports are of the highest quality remains a challenge. We recognize the responsibility that DEC and its members have in working toward services that are sufficient in both availability and quality to meet the needs of all young children who have disabilities or developmental delays, are at-risk for delay, or are gifted and talented.

Source: DEC Task Force on Recommended Practices. (1993). *DEC Recommended Practices: Indicators of Quality in Programs for Infants and Young Children with Special Needs and Their Families.* Reston, VA: Council for Exceptional Children. Permission to copy not needed—distribution encouraged.

Their visit to the program was, in every respect, different from their visit to the local center-based program. They were greeted warmly and asked to share their concerns with the program director. On hearing of the manner in which the parents had learned of Samuel's diagnosis, the director began to understand the feelings of frustration and anxiety so apparent in the parents. He advised them that his program was based on the family-centered approach to working with children and that their participation in program activities and even day-to-day intervention would be welcome. He advised the parents not to make a quick decision; instead, he invited the parents to visit the classrooms at the program and to participate in some of the parent meetings and training activities that took place on a weekly basis at the center. He told them that if they felt that what was offered would be beneficial to both Samuel and themselves, they could make a decision at that time. One week later, after several visits to the program, Samuel was enrolled.

Three years later Samuel is enrolled in an inclusionary program at the public school. His parents have learned to accept Samuel as he is and to enjoy the many activities they engage in with him. They express gratitude to the staff of the special school for helping them achieve the level of understanding and acceptance they have reached. Thanks to the special school, they are going back into an inclusionary program armed with the necessary knowledge and skills to make integration work for Samuel.

Family Involvement in Early Childhood Special Education Programs

The philosophical basis for development of early childhood special education programs has changed significantly over the past three decades. The focus of such programming has evolved from a focus on the child alone to one that is family centered. A major purpose of early childhood special education programs today is to facilitate the empowerment of families to assume management of their child's life. To facilitate enabling and empowering, it is necessary to come to consensus on definitional issues and to understand the dynamics involved in various family theories. These issues were discussed in detail in Chapter 1. Once a definition is agreed on and a basic understanding of family theories has been developed, individuals involved in early childhood special education programs are able to work toward developing positive relationships between family and professionals, leading toward family empowerment. Remembering that patterns that are developed early in any relationship, including that of parent and child, or parent and professional, are more likely to be effective and long-lasting is an important step to positive involvement in educational programs.

Interestingly, despite the requirement of the law to develop strong family involvement components in both early intervention and preschool programming and intense efforts to ensure such involvement, for the most part families remain uninvolved in program planning for their child (Fallon & Harris, 1992; Turnbull & Turnbull, 1997). No clear answers as to why this is so have appeared. Among possible reasons is the lack of adequate training of professionals involved in early childhood special education programs for working with families, or for adopting a family-centered approach to intervention. Another sad, but all too often true, response may be that parents who wish to be involved in the educational programming for their children will be, while others simply will not, regardless of efforts made by professionals to involve them.

Regardless of the progress thus far in including families in planning and implementing services to their young child with a disability, the fact that a legal mandate is in place to provide for such participation requires that professionals continue to work toward that end. The 1997 reauthorization of IDEA strengthened the family-centered focus of programs for young children with disabilities, and it is hoped that a major goal of such programs will be enabling and empowering families to become self-confident, informed, independent advocates for their children.

Dunst, Trivette, and Deal (1994) have provided a model to use in empowering families in early intervention services. This model, called the Family Enablement Project, is dynamic, with ongoing evaluation and program modification occurring after every interaction with families. The model consists of a four-step process:

1. Families alone determine their needs and wants.
2. Professionals work with the family to identify coping styles and identify components of the family system that are working effectively.
3. Professionals work with the family to identify potential resources that will assist families in achieving their needs and desires.
4. Professionals work with the family to help them achieve their goals.

This model has been adopted by many programs and found to be effective. Additional information about the project may be obtained from the Family, Infant and Preschool Program, Western Carolina Center, 300 Enola Road, Morganton, NC 28655; (704) 433-2877.

Whatever model is selected for use in facilitating empowerment of families, the purpose of empowerment must be clear. The ultimate outcome of any empowerment program should be a shift from the role of the professional as the primary leader and decision maker with regard to services for the child and family, to the families assuming the leadership role. In fact, the professional should be seen as assistant to the parent, a provider of a service deemed necessary by the family.

Parent–Professional Partnerships: Insights for New Teachers

Collaborative partnerships between parents and professionals can facilitate the provision of optimal early childhood special education services to children with disabilities. Collaborative partnerships take many forms; however, the form most often recommended is transdisciplinary teaming. This collaborative model requires willingness to give up ownership of specific roles by both parents and professionals, and instead adopting a more open-minded, sharing relationship. Table 6.3 provides a description of activities than can facilitate such role release.

In addition, parent–professional partnerships require the involvement of both parties in a variety of activities. Following are some specific situations in which parent–professional collaboration may occur, together with suggestions for ensuring successful interactions.

TABLE 6.3   *Activities to Promote Role Release for Families and Professionals on Transdisciplinary Teams*

Role Release Component	Activities
Role extension	• Read new articles and books within your discipline or about your child's condition. • Attend conferences, seminars, and lectures. • Join a professional organization in your field or a family-to-family network. • Explore resources at libraries or media centers.
Role enrichment	• Listen to parents discuss their child's strengths and needs. • Ask for explanations of unfamiliar technical language or jargon. • Do an appraisal of what you wish you knew more about and what you could teach others.
Role expansion	• Watch someone from another discipline work with a child, and check your perception of what you observe. • Attend a workshop in another field that includes some hands-on practicum experience. • Rotate the role of transdisciplinary arena assessment facilitator among all service providers on the team.
Role exchange	• Allow yourself to be videotaped practicing a technique from another discipline; invite a team member from that discipline to review and critique the videotape with you. • Work side by side in the center-based program, demonstrating interventions to families and staff. • Suggest strategies for achieving an IFSP outcome outside your own discipline; check your accuracy with other team members.
Role release	• Do a self-appraisal—list new skills within your intervention repertoire that other team members have taught you. • Monitor the performance of the service providers on your child's IFSP team. • Present the "whole" child at a clinical conference. • Accept responsibility for implementing, with the family, an entire IFSP.
Role support	• Ask for help when you feel "stuck." • Offer help when you see a team member struggling with a complex intervention. • Provide any intervention that only you can provide, but share the child's progress and any related interventions with the primary service provider and the family.

Source: From "The Transdisciplinary Team: A Model for Family-Centered Early Intervention," by M. J. McGonigel, G. Woodruff, and M. Roszmann-Millican. In Johnson, L. J., Gallagher, R. J., LaMontagne, M. J. (Eds.). (1994). *Meeting Early Intervention Challenges: Issues from Birth to Three.* (2nd ed.) (p. 107). Baltimore: Paul H. Brookes.

Parent Involvement in Assessment

Being a part of the assessment process is a new role that parents need to learn. Parents have information on their child that needs to be shared in order to develop an accurate assessment of the child's abilities. In an effort to involve parents in the process professionals should consider scheduling assessments at a time and location that is most convenient for the parents and the child. Regarding the assessment setting, Rosenbaum et al. (1990) found that where the assessment is conducted (child's home or a facility setting) is irrelevant. What is important is using the setting that the parents prefer. Prior to the scheduled assessment meeting, professionals can further parental involvement by letting parents know what type of assessments will be utilized and what type of background information may be requested, so parents will be prepared to share that information.

Parents can ensure that professionals achieve meaningful assessment results by being willing to share accurate family information such as family strengths and needs, disciplinary techniques, financial resources, and family support systems. Parents may not always feel comfortable sharing this information, but they should try to bear in mind that this information may make an impact on the services their child receives. When professionals are left to assess family strengths and needs without thorough input from family members, the assessment does not accurately reflect the family's true composition (Garshelis & McConnell, 1993).

Parent Involvement in Goal Setting

Legislation dictates that parents are to be included in the development of their child's IFSP or IEP. Often what is found is that parents are the recipients of what professionals decide is best for the child and the family. Campbell, Strickland, and La Forme (1992) found that training for both the parent and professional can lead to an increase in family involvement toward development of a family-focused IFSP. Parents can assist professionals in the development of appropriate goal setting by ensuring that they have shared accurate information regarding family dynamics such as ethnic and cultural background, parental preferences in child-rearing practices, and family priorities. When parents are involved in generating priorities for their child and the rest of their family, it is likely that professionals will see an increase in parental involvement in implementation of the goals. It would then follow that increased parent involvement in both goal setting and program implementation would foster the development of shared respect and trust between the parents and professionals. (Box 6.1 provides a brief description of a collaborative approach to problem solving.)

Parent Involvement in Program Implementation

If new teachers want parents to be involved in the implementation of the IFSP or IEP, consideration needs to be given to teaching parents how to incorporate the goals into the child's daily routine. Professionals should remember that if goals are too time consuming or are designed to be taught in isolation, the likelihood of activities being carried out will be decreased.

BOX 6.1

Family–Teacher Issues

Mr. and Mrs. Mallard are experiencing difficulty with their daughter, Casandra. Casandra, a five-year-old with mild cerebral palsy, is in a preschool for individuals with disabilities. The Mallards report that Casandra has begun to exhibit inappropriate behaviors when playing with her younger brother, Seth. Specifically, she is unwilling to share her toys and throws tantrums when required to do so. Ms. Lacross, her preschool teacher, reports that Casandra is withdrawn in the classroom and refuses to interact with the other children.

Collaborative Orientations and Responsive Practices

Ms. Lacross has contacted the Mallards and requested a meeting to discuss possible solutions for both home and school concerns. The Mallards and Ms. Lacross have agreed to collect data on the frequency and duration of the problem behaviors. Some ideas for intervention were shared and an agreement to meet again after data collection was made. That meeting will more specifically address strategies to be used in both settings to develop more appropriate social behaviors.

Likewise, parents need to speak up when they find that they cannot implement a particular goal or activity in the manner in which it was envisioned during the IFSP or IEP meeting. Communication must be developed if program implementation is going to be successful. Professionals and parents need to be open and honest with each other regarding the successes and problems encountered during the implementation stage. Communication should also be used by both parents and professionals to reinforce the positive actions the other is performing. Professionals can praise parents for carrying out activities described in the IFSP or IEP. Parents can reinforce professionals by affirming the warmth and caring shown while working with their child.

Table 6.4 provides some descriptive characteristics parents and professionals should exhibit if they are to work together collaboratively to achieve appropriate programming for children with disabilities and their families.

Family Member Questions

New teachers will face many issues when families initially attend school conferences. Families frequently ask the following questions:

- *How can I find out more about my child's specific disability?* As a teacher, it is vital that you be able to provide direction to parents when asked questions like this. Keeping a resource file, listing Internet sites, and identifying parents organizations are valuable tools for responding to individual parents. It is impossible for one individual to know all of the characteristics and behaviors of all disability categories, so being able to assist parents in accessing appropriate resources is important.
- *How can I find out what services are available for my child?* As a new teacher, having on file state and local regulations regarding services for early childhood spe-

TABLE 6.4   *Characteristics of Effective Partners in Early Childhood Special Education*

Parents	Professionals
Need to be warm, caring, and show mutual respect to others	Need to be warm, caring, and show mutual respect to others
Need to listen to information and options concerning their child	Need to listen to parents and other professionals and respond without making judgments
Have the right to have and express any and all feelings	Need to accept parents as worthy and capable of coping with their own situation
Have the right to set the pace for the parent–professional partnership	Need to accept the fact that parents know their child better than anyone else
Have the right to decide what is important—what is needed for the child/family	Need to learn to speak the truth tactfully
Have the right to know they are being listened to and heard	Need to present information in a positive, caring manner
Have the right to be themselves without feeling judged	Should nurture a parent's optimism—don't take away hope
Should accept that professionals have knowledge regarding their child that may assist in development	Should be honest about any limitations regarding their knowledge base
Should share all pertinent information regarding the child and family that may help the professionals in their work	Should support parents in putting their own ideas to work for their children
Should be willing to assist professionals in identifying goals that will benefit and empower the whole family	Should encourage parents to perform as independently as possible—don't try to solve all their problems for them
Should acknowledge the contributions made by professionals in facilitating development of the child and family	Should assist parents in experiencing a sense of control and competence in the parenting of the child with a disability

cial education will assist you in helping the parent identify needed services. In addition, keeping a resource file of private providers of a variety of services beyond those provided by early intervention is also helpful.

- *What do I tell people (my family, friends, neighbors) when they ask about my child?* Although your position is not that of counselor, you are likely to be called on to respond to this type of question. Being prepared to share case scenarios identifying how other parents may have dealt with this issue is one way to respond. Parents are most likely not asking for your opinion, but are looking for someone to listen.
- *How do I know the feelings I'm experiencing are normal?* Being aware of the different stages of grief and having a clear understanding of what each stage presents is important in order to respond to questions such as this. Being aware of warning signs

(e.g., a parent showing true signs of depression, anger, etc.) is helpful to you as a teacher in directing parents to possible resources. (Note: Physicians, psychologists, health clinics and others may have fact sheets that can provide warning signs for all types of potential emotional and/or physical problems.)

- *How do I know the decisions I'm making regarding my child are the right decisions?* As a teacher it is vital that you do not impose your own values on the family, but rather support their decisions. Just because we may not agree with the choices parents make does not mean they have made the wrong decisions. Only when the child is in jeopardy should you attempt to intervene.
- *What about my other children? How do I balance my parenting?* Again, the use of case scenarios in which families demonstrate ways in which they balance their roles and responsibilities is a good tool to share. As teachers we need to bear in mind that there may be other children in the family and our programs should be designed to incorporate the family unit, not just the child with a disability.

Family Resources and Services

New teachers may disseminate data on the following resources and services helpful to families of young children with disabilities.

Beach Center on Families and Disability
3111 Haworth Hall
University of Kansas
Lawrence, KS 66045
(785) 864-7600

Children's Defense Fund
25 E Street NW
Washington, DC 20001
(800) 233-1200
www.tmn.com/cdf/index.html

Council for Exceptional Children
1920 Association Drive
Reston, VA 20191-1589
(888) 232-7733
www.cec.sped.org

Family Voices
P.O. Box 769
Algodones, NM 87001

(505) 867-2368

March of Dimes Birth Defects Foundation
1275 Mamaroneck Avenue
White Plains, NY 10605
(888) 663-4637
www.modimes.org

NPND: National Parent Network on Disabilities
1200 G St NW Ste 80
Washington, DC 20005
(202) 434-8686

Developmental Delay Registry (DDR)
6701 Fairfax Road
Chevy Chase, MD 20815
(301) 652-2263
www.devdelay.org

Children's Hospice International
700 Princess St., Lower Level
Alexandria, VA 22314
(800) 242-4453

**National Information Center
for Children & Youth with
Disabilities (NICHCY)**
P.O. Box 1492
Washington, DC 20013-1492
(800) 695-0285
www.nichcy.org

**National Parent to Parent Support and
Information Service (NPSIS)**
P.O. Box 907
Blue Ridge, GA 30513
(800) 651-1151

www.npsis.org

**Technical Assistance Alliance for Parent
Centers**
4826 Chicago Ave., S.
Minneapolis, MN 55417
(888) 248-0822
www.taalliance.org

Sibling Information Network
The A. J. Pappanikou Center on Special
Education & Rehabilitation
249 Glenbrook Rd U-64

Storrs, CT 06269-2064
(860) 486-4985

Exceptional Parent
P.O. Box 3000
Dept. EP
Denville, N.J. 07834
(800) 562-1973
www.eparent.com

Summary

Families of young children with disabilities are often faced with the necessity of traversing the stages of grief identified on their way to acceptance. Although not all families go through all, or any of the stages, and many families move in and out of stages, it is important for professionals to develop an understanding of the stages to assist in understanding what parents may be facing. They may be facing this in addition to the requirement of learning how to work with their child.

In addition, it is vital for professionals to understand definitional issues and family theories and how these affect the empowerment of families to assume the responsibility for working with their child. The need for clear understanding of the effects of a disability on the family and its subsystems is also important in developing a clear understanding of family actions.

Family-centered programming has been mandated by law for early intervention and the requirement for strengthened family involvement, if requested, has been included in preschool programs. Service delivery options often impact on the degree of involvement of the family with their child with a disability.

The process of developing family-centered programs for delivery to families with young children with disabilities may often raise more questions than provide clear-cut answers. Nevertheless, attempts to resolve the questions by collaborative interactions should reflect a deep commitment to the understanding that society is affected positively by healthy families, and good family-centered programs can help families with a child with disabilities become healthy, strong families.

References

Allen, D. A., & Affleck, G. (1985). Are we stereotyping parents? A postscript to Blacher. *Mental Retardation, 23,* 200–202.

Anderegg, M. L., Vergason, G. A., & Smith, M. C. (1992). A visual representation of the grief cycle for use by teachers with families of children with disabilities. *Remedial and Special Education, 13,* 17–23.

Berry, J. O., & Zimmerman, W. W. (1983). The stage model revisited. *Rehabilitation Literature, 44,* 275–278.

Blacher, J. (1984). Sequential stages of parental adjustment to the birth of a child with handicaps: Fact or artifact? *Mental Retardation, 22,* 58–68.

Bradley, V. J., Knoll, J., & Agosta, J. M. (Eds.). (1992*). Emerging issues in family support.* Washington, DC: American Association on Mental Retardation.

Campbell, P. H., Strickland, B., & LaForme, C. (1992). Enhancing parent participation in the individualized family service plan. *Topics in Early Childhood Special Education, 11,* 112–124.

Children's Defense Fund. (1998). *The state of America's children: Yearbook 1998.* Washington, DC: Children's Defense Fund.

Dunst, C. J., Trivette, C., & Deal, A. G. (1994). Enabling and empowering families. In C. J. Dunst, C. M. Trivette, & A. G. Deal (Eds.). *Supporting and strengthening families* (pp. 2–11). Cambridge, MA: Brookline Books.

Fallon, M. A., & Harris, M. B. (1992). Encouraging parent participation in intervention programs. *Transdisciplinary Journal, 2* (2), 141–146.

Fox, L., Hanline, M. F., Vail, C. O., & Galant, K. R. (1994). Developmentally appropriate practice: Applications for young children with disabilities. *Journal of Early Intervention, 18* (3), 243–257.

Garshelis, J. A., & McConnell, S. R. (1993). Comparison of family needs assessed by mothers, individual professionals, and interdisciplinary teams. *Journal of Early Intervention, 17,* 36–49.

Gestwicki, C. (1996). *Home, school and community relations: A guide to working with parents* (3rd ed.). Albany, NY: Delmar Publishers.

Hanson, M. J., & Lynch, E. W. (1995). *Early intervention: Implementing child and family services for infants and toddlers who are at risk or disabled.* Austin, TX: Pro-Ed.

Howard, V. F., Williams, B. F., Port, P. D., & Lepper, C. (1997). *Very young children with special needs: A formative approach for the 21st century.* Upper Saddle River, NJ: Merrill.

Johnson, L. J., & Carr, V. W. (1996). Curriculum in early childhood education: Moving toward an inclusive specialization. In M. C. Pugach & C. Wagner (Eds.). *Curriculum trends, special education, and reform: Refocusing the conversation* (pp. 216–226). Needham Heights, MA: Allyn & Bacon.

Kubler-Ross, E. (1969). *Locus of control: Current trends in theory and research.* Hillsdale, NJ: Earlbaum.

Lamorey, S., & Bricker, D. D. (1993). Integrated programs: Effects on young children and their parents. In C. A. Peck, S. L. Odom, & D. D. Bricker (Eds.). *Integrating young children with disabilities into community programs* (pp. 249–270). Baltimore: Paul H. Brookes.

Lerner, J. W., Lowenthal, B. & Egan, R. (1998). *Preschool children with special needs: Children at-risk, children with disabilities.* Boston: Allyn and Bacon.

Notari-Syverson, A. R., & Shuster, S. L. (1995). Putting real life skills into IEP/IFSPs for infants and young children. *Teaching Exceptional Children (Winter),* 29–32.

Peck, C. A., Carlson, P., & Helmstetter, E. (1992). Parent and teacher perceptions of outcomes for nonhandicapped children enrolled in integrated early childhood programs: A statewide study. *Journal of Early Intervention, 16,* 53–63.

Rosenbaum, P., King, S., Toal, C., Puttaswamaiah, S., & Durrell, K. (1990). Home or children's treatment centre: Where should initial therapy assessments of children with disabilities be done? *Developmental Medicine and Child Neurology, 32,* 888–894.

Turnbull, A. P., & Turnbull, H. R. III. (1997). *Families, professionals, and exceptionality: A special partnership* (3rd ed.). Upper Saddle River, NJ: Merrill.

U.S. Department of Education (1998). *Twentieth annual report to Congress on the implementation of the*

7

Families of Children in Elementary Age Services

Kim Stoddard

Greg Valcante

Chapter Objectives _____

The specific focus of this chapter is to discuss the power of a family partnership for children with disabilities during the elementary years.

In this chapter we will

- Discuss the unique roles and responsibilities of families and teachers during the elementary years
- Analyze the impact of community and friends on the child's development
- Provide information on the importance of community and community agencies
- Discuss research on families from differing cultures
- Provide research-based programs that involve families with the school and community
- Discuss practical strategies for improving family conferences
- Provide insight to the teacher and family members on the many facets of developing an inclusive classroom
- Pose questions family members may ask in conferences
- List relevant family resources and materials on family research and practices
- Summarize important chapter themes

The phone call came during the winter holiday break. Katherine Geiger picked up the receiver and on the other end was twenty-one-year-old Milton Campbell. He was a former student of hers who was home on a brief leave from the military. He just wanted to let her know he was doing well and his mother suggested he call to say hello and to encourage her to "keep on teaching kids how to read." Milton had come to Katherine Geiger's classroom thirteen years ago as

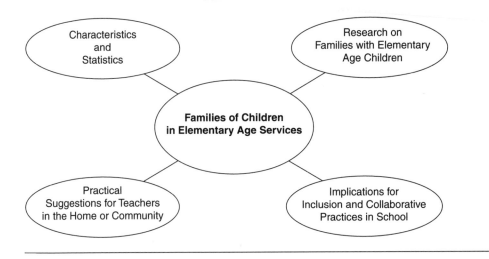

a third grader who could not read. He was often referred to the school office for numerous disruptions due to his frustration with his reading.

At the end of fifth grade, Milton was reading at his approximate grade level with very few referrals to the office. Milton's success was due to the team effort of his mother, his teacher, and Milton. Katherine Geiger followed the philosophy that the parents/guardians really know their child best and although she didn't always initially agree with Ms. Campbell's goals for Milton, she found that Ms. Campbell could usually sense what was best for Milton and knew when to push him and when to back off. Due to their strong team efforts Milton made tremendous progress throughout the next three years, enabling him to move to a consult level when entering middle school. Ms. Campbell and Milton kept in touch with Katherine Geiger as Milton moved through middle school, high school, and a two-year technical program. The effort and time it took for Ms. Campbell, Milton, and Ms. Geiger to develop a trusting relationship resulted in tremendous gains for Milton. The success and feedback Ms. Geiger received throughout Milton's growing years encouraged her to "keep on teaching kids how to read," no matter how challenging the task. Ms. Geiger was able to continually witness for thirteen years how a partnership between the family and home can be a powerful influence in the life of a student.

Characteristic and Statistics

The importance of the parents/guardians as the primary educator continues to be emphasized throughout the elementary years. When second- and third-grade children with learning disabilities were interviewed to determine their perspective on reading, the interviewers found the responses from children with learning disabilities to be similar to the responses of their peers without disabilities. When asked who taught them to read, the majority of students did not state that their kindergarten, first-grade, or special education teacher taught them to read. These students indicated that either their mother, aunt, or grandmother as the individual first responsible for teaching them to read (Stoddard, Hewitt, O'Connor, & Johnson, 1996).

Erickson describes this period of school age during which the psychosocial task of industry is the focus (Erickson, 1964). While the preschool years involved readiness skills and a strong emphasis on socialization, the elementary years' focus expands to academic skills and more time spent outside the home in organized sports and youth activities (Berry & Hardman, 1998). During this period of development the circle of friendship may begin to narrow for students with disabilities as barriers both physical and emotional are created due to the unique demands of extracurricular activities. New teachers should not assume that students are socializing with their peers without disabilities outside of school in extracurricular activities. In some cases the sports or youth activity may exclude the child with a more severe disability under the premise of safety concerns or lack of expertise on the part of the adult leaders. The child with a more severe disability may interact only with children without disabilities during the school day. For this reason the importance of inclusion and structured activities to promote inclusion are of paramount importance during the elementary school years. Building a community for all learners within the classroom has proved to be very effective in assisting the child with disabilities in becoming a part of the classroom (Stoddard & Hewitt, 1996). An activity to enhance the community of friends within a classroom is a simple strategy called a Circle of Friends (Perske, 1989). An example of a circle of friends can be found later in this chapter (see Box 7.1).

Service Delivery

It is important for new teachers to understand that certain decisions that are made during the elementary years are unique to this age level. For those parents/guardians whose children have been receiving services through early infant intervention programs, toddler programs, and prekindergarten programs, a decision must be made on where the child will receive services for the elementary years. During the preschool years, many programs are set up as more inclusive models within private preschools or run as self-contained programs within the public school setting or human resources setting. Parents/guardians must now decide if their child will receive the best services within their own zoned school. If the school indicates there are no services available for the child, the family member must decide whether to insist on those services at the home zoned school or allow the child to enroll at a school currently providing those services. In some cases the school providing the services might require a fifty-minute bus ride whereas the home zoned school is a short ten minutes away. Those parents wishing to enroll their child in their home zoned school must decide if they will be labeled as a "troublemaker" if they insist on services and must also determine whether they have the energy and knowledge to "push" the issue. The McNulty's story illustrates the dilemma many parents/guardians face when their child reaches kindergarten age.

Sam's Story

Five-year-old Sam McNulty had been receiving services for his severe disability since the age of four months. He had been diagnosed four months after birth with hololobar prosencephaly. At the age of five, Sam's current level of functioning was that of a one- to two-month-old. Sam needed several medications daily to control his body temperature and body functions. He received a shot of chloral hydrate to sleep at night and for his afternoon nap. Sam's feeding occurred through a g-tube and due to his sensitive digestive system he could be tube fed only while he slept. Sam had a pleasant personality, often smiled, and seemed to be happiest when surrounded by people and activity. Sam had been enrolled since age three within a self-contained classroom serving students with severe and profound disabilities at an elementary school approximately fifty minutes from his home. When his older brother Ian started kindergarten, Mr. and Mrs. McNulty decided that Ian would attend the same school to enable the brothers to stay together. The year progressed well, although Ian had less opportunity to make neighborhood friends due to the fact that he was attending a different school and spending an hour on the bus each day. After much discussion, the parents decided Ian would attend the zoned school five minutes from their house while Sam continued on the bus to the school with the severe and profound program. When Mr. and Ms. McNulty were asked why they did not ask the school system to provide services for Sam in their home zoned school, the parents replied that they were happy with the program at the other elementary school and things seemed to be going well for both their sons. They also were somewhat relieved that Sam had a place to attend in which he was accepted and people cared for him. They were not sure that the home zoned school would want the responsibility of a program for severe disabilities and if legally required to set up a program the parents were not sure if there would be such a strong commitment from the teachers and administrators as they felt at their current setting.

The decision for where a child in elementary school should receive services is not always so easily made as is illustrated in the McNulty case. Each family must decide what is best for their child and their situation. The McNulty's decision was effected by the relationship already established at the school where Sam had been attending since age three. Sam's need for services had been established almost since birth. However, the majority of children identified for special education services are identified during the elementary years.

The identification of a child for services during the elementary years may result in the same stages of grief as noted in Chapter 6 for parents of children with more severe disabilities. In Figure 7.1, Jadene Ransdell's Grief and Coping Cycle (1994) indicates how the perspective of the family member changes with time. As noted earlier, not all parents/guardians pass through each stage of grief nor do they necessarily pass through in a specific sequence. All parents have dreams for their children and even the acknowledgment of a mild disability can be difficult for some parents/guardians. The majority of children with disabilities receives services in resource programs during the elementary years. This picture may change as more services are provided for students within more inclusive environments.

Research on Families with Elementary Age Children

One of the primary roles of families is to raise children. It has been observed that while some do it very well and some not so well, most do it adequately (Risley, 1997). Researchers who study the families of children with disabilities have found that children with dis-

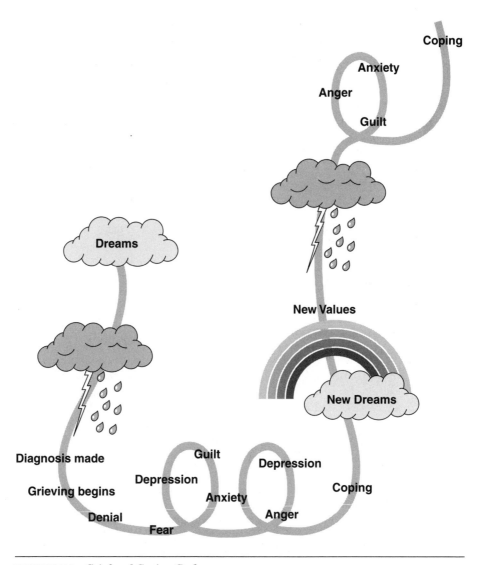

FIGURE 7.1   *Grief and Coping Cycle*

Source: Printed with permission of Jadene S. Ransdell, The Different Drummer, Inc. Copyright © 1992.

abilities can present significant challenges for families by making inordinate demands on the family's time, psychological well-being, relationships, finances, and freedom of movement (Brantlinger, 1991). However, new teachers have traditionally received little training in collaborating with families to create what Turnbull and Turnbull (1997) call reliable alliances for children. Batsche and Knoff (1994) note that the greatest obstacle to successful intervention for children with ADHD is the failure of families, educators, and health professionals to work together collaboratively.

Issues in Definition and Identification of the Child with Special Needs

Many families face serious challenges during the process of having their child identified and diagnosed with a disability. Some have been traumatized or misled by professionals and have become suspicious and untrusting before their child ever enters the doors of the elementary school. Others are still in the process of having their child assessed and diagnosed during the elementary school years. It is not uncommon to hear of families who were told "give her time" or "he'll grow out of it" or "you just need to be more consistent in your discipline," only to find later that their child had a disability and could have benefited from early intervention services if the disability had been identified. The logical progression of describing the child's symptoms, having cognitive strengths and needs evaluated, getting an appropriate diagnosis made, and beginning interventions has "rarely been the experience of most families with an autistic child" (Parks, 1983). For many families, by the time their child with a disability arrives at elementary school, they have been to see a large number of diagnosticians, have heard many different opinions, and have become disillusioned by the process. New teachers should be sensitive to families' negative experiences even before children enter elementary schools.

Challenges for Families

Just as there are many similarities and differences between children with and without disabilities, there are many similarities and differences between families who have a child with disabilities and those who do not. Just as each child is unique, each family is unique. Clearly, many families of children with disabilities have significantly more contact with professional care providers than families of typical children, including contacts in professionals' offices and having professionals into one's home.

Isolation.   Turnbull and Ruef (1996) found that the families they studied reported only minimal connection to community groups and activities. Because their children found many community settings crowded, confusing, and unpredictable, many families avoided becoming involved in clubs, organizations, and recreational activities. Additionally, families mentioned difficulties related to sustaining energy levels in the face of problem behaviors, busy schedules, and financial hardship. Sometimes the chronicity of dealing with a child's disability day after day becomes the greatest challenge for a family.

In a qualitative study, Cook (1996) looked at two families who have children with special needs and found that the children had significant effects on mothers, fathers, siblings, and on the marriage relationships in both cases. Both mothers felt that having a child with autism had changed their personal identities and made them stronger persons in the end, but had initially caused them to isolate. Both fathers also reported that their roles in the family were redefined with the arrival of a child with special needs. They felt that fathering a child with autism helped them to learn to give each child, including their typically developing children, more time and attention. Challenges for siblings included having differential expectations placed on them because of their sibling with special needs and having difficulty establishing a relationship with their sibling with special needs. Both families also reported that having a child with disabilities challenged, compromised, and strengthened their marriages. Accordingly, new teachers should note varied reactions to the child's impact on the family.

Problem Behaviors. Turnbull and Ruef (1996), interviewed seventeen families who have a child with mental retardation and problem behavior. They found that these families had acquired some successful approaches to dealing with the family member who exhibits problem behaviors. Included among these family adaptations and approaches were strategies for providing added structure for home routines. Families found that they were able to prevent occurrences of problem behavior by creating a more structured and predictable daily schedule. Families sacrificed the ability to make spur of the moment or spontaneous decisions to make simple changes in daily routine (e.g., deciding to go to a restaurant instead of eating dinner at home) that others take for granted. Families in this study also reported a need for more outside assistance in creating structure and in managing daily routines. Dunlap, Robbins, and Darrow (1994) found that some families have to deal with children's aggressive and destructive behavior that occurs quite frequently (more than once per day). The families in this study reported that the resource they most needed was "skill building," including both child and parents learning new skills. Relationships with siblings and extended family members are challenged by a child with mental retardation and problem behavior (Turnbull & Ruef, 1997). Furthermore, many parents report the absence of even one friendship for their children with problem behavior and exclusion from participating in preferred religious activities. Families found that teachers who had energy, enthusiasm, and a positive attitude; were open to change; took the time to get to know the children for who they really were; took a personal interest in each child; and went out of their way to do something for the family were the most helpful (Turnbull & Ruef, 1997).

When mothers of typically developing children were compared with mothers of children with intellectual disabilities (Harris & McHale, 1989), some striking differences were found in their activities. Mothers of children with intellectual disabilities spent significantly more time in both care giving and playing with their children as well as more total time in child-oriented activities. In fact, the amount of time these mothers needed to spend in "leisure" activities with their children who had intellectual disabilities became a problem area for them. Keeping their children busy, occupied, or entertained was found to be just as demanding and time consuming as tasks labeled "caregiving."

Research on Families from Differing Cultures

The very meaning of words such as "disability," "handicap," or "retardation" can be significantly different for peoples of differing cultures (Harry, 1992a). While some labels such as learning disability are often preferred by families over other labels such as mental retardation regardless of cultural background, different cultures may have stronger feelings about the terms for differing reasons. In a study of low-income Puerto Rican families, Harry (1992b) reported that these families believed that having their child called mentally retarded was equivalent to having the child called "loco" or "crazy." Parents of children who were classified as learning disabled believed that having to learn English as a second language was the source of their child's difficulties in school. Harry's study reminds new teachers that there is a great potential for cross-cultural misunderstandings in special education and that any system of deviance classification is based on the values and expectations of the society that creates it. If the families of minority, culturally different, and economically disadvantaged children are not given a voice and heard, teachers will lose invaluable input into the collaborative education process.

Similarly, African American parents have traditionally been relegated to passive consent givers in special education rather than active collaborators (Harry, 1992b). For low-income, minority parents to move beyond these roles, new roles such as parents as assessors, parents as presenters of reports, parents as policy makers, and parents as advocates and peer supports need to be developed. Perhaps one reason for parents' lack of participation in IEP meetings is that they have already learned that they are excluded during the assessment process. Furthermore, if parents attend conferences where their presence is not influential, why should they continue to attend?

Latino families of children with severe disabilities who are most in need of support may be least likely to receive it (Rueda & Martinez, 1992). Family training programs that included topics such as legal rights and procedures in special education, immigration and amnesty, instructional programs, and community resources have been successful in empowering families within Latino communities. Regardless of their cultural background, families who are informed and welcomed as collaborators by new teachers will be more able to participate in their child's education than those who are presumed to be unable or unwilling to collaborate with educators.

Teacher Attitudes and Behaviors

Several studies have found that active, skill-building, positive interventions that focus on solutions rather than problems are effective for reducing the stress and depression experienced by some families of children with severe disabilities (Singer, Irvin, & Hawkins, 1988; Nixon & Singer, 1993; Singer, Glang, Nixon, Cooley, Kerns, Williams, & Powers, 1994). In each case parents who participated in an active program of stress management training, cognitive therapy, or coping skills instruction fared better on measures of anxiety, depression, and guilt than did parents who were either on a waiting list for such interventions or who attended informational and emotional support groups. The researchers, in each case, discussed the important role that practice exercises, homework, and an emphasis on learning and applying specific skills played in the success of the interventions. Interventions that focused on unstructured discussions of problems and divulging feelings were less successful for helping families cope with their children with significant disabilities.

Heleen (1992) suggests that teachers have traditionally run one-shot, add-on programs for families that have ensured that involvement would be minimal and tangential. Instead he suggests that schools need to expand their vision of family and community involvement, build new kinds of "windows" and "doors" and develop new mindsets about families and schools. Heleen reminds new teachers that there is no such thing as a model family involvement program because each successful program must be individualized to meet the needs of the children and families it serves and the most important aspect of a successful program is its inclusiveness, especially of those families that have traditionally been difficult to reach. Many families will not come to the school or come only when absolutely necessary because of conflicting work schedules, shyness, fear of school activities, or negative histories with schools in general. Heleen recommends family–teacher action research teams to provide a structure for inquiry in areas of need and interest.

Unfortunately, many new teachers lack formal training (in preservice and in-service preparation) in working with families. They rely on experiences prior to elementary teaching (i.e., prior jobs), colleagues, interactions with parents as individuals (e.g., field trips, class parties), interactions with parents in groups (e.g., parent education programs), and community contacts (e.g., teaching assistants) as sources of knowledge for working with families (Allexsaht-Snider, 1995). Most of what teachers know about working with families has traditionally come from on-the-job training. Teachers generally have not had access to any written texts as resources for guiding their interactions and contacts with families.

School–Home Communication

The importance of the relationships that develop between families of children with disabilities and new teachers cannot be overemphasized. Teachers are generally the professionals with whom the family has the most frequent and most direct contact (Westling & Fox, 1995). New teachers can communicate with families in open, honest, and respectful ways. A daily log or journal which travels back and forth from home to school with the child is one common way to establish positive, ongoing communication (Westling & Fox, 1995). Both group and individual meetings with parents can be used to build collaboration and ensure cooperative relationships. For meetings to be successful, whether they are requested by the family member or the teacher, it is essential that the purpose of the meeting be made explicit, that sufficient time be allotted for all, and that all necessary parties attend. Meetings that are lacking in purpose, time, or participants are likely to be counterproductive and leave both parents and teachers feeling they have wasted their time. When dealing with upset or angry parents, it is important that novice teachers remain calm, listen carefully, and when complaints are exhausted ask if there are more. Teachers then summarize the family's concerns. They should try to reach agreement on a future course of action. Offers of help should not be demeaning or disempowering. Family support professionals have found that empowering families to make informed choices and decisions, solve their problems with support instead of having them solved for them and being permitted to reciprocate to help-givers are all important aspects for teachers' consideration. All parents have needs for information regarding their child's school program and progress just as teachers have needs for information from the family about the student's strengths and weaknesses. The extent of family involvement in the education of the child and the school program is as individual and unique as each child. While parent/guardian participation in the IEP process is mandated by federal law, the extent of involvement depends on the individual family's preferences, abilities, and competing priorities.

Implications for Inclusion and Collaborative Practices in School

Parents/guardians of children with disabilities face new and even more challenging decisions with the emphasis on full inclusion. As noted in the McNulty case, the parents decided to keep their child in a self-contained classroom in which only children with severe and profound disabilities were receiving services. The following case studies illustrate different facets new teachers can consider in making decisions for children with disabilities and their families. Bianco's case study demonstrates the powerful voice of children in communicating the needs of families.

BOX 7.1 • *Bianco's Story*

Family–Teacher Issues

Bianco Ciaco was a third-grade student with a moderate mentally disabling condition. Bianco was new to the school and the school district, having moved from out of state this past summer. Patrino Ciaco, her mother, wanted Bianco to continue in the general education classroom for fourth grade as she had the last four years in the other school district. Although Bianco was functioning at a first-grade level, Ms. Ciaco believed the social skills and language models Bianco would pick up in the general education classroom were very beneficial to her daughter's development.

When enrolling her daughter in school Ms. Ciaco was told by the principal of the school and the special education supervisor that her daughter would receive the best services within a self-contained classroom or self-contained school for children with mentally disabling conditions rather than a general education classroom. The principal, Mr. Jonas, candidly stated that in discussing with the teachers the possible class placements for her daughter Bianco, all the fourth-grade teachers indicated they could not handle a child with Bianco's disability. Ms. Ciaco was devastated to believe that no one wanted her daughter in their class. She was further dismayed that these teachers looked at her daughter as a disability. She realized that these teachers didn't see a child with a heart-warming personality and hard working attitude; they saw a child that they couldn't teach like the other children and who wouldn't learn all of the required fourth-grade curriculum.

Collaborative Orientations and Responsive Practices

Ms. Ciaco believed that if the teachers could see Bianco as a child first rather than a disability they might just change their minds and be willing to accept Bianco in one of their classrooms. She set up another conference with all six of the fourth-grade teachers, the principal of the school, her daughter Bianco, her oldest daughter, Katrina, who was 14, and herself. She brought refreshments to the meeting and asked them to listen to her story and help her decide how best to meet Bianco's needs. At the conference she first had Bianco introduce herself and talk about her teachers that she had for the previous four years, what she felt were the most memorable events from school, how she felt after moving to a new state and coming to a new school. As Bianco talked, Ms. Ciaco could see the tension in the teachers' faces relax. Although Bianco's speech was not always clear, the teachers were comfortably listening to a little girl who was excited and very scared about being in a new place. They listened to her memorable events that always included the involvement of a teacher or a friend she made at school. It was clear from Bianco's comments that school was a very important place of learning and socializing for her. Ms. Ciaco asked Bianco to wait in the next room and she asked Katrina to talk about Bianco's life at school and home.

Katrina spoke with love for her sister but also talked a little bit about sibling rivalry, the frustration of sharing a room, and the fact that Bianco never leaves her alone and always wants to borrow her clothes even though they would never fit Bianco. The teachers laughed with Katrina as she shared these stories because all of them could appreciate the frustrations of living with a younger sibling. The room became much more quiet as she talked about the heartbreaking stories of Bianco being made fun of in their neighborhood and how Bianco was not wanted in the Sunday school or in the after-school soccer program because the leaders said Bianco was too low functionally for the other children in the group and they didn't know how to handle her. Katrina's frustration with the situation was obvious when she asked, if the adults wouldn't give her sister a chance, how would the kids ever give her a chance? Katrina ended her talk by explaining how Bianco had a tough time when they first enrolled in one of their schools; the children did make fun of Bianco in second grade, but the teacher set up a Circle of Friends for Bianco and had Ms. Ciaco come in and provide the More Alike than Different training to the entire class. The children in the second-grade class did seem to understand Bianco a little bit better and Katrina felt it was due to her mom's talk and the Circle of Friends. Ms. Ciaco added that the Circle of Friends continued in third grade and Bianco's friendships were maintained throughout the year. She smiled as she told the teachers how Bianco was invited to several birthday parties this last year. This was one of the reasons for their fears about moving to a new state and a new school. All the progress that had been made these past three years could be undone in such a short time. Ms. Ciaco asked that Katrina leave and wait with Bianco in the other room.

Ms. Ciaco then shared a brief scrapbook of Bianco's. She showed her baby pictures and pictures of the family celebrating birthdays, fourth of July, and other special events. She also showed work products of Bianco's. She talked about Bianco's strengths and why she wanted Bianco in the general education classroom. She explained to the teachers that she realized Bianco would not follow an academic track into middle or high school. However, she wanted Bianco to stretch as far as she could and Ms. Ciaco saw that the students in the general education class seemed to encourage Bianco to try her best and achieve beyond everyone's expectations. Ms. Ciaco asked the teachers if they had any questions. She also asked them to please reconsider their decision about accepting Bianco at their school and that she would be willing to work with the teachers in whatever capacity she could. She concluded by asking Mr. Jonas if a teacher who accepted Bianco would have his or her progress as a teacher judged based on whether Bianco finished the year on grade level. Mr. Jonas assured the teachers that progress would need to be made as documented on the IEP, not as measured by the standards for fourth grade.

Ms. Ciaco received a call from Mr. Jonas the day after the conference. He reported that after the conference, five of the six teachers came to him and asked if Bianco could be in their class for the next year. Mr. Jonas thanked Ms. Ciaco for taking the time to talk to the teachers and to open the eyes of the teachers to enable them to see a child first rather than a disability.

When Ms. Ciaco left the conference room she was not sure what would happen. The teachers seemed to relax once Bianco began talking and it was obvious through their body language that they were listening. Ms. Ciaco also knew that she had not come in demanding certain services, although she had the legal right to demand these services. She came in with an attitude that she was looking out for Bianco's best interest and she asked the teachers to help her make that decision. She set up a comfortable atmosphere by offering refreshments during the meeting. But most important, she allowed her daughters to show the teachers that they are

(continued)

BOX 7.1 • Continued

a family just like other families and they want what all families want. The topics of conversation, including Bianco's highlights of past years and Katrina's discussion on sibling rivalry, and the family pictures enabled the teachers to relate the Ciacos' life experience to their own life experiences. The teachers were further encouraged and felt some sense of control and support from administration when it was clear that their decision was voluntary and that they would not be held responsible for Bianco reaching mastery on the fourth-grade curriculum.

Points to Remember
As in Bianco's family situation, new teachers can learn much from family experiences. Examples include the following:

- Consciously make an effort to see the child first rather than the disability.
- Awareness of body language is critical; 82 percent of communication is nonverbal.
- Set up a comfortable atmosphere for teacher-family conferences; be aware of lighting, room arrangement, room temperature, and include refreshments if possible.
- Voluntary participation of a general education teacher results in a higher percentage of success for the child with the disability.
- Principal/administrative support is a critical component for success.
- Implementing programs such as More Alike than Different enables all students to understand disabilities better.
- Implementing strategies such as a Circle of Friends assists with developing an inclusive community within the classroom.

In the next case study, a teacher realizes how judgmental her perspective had been despite her best efforts.

Donna's Story

Donna had been teaching children in special education for fifteen years. She was considered one of the best throughout her many years teaching and was looked up to by the other teachers on the staff and within the school district due to not only her longevity in the field but also her ability to maintain a positive spirit teaching in a school considered to be at risk due to the fact that many of the children came from families living below the poverty level and with a high percentage of these families headed by single mothers. Donna was nominated for Teacher of the Year two times and received outstanding evaluations on a yearly basis. Donna involved herself in the Council for Exceptional Children at the professional level and attended most yearly state meetings for the group. She continued to attend graduate school working on an advanced degree in special education with certification in administration and supervision while teaching full time.

This past summer Donna was asked by the school district to become the assistant principal for her elementary school of 750 students due to her outstanding leadership abilities and proven track record. She readily accepted the challenge because she knew that as an administrator at this school she could ensure that her students in special education were given an equal opportunity for learning.

Donna believed that the children in her school came to school at a disadvantage. Donna often purchased shoes, jackets, and school supplies for many of the children. She believed that their misbehavior was often the result of too little sleep, poor diet, and lack of structure at home. She believed that if the home life of the children she taught was more structured and had some consistency throughout the preschool and elementary years there would be quite a reduction in the number of children identified as emotionally disabled. Donna felt sorry for the parents and guardians of the students she taught, but she believed that if these adults focused more on their children and less on themselves the children would be so much farther along in their development.

She had held this view for the last fifteen years. Due to the personal problems of her brother and sister-in-law, Donna was able to finally put her own beliefs about child care into action. Although her brother and his wife worked hard at handling their problems, they needed outside counseling and were unable to care for their two elementary age boys. After a family conference it was decided that Donna would be the best temporary guardian for the boys due to her background in special education and the fact that she had no other children.

Donna set up a warm, loving, and consistent home life for the boys. Their structured home schedule included daily responsibilities for the boys along with points earned for complying with requests and consequences for noncompliance. In addition, she set both of them up for weekly counseling sessions to help them adjust to the separation from their parents. Soccer and baseball were the sports the boys enjoyed, so both were able to participate in these activities after school. Each evening dinner was eaten at 6:00 P.M. and the three discussed the events of the day. Bedtime was scheduled for 8:30, with a story read aloud until 9:00 P.M. Donna believed she was providing the necessary structure and love to reassure and guide the boys during the important elementary years of development. She only wished the parents and guardians of her students felt the same sense of responsibility in setting up their home lives.

The first two weeks with the boys were like clockwork. The boys were excited to be with their aunt and, as Donna had assumed, the boys needed and wanted the structure she provided. However, things began to unravel after three weeks. Allan's teacher called her at the school where she was now assistant principal. The principal asked Donna to pick up her nephew because he was fighting, cursing, and could not be subdued by the teacher, guidance counselor, or school principal. Donna had an important faculty meeting that afternoon in which she was to give an update on the school improvement plan. She had no choice but to leave her school and pick up her nephew. Someone had to step in for Donna to run the faculty meeting. She decided to provide an appropriate consequence at home and knew that with her behavior management program in place Allan's behavior would turn around.

Things did not turn around. Her nephew continued to have problems, and Donna was called almost daily at her school for a phone call or to pick Allan up due to his disruptive behavior. When she took Allan to counseling she explained the unfortunate situation to the therapist. Donna felt like a failure as a parent. She also sensed that the teachers and principal at Allan's school along with the therapist felt that Donna was not being consistent enough at home. They questioned her about the schedule at home; Was there a consequence for misbehavior? They asked if Allan took his medication regularly and if he had a routine schedule. She could not understand why her behavior management plan that worked so well with her students at school was not working with her nephew at home. She knew how to manage and care for students with emotional disabilities and she was not being successful. On many of the nights when she cried herself to sleep she also was upset that the educators and therapist would judge her so harshly. She realized they never actually said that she was doing a bad job—it was the type of questions they asked and what was left unsaid. No one ever said, "I know this is tough" or "You're doing the best you can," or "How can we help?"

Points to Remember
Donna learned valuable information that new teachers should consider. These include the following points:

- Carefully choose the words to explain a situation; watch judgmental tones.
- Parents or guardians are doing the best they can within their own circumstances.

BOX 7.2

Family–Teacher Issues
Donna realized that she had been just like these professionals in her past dealings with parents and guardians. When Donna called the parents/guardians of her students at home or work, she expected them to respond immediately or come to school if necessary. When they didn't come she also judged them as too busy to care; she never thought about the fact that there might be repercussions from their job if they left in the middle of the day or that they might even lose their job for leaving too many times or receiving too many phone calls at work. As a teacher she often felt that the parents were not really doing the best they could under their particular circumstances. Now she saw herself as a professional in the field trying to help her own family member be successful, and she was at the end of her rope. She understood much more clearly how a parent or guardian might be doing all that they are physically and emotionally capable of doing and the child's behavior could still continue to be a difficult challenge.

Collaborative Orientations and Responsive Practices
Donna wished she could go back through the last fifteen years and take back all those judgmental thoughts she had about certain parents/guardians and wished she could say all those needed words of encouragement. She changed her philosophical orientation throughout the trying months with her nephew. She vowed that when she worked with parents she was going to believe the parents/guardians were doing the best they could under their own circumstances She also decided that in every parent/guardian conference or phone call she would always add some words of encouragement to the parent/guardian, not in a "telling" or judgmental tone but to show the family member that she understood just a little bit what the parent was going through on a daily basis.

- Parents/guardians must feel a sense of warmth and caring in their dialogue with school personnel.
- Be aware that interrupting a parent/guardian at work could affect the income for the family.
- Parents/guardians need to hear words of encouragement about their efforts.

Practical Suggestions for Teachers in the Home or Community

The importance of building a bridge between home and community is paramount for success for the elementary-age child. The following case studies demonstrate the important components to building a bridge that allows open communication and effective planning.

Raymond's Story

Karen Ballou was a recent graduate from the university with two years' experience teaching children with mild to moderate disabilities in a local elementary school. The school year was drawing to a close and Ms. Ballou had scheduled a conference with Raymond Davison's mother to update his IEP and talk about his upcoming year in fifth grade. Raymond was a fourth grader identified as mildly mentally disabled. Raymond had learn to write his name and a few simple words but continued to struggle with writing complete sentences on a word processor. He had accomplished much this year and was reading at the kindergarten/first-grade level. He was also able to complete simple addition and subtraction facts.

Ms. Davison began the conference by indicating that she would like the focus for fifth grade to be on the skills necessary to enable Raymond to be successful academically in middle school. She noticed that he was reading only at a first-grade level and would never be ready for middle school unless there was a stronger push academically, specifically in language arts and mathematics. Ms. Ballou was taken aback by the mother's comments because Karen thought Ms. Davison understood that Raymond was not functioning on a regular academic track, and Ms. Ballou believed Raymond needed to focus more on functional skills than on a strong academic component.

Ms. Ballou began the conference by allowing Ms. Davison to talk about what she believed should be the objectives for Raymond's new IEP. Karen listened intently, took notes, withheld her own personal comments, and did not pass judgment on Ms. Davison's views. When Ms. Davison finished her perspective, Ms. Ballou began to talk about Raymond's progress and shared documentation of this progress based on portfolio information she had gathered this past year. The portfolio contained written samples of his handwriting and sentence writing, math worksheets Raymond had completed, computer-generated attempts at stories, and a tape recording of his oral reading. Karen also included documentation of his mastery of functional skills such as counting money, use of a calculator, setting a table, preparing a simple meal, riding the transit system, and eating in a restaurant. Most of these skills were documented through a skills checklist and pictures within a portfolio.

After Ms. Ballou shared the progress she had documented for Raymond she asked Ms. Davison how she felt about his progress and where Ms. Davison believed the focus should be for Raymond for next year. Ms. Davison again indicated her fears about Raymond not being ready for middle school academically. Although Ms. Ballou felt that Ms. Davison was in denial about Raymond's abilities and future progress, she also believed that parents know their children best and the teacher should not be the one to determine the goals for the student, but that it is a joint decision. Karen did share with Ms. Davison that she understood where Ms. Davison would like Raymond to be progressing and they could work toward that goal. Karen then went on to add that she thought it would be helpful to take the assessment data from the portfolio and make new objectives with that data so there would be documentation of progress. Ms. Ballou never stated her beliefs about Raymond's academic limitations. It would serve no productive purpose and she knew from past experience that stating academic limitations sometimes sets limitations.

Through the dialogue both parent and teacher were able to reach common ground on the goals for Raymond. Karen at one time had thought it was important that parents had a true (according to the teacher) understanding of the disability and resulting prognosis for the future. She soon realized that with time the prognosis will become evident and as a teacher she should not put limitations on any child. She also realized that a prognosis is never guaranteed, and parents of children with disabilities, just as all parents/guardians, should pursue their dreams. The adjustments will come with time and the reality of the situation.

Ms. Ballou and Ms. Davison wrote new goals based on the results of last year's portfolio assessment. Ms. Ballou assured Ms. Davison that she would keep in mind the ultimate goal for Raymond and continue to work toward that goal this next year.

Points to Remember
Ms. Ballou gained valuable insights from her work with Ms. Davison. These insights are important to novice teachers.

- Allow the parents/guardians to share their perspective first in the development of the learning plan of the IEP.
- Take written notes on parents' comments, ideas, concerns, and insights.
- Provide written documentation (portfolio, other assessment tools) to show academic and behavioral progress.
- Always keep in mind that families really do know their children best.
- Set goals jointly with parents/guardians based on documentable progress.
- Do not set limitations on a child's prognosis; time will determine the progress.
- Allow parents/guardians of children with disabilities to have dreams for their children, just as all parents have dreams for their children.
- Time and development of the child will determine the future; do not forecast the child's progress to the parents (just like weather forecasts, they are often wrong).

John's Story

John Hess was an elementary school student who had been identified as developmentally delayed by his schools and by medical professionals. Christina Martinez had been his teacher for the past two years and had developed a positive, collaborative relationship with John's family based on trust and mutual respect. As he approached his sixth birthday, it became time for his educational and psychological re-evaluation. Part of the re-evaluation process was to determine his eligibility for specific services that were available to students in specific disability categories. The developmental delay category would no longer be available to John because of his age. John's family informed Christina and the evaluation team that he had received a diagnosis of autism from his neurologist and that they were certain from the abilities he demonstrated at home and in the community that his autism did not include intellectual impairment. They strongly believed that he was not intellectually disabled, although his communication impairment affected his performance on standardized tests, especially verbal intelligence tests. John's parents did not want their son labeled as mentally disabled. Christina, an experienced teacher who was quite skilled at working with families, knew there were several things she could do to facilitate a smooth transition for John and his family, so she arranged to meet with Mr. and Mrs. Hess.

At the start of the meeting Christina reviewed the re-evaluation process with John's parents. She listened to their hopes and dreams about John's future and their concerns about his movement to a new class. Christina wrote down Mr. and Mrs. Hess's ideas for how they would like the reevaluation to proceed. The family felt it would be necessary for the school psychologist to get to know John and develop a rapport with him prior to administering any standardized tests. They wanted John to be evaluated with nonverbal measures of intelligence as much as possible and they wanted to know about their options for future models of service delivery for John. Christina offered to have the school psychologist call John's parents to set up a meeting. She arranged for Mr. and Mrs. Hess to visit potential classrooms and accompanied them on their visits. Christina assured John's parents that she would thoroughly and accurately document John's progress as part of the re-evaluation. At the conclusion of the meeting, Christina summarized the discussions and action plans agreed upon.

Points to Remember
Christina practiced effective behaviors that demonstrated her commitment to John's family. These behaviors can be demonstrated by novice teachers as well.

- Show that you are attentive to parents by listening to their concerns and writing down what they say.
- Use face-to-face meetings with sufficient time allotted for dialog help to build collaboration.
- Provide parents with the jargon-free information they need to make decisions and to participate on their child's educational team.
- Facilitate parents' requests to share information with other professionals (school psychologist) and learn more for themselves (visiting classrooms), thereby empowering the family.
- Document your meetings with parents and summarize decisions reached.

Carla's Story

Carla Hill was a ten-year-old girl with significant mental disabilities. She lived with her grandparents and attended a church in the community with them. Her teacher, Mr. Valentine, received a call one day from a church minister who was looking for help with Carla.

The minister explained that Carla had wandered off from her grandparents during church services for the past two Sundays and was found in a video arcade two doors down the street from the church each time. Being somewhat elderly, Carla's grandparents had some difficulty managing her behavior. The minister also mentioned that he was having difficulty including Carla in the church youth group and did not know how to promote her participation in social and educational activities. Mr. Valentine offered to meet with the minister along with Carla and her grandparents at the church one evening. At the meeting, Mr. Valentine shared some suggestions for Carla's grandparents to prevent her from wandering from church during Sunday services, such as seating her between them, and offered to visit the youth group on the following evening. After observing Carla in the youth group, Mr. Valentine met with the minister and with the typically developing youth to discuss using the principles of partial participation to engage Carla in activities and developing a "buddy system" to facilitate her peer support in the activities. One year later, Mr. Valentine received another call from the minister to let him know that Carla had been very successful in the youth group, had been very well received by the other children, and had made some important social connections. The minister thanked Mr. Valentine for his two evenings at the church and remarked that the other children had profited by having Carla as a member of their group.

Points to Remember

Carla Hill and her grandparents provided Mr. Valentine valuable knowledge that assisted Mr. Valentine's family skills and dispositions. New teachers can put into practice the following points:

- Children with disabilities and their families may be excluded from typical community organizations and activities because of the organizations' lack of experience with persons with disabilities. Remember to stress inclusion and experience for persons with disabilities and their families.
- Teachers can have a positive impact on the community connections of the children they teach.
- Providing information to families and community members can help facilitate the inclusion of children with disabilities into typical extra-school environments and activities.
- Taking a little extra time outside of the school day schedule to meet with families and community members can pay off in great dividends for the child, family, and community.

Family Member Questions

Family conferences are a valuable component in the bridge between home and elementary school. Conferences should be held a minimum of three times per year and may be held as often as once a week, depending on the needs of the student. The topics for conferences vary, but to increase the effectiveness of a conference it may be effective to send home a note or planning form that asks parents/guardians for their input for the conference and any concerns or items that need to be discussed. The form may include questions such as

"What do you see as your child's strengths?" or "What are your greatest concerns regarding your child's progress?" This enables the teacher to plan accordingly and to have all needed documentation readily available if needed. The following are questions that often arise. However, there is no one right answer. It is important for new teachers to remember the goals for the children they are teaching and how much progress is being made toward those goals.

- *My child is struggling so much with academics—should I tell him that he will have to quit after-school sports until his grades improve?* All children need to feel successful in some arena during the day. If teachers know the child is feeling success in after-school sports, then allow him to continue. Perhaps cutting down the number of practices might help. The child with the learning disability is not failing on purpose in the elementary years, so punishing the child by taking away something in which he finds success can do more damage than good.
- *I heard facilitative communication (or any strategy that has an unproven research base) is effective. I would like to try it with my child; what do you think?* The use of facilitative communication (or any strategy that has an unproven research base) has not been found to be effective. It might be wise for teachers and parents to research this method more carefully and get back together in three weeks to look at the research and then talk about a plan.
- *Do you think my child will be able to receive a regular diploma? It will just break my heart if she doesn't graduate from high school and go on to college.* Teachers can reply, "I think we cannot yet determine how far your child will advance. I think we need to look at what her strengths are and in which areas she needs improvement. We also need to remember that she can graduate from high school with a special diploma and we want to keep all options open. All students do not go to college, and there are many useful, exciting, and rewarding careers that can be accomplished without a college diploma."
- *I don't know whether to tell my children, my relatives, and the peers in my child's class about his disability.* An appropriate response might be, "The choice is really yours. It might be helpful to talk to other parents of children with this disability; let me find a resource connection. You might also want to read a little more about the disability, which would help in your discussion with others. Let me see if I can round up some resource materials. You do not need to feel embarrassed about having a child with a disability. It might help increase the understanding and acceptance of your child by others if they are more knowledgeable."
- *I am having a lot of trouble in my personal life and just need someone to talk to about my problems. Since you understand my situation so well, perhaps you can help.* The new teacher might say, "I am so sorry about your situation. It is helpful to let me know that things might be stressful for your child in the classroom at this time. I would be happy to put you in touch with the guidance counselor. I am not a counselor but I'm sure one can help you."

In all discussions with parents/guardians, new teachers should remember that the parent/guardian knows their child best. In addition, the focus for problem solving should follow the belief that the group makes decisions based on what's best for the child and family, not what's most convenient for the teacher or other professionals who interact with the child. It is also important that new teachers document notes and follow through on all suggestions and plans.

Family Resources and Services

Family resources and services at the elementary level include the following:

ORGANIZATIONS

National Information Center for Children and Youth with Disabilities (NICHY)
P.O. Box 1492
Washington DC 20013-1492
1-800-695-0285 (Voice/TT)
1-202-884-8200 (Voice/TT)
1-202-884-8441 (Fax)
e-mail: nichy@capcon.net
www.aed.org/nichy

NICHY is an information clearinghouse that provides free information on disabilities and disability-related issues. Children and youth ages birth through twenty-two are the focus. Publishes State Resource Sheets available for each state and U.S. Territory which provide a summary of many of the services offered in each state and link individuals to a variety of resources. Also publishes Disability Fact Sheets which provide a succinct, easy to read overview of each disability listed in IDEA as well as information on other disabilities. Fact Sheets provide a brief introduction to the disability as well as references and organizations for further inquiry.

Schools Are For Everyone (SAFE)
P.O. Box 583
Syracuse, N.Y. 13210

Beach Center on Families and Disability
3111 Haworth Hall
The University of Kansas
Lawrence, KS 66045-7516

785-864-7600
e-mail: Beach@dole.lsi.ukans.edu
www.lsi.ukans.edu/beach/beachhp.htm

The Beach Center actively involves parents in planning, conducting and reviewing research, providing training in areas of parent to parent mutual support, friendships, empowerment, transition planning, assistive technology procurement, fathers, family-centered service delivery, early childhood programs, family support policy, and abuse and neglect of children with disabilities.

Autism Society of America (ASA)
7910 Woodmont Avenue, #650
Bethesda, MD 20814
(301) 657-0881
(800) 3AUTISM

Arc of the U.S.
500 E. Border St., #300
Arlington, TX 76010
(800) 433-5255
(800) 277-0553 (TTY)
(817) 277-3491 (Fax)

National Parent to Parent Support and Information System
P.O. Box 907
Blue Ridge, GA 30513
(800) 651-1151

Provides information and referral services to individuals with disabilities and their families through its national database service that facilitates one-to-one matches between parents who have children with rare disabilities.

Helen Keller National Center for Deaf-Blind Youths and Adults (HKNC)
Technical Assistance Center
111 Middle Neck Road,
Sands Point, NY 11050
(516) 944-8900
(516) 944-8637 (TTY)
(516) 944-7302 (Fax)

National Association of Protection and Advocacy Systems
900 Second Street, N.E., #211
Washington, DC 20002
(202) 408-9514
(202) 408-9520 (Fax)

National Parent Network on Disabilities
1727 King Street, Suite 305
Alexandria, VA 22314
(703) 684-6763 (V/TTY)
(703) 836-1232 (Fax)

Children and Adults with Attention Deficit Disorder (CHADD)
499 N.W. 70th Avenue, Suite 101
Plantation, FL 33317
(800) 233-4050
(305) 587-4599 (Fax)
www.chadd.org/

United Cerebral Palsy Associations, Inc.
1660 L St., NW, Suite 700
Washington, DC 20036-5603
(800) 872-5827
(202) 842-3519 (Fax)
www.UCPA.ORG

PUBLICATIONS

Families and Disability Newsletter

Published three times a year by the Beach Center on Families and Disability at the University of Kansas. There is no subscription charge. Funding is provided by the National Institute on Disability and Rehabilitation Research (NIDRR), U.S. Department of Education, Office of Special Education and Rehabilitative Services. Publications include research results published by University of Kansas researchers.

Beach Center on Families and Disability
3111 Haworth
The University of Kansas
Lawrence, KS 66045-7516
(785) 864-7600 (V, TTD)
(785) 864-7605 (Fax)
e-mail: Beach@dole.lsi.ukans.edu

Exceptional Parent
Published twelve times per year by Psy-Ed Corp.
555 Kindermack Rd.
Oradell, NJ 07649
www.eparent.com

Editorial mission includes energizing parents and professionals and sharing ideas and experiences so parents, professionals, people with disabilities, and other advocates can learn from one another and better collaborate to serve all children and families.

Uncommon Fathers: Reflections on Raising a Child With a Disability
Donald J. Meyer, Editor
Woodbine House, Inc.
6510 Bells Mill Rd.,
Bethesda, MD 20817
(800) 843-7323

A collection of nineteen personal accounts, essays, and case studies of fathers and their children with disabilities written by the fathers.

The 3 R's for Special Education: Rights, Resources, Results
Paul H. Brookes Publishing Company
P.O. Box 10624
Baltimore, MD 21285-0624

A guide for parents and a tool for educators, this videocassette provides information and advice for special educators who need answers to the questions parents ask.

Negotiating the Special Education Maze: A Guide for Parents and Teachers
By Winefred Anderson, Stephen Chitwood, and Deidre Hayden

This text explains all phases of the special education process in simple language. It also shows parents how to advocate for their child and maintain collaborative relationships with educators and other professionals.

The Council for Exceptional Children
P.O. Box 79026, Dept. K7082
Baltimore, MD 21279-0026
(888) CEC-SPED
(703) 264-9494 (Fax)
e-mail: cecpubs@cec.sped.org

Families, Professionals, and Exceptionality: A Special Partnership
by Ann P. Turnbull and H. Rutherford Turnbull, III
Merrill-Prentice Hall
Columbus, Ohio 43216

A comprehensive source of information on family/professional collaboration addressing all types of disabilities and the wide diversity of families.

Summary

This chapter focused on issues and needs of families of children in elementary age services. The following points were emphasized:

- During the elementary years the child's opportunities for social situations may expand or narrow, depending on the severity of the disability and planning on the part of the family members, teacher, and community agencies.
- The highest percentage of children identified for services for students with disabilities occurs during the elementary years.
- There are many similarities and differences between families who have a child with disabilities and those who do not.
- Families report that having a child with a disability challenges, compromises, and strengthens marriages.
- Many parents report the absence of even one friendship for their children with problem behavior.
- Families report that teachers who are open to change, have energy, enthusiasm, a positive attitude, take a personal interest in the child, and go out of their way to do something for the family are most helpful.
- There is a great potential for cross-cultural misunderstanding in special education due to the fact that the classification system is based on the values of the society that created it.

- There is no such thing as a model family involvement program because each successful program must be individualized to meet the needs of the children and family it serves.
- Empowering families to make informed choices and decisions, solve their problems with support instead of having them solved for them, and being permitted to reciprocate to help-givers are important aspects of family support.
- Teachers need to allow families of children with disabilities to have dreams for their children just as all families have dreams for their children.
- Teachers should not forecast a child's prognosis; time and development will determine the future.
- Teachers can take a little extra time outside of the school day schedule to meet with families and community members. This will pay off in great dividends for the child, family, and community.

There are many facets of the home–school partnership for children with disabilities during the elementary years. During this developmental period the needs of the child expand to include a stronger emphasis on academic skills and social skills. Challenges for the child in the academic and social domain vary depending on the severity of the disability. One challenge a family may face during this period includes a decision about what is the best service delivery model for their child when entering kindergarten if previously in a special education program. The elementary years are when the highest percentage of children are identified as needing services for special education, thus for many families it is the time for the child to be first identified for services for a disability. The realization that their child has a disability may result in various stages of the grief cycle for parents or guardians.

The elementary years require the development and planning of a reliable alliance between the family and school. The planning between members of the family, school, and community affects the acceptance and involvement of the child in the classroom and in extracurricular activities. There is no one family involvement program that will effectively meet the needs of all families, thus the planning must be unique to the needs of each family. The needs of families also may vary based on differing cultures. As Harry (1992) states, the input of families who are culturally different is invaluable to the collaborative education process.

Novice teachers who are collaborative and responsive in their way of working will be needed for true family–school partnerships to be developed. These professionals must possess and practice effective communication and problem solving skills. In addition, they must be able to assist families in accessing the necessary resources that are established within the local community and within the profession. The power of the family–school partnership at the elementary level will be realized when family members and members of the school work to develop a collaborative team whose ultimate goal is to meet the needs of the child within that family.

References

Allexsaht-Snider, M. (1995). Teachers' perspectives on their work with families in a bilingual community. *Journal of Research in Childhood Education, 9* (2), 85–95.

Batsche, G. M., & Knoff, H. M. (1994). Children with attention deficit hyperactive disorder: A research review with assessment and intervention implications for students and families. *Special Services in the Schools 9* (1), 69–95.

Berry, J. O., & Hardman, M. L. (1998). *Lifespan perspectives on the family and disability.* Boston, Mass.: Allyn & Bacon.

Brantlinger, E. (1991). Home-school partnerships that benefit children with special needs. *Elementary School Journal, 91,* 249–259.

Cook, D. G. (1996). The impact of having a child with autism. *Developmental Disabilities, Special Interest Newsletter American Occupational Therapy Association, Inc., 19* (2), 1–4.

Dunlap, G., Robbins, F. R., & Darrow, M. A. (1994). Parents' reports of their children's challenging behaviors: Results of a statewide survey. *Mental Retardation, 32,* 206–212.

Erickson, E. H. (1963). Childhood and society (2nd ed). New York: Norton.

Heleen, O. (1992). Is your school family friendly? *Principal, 72* (2), 5–8.

Harris, V. S., & McHale, S. M. (1989). Family life problems, daily caregiving activities, and the psychological well-being of mothers of mentally retarded children. *American Journal of Mental Retardation, 94,* 231–239.

Harry, B. (1992a). Making sense of disability: Low-income Puerto Rican parents' theories of the problem. *Exceptional Children, 59,* 27–40.

Harry, B. (1992b). Restructuring the participation of African-American parents in special education. *Exceptional Children, 59,* 123–131

Nixon, C. D., & Singer, G. S. (1993). Group cognitive-behavioral treatment for excessive parental self-blame and guilt. *American Journal on Mental Retardation, 97,* 665–672.

Parks, S. L. (1983). Psychometric instruments available for the assessment of autistic children. *Journal of Autism and Developmental Disabilities, 13,* 255–267.

Ransdell, J. (1994). *Grief and Coping Cycle.* JULE Parent Services. Pinellas County School Board, Largo, Florida.

Perske, R. (1989). *Circle of friends.* Nashville: Abingdon Press.

Rueda, R., & Martinez, I. (1992). Fiesta educativa: One community's approach to parent/guardian training in developmental disabilities for Latino families. *Journal of the Association for Persons with Severe Handicaps, 17,* 95–103.

Singer, G. H. S., Irvin, L. K., & Hawkins, N. (1988). Stress management training for parents of children with severer handicaps. *Mental Retardation, 26,* 269–277.

Singer, G. H. S., Glang, A., Nixon, C., Cooley, E., Kerns, K. A., Williams, D., Powers, L. E. (1994). A comparison of two psychosocial interventions for parents of children with acquired brain injury: An exploratory study. *Journal of Head Trauma Rehabilitation, 94* (4), 38–49.

Stoddard, K., & Hewitt, M. (1996). Teacher for all children program. Innovation through collaboration: Emerging practices in Florida. Presented at the CSPD meeting, St. Pete Beach, FL.

Stoddard, K., Hewitt, M., O'Connor, D., & Johnson, L. (1997). Looking at students' perceptions concerning inclusive practices. Paper presented at the meeting of the National Council for Exceptional Children, Salt Lake City, UT.

Turnbull, A. P., & Ruef, M. (1996). Family perspectives on problem behavior. *Mental Retardation, 34,* 280–293.

Turnbull, A. P., & Ruef, M. (1997). Family perspectives on inclusive lifestyle issues for people with problem behavior. *Exceptional Children, 63,* 211–227.

Turnbull, A. P., & Turnbull H. R. III. (1997). *Families, professionals, and exceptionality: A special partnership.* Upper Saddle River, NJ: Merrill-Prentice Hall.

Westling, D. L., & Fox, L. (1995). *Teaching students with severe disabilities.* Columbus, Ohio: Merrill.

8

Working with Families of Adolescents

Kate Algozzine

Dorothy J. O'Shea

Bob Algozzine

Chapter Objectives

In this chapter we will

- Describe typical and special needs of adolescents and implications for parents' child-rearing techniques
- Examine life in middle and high schools as it relates to students with disabilities and their families
- Provide practical teacher suggestions for working with parents toward a successful inclusion experience in classrooms and schools
- Describe how teachers can work collaboratively with parents in helping adolescents participate in community activities
- Pose questions caretakers may ask and provide answers teachers might give regarding inclusion of special needs adolescents in school and in the community
- List relevant resources for parents of middle and high schoolers
- Summarize important chapter themes

Maria has been in special education since second grade. During the first weeks of her first year in middle school, her mother noticed some changes in Maria's attitude toward school. When Mrs. Lopez talked with her daughter, she learned that Maria was feeling overwhelmed by all the schoolwork she was expected to do. Maria was participating in an "inclusion" model where she spent most of her instructional time with students without disabilities; during her special education instruction, Maria left her general education classroom and went to "special ed" for remedial assistance. In addition to the work assigned by the special education teacher, Maria's general education teacher expects her to finish assignments completed by her classmates while Maria is in the special

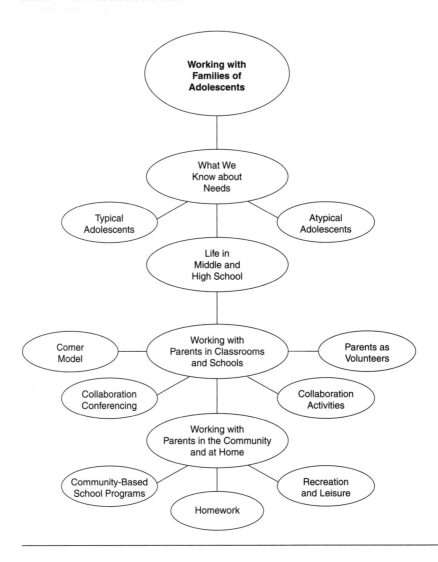

class. For the past two weeks, Maria has had "piles" of homework. When Mrs. Lopez asked the special education teacher for assistance, she informed Mrs. Lopez that Maria was having so much homework because she was not doing her work in school.

Adolescence is the transition into adulthood when the focus draws away from family to school and community participation. The adolescent years pose varied challenges for parents. Working effectively with families of children in their teens involves helping them understand the changes they will observe during this transition and supporting them in their efforts to guide their children toward responsible independence. As new teachers of middle and high school students work toward these goals, they must be ever aware that school and community integration is a collaborative effort, with students and their caretakers being indispensable members of the team.

A few years ago the major worries of adolescents focused on the deaths of their parents, being rejected by the opposite sex, impregnating a girl or being impregnated, and failing in school (Beale & Baskin, 1983). Although teens today still fear the deaths of their parents and failing in school, they also have three serious concerns that are new: contracting the AIDS virus, loved ones or oneself being a victim of violence, and not being able to find work (Gribin, 1994).

These concerns mirror today's statistics. AIDS is now the sixth leading cause of death among youth ages thirteen to twenty-four (Stratton, 1995). In 1996, 50 percent of ninth graders, 42 percent of tenth graders, 41 percent of eleventh graders, and 35 percent of twelfth graders reported being involved in a physical fight during the previous year (U.S. Department of Health and Human Services, 1996). In 1993, an estimated 270,000 guns were carried to school each day, according to the U.S. Justice Department. According to a recent survey of 700 American cities conducted by the National League of Cities, school violence in 1993 caused the death or serious injuries of students in 41 percent of these large cities (Queen, Blackwelder, & Mallen, 1997). A University of Maryland School of Medicine study reported that out of 168 teenagers who visited an inner-city clinic for routine medical care, 24 percent had witnessed a murder and 72 percent knew someone who had been shot. One out of every ten girls who visited the Baltimore clinic had been raped (Zinzmeister, 1990). And of the 37 million young people ten to nineteen years old now living in the United States, more than 14 million are living in poverty (Stratton, 1995).

Teens today are faced with far more serious challenges than in years past. Unfortunately, the two entities that would ordinarily be the havens for help, guidance, and security, the home and community, are no longer as stable as they used to be. Teens live in diverse environments in which a hurry-up society works against a sense of community and in which the number of dysfunctional families is growing.

Educators have seen many changes in students, but children have remained the same in that they respond positively to love, honesty, an open ear, and a helping hand. All adolescents are at risk for feelings of hopelessness and life-threatening mistakes, yet they can also be inspired by collaborative efforts to help them acquire social competency, develop problem solving skills, gain autonomy and control over decision making, and develop a sense of purpose. Essential in these efforts is information to assist families in meeting their school inclusion needs and to aid communities in decision making that affects children.

What We Know about Typical and Special Needs Adolescents

During the adolescent years, teens are dramatically changing physically and emotionally. Adolescents suddenly faced with new faces and bodies become overly concerned with the way they look and overly sensitive to how others perceive them. Demanding independence from their parents, they become entirely dependent on the opinions of their peers, even though peer values may be in marked contrast to those they have previously been taught.

BOX 8.1

Family–Teacher Issues
Administrators in the Mackenzie School District decided to tackle the low achievement and high drop-out rates that have plagued students in several high schools for years. During the summer, they conducted a series of teacher focus groups. Among the problems identified were a consistent lack of motivation, elevated levels of within-district mobility, and heightened teacher apathy.

Collaborative Orientations and Responsive Practices
Administrators decided to conduct monthly "town meetings" at each high school in the district. Local business and community college professionals agreed to serve as guest speakers addressing the following topics identified by parents and teachers as critical concerns: (a) school violence, (b) teen sexuality, (c) drug and alcohol abuse, (d) depression and suicide, (e) date rape, and (f) learning strategies instruction. Parents suggested that each session be organized as a panel discussion with students, teachers, parents, and community leaders servings as members.

They argue that they should be left on their own, yet in this time of risk taking, their actions indicate that they still need both security and supervision.

It is hard for any parent to remain calm and supportive during this time of "de-idealization" of parenthood (Felber, 1997; Tubman & Lerner, 1994). Allowing more independence and offering less protection is difficult, and it is especially tough for parents of teens with disabilities. Parents of adolescents with special needs find it challenging to encourage independence because dependence might seem easier. After all, fewer peers might mean less exposure to different values and beliefs and therefore less rebellion and conflict. Fewer opportunities to attend social activities might mean fewer opportunities to try drugs and alcohol. The flip side of this dilemma, however, is that if parents do not help their children toward independence, adolescence may bring greater isolation, a growing sense of indifference, and confusion and fear about emerging sexuality (Turnbull & Turnbull, 1997). New teachers of middle and high school students are part of the team that will help parents provide the necessary balance between security and opportunity necessary for each adolescent to reach the level of independence he or she can achieve. Although parents of a teen with special needs require guidance specific to their child's disability, the needs presented in Table 8.1 are those shared by all adolescents and can be provided by parents and professionals alike. Parental involvement has been demonstrated to influence a wide variety of adolescent perceptions and behavior (see Table 8.2).

Life in Middle and High School

When adolescents enter middle school, they risk losing two familiar support networks. One is their elementary school where they spent most of their day with one teacher and knew many students and professionals. The other is their parents, who were probably quite involved with their beginning school years, working as volunteers in the school and maintaining close contact with teachers.

TABLE 8.1 *What Teens Need*

- Promise of parents and professionals that they are committed to helping them succeed and reach their level of independence
- Opportunities to experiment with independence with guidance and support from parents and professionals
- Opportunities to communicate openly with significant others about feelings, thoughts, and actions without being judged
- Positive role models, of any age
- Trust of significant others
- Clear limits, consequences for actions, and discipline that is consistent
- Assurance from teachers, counselors, parents, and significant others that they will be loved, even if they make mistakes
- Opportunities to shine both in school and in the community
- Opportunities to receive accurate information

Teens face a very different school experience in middle school and high school than that in elementary school. They deal with an unfamiliar population of staff and students, often much larger than in their elementary school. They change classes, dealing with a variety of teachers with different instructional methods and teaching styles. Instead of spending most of their day with one teacher, contact time typically dwindles to about an hour a day. When elementary classes have over twenty-five students, there are complaints that the teacher won't have time to get to know and help each of his or her students, yet middle and high school teachers may have up to five classes and more than 125 students.

At this time, parents may pull away from contacting and visiting their teen's schools. They may do this at the teen's request. Because at this age teens want to be as independent as possible, they might be embarrassed by parental contact, seeing it as a lack of trust that they can handle the situation. If parents haven't talked before school begins with one single

TABLE 8.2 *Perceptions and Behaviors Influenced by Parent Involvement*

- Internal locus of control (Baumrind, 1991; Trusty & Lampe, 1997)
- Self-esteem (Chubb & Fertman, 1992)
- Higher career aspirations (Farmer, 1985; Wilson & Wilson, 1992)
- Higher educational expectations (Trusty, 1998)
- Career decision making (Palmer & Cochran, 1988; Penick & Jepsen, 1992)
- Positive school attitudes (Chubb & Fertman, 1992; Trusty, 1996)
- Psychosocial competence (Lamborn, Mounts, Steinberg, & Dornbusch, 1991)
- Lower levels of drug use (Barnes & Farrell, 1992)
- Academic success (Paulson, 1994; Steinberg, Lamborn, Dornbusch, & Darling, 1992)
- Adaptive school behaviors (Trusty, 1996)

BOX 8.2

Family–Teacher Issues

Lauren was an only child for ten years before his brother was born. Lauren's teacher, Mr. Pate, noticed some changes in his behavior and contacted Lauren's parents to discuss them. Mr. Pate observed less independent and more attention-seeking behavior in Lauren. His parents also thought Lauren was more distractible and easily upset at home. Everyone agreed that the new baby had changed Lauren's world.

Collaborative Orientations and Responsive Practices

Mr. Pate decided to get Lauren involved in more activities at school. The annual wrapping paper sale and holiday show projects were about to start, and he decided to ask Lauren to be his "assistant" for the next few months. Working with Lauren and his parents, Mr. Pate organized a work schedule for several days after school. He asked Lauren's parents to be involved by checking with Lauren each day when the extracurricular activities were completed. He asked Lauren to keep a diary of the work he had done as his assistant and suggested that the diary be used to keep his parents informed about his new job.

person responsible for their child's school life, they may be unsure whom to contact. The school may not be a neighborhood school and transportation may be a problem. New teachers or administrators without formal training or positive experiences with parents can view parental involvement as threatening and discourage what they perceive as interference.

What do these changes mean for teens with disabilities? For many students with disabilities, the teen years may mark their first experience receiving "split instruction"—some instruction in regular settings and some in special education settings. Often, students are placed in content area classes for instruction, where collaboration and supportive services are supplied by the special education teacher. This means that they will be coping with trying to please a variety of teachers and students, experiencing the physical and psychological changes of typical adolescents, and then continuing to contend with the challenges of their particular disabilities. More than at any other time in their school careers, teens with special needs will be at risk for failure because of poor self-concept, inability to problem-solve, social ineptitude, attention deficits, and lack of motivation (Lerner, 1997). Added to this is the fact that by the time they get to high school, teens may have experienced many years of failure and have begun to seriously doubt that they can ever achieve (Luther, 1993).

Comfort, Giorgi, and Moody (1997) report that a series of four youth conferences was sponsored by a school–university partnership in Virginia for the purpose of determining major problems in high schools. Students were selected from rural, suburban, and urban high schools to represent diversity in terms of race, gender, grade levels, program, and academic performance. Three major problems were cited: lack of a connected and focused curriculum, inflexible instructional system, and lack of a sense of community. Students saw the high school curriculum as fragmented and abstract. Subject matter was disconnected from the real world. Detail seemed to be learned for its own sake, not because it was related to achieving understanding of overarching concepts or skills. For adolescents with disabilities, these criticisms spell trouble with a capital "T" and put them at risk for continued failure. More than any other teens, those with special needs learn best when skills and content relate to that which builds on previous learning or experiences (Lerner, 1997). They need a flexible instructional system which can meet their individual needs and a curriculum in which they can learn strategies and adaptations for living in the real world (Beakley & Yoder, 1998). The more isolated they feel from their school community, the less motivated they will be to succeed in that environment.

The statistics for students with learning disabilities show just how difficult it is for teens with special needs to succeed in middle and high school. Over 21 percent drop out of school, and the reason for leaving is unknown for almost 18 percent (U.S. Department of Education, 1994). According to a recent survey, almost one out of three youths with learning disabilities fail their regular high school courses, and most experience failure before reaching high school (Wagner, 1990).

For parents who are already spending lots of time and energy meeting the needs of a teen with a disability, the transition from elementary school to inclusion in regular classes at the middle and high school level is especially tough. Unfamiliarity with the school, lack of time and energy, and cultural and language differences all act as hindrances to parent involvement in their child's middle and high school life. Some teachers may expect too much from parents and may read their inability to carry out educational and therapeutic interventions with their child as lack of care. Others may expect too much from the student, foregoing necessary follow-up by parents. Holmes and Croll (1989) report that if parents regularly sign a diary of homework assignments students spend more time on their homework. Yet Salend and Schiff (1989) found that 38 percent of LD teachers never had parents sign homework and 45 percent only occasionally requested a parent signature.

In 1988, the Parent Advisory Committee of the Washtenaw Intermediate School District (WISD) in Ann Arbor, Michigan, responded to the fact that parents of children with disabilities felt isolated and unaware of existing resources that could help meet their needs (Sussell, Carr, & Hartman, 1996). One of the steps the committee took to improve communication was to send a newsletter to parents and staff with a survey asking them to identify their needs. Families requested more information about resources available in the community, programs and services available after graduation, more written information, more classes and presentations, more information about school evaluations and program planning, more support groups, and more active leisure time for adolescents. Similar findings have emerged in other studies of parent concerns and issues, especially with regard to resources and services available in meeting special learning needs of students with high and low incidence disabilities.

Working with Parents in Classrooms and Schools

Special education legislation has formalized the belief that parents need to be included in the design and delivery of educational services to their children (Sussull, Carr, & Hartman, 1996). P.L. 94-142 included parents in the process of determining each child's individualized education program (IEP). P.L. 99-457 (Part H) acknowledges that individual families, as well as individual children, have unique strengths and needs that should be considered in developing intervention plans. The Individuals with Disabilities Education Act (reauthorization of P.L. 94-142) directs that parents will be actively involved in developing IEPs which include a statement of how the students' families will regularly be informed of progress toward annual goals.

Not only legislation but also research has supported the extension of the parent role to include that of advocate, teacher, case manager, and program evaluator (Allen & Hudd, 1987). Parent involvement, care, support, and monitoring have been linked to many adolescent perceptions and behaviors, including attitudes, aspirations, and achievement.

Despite legislative support and research findings, parental and professional satisfaction with family involvement in individual educational planning has typically been low (Benz & Halpern, 1987). This dissatisfaction and low level of family involvement has been attributed to such causes as lack of knowledge of available services (Gilliam & Coleman, 1981), feelings of token participation (Brinckerhoff & Vincent, 1986), competing priorities, and time or scheduling conflicts (Ayres, Meyer, Erevelles, & Park-Lee, 1994). However, with the national trend toward inclusion of students with disabilities into general education classrooms, professionals recognize that the need for family–teacher collaboration is crucial for student academic success.

A Model for Parent–School Collaboration

A model developed by James Comer at Yale University illustrates how a range of special activity and volunteer options for parents can be merged within a school. Comprising the Comer Model are the following:

• School planning and management team. This team represents families, professional staff, and all nonprofessional support staff to carry out the three management options of (a) developing and implementing a comprehensive school plan, including a focus on school climate and academics, (b) staff development to implement the plan, and (c) evaluation and modification of the school program as needed. The major goals include creating a sense of direction and providing a sense of program partnership and purpose to all volunteers.

• Mental health team. This team focuses on students' developmental and behavioral needs and shares knowledge and skills related to child development and teacher/administrator relationships. The team's goal is to address difficult issues as soon as they appear and to prevent problematic issues from escalating.

• Parent program. This program supports the social program of the school and provides input to the other two teams. Representatives from this group attend school planning and management team meetings. They help establish the school calendar and plan school events such as parties, field trips, and athletic programs.

Collaboration through Conferencing

Every teacher of a teen with a disability will meet with parents to conference about educational programming. These conferences will determine coursework students will take and the setting in which they will learn. During these conferences, parents and teachers will formulate educational goals for the student and will establish plans to evaluate progress toward those goals. Teachers will discuss the various forms of modified instruction and testing they use and the strategies that have proven successful in the past. Jordan, Reyes-Blanes, Peel, Peel, and Lane (1998) refer to this type of conference as a *purposeful confer-*

ence. Purposeful conferences are used when the parent and educator have particular topics to discuss such as academic progress, behavior, or IEP changes. In a purposeful conference, participants meet with a specific goal in mind in a structured environment.

The *casual conference* is another type that has a great influence on the productiveness of the purposeful conference. In a casual conference, information is exchanged and rapport is built in an informal setting (Jordan, Reyes-Blanes, Peel, Peel, & Lane, 1998). Casual conferences are far more likely to make parents feel at ease and establish a tone of openness that will set the groundwork for purposeful conferences. Phone calls, feedback written on student work, newsletters, and invitations to visit the classroom are all excellent ways to communicate informally with parents.

Casual conferences not only help parents get to know teachers, but also help teachers learn about the diverse cultures, goals, beliefs, values, and expectations of their students and parents. Research indicates that many preservice teachers expect to teach students who are similar to themselves when they were in school (Kagan, 1992). Our increasingly diverse culture makes this "sameness" situation unlikely. Parent expectations may differ radically from teacher expectations. An understanding of student academic and social behavior will come when the teacher becomes familiar with factors such as the value the family places on education, the amount and types of student and family responsibilities, family expectations for appropriate behavior and academic performance, and the level of parent involvement (Ramey & Ramey, 1994).

If new teachers have a clear understanding of the family dynamics before a purposeful or formal conference is held, success is more likely (Jordan, Reyes-Blanes, Peel, Peel, & Lane, 1998). In a study by Palmer, Borthwick-Duffy, and Widaman (1998), parents of children with significant cognitive disabilities were more likely to have positive perceptions of inclusive practices when they placed a relatively higher value on the school's role in developing social skills. These parents were more likely to trade off "special education" benefits such as a specialized curriculum, easier access to ancillary services, and more individualized instruction for the social benefits that they consider more attainable in a general education setting. Knowing through casual conferencing that a family places a high value on socialization for their teen with a disability will greatly help teachers involved in the educational planning for that adolescent. They will go into the purposeful conference relatively sure that the student's parents will support placement in general education classes if the socialization process is going well for their teen.

Shanda Clark's experience is a good example. When Shanda entered middle school in Lake City, Florida, and was placed in a general education math class, her teacher, Mr. Stavrakas, called to introduce himself to Shanda's parents. During the conversation, Shanda's mother shared that she wanted social acceptance more than anything for her daughter. However, sometimes the family preferred to do things with Shanda themselves instead of encouraging her to socialize because they feared her peers would ridicule her and reject her company. With the help of Mr. Stavrakas and Shanda's resource teacher, a friendship group consisting of four classmates, the two teachers, and Shanda was arranged. By the time the first conference of the year was held, the friendship group had helped Shanda join Future Teachers of America and chorus and attend several athletic events. Needless to say, Shanda's parents came to their first conference pleased and ready to support Shanda's inclusion in general education coursework. They felt comfortable in agreeing to try to step aside and let others help handle any socialization problems Shanda might experience.

Effective conferencing beginning in middle school ensures that there are no surprises for the family at the end of high school. All participants can use purposeful conferencing to develop realistic goals for student progress as well as to explore long-range options. Parents and students can make informed decisions about course selection, advise on curriculum modifications, and set realistic expectations for postsecondary education or work. Successful purposeful conferencing depends not only on setting the groundwork with casual conferencing, but also understanding and following these suggestions:

- The aim of a formal or purposeful conference should be to develop, evaluate, and redevelop short- and long-term goals. The actions and roles to be taken by the educators, family members, student, and other professionals should be clarified. An evaluation time line and method of assessment should also be planned (Jordan, Reyes-Blanes, Peel, Peel, & Lane, 1998).
- Some families may have an extended family network whose members may play an important role in the teens' development (Hurtado, 1995). Invite both parents and other significant members of the family. Student-made invitations, phone calls, and reminders can all actively solicit family participation.
- Include students and inform all conference participants that the important skills of self-regulation, progress monitoring, and communication must be developed through the students' taking ownership of their educational experiences.
- Prepare an outline and distribute it to all conference participants.
- Listen to parents to gain insight into their teen's disability. Only teens and their caretakers can provide a clear picture of how their disability affects them.
- Let parents know that you celebrate their child's individuality. Once you demonstrate a genuine interest in and get to the teen as an individual, parents will be more likely to talk honestly about their needs.
- Have students bring to the conference materials they wish to share. Have them discuss their perspectives about their classroom performance and strategies that work within the classroom that can be tried at home. For instance, if Traci is less distracted and more focused when the lights are dim, discuss ways these conditions can be established at home when Traci is doing her homework.
- Try not to schedule back-to-back conferences. Set a time limit for the conference with extra time in case it lasts longer.
- Prepare a comfortable place for all conference participants to sit that is at eye level with the teacher and has no physical barriers between them (Jordan, Reyes-Blanes, Peel, Peel, & Lane, 1998).
- If home visits are possible for you, give parents a choice. The student's home may serve as an appropriate setting for a parent conference, particularly if transportation is a problem for family members. Ramey and Ramey (1994) have advocated parent contacts that provide a high level of comfort. Home visits may offer a high level of comfort to some parents because the surroundings are familiar, but other parents may find them intrusive.
- Recognize that language and cultural barriers may make understanding difficult for family members (Jordan, Reyes-Blanes, Peel, Peel, & Lane, 1998). Go slowly and check for understanding.

- Educational jargon is often meaningless to parents. Present information clearly, describing behavior in explicit terms (e.g., the number of times a student drops his or her pencil in a fifteen-minute period of time, the number of times he or she shouts out during a lesson).
- Present documented observations about each student as a learner and member of the classroom community.
- Refrain from judging family roles based on personal experience or the perception of a normative group. Expect differences, expect diversity from prevailing cultural norms, expect the unexpected (Reyes-Blanes & Daunic, 1997). A family's reaction to a disability may be based on tradition, religion, economic level, or prior knowledge and experience. To some, a child's disability is viewed as a parent's punishment or curse; in other cultures, a disability is seen as a challenge, a test of faith or worth, or a natural occurrence (Harry, 1992).
- Acknowledge that family members will be teens' primary advocates (Jordan, Reyes-Blanes, Peel, Peel, & Lane, 1998).
- Explore the family's ideas of what constitutes appropriate behavior or academic performance. Communicate clearly your expectations for behavior and academic performance and note differences and ways to overcome them.
- At the close of the conference, summarize major points and check again to make sure family members have understood critical issues addressed within the conference. A mutually acceptable plan of action should be devised, with family members and teachers aware of their roles (Kroth & Edge, 1997).
- Ask parents for their preferred method of follow-up to the conference (e.g., phone calls, notes, or another conference) and try to honor them (Jordan, Reyes-Blanes, Peel, Peel, & Lane, 1998).

To prepare students for participation in conferences, new teachers can involve them from day one in activities that help them keep track of their academic and behavioral success. For instance, Dan, a seventh-grade student with mild disabilities, was having difficulty with several inappropriate behaviors that were negatively influencing his academic performance and his relationships with his teachers. His resource teacher, along with his English and social studies teacher, met with Dan and showed him how he could create a chart listing four positive skills to replace the inappropriate behaviors. After Dan wrote the positive skills, they agreed that Dan would pick one of them to work on that week. Every day he was able to successfully achieve those positive behavioral skills, the teacher would write his or her initials for that day. Dan and the teachers agreed that achieving each skill at least four times a week would indicate mastery. Once Dan mastered a skill for two weeks in a row, he would add another skill to master. The charts became a record of improvement that he used during his conference with family members to discuss his goals and progress.

Portfolio assessment is defined as "the use of records of a student's work over time in a variety of modes to show the depth, breadth, and development of the student's abilities; it is the purposeful and systematic collection of student work that reflects accomplishment relative to specific instructional goals" (Pierce & O'Malley, 1992, p. 2). Portfolios can include, among other things, work samples, self-evaluation logs, peer or teacher evaluations, and progress graphs. Advocates for portfolio assessment indicate that portfolios help students create "real-world" products they can share with their parents (Cole, Struyk, Kinder, Shee-han, & Kish, 1997). Portfolios provide an excellent means of communicating with parents and families (Lerner, 1997).

New teachers may establish a more formal method of teacher–parent collaboration through the forming of a task force of teachers, support staff, parents, and students. This task force would analyze the student's present program, form a mission statement defining what everyone would like the inclusion program to achieve, develop a parent involvement policy, determine what resources are needed for successful implementation of the program, and develop a method of evaluating the program. Williams and Fox (1996) note the actions for which a task force or planning team would be responsible:

- Identifying areas of concern such as academics, social acceptance and friendships, health and safety, self-concept, or self-esteem
- Identifying the skills that student needs to be successful in the new environment
- Determining if the student's needs can be met through general education activities
- Determining the needs that can also be addressed in the home

FIGURE 8.1 *Positive Behaviors Chart*

Name _____   Week _____

Teacher(s) _____

Class(es) _____

1. I will remember to bring my math text to math class every day. (Each goal is handwritten.)

Monday	Tuesday	Wednesday	Thursday	Friday

2. I will remember to bring my science text to science every day.

Monday	Tuesday	Wednesday	Thursday	Friday

3. I will sit in my assigned seat at the front of the room in science class every day.

Monday	Tuesday	Wednesday	Thursday	Friday

4. I will have my math homework ready and on the desk at the start of math class every day.

Monday	Tuesday	Wednesday	Thursday	Friday

- Developing the student's schedule
- Identifying tasks necessary to support the achievement of a student's plan
- Summarizing and monitoring the student's program
- Planning movement to the next grade or beyond high school
- Helping students become knowledgeable about their educational needs through participation in their conferences prepares them for life in postsecondary institutions whether academic, technical, or vocational. It is here that students will be required to take responsibility for documenting any disability and requesting appropriate services. They will be expected to self-advocate. Two important learning experiences students take from conferencing is learning to self-monitor and to taking the lead and describing their strengths, needs, goals, and progress toward goals. Many families find that simple self-monitoring charts (see Figure 8.1) are useful in helping adolescents keep track of important school survival skills.

Collaboration through Special Activities

Communication doesn't need to be in the form of a conference. Special speakers and open forums can serve as tools for parents' involvement in their teens' education. For instance, new teachers could plan a dance contest for students following a Parent Night presentation. Students could make invitations and pull parent names from a hat to invite as judges. Teachers can communicate necessary information to family members and provide them with information (see Figure 8.2) before the big dance, then socialize with them during the contest.

When teens have recently been placed in inclusive settings, Parent Night is an excellent way to introduce their families to others' families. However, their questions may differ from those of families whose children do not have special needs and may be difficult for them to ask in a group. For example, parents of a teen with challenging behavior might attend their child's classes and worry about the teachers' frustrations related to their child's

BOX 8.3

Family–Teacher Issues

Paige Jones is a first-year seventh-grade social studies teacher. She has a "challenging class" of nineteen students right after lunch. Several of the students in this class have IEPs. Paige wants to take a field trip to the local newspaper office, but she is reluctant to go because she doesn't feel qualified to manage the behavior of her "special students." She knows all of her students need exposure to the real world, but she also recognizes her limits, especially in light of the heavy monitoring she is experiencing as a new teacher.

Collaborative Orientations and Responsive Practices

Paige talks to her grade-level mentor who suggests she meet with Mr. Bottlepaste, the behavior management teacher. She explains her dilemma to him and asks for help. Mr. Bottlepaste reviews a few simple management strategies that have been successful in his classes (e.g., tickets for good behavior, in and out of the classroom; peer coaching; peer competitions in a "good behavior game") and suggests that Paige invite a few parents to go on the field trip. He also suggests that the parents be asked to prepare brief "speeches" describing their jobs and a few of their memories from high school field trips before the trip.

FIGURE 8.2   *Request for Parent Involvement: Handout for Parent Night*

PARENTS: WE NEED YOU

We would appreciate your help in making your child's education the best it can be.
Here are some ways you can become involved:

Help plan your teen's schedule.

Provide study time and a quiet study environment.

Review homework assignments after they are completed.

Highlight the strengths and gifts of your teen.

Post examples of great work.

Don't wait for us to call you, schedule your own conferences as needed.

Talk to your teen about school and life goals.

Provide educational resources.

Combine educational and family activities.

Help your teen develop friendships; teach them how to make and keep friends.

Encourage improvement.

Praise good performance.

behavior, as well as about the frustration of other parents because their child's behavior is disrupting the class. To address their individual concerns, new teachers can rely on casual conferences to assure them that all is going well or to notify them that a more formal get-together might be needed to deal with problems their child may be encountering.

Schools may design their own parent-learning sessions, with teachers, parents, and community members serving as leaders. At Lassiter Middle School, Louisville, Kentucky, the assistant principal initiated "Parent at Lassiter" workshops. Conducted in the evening, these sessions covered topics of concern to middle school parents, teachers, and students. One workshop, on drug abuse, focused on causes, prevention, and intervention, with an emphasis on how parents can help prevent their children from becoming involved with drugs. Community members are frequently invited as guest speakers. For instance, the director of a local treatment center for youth with drug problems led the workshop on drug abuse (Fleming, 1993).

A similar method of linking schools to the family is to invite parents and family members to staff development workshops. School professionals have found that parents become more knowledgeable and more supportive of school programs, curriculum, and instruction issues when they are part of teacher training sessions where topics like discipline and homework affect them. Allowing parents in training allows new teachers and parents to establish a common understanding that can help them work together more effectively.

Parents as Volunteers

In the middle and high school years, some teens may not want their parents to volunteer in their classrooms, but that shouldn't stop the parents from helping out within the school. Parents can assist new teachers by developing instructional materials, adaptive equipment, or games, as well as copying and collating instructional materials. As volunteers in the schools, caretakers of students with disabilities may be able to provide expertise on exceptionality-related issues. They can provide assistance with supplementary aids and services such as providing sign language interpretation for school assemblies, plays, and musical performances (Luetke-Stahlman, Luetke-Stahlman, & Luetke-Stahlman, 1992). Students who would like their parents to help out in their classes can invite them to share their expertise, to give tips on job hunting, help with foreign languages, or assist in science labs. Parent Night is an excellent time to introduce the jobs that are available and conferences are a good time for follow-up.

Some schools have organized family resource centers within the school building where families may come to learn about volunteer activities and meet other families. Kosciuszko Middle School in Milwaukee established a room where parents can meet, make phone calls, and engage in problem solving. An average of five to fifteen parents stop by the room each week. They are supported by a school staff member, three parents who are paid $6.00 an hour for sixteen hours of work each week, and a network of volunteers (Lynn, 1994). Other schools have parent coordinators who identify parent expertise and school needs and link the two together.

Working with Parents in the Community and at Home

New teachers of adolescents with disabilities have a responsibility to prepare each of their students for an adult life with as much autonomy as possible. Just as elementary teachers prepare their students for the transition from elementary to high school level, so the middle and high school teachers must prepare their students for the transition from youth to adulthood.

As we discuss in Chapter 9, the need for transition plans and services to prepare adolescents with disabilities for adult life is recognized in the reauthorization of the Individuals with Disabilities Education Act (IDEA). The law requires that an individualized transition plan be written for students with disabilities beginning at age fourteen as part of the IEP. It views transition services as a coordinated set of activities that are based on the needs of the individual student and ensures that students complete secondary school prepared for employment or postsecondary education, as well as for independent living (Lerner, 1997). New teachers help students prepare for adulthood by doing the following:

- Creating community-based programs that help students learn and master independent work and living skills
- Creating homework programs that provide opportunities for students not only to practice skills, but also to acquire work habits that promote self-reliance
- Working closely with parents in offering teens leisure and recreational options to play and socialize with their peers

Community-Based School Programs

The success of community-based programming for students in middle and high school depends on the family's ability to communicate to the school the activities that they believe are appropriate and important for their child, the support they provide to the program, and follow-up at home to maintain the skills introduced during community activities. Beakley and Yoder (1998) offer the following teacher tips on how to involve parents in a community-based program:

- Inform parents about the goals and expected outcomes of the program; collect information from parents about the areas that they want emphasized.
- Use information gained from parents to document entry-level skills of each student and to determine individual student goals.
- Implement the program by grouping students according to the locations their parents recommended.

Homework

Home-to-school communication about homework is essential in maintaining a homework program that promotes independence in teens with disabilities while maintaining essential skills. An open line of communication guides family members in their efforts to monitor, interact, and support teens in their efforts to complete homework assignments. It helps parents avoid trying to teach school subjects or read or direct the assignments that are the students' responsibilities. Through casual and purposeful conferences, new teachers can find out from parents if students

- Understand homework directions without help from family members
- Complete homework assignments within the time period recommended
- Can explain how homework assignments relate to what they are learning in class

Epstein, Simon, and Salinas (1997) describe a successful homework program designed to help parents support their students' in-class performance, become more informed about the curriculum, and help with their teens' homework. Researchers at Johns Hopkins University and teachers in Maryland, Virginia, and the District of Columbia have developed the Teachers Involve Parents in Schoolwork (TIPS) Interactive Homework process. The TIPS process enables teachers of any grade level or subject to design homework that requires children to talk to someone at home about something interesting they're learning about in class. Some of the activities may include interviewing family members, asking for reactions to in-class lessons, or reading stories aloud that they have written. All TIPS activities include a section for home-to-school communication in which parents indicate whether the student was able to explain the homework assignment, whether they enjoyed working on the activity together, and whether the parent learned something about what the student is learning in class. Parents may add observations, comments, or questions for the teacher (see Table 8.3).

TIPS activities may be assigned once a week, every other week, or on some other regular schedule. Teachers usually give students more than one day to complete the activities (e.g., two weekdays or a weekend) to accommodate families' busy schedules. The TIPS process is designed to keep all families aware of what their children are learning in school, including parents who work outside the home, have little formal education, speak languages other than English, have many children at home, or others whom teachers sometimes find hard to reach.

TABLE 8.3 *Homework TIPS*

Here are some hints to help ease typical homework frustrations of middle school students:

- Teach your child to use a few organizing skills (e.g., have assignment, have materials, review expected product, include review time) before he or she begins doing homework.
- Set up a specific place, free of distractions, for your child to do his or her homework.
- Agree on time frame for doing homework and stick to it.
- Ask for assignment modifications such as doing odd- or even-numbered problems rather than the entire worksheet.
- Avoid power struggles between you and your child during homework time.

Nelson, Epstein, Bursuck, Jayanthi, and Sawyer (1998) surveyed middle school students to determine preferences for homework adaptations. The highest ratings were for teachers giving homework assignments that are finished at school; the lowest ratings were for teachers giving different assignments to different groups of students within a class. Productive homework assignments for teens with disabilities provide the following:

- A chance for parents to gain information about the school curriculum and their children's work
- Student practice time with school lessons
- Openings for students to receive encouragement from home
- An opportunity for teachers to appreciate parental support for the academic success of students

Building Independence through Leisure and Recreational Community Experiences

Playing cooperatively with peers, participating in recreational activities, planning for those activities to occur, and making self-determined leisure choices are central to all students' growth and development. But many students with disabilities have few opportunities to learn and practice play, recreation, and social skills (Turnbull & Turnbull, 1997). In a study by Sonderlund, Epstein, Quinn, Cumblad, and Peterson (1995), for example, parents of children and youths with emotional and behavioral disorders named finding recreational activities for their children as one of their top three needs. Typically, schools have not encouraged or supported people with disabilities to be self-determining in leisure (Turnbull & Turnbull, 1997).

Successful leisure experiences can provide opportunities for students with disabilities to learn and practice skills that enhance educational outcomes regularly included in the individualized education programs. If students learn leisure skills in context, families will often participate in the process. Because most students spend much of their leisure time at home with their families, families are natural partners in leisure education for students with disabilities. Novice teachers and parents may integrate students' academic and life-skill goals and objectives into existing IEPs, and facilitate those goals through new leisure experiences in contextual learning situations (i.e., learning that connects subject matter content with the context of application). For instance, a math goal of counting money and making change could be practiced when the student attended sports activities and communication goals could be practiced when the student needed to ask directions to his or her seat, or call the ticket center for scheduling information.

Johnson, Bullock, and Ashton-Shaeffer (1997) describe a program they developed that facilitates contextual learning for school-aged students with disabilities by developing individualized, community-based leisure education programming in concert with students' families. The program described is entitled Family Link in Leisure Education (FLLE) and included students ranging in age from five to twenty-one years. Students and their families were seen one to two times per week for twenty to forty weeks by a Certified Therapeutic Recreation Specialist (CTRS) or a master's-level therapeutic recreation student. CTRS's, certified by the National Council on Therapeutic Recreation Certification, have worked in school systems since the 1975 passage of P.L. 94-142, the Education for All Handicapped Children Act, and work in schools as both consultants and direct service providers.

Students, teachers, and families all completed assessments that included sections on needs, interests, and strengths. FLLE staff, together with families and students, set goals that included specific activities, skills, and programs of interest to the students. Staff members spent considerable time in the families' homes interviewing both the parents and the students. These home interviews allowed the staff to see the context of the children's play, as well as family dynamics.

Each learning plan was based on the student's interests and his or her desire to explore specific activities and interactions. Families were involved in their child's learning in natural settings so that they could support and reinforce their child's interests. Families provided assessment information, support, resources, and ideas for contextual learning.

Several families who benefited from their involvement with the project had very little knowledge of recreation opportunities and resources for their child in their community. They were unaware that programs existed, that there were printed resources available, and that community recreation programs were open to their child's participation. Families from inner-city neighborhoods specifically benefited from scholarships and fee waivers that they did not know existed. Several families were waiting for someone to indicate that play, recreation, and leisure were important aspects of their child's life and deserved attention. These families quickly followed through with plans.

FLLE provided a model for facilitating students' self-determination leisure choices based on their individual interests. Families became part of the process and were involved in their child's growth and development. Johnson, Bullock, and Ashton-Schaeffer (1997) provide the following suggestions for contextual learning with families:

- Spend lots of time exploring interests.
- Prepare students, families, and the community for inclusion. Give the responsibility to communicate with recreation and community leaders about being part of their programs to the student, if possible.
- Keep it simple. By starting with simple, successful activities, many students and families moved to more complex activities. One student, for example, participated in his school's Habitat for Humanity Club before working at the building site with community volunteers.

- Help students find places to fit in. Staff attitudes, architectural barriers, and assistive technology are just some of the issues that need to be evaluated before students participate.
- Not all families need intensive, long-term assistance. Getting families started on the right track can be the most critical factor in facilitating their child's learning through and enjoying leisure experiences.
- Challenge limits. Students in special education can be surrounded by limits and small expectations. Families sometimes need permission to succeed and to move beyond others' expectations. If you limit your students' participation to "special programs" you have sold them short.

Sports for children can be an effective means of increasing home–school communication and encouraging family involvement in learning. The new emphasis in adapted physical education is inclusive sport that brings family members together in events that use the community facilities and promote transition into independent living that includes a healthy, active lifestyle.

Baseball and soccer programs can provide ways to include students with disabilities and their families in sports programs as a complement to Special Olympics. Arlington, Texas, is one of many communities that is embracing new inclusive approaches to baseball, soccer, and other sports, as well as supporting traditional Special Olympics programs. Little League baseball's Challenger Division and the United States Youth Soccer Association's TOPSoccer (The Outreach Program for Soccer) provide opportunities for children with mental or physical disabilities and their family members or volunteers to play games in the same ballparks and wear the same uniforms as other children in the community. Castaneda and Sherrill (1997) detail the benefits of these programs which began less than ten years ago as ways to include children and youth with various physical or mental disabilities. In contrast, Special Olympics, which was founded in 1968, is limited to children and adults with mental retardation. The new programs are supplementing Special Olympics, not replacing it, and they reflect the combined desire of parents and teachers to expand sports opportunities for all children, youth, and adults with disabilities.

Both the Challenger Division and TOPSoccer programs in Arlington were initiated by parents. The mother of a twelve-year-old girl with a disability led the advocacy effort that resulted in the formation of a Challenger Division at North Arlington Little League. Excellent newspaper coverage attracted the attention of an adapted physical education specialist in the Arlington Independent School District. The specialist became involved as a coach, recruiter, and organizer of the Challenger Division. A mother of a child without disabilities, after attending a state youth soccer association conference where TOPSoccer was described, requested the Arlington Soccer Association to start a TOPSoccer program. This also attracted the attention of the adapted physical education specialist, parents, and other special educators in the district.

An informal support group for parents and families also emerged during the past three baseball seasons. The time that these parents spent at practices and games was emotionally helpful because it brought people together who were confronted with the same child-rearing concerns. Parents and families were also provided the opportunity to participate in traditional activities such as team mom or dad, volunteer coaches, and umpires.

Siblings expressed satisfaction in watching their brothers and sisters participate in an enjoyable activity. Siblings also enjoyed the role reversal of cheering for the Challenge

TABLE 8.4 *Tips for Starting an Inclusive Sports Program*

- Contact the local Little League chapter or youth sports organization and express a desire to create a division for children and youth with disabilities. Volunteer to become a member of the Little League or program board.

- Contact your school district's special education department or special education personnel within the district (especially an adapted physical education specialist). Ask for assistance in recruiting players, coaches, and volunteers. The adapted physical education specialist can also serve as an excellent resource in working with children and youth with disabilities in a sports setting (teaching sports skills, behavior management, modification of rules, equipment).

- Create and distribute informational flyers throughout the district (permission from building administrators or special education department is required in most cases) and within the local community. Follow through with additional flyers that describe sports programs, benefits, registration dates and times, and fees (if applicable).

- Contact local media and inform them of the development of the program.

- Contact local support groups for parents of children of disabilities.

players instead of having their brothers or sisters with disabilities in the stands cheering for *them*. Tips for starting an inclusive sports program suggested by Casteneda and Sherrill (1997) are presented in Table 8.4.

Participating in sports and leisure will help impact on teens and their families the need for creating a weekly schedule that includes sports and leisure activities, homework time, travel, and snacks and dinner. Scheduling is an excellent topic for a workshop for parents and teens with disabilities in middle and high school.

Perspective on Working with Families of Adolescents

The role of education professionals has been expanded with the advent of the inclusion movement, student self-determination, increased family participation, and focus on community integration and student participation. The Individuals with Disabilities Education Act (IDEA) mandates parent participation in the process of developing educational programs for students with disabilities. By fostering and supporting positive relationships with parents, new teachers and other professionals gain a window into the lives of their students in the world outside of school. Information gained from parents enables schools to be more effective in promoting positive learning environments for all students.

Good family communication serves multiple purposes. It provides new teachers with information about students and the expectations of parents and it provides reliable and current information for use in making decisions about school progress. Of course, communication means more than simply relaying information. It also provides a basis and opportunities for developing shared commitment and trust.

School is a challenging time for adolescents, especially those with disabilities. As they progress from elementary school to middle and high school, their need for independent living skills and preparation for work increases greatly. Elementary programs provide students with a functional knowledge base in reading, math, and social skills. Older students should not only build on this knowledge, but also learn a set of strategies and adaptations for living in the real world. This increased need adds to the importance of involving families in educational programs by encouraging parents and students to visit the classrooms and meet with teachers, assistants, and other students. The visits serve to foster ways to smooth transitions between schools and to begin the process of communication between family and school. In some cases, a handbook including school information, curriculum information, student reports and checklists, behavior programs, and permission slips is provided to assist families in transition. In many cases, this process also extends to community involvement. For example, through the use of real materials, role playing, functional academic lessons, and in-school jobs, many teachers have been able to assimilate community skills into their classrooms, and then generalize them into the community. An ultimate goal of middle and high school programs is to enable students to use practical skills in the real world. Sometimes the most creative part of the process is working out ways to have students spend as much time in the community as possible and finding ways for families to support these efforts.

The process is facilitated by structures that allow parents, teachers, and students to meet as members of the same team, and know they are working with and trying to nurture the same educational goals. Conferences represent a useful method for supporting communication with families. When parents and professionals meet to discuss school problems and progress, parents need to feel that they are valued participants and respected members of educational teams. The challenge of continued, productive family involvement is formidable, but successful models are available and documented.

Family Member Questions

The following are important questions new teachers may face in middle school or high school conferences.

• *What kind of input can I have when my child's IEP is developed? What is my role in the IEP process?* Parents are expected to be equal participants along with school personnel, in developing, reviewing, and revising the IEP of their child. This role is an active one in which the parents provide critical information regarding the strengths of their child and express their concerns for enhancing the education of their child, participate in discussions about the child's needs for special education and related services and supplementary aids and services, and join with the other participants in deciding how the child will be involved and progress in the general curriculum and participate in state and districtwide assessments, and what services the agency will provide to the child and in what setting.

• *I'm still confused. The IEPs that have been developed for my child don't include objective measures of progress. How can they be written differently? How will I know whether he is actually making progress?* List your child's weaknesses (i.e., writing, arithmetic, spelling, typing). Next, list your child's present levels of performance in measurable terms. For example:

Present Levels: My child reads a passage of text orally at the 7.2 grade equivalent level as measured by the Woodcock Johnson.

or

My child is reading a passage of text orally at the 45 percentile level as measured by the WRAT.

These examples apply to all disabilities—learning disabilities, autism, speech language deficits, mental retardation, and cerebral palsy. It is important to know specifically where students' deficits are, what skills are deficient, and what behavior needs to be changed.

The starting point should be observable and measurable percentile ranks, grade equivalents, age equivalents or standard scores. Where should this skill be one year later? Use objective measurable terms, not subjective terms. Write down a goal that the student should achieve after one year of an appropriate special education. (Special education should be designed to remediate the child's weaknesses.)

Sample Goal for Parents

By May 15, [one year later], my child will be able to read a passage of text orally at the XYZ [insert the appropriate increased level here] grade equivalent level as measured by the Woodcock Johnson.

or

By May 15, [one year later], my child will be able to read a passage of text orally at the XYZ [insert the appropriate increased level here] percentile level as measured by the WRAT.

Now, there is an objective measurable starting point and ending point, using norm referenced data. New teachers can help parents determine how to get from Point A to Point B. The map from Point A to Point B includes short-term objectives and benchmarks.

Family Resources and Services

The following resources may help families of adolescents with disabilities.

C.H.A.D.D. (Children and Adults with Attention Deficit Disorder)
499 N.W. 70th Avenue, Suite 101
Plantation, Forida, USA, 33317
(305) 587-3700
(800) 233-4050
(305) 587-4599 Fax

C.H.A.D.D. is a national organization working toward helping children and adults with ADD achieve success. C.H.A.D.D. publishes a regular newsletter and an expanded magazine-style publication covering the latest developments in ADD research, diagnosis, and treatment. There is also a Fact Sheet series and regular updates on breaking news. On the state level C.H.A.D.D. is developing ADD councils to help local and state school systems implement the U.S. Department of Education Federal Policy on ADD which tells schools how to serve students with attention deficit disorders through IDEA and Section 504 of the Rehabilitation Act.

Beach Center on Families and Disability
3111 Haworth Hall
University of Kansas
Lawrence, KS, 66045
(913) 864-7600
www.Isi.uknas.edu/beach/beachhp.htm

Funded by the National Institute on Disability and Rehabilitation Research (NIDRR) of the U.S. Department of Education, the Center offers newsletters, advocacy how-to publications, opportunities for parents to make connections with other parents of children with disabilities, and information on coping strategies for a disability diagnosis and laws that affect families.

Parent to Parent Program
Beach Center
(913) 864-7600

Using mutual support, veteran parents of children with disabilities offer emotional and informational support to rookie parents in one-to-one matches. Beach Center provides information about local programs.

PEAK Parent Center
6055 Lehman Drive, #101
Colorado Springs, CO 80910
(719) 531-9400

Provides information and support regarding inclusion of students with disabilities.

Parents Let's Unite for Kids
1500 N. 30th
Billings, MT 59101
(406) 657-2055

Provides information on assistive technology for individuals with disabilities.

National Information Center for Children and Youth with Disabilities
(800) 695-0285

Provides publications, such as fact sheets on specific disabilities, state resource listings, and booklets.

Educational Resources Information Center Clearinghouse on Disabilities and Gifted Education
(800) 601-4868

An excellent source of information including free publications that summarize research findings.

Guide to Disability and Rehabilitation Periodicals
NARIC
8455 Colesville Rd. #935
Silver Springs, Maryland 20910
(800) 346-2742
email: naric@capaccess.org

Guide to seventy magazines and over 5,000 newsletters covering disability-related topics.

Exceptional Parent
(800) 247-8080

Excellent magazine covering families and disabilities. Has the section "Parent Search and Parent Respond" for parents to contact each other for information and other needs.

Making School and Community Recreation Fun For Everyone: Places and Ways to Integrate
by Sherril Moon
Published by Paul H. Brookes

Friendships and Community Connections Between People with and without Developmental Disabilities
Edited by Angela Novak Amado
Published by Paul H. Brookes

A Guide to Thoughtful Friendships: Facilitation for Education and Families
by C. Beth Schaffner and Barbara Buswell
Available from the PEAK Parent Center
611 North Weber, Suite 200
Colorado Springs, CO 80903

Summary

Adolescence is the transition period from childhood into adulthood when the focus draws away from family to school and community participation. Today's adolescents are faced with more serious challenges than in years past. Unfortunately, the two areas of adolescent life that would ordinarily be the havens for help, guidance, and security—the home and community—are no longer as stable as they used to be. Today, adolescents live in diverse environments where a hurry-up society works against a sense of community, and where the number of dysfunctional families is growing. The adolescent years also pose important challenges for parents. Working effectively with families of children in their teens involves helping them understand the changes they will observe during this transition and supporting them in their efforts to guide their children toward responsible independence. For students with disabilities, the middle school and high school years may mark their first experience receiving some instruction in regular settings and some in special education settings. This means that they will be coping with trying to please a variety of new teachers and students, experiencing the physical and psychological changes of typical adolescents, and then continuing to contend with the challenges of their particular disabilities. The role of new teachers has been expanded with the advent of the inclusion movement, student self-determination, increased family participation, and focus on community integration and student participation. By fostering and supporting positive relationships with parents, new teachers and other professionals gain a window into the lives of their students in the world outside of school. Information gained from parents enables schools to be more effective in promoting positive learning environments for all students.

References

Allen, D., & Hudd, S. (1987). Are we professionalizing parents: Weighing the benefits and pitfalls. *Mental Retardation, 25* (3), 133–139.

Ayres, B., Meyer, L., Erevelles, N., & Park-Lee, S. (1994). Easy for you to say: Teacher perspectives on implementing most promising practices. *The Journal of the Association for Persons with Severe Handicaps, 19,* 84–93.

Barnes, G. M., & Farrell, M. P. (1992). Parent support and control as predictors of adolescent drinking, delinquency, and related problem behaviors. *Journal of Marriage and the Family 54,* 763–776.

Baumrind, D. (1991). The influence of parenting style on adolescent competence and substance use. *Journal of Early Adolescence, 11,* 56–95.

Beakley, B. A., & Yoder, S. L. (1998) Middle schoolers: Learn community skills. *Teaching Exceptional Children, 30* (3), 16–21.

Beale, C. J., & Baskin, D. (1983). What do our teenagers fear? *Child Psychiatry Quarterly, 16* (1), 1–10.

Benz, M., & Halpern, A. (1987). Transition services for secondary students with mild disabilities: A statewide perspective. *Exceptional Children, 53,* 507–514.

Brinckerhoff, J., & Vincent, L. (1986). Increasing parental decision-making at the Individualized Educational Program meeting. *Journal of the Division for Early Childhood, 17,* 97–106.

Castaneda, L., & Sherrill, C. (1997). Challenger Baseball & TOPSoccer. *Teaching Exceptional Children, 30* (2), 26–29.

Chubb, N. H., & Fertman, C. I. (1992). Adolescents' perceptions of belonging in their families. *Families in Society, 73,* 387–394.

Cole, K. B., Struyk, L. R., Kinder, D., Sheehan, J. K., & Kish, C. K. (1997). Portfolio assessment: Challenges in secondary education. *High School Journal, 80* (4), 261–272.

Comfort, R. E., Giorgi, J., & Moody, S. (1997). In a different voice: A student agenda for high school re-form. *High School Journal, 80* (3), 179–183.

Epstein, J. L., Simon, B. S., & Salinas, K. C. (1997). Involving parents in homework in the middle grades. *Research Bulletin,* Center for Evaluation, Development, and Research, Phi Beta Kappa, No. 18.

Farmer, H. S. (1985). Model of career and achievement motivation for women and men. *Journal of Counseling Psychology, 32,* 363–390.

Felber, S. A. (1997). Strategies for parent partnerships. *Teaching Exceptional Children, 30* (1), 20–23.

Fleming, B. (1993). From visitors to partners: A summary of effective parent-involvement practices: From parents to schools. In R. C. Burns (Ed.). *From visitors to partners,* (pp. 77–89). Washington, DC: National Education Association.

Gilliam, J., & Coleman, M. (1981). Who influences IEP committee decisions? *Exceptional Children, 47,* 642–644.

Gribin, K. S. (1994). What do adolescents worry about: A quantitative study. *Progress: Family System Research and Therapy, 3,* 121–135. (www.pgi.edu/gribin.htm)

Harry, B. (1992). Making sense of a disability: Low income, Puerto Rican parents' theories of the problem. *Exceptional Children, 59,* 27–40.

Holmes, M., & Croll, P. (1989). Time spent on homework and academic achievement. *Educational Research, 31,* 37–45.

Hurtado, A. (1995). Variations, combinations, and evolution: Latino families in the United States. In R. Zambrana (Ed.). *Understanding Latino families: Scholarship, policy, and practice* (pp. 40–61). Thousand Oaks, CA: Sage.

Johnson, D. E., Bullock, C. C., & Ashton-Schaeffer, C. (1997). Families and leisure: A context for learning. *Teaching Exceptional Children, 30* (2), 30–34.

Jordan, L., Reyes-Blanes, M. E., Peel, B., Peel, H. A., & Lane, H. B. (1998). Developing teacher-parent partnerships across cultures: Effective parent conferences. *Intervention in School and Clinic, 33* (3), 141–147.

Kagan, D. H. (1992). Professional growth among preservice and beginning teachers. *Review of Educational Research, 62,* 129–169.

Kroth, R. L., & Edge, D. (1997). *Strategies for communication with parents and families of exceptional children.* Denver: Love.

Lerner, J. (1997). *Learning disabilities: Theories, diagnosis, and teaching strategies* (7th ed.). Boston: Houghton Mifflin.

Luetke-Stahlman, B., Luetke-Stahlman, B., & Luetke-Stahlman, H. (1992). Yes, siblings can help. *Perspectives, 10* (5), 9–11.

Luther, S. S. (1993). Methodological and conceptual issues in research in childhood resilience. *Journal of Child Psychology and Psychiatry and Allied Disciplines, 34,* 441–453.

Lynn, L. (1994). Building parent involvement. National Association of Secondary School Principals. *Practitioner, 20* (5), 1–4.

Nelson, J. S., Epstein, M. H., Bursuck, W. D., Jayanthi, M., & Sawyer, V. (1998). The preferences of middle school students for homework adaptations made by general education teachers. *Learning Disabilities Research and Practice, 13,* 109–117.

Palmer, D. S., Borthwick-Duffy, S. A., Widaman, K. (1998). Parent perceptions of inclusive practices for their children with significant disabilities. *Exceptional Children, 64* (2), 271–282.

Pierce, L. V., & O'Malley, J. M. (1992). *Performance and portfolio assessment for language minority students.* Washington, DC: National Clearinghouse for Bilingual Education.

Queen, J. A., Blackwelder, B. B., & Mallen, L. P. (1997). *Responsible classroom management for teachers and students.* New Jersey: Prentice Hall.

Ramey, S. L., & and Ramey, C. T. (1994). The transition to school: Why the first few years matter for a lifetime. *Phi Delta Kappan, 76,* 194–198.

Reyes-Blanes, M. E., & Daunic, A. (1997). Cultural dynamism: An alternative view of cultural diversity. Manuscript submitted for publication.

Salend, S. J., & Schiff, J. (1989). An examination of the homework practices of teachers of students with learning disabilities. *Journal of Learning Disabilities, 22,* 621–623.

Soderlund, J., Epstein, M. H., Quinn, K. P., Cumblad, C., & Peterson, S. (1995). (Parental perspectives on comprehensive services for children and youth with emotional and behavioral disorders. *Behavioral Disorders, 20* (3), 169.

Stratton, J. (1995). *How students have changed: A call to action for our children's future.* Arlington, VA: American Association of School Administrators.

Sussell, A., Carr, S., & Hartman, A. (1996). Families R us: Building a parent/school partnership. *Teaching Exceptional Children, 28* (4), 53–57.

Tubman, J. G., and Lerner, R. M. (1994). Affective experiences of parents and their children from adolescence to young adulthood: Stability of affective experiences. *Journal of Adolescence, 17,* 1–14.

Turnbull, A. P., & Turnbull, H. R. III. (1997). *Families, professionals, and exceptionality: A special partnership* (3rd ed.). New Jersey: Prentice-Hall.

U.S. Department of Health and Human Services, Office of the Assistant Secretary for Planning and Evaluation. (1996). *Trends in the well-being of America's children and youth.* Washington, DC: Author. (youth.os.dhhs.gov/youthinf.htm#new)

U.S. Department of Education. (1994). *To assure the free appropriate public education of all children with disabilities.* Sixteenth Annual Report to Congress on the Implementation of the Individuals with Disabilities Education Act. Washington, DC: U.S. Government Printing Office.

Wagner, M. (1990). *The school programs and school performance of secondary students classified as learning disabled: Findings from the National Longitudinal Transition Study of Special Education Students.* Menlo Park, CA: SRI International.

Williams, W., & Fox, T. J. (1996). Planning for inclusion: A practical process. *Teaching Exceptional Children, 28* (3), 6–13.

Wilson, P. M., & Wilson, J. R. (1992). Environmental influences on adolescent educational aspirations. *Youth & Society, 24,* 52–70.

Zinsmeister, K. (1990). Growing up scared. *Atlantic, 265* (6), 49–66.

9

Families of Adult Individuals with Disabilities

David Bateman

Chapter Objectives _____

In this chapter we will

- Describe and discuss some important facts about adults with disabilities
- Describe some of the major challenges that adults with disabilities and their families encounter
- Discuss the role of the non-disabled siblings
- Examine important transition issues for adults with disabilities
- Discuss the role of the school in attempting to provide parents and students support as they develop plans regarding the transition to life beyond the school years
- Pose questions that families ask with answers regarding the many concerns regarding adults with disabilities
- Describe major laws affecting adults with disabilities
- Provide useful resources for families with an adult member with a disability
- Summarize important chapter themes

Mary's father, Greg Riggs, suspected that a problem existed when he met with the doctor shortly after Mary's birth. He feared something was wrong because of the difficulty Mary's mother, Pam, experienced during the pregnancy and also during the delivery. The doctor informed Greg that Mary had Down syndrome and suggested the family place her on a waiting list for a local state institution providing care for such children. The message from the doctor seemed too heavy a weight for Greg to bear. When he shared the information with Pam, she told Greg that she planned to bring Mary home where they would provide all the support services she needed.

Mary spent most of her school years in a special class for students with moderate to severe mental and physical disabilities. Although the principal was

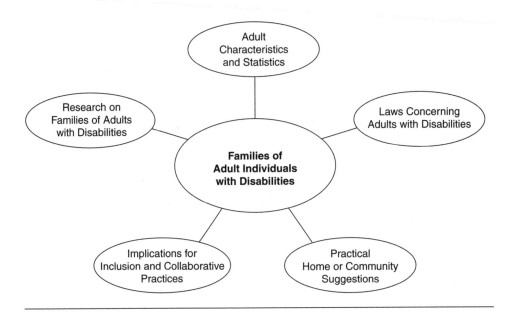

generally opposed to inclusion, Mary was placed in some regular education classes during elementary school. However, during high school the education and support staff seemed more willing to include Mary in regular school programs. Mary made friends in the regular classes and participated in a variety of school functions. She became involved in a work-study program during her last two years of school, first working at McDonald's and later at a local hotel with supports from coworkers when necessary. Mary was experiencing many of the joys of a normal teenager.

With pride, Mary's father thought about all that she had accomplished despite her doctor's early predictions. However, as Mary's graduation approached, Greg feared for her future. What would become of Mary after leaving the supportive environment of high school? Would she be able to maintain a job? Would she be able to live independently? And how would her family support her?

Adults with special needs face the many challenges that we all encounter as we move through the different phases of the life cycle. For individuals with disabilities, as well as their families, one of the most confusing and often most stressful periods involves the transition from school to the world of adulthood. In this chapter we identify some of the more pressing concerns and challenges that individuals with disabilities and their families encounter during adulthood. Areas of focus and concern include living arrangements, employment, and recreational and leisure time activities. This chapter also discusses the role of new teachers in attempting to provide guidance and support for individuals with disabilities and their families when developing transition plans.

Adult Characteristics and Statistics

What happens to students with disabilities and their families after they leave high school? Unfortunately, most of the research regarding families with members who have disabilities has focused on childhood (Hayden, 1992) rather than on postschool life. However, several studies have attempted to track individuals with disabilities into adulthood to determine whether they were able to make a smooth transition into independent living. Notably, Brolin (1995) suggests that individuals with disabilities do not have access to resources and services necessary to enhance their participation in the community. Brolin concludes that only one-third of those individuals who were studied could be considered to be leading relatively satisfactory lives. Similarly, Wehman (1997) argues that young adults fail to find stable employment because the journey from school to work consists of several years of dead-end, low-paying jobs.

One of the most comprehensive studies of adults with disabilities was conducted by SRI International. In their longitudinal transition study, approximately 8,000 former special education students, ages thirteen through twenty-one, were tracked for a five-year period. Brolin (1995) outlined four of the major findings of this massive study:

1. Approximately 29.2 percent of those individuals who had been labeled (eleven disability categories) had been employed full-time for one year or more upon leaving school. Individuals with learning disabilities had the highest employment rate (37.9 percent) and individuals with multiple disabilities and orthopedic impairments the lowest employment rate (1.3 percent).
2. The average wage of the former students was $4.35 per hour. Individuals with learning disabilities had the highest wage at $4.63 and individuals with visual impairments the lowest at $3.12.
3. The young adults who were studied indicated their social experiences were quite limited. Such social isolation became more pronounced the longer they were out of school.
4. The individuals studied had major deficits in important life skill areas such as using the telephone directory, counting change, telling time, and reading common signs.

Another fairly comprehensive study was done for the National Organization on Disability by Louis Harris Associates in 1998. This study found adults with disabilities fared much worse than their nondisabled counterparts in employment, income, education, along with gaps in frequency of socializing, entertainment, and access to transportation and health care (Harris, 1998). Specifically, the poll found:

• In employment, among adults with disabilities of working age (eighteen to sixty-four), three out of ten (29 percent) work full- or part-time, compared to eight out of ten (79 percent) of those without disabilities, a gap of fifty percentage points.
• In education, one out of five (20 percent) adults with disabilities aged eighteen and over has not graduated from high school, compared to only one out of ten (9 percent) adults with no disabilities.

- In frequency of socialization, only seven out of ten (69 percent) adults with disabilities socialize with close friends, relatives, or neighbors at least once a week, compared to more than eight out of ten (84 percent) of the nondisabled population.
- Just over half (54 percent) of adults with disabilities go to church, synagogue, or another place of worship at least once a month, compared to almost six out of ten (57 percent) of those without disabilities.
- About a third (33 percent) of adults with disabilities go to a restaurant at least once a week, compared to six out of ten (60 percent) of those without disabilities.
- Only six out of ten (62 percent) adults with disabilities was registered to vote in the 1996 presidential election, compared to almost eight out of ten (78 percent) among the nondisabled population, representing a gap of sixteen percentage points, according to the Current Population Survey.
- Fully a third (34 percent) of adults with disabilities lived in a household with an annual income of less than $15,000 in 1997, compared to only about one in eight (12 percent) of those without disabilities.
- Inadequate transportation is considered a problem by three out of ten (30 percent) adults with disabilities (17 percent "major problem," 13 percent "minor problem"), but by only one out of six (17 percent) adults without disabilities (7 percent "major problem," 10 percent "minor problem"), a gap of thirteen percentage points.
- One out of five (21 percent) adults with disabilities did not get medical care that they needed on at least one occasion during the past year, compared to one in ten (11 percent) adults without a disability, a gap of ten percentage points.
- Only about one in three (33 percent) adults with disabilities is very satisfied with life in general, compared to fully six out of ten (61 percent) nondisabled adults.

Clearly there are problems that still need to be overcome, both by individuals with disabilities and their families.

The transition from school to adulthood for an individual with disabilities is often a complex and lengthy process. Schools must provide a solid preparation program that truly prepares the individual for the many challenges that lie ahead. The program must also include ongoing support for the individual and his or her family as they leave the educational system.

The essential elements of an effective transition system should include the following components (Bateman, 1994):

1. Effective high school training regarding the demands of community living
2. An array of adult services aimed at meeting the unique vocational, residential, and leisure needs of the disabled individual
3. A cooperative system of transition planning that ensures access to needed postschool services

Transition is a process involving many individuals and agencies in cooperation with the family that attempts to develop and implement an effective plan to support the individual with disabilities as they move into adulthood (Wehman, 1997). Brolin (1995) suggests that many adults with disabilities encounter significant problems as they attempt to assume the many roles of adulthood including independent living, achieving successful employment, and developing leisure and recreational pursuits. This time of transition continues to be quite stressful. Brolin (1995) states that some individuals with disabilities will achieve success and live productive lives but the majority will most likely become either unemployed as low-level members of a secondary labor market. He also believes that although some will become successful, many will be dependent on their families, many will get in trouble with the law, and they will have limited friendships and recreational outlets. Major areas of concern for the individual and the family continue to include living arrangements, meaningful employment, and development of recreational and leisure time activities (Hobbs, Perrin, & Ireys, 1985).

Research on Families of Adult Individuals with Disabilities

New teachers should remember that an adult with a disability does not always threaten the well-being of a family. Feelings of family members about an adult with a disability can range from rejection and denial to acceptance, from intense hate to intense love, from total neglect to overprotection. Historically, people believed that families with a member who had a disability always experienced unrelieved grief, despair, and sorrow, but today we know that such families often experience many joys as well as moments of appreciation and satisfaction (Ziegler, 1992). In fact, some parents and siblings assert that having a family member with a disability has actually strengthened and enriched the family (Powell & Gallagher, 1993). For most caregivers, the family members with disabilities often give their lives purpose (Heller & Factor, 1993). One mother said her son gave her life meaning by teaching her greater love, compassion, and patience. This mother's reaction is often repeated by parents, especially mothers, of adults with disabilities (Heller & Factor, 1993).

Studies show that families of adults with disabilities resemble families with nondisabled adult children more often than not (Haring, Lovett, & Saren, 1991). However, this is not to diminish the fact that the challenges and burdens faced by family members of individuals with disabilities can be great (Miller, Burmester, Callahan, Dieterle, & Niedermeyer, 1994). One of the most immediate needs on moving into adulthood for individuals with a disability and their family members involves selecting a place of residence. A large number of adults with disabilities continue to live with their families for most of their lives. In fact, according to Heller and Factor (1993), most families of adults with developmental disabilities provide life-long family-based care, although out-of-home placement increases slightly as parents age or develop disabilities themselves. Most persons with developmental disabilities remain at home until parental death or disability occurs. Parents often worry about their ability to continue to provide care for their adult children into old age.

Heller and Factor (1993) conducted a 2.5 year follow-up of an earlier study of 100 family caregivers of individuals with mental retardation age thirty and older living at home to attempt to determine older parents' perception of their caregiving burden and ultimately their desire to place their adult children in residential facilities. They discovered that the level of support services that are available often play a significant role in reducing perceived burdens of older parents of an adult with mental retardation living at home. In their opinion, support programs designed to enhance the caregiving capacities of families are strongly needed. The highest unmet need that was identified by the families was information on available residential services. Other needs included out-of-home respite care, social and recreational services, in-home respite care, life management, information on guardianship, information on financial planning, and family counseling for all family members. Seekins, Offner, and Jackson (1991) discovered that many parents who care for an adult with disabilities, who may have had little or no involvement with the formal support services system when their children were younger, finally seek help from that system when they are faced with an imminent crisis involving the care of their adult child.

When a student with a disability leaves school and enters the adult world, many parents receive a considerable shock that they were not prepared to encounter. First, there is the realization that state or federal laws no longer mandate the services their child was entitled to during school years. Second, many parents know very little, if anything at all, about adult service systems in the neighborhood or community (Miller, et al., 1994). This supports the contention that transition planning should attempt to prepare the family for the different service and support systems that are available for the adult with disabilities. The discussion should be initiated while the individual is attending school. In addition, an effort should be made to develop a seamless transition system from school to adulthood so that needed services are not lost during the transition process.

One of the most important concepts in family support is that it must be family centered and attempt to meet all members' varying needs (Griffiths & Unger, 1994). The needs of each individual family and the needs of each family member should define what supports are essential. As new teachers attempt to design support services and programming necessary to support adults with disabilities, it is critical to include the needs of all family members, including siblings, in the effort. Families have requested information on many topics, including in-home and out-of-home respite care, available support services, advocacy groups and organizations, financial assistance for family needs, and other supports as determined by each family member (Friesen and Wahlers, 1993). Families should be provided information regarding guardianship, estate planning, wills, and trusts; assistance for the young adult or family member with career or vocational choices; and, if appropriate, address the issues and responsibilities of marriage and family (Turnbull & Turnbull, 1995). Although there are no simple solutions to the myriad of problems that arise in families with an adult with disabilities, careful planning for the future or permanency planning, which considers the entire family's needs and concerns, is likely to be very helpful (Griffiths & Unger, 1994).

Siblings in particular play an important role of support for adults with disabilities and can contribute to future planning (Seltzer, 1993). Although a relatively large body of literature pertains to parental reactions, there is limited information about siblings of individuals with disabilities (Alper, 1994). In families with adults with disabilities, siblings can act as parental surrogates, caretakers, or simply as siblings. While many parents have increasingly higher expectations of siblings to become more involved in caregiving as the children with disabilities grow older, siblings are typically only minimally involved in the planning process (Alper, 1994).

Minimal research has been conducted on reactions of the nondisabled siblings. Liska (1996) refers to them as the "other" children who were always around but somehow remained invisible. Krauss, Seltzer, Gordon, and Friedman (1996) state that the nondisabled siblings are often overlooked by parents and service providers when considering sources of support for the adult with disabilities. The research that has been conducted indicates many areas in which the nondisabled sibling can be looked to for support and guidance. Gartner, Lipsky, & Turnbull (1991) identified some of the areas, including temporary respite care, guardianship, and involvement in career and living choices.

If families decide, out of exasperation or financial restrictions, that they can no longer provide in-home care for their adult children they often encounter long waiting lists for out-of-home placements in group homes or other facilities (Griffiths & Unger, 1994). This is an area in which the nondisabled sibling can provide support for the parents. Unfortunately, parents often feel uncomfortable involving the nondisabled sibling when they reach a point of desperation (Griffiths & Unger, 1994). Many parents seldom involve the nondisabled sibling in any matters because they do not want to burden the siblings with what they consider as their responsibility. This is an issue that should be addressed as early as possible, with expectations clearly delineated.

To determine the long-term effects of having a brother or sister with a disability, ninety men and women who were nondisabled siblings of adults with disabilities were questioned (Cleveland & Miller, 1977). They reported that the nondisabled siblings were able to make a positive adjustment and had developed good relationships. They also discovered that the parents did not ask the nondisabled siblings to assume responsibilities that were beyond their ability. Also, the nondisabled siblings related that their parents were

BOX 9.1

Family–Teacher Issues

Vincent, age thirty-nine, displays tremors in his hands or arms when performing writing activities. Sometimes he displays poor balance and lack of body strength. His vocational advocate, Mr. Whipple, wants to refer Vincent to the local clinic in the Ardent Hospital. Most likely, Mr. Whipple is observing signals of motoric difficulty in Vincent. Mr. Whipple, however, is fearful that Vincent's parents won't respond because at age seventy-five and eighty-one, neither parent drives. Mr. Whipple is afraid that Vincent's problems will be given a low priority, due to his parents' lack of transportation.

Collaborative Orientations and Responsive Practices

Mr. Whipple desires to involve Vincent's parents, but doesn't know how to respond. Mr. Whipple decides to elicit the support of Vincent's counselor, Mrs. Packles. Mrs. Packles tells Mr. Whipple that she has worked with Vincent's parents in the past and they will respond if they believe they are not being pressured. Further, Mrs. Packles passes on to Mr. Whipple the most recent Ardent social service: free transportation to and from services for individuals with no other means.

Mr. Whipple decides that Vincent's tremors in his hands or arms can't wait. He must call Vincent's parents to secure Vincent immediate help. He calls Vincent's parents to ask whether they or he can accompany Vincent to the hospital.

After conferring with the parents, Mr. Whipple decides to help by offering to arrange transportation for both Vincent and his parents to Ardent's local clinic. Vincent and his parents arrive at the local clinic for their scheduled appointment a week later.

able to meet their many needs, that they did not feel neglected, and that the experience did not have a negative impact on their life in any way.

Some of the issues siblings of adults with disabilities must face include responsibility for financial support, issues of guardianship, concerns regarding genetic counseling, and supporting career and living options and choices. These are a few of the many concerns that siblings encounter related to their adult brother or sister with a disability (Alper, 1994).

If families decide out of exasperation or financial constraints that they can no longer provide in-home care for their adult children, they face the additional stress of long waiting lists for residential placement in group homes or other facilities (Griffiths & Unger, 1994). Siblings often can be a source of support and comfort when parents can no longer continue to meet all the needs of the adult with a disability. Unfortunately, in many cases parents are reluctant to ask their nondisabled children to take on the caregiving responsibilities (Griffiths & Unger, 1994).

In a study that examined the relationships of forty-six sisters who had siblings with moderate to profound developmental disabilities, Begun (1989) discovered that the relationships were positive but nonintimate. She attempts to explain her findings by stating that lack of intimacy was a result of an inability to interact with a person of limited language and social competence.

Krauss et al. (1996) investigated the current relationship patterns and future adult role expectations of 140 adults with a sibling who had a disability and resided at the family home. They discovered that nondisabled siblings were willing to provide support for their sibling with a disability in a variety of ways. They were willing to maintain regular contact, provide emotional support, and were sensitive to the varying needs of their sibling with a disability. Many were willing to provide a residence for their sibling with a disability when their parents were no longer able to do so. This was especially true if the mother was vulnerable. The willingness to provide needed support was somewhat related to the level of involvement the nondisabled sibling had with their brother or sister with disabilities. The results of this study, as well as others, seems to indicate that nondisabled siblings are often willing to provide necessary support to their family.

It seems apparent that when developing transition plans that will provide direction for the family as the individual with disabilities leaves the school setting and moves to the world of the adult, new teachers should work toward involving the entire family in the process. Certainly, all family members are affected in some way by the presence of a child with a disability. All family members should attempt to identify their individual needs and attempt to outline strategies to support and meet their needs in the transition planning process. The current research tends to support active involvement by the nondisabled siblings in the planning process and the support efforts as needed throughout life.

Family Roles/Tasks within Families of Adults with Disabilities

The transition from high school to adulthood for individuals with disabilities can produce concern and stress for their families (Thorin & Irvin, 1992). Parents are often involved in helping the young adult with disabilities make many critical life decisions. Parents are required to move from a familiar system within the public schools into an unfamiliar and uncertain adult services system (Summers, 1986). Moreover, unlike the educational system, which entitles all children to receive services, the adult service system requires eligibility (Moon, Inge, Wehman, Brooke, & Barcus, 1990). In the process, the role of advocate, decision maker, or life manager is often thrust by default upon parents of young adults with disabilities (Russell, Grant, Joseph, & Fee 1993).

Implications for Inclusion and Collaborative Practices in Schools and Classrooms

As a part of the transition process, social agencies and organizations that have never talked with one another (but probably should have) are expected to work together to meet the needs of individuals with disabilities. This component is the heart of how transition services are to be provided. Transition services now rely on individuals outside of the realm of school systems. This includes agencies with fixed mandates to serve only one segment of the population, agencies that have a limited number of open positions for the individuals they serve, agencies that have long waiting lists, and organizations that either duplicate the services provided or are also limited in what they can do for individuals with a disability and their families.

A major component of transition services is a coordinated set of activities (Bateman, 1994). The school districts have it incumbent on them to provide the coordination necessary to meet the needs of the student with a disability, and these aspects are detailed in the student's IEP. Why is the coordination of activities crucial to the success of effective transition services? For transition services to be effective, multiple individuals from many parts of the student's life need to be involved. Coordination of these individuals is necessary to ensure the necessary services for life after high school. This avoids duplication, makes sure that all the services necessary are provided, and ensures that individuals who need services receive the assistance they need.

It is important that new teachers recognize that the agencies with which the school systems must work do not have a legal mandate to provide their services. The school system has the only legal mandate, and therefore it is imperative that the schools convene the meetings to discuss transition services and ensure that the services provided are coordinated among the different agencies and are not duplicative of what other agencies are providing. As the agency responsible for convening the transition meetings (in most states), schools should expand their realm to include postschool life as well.

There are three levels of collaboration among agencies. The first level is that of agencies arriving at a specific understanding of who does what, when, and how often (Audette, 1980). The second level is that of agencies agreeing to sharing resources. The different agencies develop decision rules about who pays for what and under what circumstances (Cohen, Vitalo, Anthony, & Pierce, 1980). The third level is that of agencies pooling their resources for planning and administration, staff training, and community services (Wehman, 1992). Schalock (1985) states that collaboration among agencies works better when initiated at the local level instead of by federal or state agencies.

No longer can one agency meet all the needs of every individual. Some individuals will require counseling, transportation services, employment assistance, physical therapy, or other health-related services. An individual living in the community will need to be able to take advantage of the best the different services have to offer instead of relying on just one service provider. Organizations working with individuals with disabilities are realizing that they need to work together to provide the best services (Wehman, 1997).

Still, effective interagency coordination is difficult to achieve. Effective coordination requires planning, conflict resolution, and a genuine commitment to the welfare of the person involved (Summers, 1986). Although more agencies are working together to meet the needs of individuals with disabilities, there are still some problems with collaborating agencies. Some agencies have a very specific method of dealing with a situation with which others would not philosophically agree. Some agencies also find it difficult to work together because they have problems working with others, do not want to share their services with others, or are afraid that they will lose control over the service they provide to the community (Wehman, 1997). With these problems in coordinating services among different agencies it is often difficult to meet the needs of individuals with disabilities (Wehman, 1995).

Practical Home or Community Suggestions for New Teachers

The role of the new teacher includes providing effective and appropriate training while the individual with disabilities attends school. The primary focus should be to prepare the student for life beyond the school years. Also, it is the responsibility of the school to provide support and guidance when it is time to plan for the school to work transition. One of the most telling ways to evaluate the impact of the educational system on its students is what happens after they leave the school system (Brolin, 1995). Another important point is that one of the most critical and pressing responsibilities of new teachers and other support personnel is to help pupils with physical and perhaps multiple disabilities prepare for present and future life work endeavors (Bigge, 1991). One of the most critical issues that students, parents, and professionals often encounter involves the relationship between what is taught in school and the needs of the individual with disabilities during the adult years (Turnbull, Bateman, & Turnbull, 1993).

For instance, it is imperative that the curriculum provide training in skills needed in adulthood. Also, it is just as essential that transition planning outlining movement from school to work be initiated as early as possible and involve all who will have a role to play in the process, especially the individual with disabilities and his or her family. The transition from school should be planned in a collaborative manner between the individual, the family, and the school. The Individuals with Disabilities Act (IDEA) mandates that the Individualized Education Program (IEP) includes transition services before or by the age of sixteen (Wehman, 1995). This aspect of the IEP should receive more serious attention than it often does. Also, the parents, the student and, if applicable, the siblings need to be encouraged to become more active participants in the development and implementation of the transition plan. This aspect of the IEP seems to offer the most hope that life beyond school will be both productive and satisfying for those with disabilities.

Unfortunately, programs intended to enhance transition from school to employment have not been developed sufficiently, and this continues to be a serious concern to educators, parents, and policy makers (Bateman, 1994). It seems apparent that there is much the new teacher can do to provide training and support for students with disabilities and their families as they plan for the transition to the adult world. It is just as evident that all family members should be involved in the development and implementation of the plan.

Basic Steps New Teachers Can Provide

1. Engage in learning opportunities to meet basic obligation to work effectively with families.
2. Ensure systematic two-way communication (school to home and home to school) about the school, school programs, and students' progress.
3. Engage in learning opportunities to work together with families so that a wide range of support and resource roles for students and the school is available.
4. Emphasize strategies and techniques for connecting children and learning activities at home and in the community with learning at school.
5. Encourage families to actively participate in school decision making and to exercise their leadership and advocacy skills.
6. Encourage families to gain the skills to access community and support services that strengthen school programs, family practices, and student learning and development.

BOX 9.2

Family–Teacher Issues

Transition services recognize Tara's and Bill's levels of career development and assess their work-related behaviors, skills, and aptitudes. Miss Carson would like to write a news article for the adult program's paper to inform all families of the importance of vocational assessments for their family member at the start of the adult program—not when their family member is ready to graduate and begin looking for a real job.

Collaborative Orientations and Responsive Practices

Miss Carson is so adamant about expressing the importance of vocational assessment and preparation that she writes a clear, persuasive, and moving message to the families. In the news article, Miss Carson personally recognizes important vocational sites that have worked well with families in the past. She also names specific vocational assessment devices that seem useful in guiding the career choices of individuals with disabilities. Finally, she offers to arrange presentations by former graduates who participated in and profited by early transition services started at the beginning of the adult program.

A week after the news article appeared in the school paper, more than 60 percent of families sign up for the vocational assessment seminar to be held later this month. Miss Carson is pleased with the parental response.

Laws Concerning Adults with Disabilities

New teachers should be familiar with the following laws affecting adults with disabilties.

The Rehabilitation Act of 1973

The first major piece of legislation to have an impact on the education and services for students with disabilities was the Rehabilitation Act of 1973 (P.L. 93-112). Commonly referred to as the "Rehab Act," or "Section 504," because of a main provision within the whole law dealing with individuals with disabilities, this authorized federal funds for compliance with regulations concerning the education of students with disabilities (and withholding of funds for noncompliance). The main component of Section 504 of the Rehab Act states: "No otherwise qualified individual with handicaps shall solely by reason of her or his handicap, be excluded from the participation in, be denied the benefits of, or be subjected to discrimination under any program or activity receiving Federal financial assistance" (29 U.S.C. Sec. 706).

In addition to students with disabilities, this act protects any person who meets one of three life-defining criteria. Any person who:

(i) has a physical or mental impairment which substantially limits one or more of such person's major life activities
(ii) has a record of such an impairment, or
(iii) is regarded as having such an impairment (29 U.S.C. Sec. 706)

is considered as having a disability under the law. For the purposes of Section 504, major life activities include caring for one's self, performing manual tasks, walking, seeing, hearing, speaking, breathing, learning, and working. An important aspect is that individuals who are intentionally and unintentionally discriminated against are protected. Under Section 504, individuals who have a disability and therefore might need assistance qualify for the related services necessary for them to benefit from education. Also, Section 504 has provisions for nondiscriminatory employment.

The Americans with Disabilities Act of 1990

The definition used for Section 504 for an individual with a disability and the descriptors of major life events are the same definitions used in the Americans with Disabilities Act (ADA), and although the Rehab Act was passed in 1973, individuals with disabilities continued, as a group, to occupy an inferior status in our society, and were severely disadvantaged socially, vocationally, economically, and educationally (42 U.S.C. 12101, et seq., Sec. 2[a][6]). Therefore, the law was strengthened through its subsequent amendments and with the passage of the Americans with Disabilities Act (ADA) in 1990 (P.L. 101-336). The language of ADA is analogous to the language of the Rehab Act in this respect:

"Subject to the provision of this title, no qualified individual with a disability, shall by reason of such disability, be excluded from participation in or be denied the benefits of services, programs, or activities of a public entity, or be subjected to discrimination by such entity" (The Americans with Disabilities Act of 1990, Section 12132).

The Rehabilitation Act of 1973 and the Americans with Disabilities Act of 1990 are important to adults with disabilities because they allow statutory venues for remediation of complaints. This provides individuals with disabilities and their families an avenue through which they can file complaints against public schools. If these complaints are found to be valid, the schools can potentially have all their federal funds terminated. A typical example is a student with a physical disability who does not require special assistance from school personnel relating to his education, and, therefore, is not classified as needing special education but still meets the definition of having a disability under the three-part definition of Section 504 of the Rehab Act. Under Section 504 it would be illegal to discriminate against this child regarding activities, events, or classes. Section 504 of the Rehab Act and ADA are broader and more inclusive than later special education laws.

The ADA strives for "equality of opportunity, full participation, independent living, and economic self-sufficiency" (42 U.S.C. 12101, et seq., Sec. 2[a][8]) for persons with disabilities. The main purpose of the ADA is to provide civil rights to the 43 million Americans with disabilities who have been unable to access their communities and necessary services. It has been argued that the ADA was developed to prevent businesses from expanding and to wreck small business (see Wehman, 1993), however, its main interest is to promote equal access and freedom for people with disabilities. Others state the ADA is an extension on the installment of a contract between individuals with disabilities, their family members, and the government for a lifetime of services and accessibility that starts with special education services received in schools (Turnbull, Bateman, & Turnbull, 1993). The intent of the ADA is to open up more of society to people with disabilities. It is clear, however, that the norms of society will be changed by the ADA.

Family Member Questions

The list of questions that might be asked by family members is long and involved. Family members will be frustrated to learn that the maze they have negotiated (Anderson, Chitwood, & Hayden, 1996) is now a completely different maze, and they can forget everything they knew before about whom to contact, where to go for help, and the amount of help or assistance that might be provided. The answers that are provided are short, and give very basic information. For more information, and much more involved answers, new teachers are encouraged to contact the organizations listed in the Family Resources and Services section.

- *Where does my son or daughter go after they finish high school?* While the student is in high school it is imperative that a transition plan be developed that will elaborate what services will be provided for the student with a disability, who will provide those services, and what can be done in high school to get ready for those services. Additionally, there should be concerted attempts to get the individual involved in the community so that informal support networks (friends, siblings, and neighbors) can assist in the transition into the community.
- *Where is the best place to talk with others?* Have the parents contact a local Parent-to-Parent group. The Parent-to-Parent program is one in which parents of children with disabilities help other parents whose child has mental retardation, cerebral

palsy, epilepsy, autism, or other disabilities. The purpose is to provide supportive, experienced parents to help the parents through the difficulties of accepting that their child has a disability, learning about the disability, and finding the proper services to aid their child in his or her development.

- *What will happen to my son/daughter after I am gone?* Many parents fear that after they are gone no one will be around to assist in the care of their child who has a disability. All parents, not just parents of a child who has a disability, need to develop a will and discuss guardianship issues with someone they feel is responsible. New teachers can discuss with parents about what would happen in an ideal world, and who would take responsibility. They can have the parents make sure the responsible person is aware of the guardianship role and can help make decisions. They can have them think about a less than ideal world, who would become responsible, and plan accordingly. There is good information in the book *Planning for the Future: Providing a Meaningful Life for a Child with a Disability after Your Death* by L. M. Russell, A. E. Grant, S. M. Joseph, & R. W. Fee (1993), Evanston, IL: American Publishing.

- *Where can I get more information about life after high school for my son/daughter?* Each of the organizations listed in the following resource list has a wealth of information available for families and for individuals with disabilities. New teachers can take advantage of the Web addresses and help others make sense of the information.

Family Resources and Services

The following resources and services may be useful to families with an adult member with a disability.

American Association on Mental Retardation
1719 Kalorama Road NW
Washington, DC 20009-2684
www.aamr.org

American Cancer Society
1599 Clifton Road
Atlanta, GA 30329
www.cancer.org

American Council for the Blind
1155 15th Street NW, Suite 720
Washington, DC 20005
www.acb.org

American Diabetes Association National Service Center
P.O. Box 25757
1660 Duke Street
Alexandria, VA 22313
www.diabetes.org

American Heart Association
7320 Greenville Avenue
Dallas, TX 7231
www.amhrt.org

American Network of Community Options and Resources (ANCOR)
4200 Evergreen Lane, Suite 315
Annandale, VA. 22003
www.ancor.org

American Parkinson Disease Association
116 John Street, Suite 417
New York, NY 10038
www.apdaparkinson.com

American Speech-Language-Hearing Association (ASHA)
10801 Rockville Pike
Rockville, MD 20852
www.aha.org

The Association for Persons with Severe Handicaps (TASH)
7010 Roosevelt Way NE
Seattle, WA 98115
www.tash.org

Autism Society of America
7910 Woodmont Ave, Suite 300
Bethesda, MD 20814
www.autism-society.org

Council for Exceptional Children (CEC)
1920 Association Drive
Reston, VA 20091
www.cec.sped.org

Council for Learning Disabilities
P.O. Box 40303
Overland Park, KS 66204
www.1wintrop.edu/cld

Cystic Fibrosis Foundation
6931 Arlington Road, Suite 200
Bethesda, MD 20814
www.cff.org

Goodwill Industries of America
9200 Wisconsin Ave.
Bethesda, MD 20814-3896
www.goodwill.org

Learning Disabilities Association
4156 Library Rd
Pittsburgh, PA 15234
www.ldnatl.org

National Association of Rehabilitation Facilities
PO Box 17675
Washington, DC 20041

National Association for the Visually Handicapped
22 W. 21st Street
New York, NY 10017
www.navh.org

National Council on Disability
800 Independence Ave SW, Suite 814
Washington, DC 20591
www.ncd.gov

National Down Syndrome Congress
1800 Dempster Street
Park Ridge, IL 60068
www.members.carol.net/ndsc

National Institute of Communication Disorders
Hearing and Deafness (NICHD)
National Institute of Health
Bethesda, MD 20892
www.nih.gov/nidcd

National Mental Health Association
1800 N. Kent Street
Arlington, VA 22209
www.nmha.org

National Rehabilitation Information Center (NARIC)
Catholic University of America
620 Michigan Avenue NE
Washington, DC 20017
www.naric.org

President's Committee on Employment of People with Disabilities
1331 20th Street NW, Suite 300
Washington, DC 20004
www50.pcepd.gov/pcepd/

Summary

This chapter's purpose was to examine the major challenges that await individuals with disabilities as they transition from school to adulthood. It is essential that novice teachers are familiar with the issues and challenges so that they might adjust the curriculum accordingly. Also, it will help to outline a transition plan that will attempt to help individuals and their family prepare for the future. New teachers face a myriad of different issues, concerns, tasks, and questions as they interact with family members and community professionals. The major concerns and issues that young adults with disabilities encounter were outlined and discussed in this chapter.

Major issues that were presented in this chapter include:

- Society often underestimates adults with disabilities and their potential to learn to live with little or minimal support in the community.
- Federal legislation has outlined a process called transition, so schools should attempt to provide support and guidance to families preparing to meet the challenges of adult life with a disability.
- Community adjustment should be one of the main goals of the transition plan and it should attempt to focus on the skills needed to find employment, establish residence, and enjoy recreational and leisure time activities.
- There is a variety of options for adults with disabilities in the areas of employment that include sheltered options, supported options, and competitive employment.

All family members should be involved in the transition planning process and there should be an attempt to develop a plan that meets the needs of all family members. The transition plan should provide the bridge between the curriculum and the demands of adult life. If possible, service agencies that will be involved in providing support to the adult with disabilities should be involved in the transition process. New teachers should consider all of the issues that have been outlined in this chapter when reviewing the curriculum and also when developing the transition plan.

References

Alper, S. K. (1994). Families of students with disabilities: Consultation and advocacy. Needham Heights, MA: Allyn & Bacon.

Americans with Disabilities Act, PL 101-336. (July 26, 1990). 42 U.S.C. 12101, et seq. *Federal Register, 56* (144), 35544–35756.

Anderson, W., Chitwood, S., & Hayden, D. (1996). *Negotiating the special education maze.* Rockville, MD: Woodbine House.

Audette, R. H. (1980). Interagency coordination: The bottom line. In J. O. Elder & P. R. Magrab (Eds.). *Coordinating human services to handicapped children: A handbook for interagency collaboration* (pp. 25–34). Baltimore: Paul H. Brookes.

Bateman, D. F. (1994). Transitional programming: Definitions, models, and practices. In A. Rotatori & J. O. Schwenn (Eds.). *Advances in Special Education, Vol. 8,* (pp. 109–136). New York: JAI Press Inc.

Begun, A. (1989). Sibling relationships involving developmentally disabled people. *American Journal on Mental Retardation, 93* (5), 566–574.

Bigge, J. L. (1991). *Teaching individuals with physical and multiple disabilities.* New York: Macmillan.

Brolin, D. E. (1995). *Career education: A functional life skills approach* (3rd ed.). Englewood Cliffs, NJ: Prentice Hall.

Cleveland, D., & Miller, N. (1977). Attitudes and life commitments of older siblings of mentally retarded adults: An exploratory study. *Mental Retardation, 15,* 38–41.

Cohen, M. R., Vitalo, R. L., Anthony, W. A., & Pierce, R. M. (1980). *The skills of community coordination, Book 6.* Baltimore: University Park Press.

Friesen, B., & Wahlers, D. (1993). Respect and real help: Family support and children's mental health. *Journal of Emotional and Behavioral Problems, 2* (4), 12–15.

Gartner, A., Lipsky, D. K., & Turnbull, A. P. (1991). *Supporting families with a child with a disability.* Baltimore: Paul H. Brookes.

Griffiths, D. L., & Unger, D. G. (1994). Views about planning for the future among parents and siblings of adults with mental retardation. *Family Relations, 43,* 221–227.

Haring, K. A., Lovett, D. L., & Saren, D. (1991). Parent perceptions of their adult offspring with disabilities. *Teaching Exceptional Children, 23* (2), 6–10.

Harris, L. (1998). *The National Organization of Disabilities Survey.* New York: Louis Harris and Associates, Inc.

Hayden, M. (1992). *Waiting for community services: Support and service needs of families with adult members who have MR/DD.* Policy Research Brief, University of Minnesota: Research and Training Center on Residential Services and Community Living.

Heller, T., & Factor, A. (1993). Aging family caregivers: Support resources and changes in burden and placement desire. *American Journal on Mental Retardation, 98* (3), 417–426.

Hobbs, N., Perrin, J. M., & Ireys, H. T. (1985). *Chronically ill children and their families.* San Francisco: Jossey-Bass.

Krauss, M., Seltzer, M., Gordon, R., & Friedman, D. (1996). Binding ties: The roles of adult siblings of persons with mental retardation. *Mental Retardation, 34* (2) 83–93.

Liska, V. (1996). *The siblings: A lifelong journey of care.* Paper presented at the Annual World of Congress for the International Association of Scientific Study of Intellectual Disabilities, Helsinki, Finland.

Miller, N. B., Burmester, S., Callahan, D. G., Dieterle, J., & Niedermeyer, S. (1994). *Nobody's perfect: Living and growing with children who have special needs.* Baltimore: Paul H. Brookes.

Moon, M. S., Inge, K. J., Wehman, P., Brooke, V., & Barcus, J. M. (1990). *Helping persons with severe mental retardation get and keep employment: Supported employment issues and strategies.* Baltimore: Paul H. Brookes.

Powell, T. H., & Gallagher, P. A. (1993). *Brothers and sisters: A special part of exceptional families* (2nd ed.). Baltimore: Paul H. Brookes.

The Rehabilitation Act of 1973 (PL 93–112). 29 U.S.C. Section 794.

Russell, L. M., Grant, A. E., Joseph, S. M., & Fee, R. W. (1993). *Planning for the future: Providing a meaningful life for a child with a disability after your death.* Evanston, IL: American Publishing.

Schalock, R. L. (1985). Comprehensive community services: A plea for interagency collaboration. In R. H. Bruininks & K. C. Lakin (Eds.). *Living and learning in the least restrictive environment* (pp. 37–63). Baltimore: Paul H. Brookes.

Seekins, T., Offner, R., & Jackson, K. (1991). *Demography of rural disability.* Missoula, MT: Montana University Affiliated Rural Institute on Disabilities.

Seltzer, M. (1993). Siblings: The next generation of family supports? *IMPACT, 6,* 18–19.

Summers, J. A. (1986). Putting it all together. In J. A. Summers (Ed.). *The right to grow up: An introduction to adults with developmental disabilities* (pp. 287–328). Baltimore: Paul H. Brookes.

Thorin, E., & Irvin, L. (1992). Family stress associated with transition to adulthood of young people with severe disabilities. *Journal of the Association of Persons with Severe Handicaps, 17* (1), 31–39.

Turnbull, A. P., & Turnbull, H. R. (1995). *Families, professionals, and exceptionality* (3rd. ed.). Englewood Cliffs, NJ: Merrill/Prentice-Hall.

Turnbull, H. R., Bateman, D. F., & Turnbull, A. P. (1993). Family empowerment. In P. Wehman (Ed.). *The Americans with Disabilities Act* (pp. 157–174). Baltimore: Paul H. Brookes.

Wehman, P. (1992). *Life beyond the classroom: Transition strategies for young people with disabilities.* Baltimore: Paul H. Brookes.

Wehman, P. (1993). *The ADA mandate for social change.* Baltimore: Paul H. Brookes.

Wehman, P. (1995). *Individual transition plans: A curriculum guide for teachers and counselors.* Austin, TX: PRO-ED.

Wehman, P. (1997). *Exceptional individuals in school, community, and work.* Austin, TX: PRO-ED.

Ziegler, M. (1992). Parent advocacy and children with disabilities: A history. *OSERS News in Print, 5* (1), 5–6.

Part III

Family Services

The chapters in Part 3 expand on new teachers' knowledge base to include research and practical approaches in teachers' responsiveness to families. While Parts 1 and 2 primarily target new teachers, Part 3 family services relate to new teachers' work with other professionals (who also work with and influence students and families). Home, school, and community professionals all help to improve new outcomes and future practices when they understand family-centered programs and services. Thus, as new teachers apply collaborative orientations and responsive practices, teachers use flexibility and multiple methods for meeting family needs. However, they do not work alone, but rather benefit from the experience and expertise of other professionals.

Part 3 discusses strategies for novice teachers in eliciting the aid of professionals representing related services in schools, family agencies and resources, and services from the local, state, or national community. School professionals, as related service providers, include speech and language therapists, physical therapists, occupational therapists, school counselors, school psychologists, or social workers. Other professionals from the community include counselors, community agency workers, and family therapists who also work with parents, siblings, grandparents, and so forth across various settings.

Through the use of various vignettes and case study examples, Part 3 authors examine the respect for divergent thinking when group members originally disagree, then eventually arrive at workable solutions. They summarize key points promoting increased family–professional communication. They promote practical strategies, addressing ways new teachers can use these practices in their family work. Finally, they encourage teachers' reflections on professional sharing of expertise and valuing the input of other profession-als' contributions. Authors offer practical suggestions, questions, family resources, and services useful to teachers.

Chapter 10: Related Service Providers' Work with Students, Families, and Teachers

Lawrence J. O'Shea and Adrienne P. Lancaster describe related service activities in schools, analyzing how these professionals can support new teachers in their family issues. Related service providers also deal with, influence, and have effects on the individual with special needs and his or her family. New teachers require information on the type and level of contacts these other individuals have with families. Accordingly, these authors stress that offering varied family service perspectives strengthens new teachers' understandings of multiple views in identifying and responding to family issues effectively.

Chapter 11: Community Professionals' Roles with Families

So that new teachers understand others' work with family members, Diana J. Hammitte and Betty M. Nelson contend that certain group conditions in communities must occur before collaborative orientations and reflective practices can be valued, respected, and ac-cepted. Thus, Hammitte and Nelson examine data to increase new teachers' understanding of the work by community-based professionals. The authors examine how, as our society becomes more aware of the need for community participation in the development of future generations, new teachers must understand how such community involvement can be ac-cessed for families of children with disabilities. Thus, these authors examine ways and means in which families can access the collaborative services of professionals with teach-ers' assistance. The authors also address barriers to effective collaborative partnerships and strategies for overcoming such barriers.

Chapter 12: Improving Outcomes and Future Practices: Family-Centered Programs and Services

In this final chapter, Sylvia Nassar-McMillan and Bob Algozzine reiterate the importance of new teachers' collaborative orientations and responsive practices. These authors' pri-mary focus is on outcome design issues important to teachers (e.g., characteristics of effec-tive and ineffective family services). They discuss such factors as describing what is known about working with families in supporting the education of their children. Addi-tionally, they summarize barriers to family participation in schooling, and reiterate the im-portance of new teachers seeking out and applying family-oriented knowledge, skills, and dispositions.

Finally, these authors extrapolate from the developments in current theories, research, and practice trends into the future. By speculating on service implications of shared "ownership" of family problems, use of sharing and expertise across funding sources, incentives/commitment to group goals on family programs and services, and projected future in-service programs to further practicing teachers' work, these authors consider how teachers, families, and other professionals address and improve together family-centered programs and services.

Related Service Providers' Work with Students, Families, and Teachers

Lawrence J. O'Shea

Adrienne P. Lancaster

Chapter Objectives _____

In this chapter we will

- Define related services
- Describe examples of related service providers' activities
- Pose questions and answers that may arise during school-based conferences related to related service providers' activities
- List resources related to the work of related services providers
- Summarize important chapter themes

> *Jean Ann has been more than an older sister to Suzie. When Suzie was born thirty-six years ago, Jean Ann was very excited about her sibling's arrival. She looked forward to Mom and Suzie coming home from the hospital. But from the very beginning, Suzie had a myriad of health-related problems. Family members and friends noticed that Suzie was not developing as did other children her age. Suzie needed constant medical care and her mother's complete attention. Jean Ann and her brother, Kent, had to assume many family roles. Jean Ann and her brother helped their parents wash, fold, and put away the laundry; do the dishes; go grocery shopping; complete the lawn care; and finish most other household routines. This way of life continued long after Kent was killed in an automobile accident and their father passed away.*
>
> *Currently, her mother and sister live in Jean Ann's home. At age forty-one, Jean Ann is "surrogate mother" to both. Jean Ann makes most decisions*

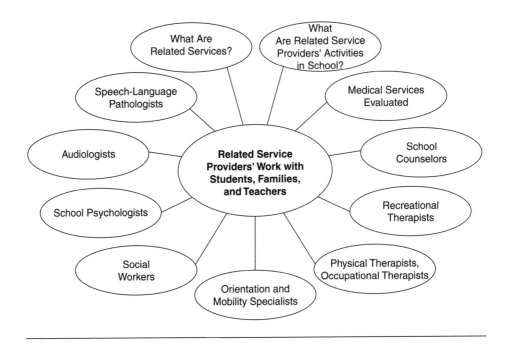

for Suzie's care, in collaboration with her mother. Follow-through on the care, however, is Jean Ann's sole responsibility.

Complicating the family dynamics is Jean Ann's daughter, Beth, who attends school in the local district. Beth, age eleven, desperately wants to join in after-school activities. Beth's father left the family when she was two years old. Jean Ann believes that Beth wants a "super parent," because of her father's absence. That is, Beth says she wants her mother to be a Girl Scout leader and a coach for the after-school swim club. Beth wants her mother to be active in the Parent Teacher Association. Beth wants her mother to be a Bible study volunteer. However, Jean Ann has little time to join in school or community events. In addition to providing physical care to her family, Jean Ann provides financial support through her home business. The business offers a meager family income. Jean Ann must balance home and office responsibilities on a daily basis.

Jean Ann never complains about her surrogate mother status. She would describe her experiences in both positive and negative terms. Nonetheless, Jean Ann doesn't know what would happen if she were unable to be there for her sister, her mother, and her daughter.

Jean Ann's concern now is planning for Suzie's long-term care. Jean Ann also worries about her mother, who is losing her hearing and showing senility signs. Jean Ann continually worries about Beth and Beth's adjustment to the family living arrangements. Jean Ann constantly asks herself: "Shouldn't Beth understand my position and my reasons for not joining in her activities?"

> *Jean Ann wants to help Beth, but can't find the time and energy to do so. Jean Ann is tempted to call Beth's school to get some advice. Beth is beginning to display many problem behaviors at home and school. Beth's teacher hinted that due to the frequency, duration, and intensity of her school tantrums, Beth has emotional needs, requiring a special education referral. Although she professes to love both Suzie and her grandmother, Beth's continued home tantrums indicate that she wants her mother's sole attention. Jean Ann is at her wit's end.*

Similar to other families, Jean Ann is wise to contact school professionals. Many professionals, working along with classroom teachers, offer an array of related services and resources. These professionals can provide much assistance concerning Beth's family and school needs. Further, they can help Jean Ann to focus on her own needs as she cares for her aging mother, her sister with a disability, and her preteenage daughter.

What Are Related Services?

Federal law identifies related services. That is, the Office of Special Education Programs (1999) and the U.S. Department of Education (1997) stressed that *related services* entail "transportation, and such developmental, corrective, and other supportive services (including speech-language pathology and audiology services; psychological services; physical and occupational therapy; recreation, including therapeutic recreation; social work services; counseling services, including rehabilitation counseling; orientation and mobility services; and medical services, except that such medical services shall be for diagnostic and evaluation purposes only) as may be required to assist a child with a disability to benefit from special education, and includes the early identification and assessment of disabling conditions in children." (pp. 5–26).

Related service providers can offer assessments, observations, resources, and specific strategies to assist students and families. Importantly, many related service providers work very closely with new teachers and community-based personnel to implement collaborative orientations and responsive practices unique to a family's situation.

In Jean Ann's situation, Beth is in the ranks of at-risk status for special education, meaning that her teacher's referral places Beth in the "thought to be exceptional" student group. Teachers and other school professionals can work with Jean Ann to consider whether or not Beth now requires special education and related services. By enlisting the support of related service professionals, Beth and Jean Ann can secure individualized assessments and recommendations concerning Beth's qualifications and need for specific help.

What Are Related Service Providers' Activities in Schools?

Related service providers, as school professionals, can offer help to families and new teachers in a number of areas. In the following sections, we describe related service providers' activities. We identify examples of speech-language pathology, audiology, psychology, physical therapy, occupational therapy, recreation therapy, social work, counseling, orientation and mobility, and medical diagnostic and evaluation services. Additionally, we discuss applications to Jean Ann's and Beth's family.

Speech-Language Pathology and Audiology Service Providers

Speech-language pathology and audiology service providers concentrate in the communications area. Speech-language pathologists and audiologists help to determine the similarities and differences among the communication needs of students with and without exceptional needs. Thus, they focus on whether or not students display characteristics of normal, delayed, or disordered communication patterns. Normal communication patterns indicate that the student has age appropriate speech, language, and hearing development. Delayed communication patterns suggest that although speech, language, or hearing is slow to emerge, the student does possess a repertoire of communication skills. Disordered communication patterns suggest deficiencies in speech, language, or hearing emergence or the developmental appropriateness of communication patterns.

Speech-Language Pathologists.   Speech-language pathologists provide observations, assessments, and therapeutic strategies in students' *receptive language* (skills involved in understanding language, such as those used in listening to and comprehending words). These specialists also consider students' *expressive language* (skills involved in speaking and writing language). When there are specific issues related to students' *articulation* (problems in phoneme or sound pronunciations), *voice* (appropriateness of voice tone or voice quality related to age or gender), *fluency* (speaking smoothness or language flow), or *language* (language delays, deficiencies, or disorders), the speech-language pathologist may indicate that individualized or small-group therapy sessions are appropriate.

Speech-language pathologists perform many specific school activities that are useful to new teachers. These include the following:

- Locate and identify those students whose speech or language deviates from the normal speech of the area
- Function as a member of the multidisciplinary team in the identification and reevaluation of students
- Schedule and conduct therapy classes according to the content of the Individual Education Program (IEP) for students with speech and language problems to ensure the most effective results
- Notify parents, teachers, nurses, administrative personnel, and any others concerned with students' welfare or inclusion in therapy
- Supply information to and counsel with the family and personnel just mentioned in order to achieve the best possible therapy results
- Refer students, through the proper authorities, to the appropriate agencies for supplemental diagnosis and assessment as indicated by specific student needs
- Keep adequate records on students receiving speech-language therapy in order to ensure the most effective continuing therapy

The specific type, level, and amount of speech or language therapy are concerns of each student's IEP team. The speech-language pathologist plans and consults with teachers, other related service providers, and family members on specifics of students' individual therapy. Further, they consult on follow-through, asking team members to assist on supplemental activities geared toward strengthening students' speech and language skills at school or home. Downing (1999) suggested that by determining students' communication needs collaboratively, in accordance with the expectations of the school and home environment, professionals and parents have a wealth of partnership ideas to facilitate good communication with students. Even for students with severe needs, communication skills can be maintained or increased when professionals and families work together.

For instance, new teachers and families may work with speech-language pathologists to ascertain the similarities and differences a preschooler has in word or sentence pronunciations, compared to peers. The team may decide that the student has slow vocabulary development and a disinterest in initiating peer interactions. A strategy, useful in supplementary school and home efforts, may entail that both the preschool teacher and the parents reinforce the young student every time he or she initiates a peer discussion. By working with the speech-language pathologist to plot out how many times per day the student initiates peer conversations, this team is demonstrating collaborative orientations and responsive practices. Such teamwork, most likely, will have a positive impact on the student's communication skills.

As this same student ages, however, the focus may switch to whether or not there are delayed decoding skills that influence reading comprehension. Compounding the student's verbal language issues may be trouble following verbal directions, poor oral or written expressions, weak grasp of verbal or written explanations, or trouble summarizing verbal or written thoughts. Again, by devising collaborative school and home interventions that support the student, significant adults work in tandem to increase the student's communication proficiency and lessen communication problems.

Audiologists.   Audiologists, on the other hand, provide specific information concerning hearing skills. Students demonstrating intense hearing difficulties most likely will require specific audiological services meant for individuals with hearing impairments or deafness. Even mild to moderate hearing difficulties can have an effect on students' language, memory, attention, social development, and organizational skills. Accordingly, it is very important that teachers and family members refer immediately to audiologists students suspected of having hearing difficulties. Audiologists can offer important supplemental hearing strategies that new teachers and family members can use to support students' school hearing services. For instance, these include tips on controlling auditory stimuli or noise distractions at home or school. Audiologists also may assist students, families, and teachers in their use of tape recorders, radios, televisions, computers, or language masters to support school hearing services. If students require more specialized hearing devices, audiologists can help to locate and fit hearing aids, language adapters, voice synthesizers, or more advanced communications technology. Thus, audiologists perform the following activities, often in consultation with speech-language pathologists:

• Locate and identify those students whose hearing deviates from the normal, especially in the speech range

- Schedule and conduct therapy for students with hearing impairments, which will encourage their development to the fullest potential during the years of formal education, with emphasis on growth in the comprehension and expression of the English language
- Interpret the needs of students with hearing impairments to teachers as well as to classmates and family members; in addition, outline their needs to the administrators of the school system
- Determine, by consultation with the school faculty, an individual educational and therapeutic program to meet the needs of students with hearing impairments
- Refer students, through the proper authorities, to the appropriate agencies for supplemental diagnosis and assessment as indicated by students' needs
- Keep adequate records on students and their hearing services in order to ensure the most effective continuing therapy

Application to Jean Ann and Beth.   In Jean Ann's family situation, Beth most likely will not require services by speech-language pathologists or audiologists. However, if Beth did, these professionals could assist in the following areas:

- Locate important resources about ways and means to increase Beth's speech-language or hearing effectiveness, verbal fluency, or opportunities to socialize with peers (without relying on Jean Ann's sole involvement)
- Provide suggestions on working to improve Beth's whole family engagement in conversations, response to questions, listening activities, and communication skills
- Provide the names and addresses of specific Web site information, or books and organizational sources on speech-language or hearing services that Jean Ann can access locally
- If appropriate, consult with Jean Ann to promote alternative forms of communication, such as gestures, body language, signing, and use of both objects or pictorial devices that might assist Beth or Jean Ann to communicate more effectively with each other, and Suzie or Beth's grandmother

Psychological Service Providers

School psychologists, the major psychological service providers in schools, concentrate in the area of assessments. That is, they administer and score student responses on group or individualized testing, which is useful for classroom and school decisions. School psychologists interpret and explain testing results, making recommendations to families and teachers.

Many school psychologists are responsible for the evaluation of students referred by teachers or other members of local education agencies as thought-to-be exceptional students, and for the re-evaluation of identified exceptional students. School psychologists' roles also include the functions of consultant to district personnel and parents, contributing member of multidisciplinary teams, and provider of information to aid in the development and maintenance of district policies and procedures relative to the identification and re-evaluation of exceptional students.

Accordingly, the activities often assumed by school psychologists are varied. These target the following:

- Administer, score, and interpret psychological tests and measurements
- Function as a major contributing member of multidisciplinary teams
- Provide psychological consultative services to district professional personnel, administrators, and families
- Observe students in the classroom, community, and home when such observation is indicated
- Prepare written psychological reports on each student referred and evaluated
- Provide for follow-up when necessary
- Recommend for referral or additional academic, diagnostic, psychiatric, or medical evaluations pertinent to the diagnosis for a particular student
- Provide professional training and support when indicated by students' needs

Recent changes to the field of school psychology, resulting from the demands of public policy and litigation concerning IDEA, are now expanding many school psychologists' roles. There is now increased emphasis on linking psychological assessments and interventions, so that information from the school assessment process leads directly to classroom intervention strategies rather than to students' diagnostic labels. Thus, current school psychologists work very closely with parents or guardians, teachers, and other school professionals to consider the usefulness of all relevant student data. Formal and informal assessments and observations provided by school psychologists, other related service providers, teachers, or families are necessary in linking students' individualized assessments to the classroom and real-world experiences (Overton, 2000; Rosenfield & Nelson, 1995).

Additionally, many school psychologists help to plan classroom-based assessments, behavioral observation systems, data gathering techniques, specially designed instruction, and strategies for facilitating students' maintenance and generalization of behavioral skills across home or school settings. However, in many schools, school psychologists manage and oversee much of the data collection and assessment processes when a student, such as Beth, is referred for special education and related services consideration. School psychologists can help new teachers to foster healthy interactions among students, families, and school personnel. School psychologists' specific roles expand the areas of assessments, interventions, and behavior support, in order that important student and family interventions may evolve.

Assessments and Behavioral Support.   School psychologists collaborate with families, teachers, other professionals, and students (as appropriate). Collaborative orientations and responsive practices can guide discussions by every team member's involvement. For instance, school psychologists can assist new teachers and families by assessing referred students, as well as by helping to ascertain whether or not classroom programming is effective. Novice teachers can consult with school psychologists having particular assessment expertise. Teachers can work with school psychologists by contributing curricular expertise and subject matter knowledge relevant to students' academic or behavioral interventions. Families can provide important academic, medical, and family history data, helping to determine accuracy in detection of students with difficulties or probable giftedness.

Many school psychologists not only assess students for important interventions and effective classroom programming, but also offer tips on family assessment issues, as discussed in Chapter 5. Often, school psychologists help to create and maintain student records, assuring compliance with legal provisions, regulations, and guidelines regarding confidentiality and ethical considerations related to students and family members' assessments.

Most school psychologists also provide resources and strategies on a variety of effective behavioral support, or behavior or classroom management strategies (Dunforth, 2000). Because of school psychologists' changing roles and their relationships with classroom teachers and family members, there is a vital need to build communication and working relationships with all individuals involved in the care and treatment of students with disabilities. Collaboration activities can take different forms, including a one-time meeting or weekly sessions with the teacher, other staff, student, parents, guardians, siblings, or a combination of significant individuals (Tiegerman-Farber & Radziewicz, 1998).

Novice teachers may need to foster rapport between family members and school psychologists, as teachers often are primary communicators between home and school. How this evolves may be a function of the stresses and family dynamics unique to each family circumstance. Rapport may depend on whether the school psychologist is part of the interactive team working with teachers and families. Nonetheless, family members must have an open and trusting relationship with important school professionals in order for assessment, behavioral support, and interventions to be effective.

Box 10.1 illustrates how Miss Weatherbee, the school psychologist, helped to assess Beth's family situation and provide important data on Beth's school and family needs to Jean Ann and Beth's teacher.

Application to Jean Ann and Beth.   Beth's school psychologist, Miss Weatherbee, would collaborate with Beth's classroom teacher, other related service providers, and Jean Ann to ascertain whether Beth requires a change in her current educational placement. Miss Weatherbee would administer to Beth individualized, formal tests in the areas of ability, achievement, processing, and social–emotional measures. Additionally, in collaboration with Jean Ann's home data, curriculum-based assessments provided by Beth's classroom teacher, or assessments and observations secured by other school professionals, Miss Weatherbee would consider whether Beth qualifies for and has a need for special education. Further, Miss Weatherbee's role includes interpreting important assessments and observations from Jean Ann, Beth's teacher, and other school professionals to determine whether Beth qualifies for and has a need for related services. Miss Weatherbee would use Beth's background information to determine the appropriateness of Beth's special education and need for emotional support. Miss Weatherbee can use the data to help other school professionals and Jean Ann plan Beth's after-school support program, appropriate to her family means. Importantly, Jean Ann and Beth's classroom teacher can consult with Miss Weatherbee for help in interpreting information and in making recommendations from informal or formal observations regarding Beth's adjustment and willingness to support Jean Ann, her mother, and her grandmother.

BOX 10.1

Family–Teacher Issues

Although they tried very hard, support from Beth's fifth-grade teachers appears to have done little in the way of modifying Beth's behavior. Beth still displays problem behaviors and tantrums now that she is in sixth grade.

Beth received once-a-week progress reports, given concerns about her overall social and behavioral progress from her classroom teacher. Jean Ann tells Beth's classroom teacher that she is concerned that Beth is having difficulty adjusting to their family's living conditions. Jean Ann tells Miss Weatherbee, the school psychologist assigned to assess Beth, that Jean Ann knows Beth is having school behavioral issues. Jean Ann tells Miss Weatherbee that Beth is throwing tantrums at home.

Collaborative Orientations and Responsive Practices

Miss Weatherbee wants to get Jean Ann's input into Beth's situation, prior to any formal assessment. Miss Weatherbee knows the importance of fostering a rapport with Jean Ann and Beth. Miss Weatherbee begins by asking for Jean Ann's observations of when and where Beth has problem behaviors. When Miss Weatherbee begins to collect data from Jean Ann, Jean Ann confides that Beth wants to join in after-school activities to be with others. Miss Weatherbee ascertains from Jean Ann that Beth's father left the family when Beth was a toddler. Jean Ann tells Miss Weatherbee that Beth wants a "super parent," because of her father's absence. Miss Weatherbee tries to probe Jean Ann about the family living situation. She asks about Beth's interactions and comfort level with Suzie. After describing Beth's behaviors, Jean Ann tells Miss Weatherbee that she needs help in making decisions about Suzie's living arrangements and in trying to reinforce Beth for appropriate behavior. Jean Ann tells Miss Weatherbee that she will try to support Beth as much as she can. However, she needs information on whether Beth's school and home behaviors really are related to Suzie and Jean Ann's lack of attention.

Miss Weatherbee tells Jean Ann she will provide a complete assessment of Beth and try to glean other important data from all school personnel working with Beth. She thanks Jean Ann for her important contributions on Beth's home behaviors and needs.

Jean Ann may need ideas on creating token systems, or other reinforcement strategies, that can help in Beth's appropriate home behaviors. Specific rewards may surface to increase or maintain Beth's acceptance of or adjustment to Suzie and her grandmother. Token systems also may help Beth's school professionals to link home and school interventions. Thus, Miss Weatherbee and Beth's teacher can offer to Jean Ann specific ways to use a schedule of reinforcement that rewards Beth for compromising during various times at home or school. Home rewards might target such behaviors as Beth's willingness to ride with peers to the Girl Scouts or swimming activities, rather than relying strictly on Jean Ann's transportation. Additionally, Miss Weatherbee may work with Beth, Jean Ann, Beth's teacher, and other school professionals to help Jean Ann modify Beth's home compliance, focusing on Beth's outburst or problem behaviors. For instance, they might teach Jean Ann strategies to "time out" Beth when she has a tantrum, or remove Beth from the situation to get Jean Ann's attention. Further, Jean Ann, Miss Weatherbee, and other school professionals may analyze together important antecedents and consequences to Beth's tantrums, seeking home or school interventions that school professionals and Jean Ann can use to increase Beth's self-awareness, self-control, self-reliance, and self-esteem skills. Thus, school professionals and Jean Ann may send home-to-school correspondence back and forth to share ideas on Beth's awareness and control of her appropriate behaviors.

In Jean Ann's family situation, Beth benefits from Miss Weatherbee's open and trusting relationship with important school professionals and Jean Ann. The following summary of Miss Weatherbee's contributions is pertinent.

- Miss Weatherbee, as school psychologist, helps to assess Beth's school needs and her family situation. Miss Weatherbee provides observations, testing data, and behavioral support strategies that may help Jean Ann and Beth's teacher to discern important information, services, and means to make choices conducive to Beth's school placement services.
- Because school psychological services now go beyond testing and placement to include consulting, planning, interviewing, conducting classroom observations, managing psychological services, and counseling for children and parents, an important decision that Jean Ann may have to make concerns whether data she receives from Miss Weatherbee support Suzie's current living arrangements. Other living arrangements (e.g., group homes, community living centers, hospital settings) may be more effective solutions than are available currently in the family. Suzie's long-term habitation, taken into consideration of Beth's school and home needs, are important data that must receive attention.
- Miss Weatherbee helps Jean Ann and Beth's teacher to analyze whether and how Beth's home and school behaviors, in terms of frequency, duration, and intensity may change, as important antecedents and consequences in Beth's home and school settings change.
- Miss Weatherbee helps Jean Ann to analyze whether Jean Ann's own parental and self-coping skills may be better met by making changes to her family living arrangements, especially regarding Suzie's habitation and Beth's behaviors.

Physical Therapy and Occupational Therapy Service Providers

Physical therapy and occupational therapy service providers are professionals concentrating on students' central nervous systems, muscular systems, or skeletal systems. Physical therapists concentrate in gross motor areas. Gross motor areas indicate issues related to an individual's neuromuscular skeletal development. That is, these professionals may work with new teachers or family members to determine students' proficiency in running, hopping, jumping, or kicking skills. Difficulties may arise in neuromuscular or skeletal influences affecting students' coordination and completion of physical tasks or lower-body requirements. Also affected may be students' skills in endurance, posture, memory and processing. Observations, assessments, and strategies may center on students' coordination and completion of physical tasks, or lower-body requirements for standing or sitting in required locations.

Physical therapists usually provide physical therapy according to a doctor's prescription and consult with the teaching staff and parents with respect to the needs of the student with physical disabilities. Many assume varied roles that include the following activities:

- Maintain physical therapy prescriptions on all students with disabilities who are in need of therapy according to the directions of the students' personal physicians.
- Submit reports to the program supervisor or classroom teacher indicating teaching strategies to be used in the physical area of students' development.
- Develop and maintain student files on those students requiring physical therapy services. It is understood that all information gathered will come under the district's jurisdiction and policy regarding the confidentiality of student records.
- Develop appropriate physical therapy guidelines and teaching strategies to be used by the classroom teachers and family members.
- Conduct therapy sessions in accordance with students' individualized prescriptions.
- When requested, participate as a member of the multidisciplinary team in the identification or re-evaluation of students "thought to be exceptional" or with identified labels.

On the other hand, occupational therapists concentrate on an individual's small muscle development, or small muscles related to upper-body, arm, and hand strength. Issues in the upper body, arm, or hand may reveal difficulties in students' fine motor skills that affect educational performance. For instance, occupational therapists can give insights into fine motor support necessary in the development of students' self-help skills (e.g., tying, buttoning, toileting skills) or in academic skills (e.g., grasping, pointing, cutting, or other tasks related to use of school implements). Occupational therapists may provide students with individual or group therapy sessions. The focus may be on maintaining or increasing students' fine motor strength, or motor coordination areas. Students' fine motor therapy may reveal issues in an unstable pencil or pen grip, trouble with tracing skills, or an inability to control small objects. Such skills are necessary for written expression tasks, as students with fine motor problems may have difficulty with letter formation or penmanship skills. Handwriting may be illegible, slow, or inconsistent according to developmental age. Areas such as an underdeveloped upper trunk in the shoulder girdle area often affect students' academic performance. Some students have resulting problems, such as in the ability to write compositions or complete motor tasks.

Other subject area skills, such as in mathematics or science, also may be affected. For instance, fine motor analysis may indicate that afflicted students have an inability to pick up and use counting manipulatives, useful in mathematics. Students may have difficulty in maneuvering measurement and weight objects in science experiments. The students' poor motor coordination and motor planning problems, further, may affect the ability to interact with peers, develop social relations, or participate in team sports. Thus, occupational therapists assume varied roles focused on the following activities:

- Maintain occupational therapy prescriptions on all students with disabilities who are in need of therapy according to the directions of the students' personal physicians
- Submit reports to the program supervisor or classroom teacher indicating teaching strategies to be used in the fine motor area of students' development

- Provide data related to students' degree of finger muscle development, hand coordination, and motor coordination activities
- Develop appropriate occupational therapy guidelines and teaching strategies to be used by the classroom teachers and family members
- Conduct therapy sessions in accordance with students' individualized prescriptions
- When requested, participate as a member of the multidisciplinary team in the identification or re-evaluation of students "thought to be exceptional" or with identified labels

Application to Jean Ann and Beth.   As is the case for speech-language and audiological services, Beth most likely will not require physical therapy or occupational therapy. More likely, Jean Ann might consult with specialists on help for Suzie and Beth's grandmother. Physical therapy or occupational therapy specialists may assist Jean Ann and the family in a variety of ways, including the following:

- Planning and conducting evaluations, managing therapy services, and counseling about Beth's motor needs, if warranted
- Naming physical therapy or occupational therapy referral sources that focus on home visits, geriatric specializations, or health care options for individuals, such as Suzy or the grandmother, who are unable to leave the home setting
- Locating names and addresses of hospitals or community service agencies that assist with respite care or direct therapeutic services, in order that Beth and Jean Ann have opportunities to leave the home, without worrying about the care, safety, or comfort of Suzie and the grandmother
- Identifying important resources and information for the family about physical therapy and occupational therapy Web sites, books or tapes, and organizational sources available locally that are free or at low cost

Recreation Service Providers

Recreation service providers support social and leisure time opportunities available to students with disabilities. Such activities include recreational swimming, horseback riding, bowling, or track and field experiences that often are appropriate for students' participation in health, sports, or social arenas. Many recreation service providers work directly in schools or in community service agencies. Many are integral to students' comprehensive evaluation plans and IEPs. Recreation service providers collaborate with new teachers and family members to encourage students' social skills; fine-tune appropriate adult-bound, leisure time goals; ascertain students' interests, pursuits, or preferences; or encourage students' and families' daily leisure activities.

Application to Jean Ann and Beth.   The direct services of recreation service providers may not be readily apparent in all students' situations, such as in Beth's case. However, Jean Ann's family may be given options in the following areas:

- Receiving the names, locations, and contacts involved in home cable services, offering affordable cable or educational television services to Beth's family members unable to leave the home

- Locating community arts, recreation, sporting, or theatrical opportunities available on a free or low-cost basis to Beth, if warranted
- Receiving the services of respite care volunteers who relieve families, such as Beth's, on an intermittent basis in order that family members can participate in leisure activities with community groups, other families with a member with a disability, or on an individual family basis

Social Work Service Providers

Social workers concentrate on the provision of social support to students with disabilities and family members. Social workers interact with new teachers and other school professionals to support students' growth and development and the development and maintenance of healthy family interactions. Social workers help to determine specific family strengths, analyze family assets and skills, and assess or intervene in unique family experiences. Such actions often occur in the home or community setting.

Many social workers are responsible for gathering information, making appropriate referrals for psychiatric or psychological services, and providing ongoing support to students who are thought to be or have been identified as students with serious emotional disturbance (SED). Among the relevant activities that many social workers accomplish are the following:

- Provide direct mental health services to school-age students with SED
- Develop and maintain a liaison with psychiatric services to facilitate referral or follow-up on students with SED
- Provide casework, group work, and consultative mental health services to give definition and treatment to those students not adjusting to the ongoing SED program
- Involve school personnel, parents, and community services as a part of the treatment process for students with SED
- Be a member of the diagnostic team and serve on the multidisciplinary team when a student appears to be in need of SED class placement or mental health intervention
- Mobilize school and community resources to enable the student to receive maximum benefit from the educational program.

Social workers work with other students with disabilities and their families as well. Many social workers must consider the effects a disabling condition may have on an individual's life. That is, as a liaison among home, school, and community entities, social workers often observe, firsthand, effects of the cultural and environmental milieu of students and families. An important philosophy for many social workers is to help families and novice teachers understand the content, type, and location of student or family services in the local community. Many social workers identify for and assist in locating specific contact names, addresses, and phone numbers of services provided by such individuals as local physicians; personnel of mental health facilities, social groups, or family agencies; local business professionals; or community and religious leaders.

Because many make home visits, social workers obtain data that new teachers can use to demonstrate respect for racial, ethnic, cultural, and religious diversity. Social workers often are on a first-name and personalized basis with parents or guardians. Social workers often assist novice teachers and other school or community professionals to value and respect choices in such family issues as family need for autonomy, independence, or deci- sion making. Social workers often obtain data on the level, nature, and desires of families' involvement in educational or social services. Social workers also promote the integration of students and families within the community, recognizing the already existing natural supports and resources of the family.

Social workers, thus, assist students, families, and new teachers in their liaison roles with school and community personnel and families. Many help in planning and providing comprehensive services in life domains that include the family's living situation or commu- nity setting. Many social workers offer to IEP teams data on students' family demographics or housing conditions. Many report on family interactions, resulting from observations in home visits. Often, social workers help new teachers and family members to understand what students bring to the classroom and what they take home with them. Social workers help new teachers to discern important data emerging from patterns in student's living arrangements or community variables. Analysis of home and community patterns can help in planning appro- priate classroom observations, assessments, and interventions. Social workers also can help new teachers to acquire family knowledge of variations in beliefs, traditions, and values across cultures when considering diversity issues families face. Social workers, further, can help family members value and respect school personnel's roles and responsibilities.

Box 10.2 illustrates the case of Mr. Harman, the school social worker, assisting Jean Ann. Mr. Harman realizes he must work with Beth's teachers and Jean Ann, viewing Beth's whole family as important.

BOX 10.2

Family–Teacher Issues

Mr. Harman wants to make a home visit to observe Jean Ann and Beth. He has a number of ques- tions he wants to ask the family. He wants to find out what is important to Jean Ann and Beth. He wants to find out Jean Ann's and Beth's perspectives of their family household. He also wants to see whether Beth displays similar home behavior, compared to her school behavior.

Collaborative Orientations and Responsive Practices

Mr. Harman arrives at Beth's home during his scheduled observation with Jean Ann. Beth will come home from school in about one hour. Mr. Harman's visit is for two hours. He wants to talk to Jean Ann, Suzie, and Beth's grandmother, first, to get a feel for their views on Beth's behav- iors at home and school. In order to help Beth's referral team plan appropriate interventions, Mr. Harman will ask Beth's family about their family customs and holidays. He'll ask whether they go to a special church or have other family member's close by who can offer some finan- cial or emotional help. He also wants to find out what Jean Ann and her mother believe are each family member's strengths and contributions to the household, including Suzie's.

Mr. Harman brings along a list of community programs that he thought might interest Jean Ann. These relate to interests Beth related to him when he interviewed Beth in school last week. Beth told Mr. Harman that she wants to be a Girl Scout and a swimmer. Mr. Harman is prepared to link the family up to specific contacts at the Community Recreation Center who can help to provide some swimming opportunities for Beth, and even quite possibly for Suzie, the grandmother, or Jean Ann.

Application to Jean Ann and Beth.   Mr. Harman was correct to initiate family contacts. He relied on existing, informal community networks available to Beth and her family, and ascertaining natural sources of support for them. Jean Ann then indicated she felt comfortable working with Mr. Harman to answer questions about Beth's home conditions. Important to Beth and Jean Ann are the following activities initiated by Mr. Harman:

- Determining the whole family's concerns, priorities, and resources as based on this family's determination of which aspects of family life are relevant to Jean Ann, Beth, Suzie, and the grandmother
- Identifying specific beliefs, customs, or traditions held by Jean Ann, Beth, Suzie, and the grandmother, and specifics of their needs or concerns (as warranted by the family's willingness to reveal)
- Naming what these family members believe to be family strengths, particularly as they relate to the provision of home, school, or community services available to Jean Ann, Beth, Suzie, and the grandmother
- Examining community interests, needs, and strengths identified by Jean Ann, Beth, Suzie, and the grandmother
- Locating specific names, locations, and contacts of social services and resources available to Jean Ann, Beth, Suzie, and the grandmother at the local, state, or national levels

Counseling Service Providers

Today's school counselors hold many responsibilities that fall under the broad category of counseling. Many focus on students' feelings, attitudes, and coping skills. School counselors frequently consult with teachers and families to design individual counseling or group programs. Many observe, assess, and intervene in students' interpersonal, life management, and coping skills.

In addition to serving students without disabilities, many school counselors assist new teachers in such areas as working directly to support school-age students with disabilities, their parents, siblings, or other family members. School counselors' activities include helping to foster healthy interactions in reaction to home or school crises. School counselors also support other school professionals and community personnel in various capacities, such as in helping high school students make school-to-work transitions, and in providing necessary counseling services to help the vocational world value and respect graduating students' strengths, needs, and skills.

School counselors are collegial, not supervisory. It is essential that they have knowledge, skills, and experiences in such areas as cognitive, communication, physical, cultural, social, and emotional conditions of individuals with and without disabilities. They also need knowledge, skills, and experiences in family roles and responsibilities, life transitions, and group dynamics. Many are in key liaison positions between home and school, thus necessitating the use of excellent communication, management, and social interaction skills. School counselors often help others in their listening, dialoguing, and interaction effectiveness (American School Counselor Association, 1998).

In many secondary and middle schools, school counselors are also responsible for designing and coordinating students' class schedules, and assisting students with making decisions about future plans for higher education, military service, or vocational careers. Often in small districts without social workers, school counselors are major liaisons with community agency personnel. Consultation with others helps multidisciplinary teams to think through problems and concerns, acquire more knowledge and skills in working with students, families or peers, and in the staff's continuing professional development activities.

School counselors can assist other school professionals in developing appropriate reflective listening skills. Thus, by using their training in counseling and support, school counselors can offer insights in the following areas:

- Helping others reflect on beliefs, values, and traditions that family members say are important to them
- Locating names and addresses of family members, friends, or community professionals who already support the family and whose support family members say they trust and desire
- Recognizing and valuing interests, needs, and strengths identified by the family members that might link the family to a wide network of supporters
- Examining coping resources important to and identified by the family (e.g., religious affiliations, community help, hospital resources) and the family's expressed desires for expanding or delimiting coping resources
- Assessing family approaches to solving problems used previously that family members say have been useful or not successful (e.g., use of family meetings, previous therapy services, and so forth to help in addressing individual or family member coping skills)
- Promoting ways to acknowledge students' specific strengths and needs family members identify in living with the member with a disability and to other family members' strengths and needs who are in the household

Box 10.3 illustrates the case of Mrs. Rothy, the school counselor, working with Jean Ann on important considerations for Beth's family adjustment. Mrs. Rothy understands that she must work very hard with Beth's mother. Mrs. Rothy views her counseling role as helping Jean Ann to understand the grandmother's and Suzie's influence on Beth's acceptance of and adjustment to the family living arrangements.

Application to Jean Ann and Beth.   In Beth's case, Jean Ann is wise to consult with Mrs. Rothy. As we discussed in Chapter 8, preadolescence and adolescence is of particular concern to parents and school personnel. At this time of life, many young people struggle to bridge successfully from childhood to adulthood without much poise or sophistication. In turn, parents or guardians often become frustrated and lack the strategies necessary to deal with a young adult. The following are important to Jean Ann and Beth:

- Beth's counselor can offer Jean Ann and Beth such data as realistic expectations for Beth's personal and social behaviors acceptable in the home or school setting.
- The counselor may work with Beth's teacher on ascertaining specific ways to prepare Beth to exhibit self-enhancing behaviors in response to societal attitudes and actions resulting from Suzie's family effect.

BOX 10.3

Family–Teacher Issues

Mrs. Rothy, the school counselor, calls Jean Ann for an appointment. Mrs. Rothy wants to discuss Jean Ann's views on strategies Jean Ann believes school personnel can use to help Beth. Mrs. Rothy has a number of questions she wants to ask Jean Ann. She wants to find out what Jean Ann believes are her friend's attitudes and actions concerning Suzy's family effect. She wants to ask Jean Ann more about Beth's home behavior.

Collaborative Orientations and Responsive Practices

Mrs. Rothy is prepared to help Jean Ann. Mrs. Rothy begins her parent interview by asking Jean Ann to reflect on Beth's school and home strengths and needs. What does Jean Ann believe are her sister's and her mother's strengths and needs?

She wants Jean Ann to talk about Jean Ann's beliefs, values, and traditions that Jean Ann and her aging mother say are important to them concerning their family needs. Because she knows the importance of reflective listening and communication skills, Mrs. Rothy is willing to work overtime today to let Jean Ann talk about Beth and her family for as long as Jean Ann needs to do so.

Mrs. Rothy tells Jean Ann that she is prepared to start a database of important family members, friends, or community professionals that Jean Ann says are trusting and whose support Jean Ann values. Mrs. Rothy wants to ask Jean Ann whether Jean Ann has free time for herself, so that she can take a break from her home office or family care responsibilities. She listens intently as Jean Ann talks about her interests, needs, and strengths as a parent. Mrs. Rothy also listens intently as Jean Ann reveals her limited contacts with other families who may be caring for individuals with disabilities similar to Suzie's.

- Beth's counselor is important in offering resources about characteristics and needs of Suzie's specific disability and insights for Beth and Jean Ann.
- Her counselor is facilitating important reflections on Beth's right to choose her role in family obligations and Suzie's long-term support.

Orientation and Mobility and Medical Service Providers

Professionals providing orientation and mobility services often work with students with visual impairments. Students may be blind or require special assistance due to limited sight, low visual acuity, or inadequate visual perception skills. Orientation and mobility specialists concentrate on providing to new teachers, students, and families such strategies as tips in moving freely to and from school areas, using the stairways to get to and from various classroom locations, and being able to smoothly access bathroom facilities, lunchrooms, physical education areas, laboratories, assembly rooms, or other school environments. Thus, orientation and mobility specialists often perform the following activities:

- Evaluate students referred by districts and parents
- Interpret the needs of the students with low vision to school administrators, nurses, teachers, and parents and discuss orientation and mobility strategies with them

- Schedule and conduct sessions with consideration toward the needs and capacities of students with low vision
- Provide special material, equipment, and aids made necessary by students with low vision, their conditions, and specific skills needed to use these special materials, equipment, and aids effectively
- Coordinate the services of public and private agencies, volunteers, counselors, and library services so as not to overwhelm, overlap, or neglect students with low vision
- Consult with families on availability of local community resources
- Keep well informed about recent research, findings, and current methodologies and techniques

Medical Services.   Medical services include work by professionals providing diagnostic and evaluation services in students' health areas. Nurses, or other health-related specialists, provide important data related to evaluations of students' nutrition, exercise, sleep, and safety precaution needs. Medical services must be related to students' educational planning and school needs. Medical service data help new teachers and family members to acquire appropriate diagnostic information, important for students' IEPs. Data help to further ascertain whether students' growth and healthy development are proceeding smoothly.

Application to Jean Ann and Beth.   Although Beth most likely does not need orientation and mobility services, Jean Ann and Beth may profit from diagnostic and evaluation information from local health centers, food groups, or safety organizations that can assist in ascertaining Beth's health or medical needs. Services should be flexible, accessible, and responsive. Thus, medical service providers may work with Jean Ann and Beth in the following areas:

- Diagnosing and evaluating health and safety information, based on relevant local, state, and national hot lines that Jean Ann might find useful for Beth
- Assessing Beth in such at-risk variables as vulnerability for drug or alcohol abuse domains
- Providing to Jean Ann resources in such areas as suicide prevention, alcohol and drug awareness, and mental health services

Summary of Related Service Providers Activities

As the examples illustrate, related service providers offer an array of help and resources. These professionals can provide much assistance to students, families, and new teachers. Many hold specialized training and expertise in their concentration areas. Related service providers are most effective when they demonstrate collaborative orientations and responsive practices.

General Questions Confronting Related Service Providers _____

Questions and answers relate to roles related service providers play with students, families, and teachers. Because related service providers increase data on family awareness factors and important home-school-community strategies, the following questions and answers often arise in school-based conference sessions. We list typical questions that parents, guardians, or new teachers may ask. We also offer practical answers.

FAMILY MEMBER QUESTIONS

A common family question is, *Is my child progressing appropriately in all school services and if not, where can I go for help*? For many families, the ability of their children to interact with others and have school success is very important. This can show whether children eventually have the necessary skills, dispositions, and attitudes to become active members of their families and communities. Many related service providers work with new teachers on relating the idea that families should be told straight out about their children's skills and progress (Cohen & Spenciner, 1998). Students' skills targeted by related service providers are important in the classroom, home, and community. It is vital to be able to identify students' specific needs and strengths areas. Collaborative orientations and responsive practices imply that related service providers and teachers collaborate with family members to help students appropriately. Related services can provide help to families through the following:

- When parents or guardians need specific resources or referrals, many related service providers act as liaisons to provide the necessary information. Many assist novice teachers in developing for families such resources as brochures describing the special education or related services.
- Many related service providers can offer specialized brochures, each describing family contacts for securing relevant student support or family interventions, relevant to the related service discipline.
- Related service providers can work with new teachers on relevant articles in professional journals, the district newspaper, school paper, or local newspaper naming specific curricula that may be useful to the students' or families' particular concerns.
- Related service providers can offer to families the names, addresses, and costs of specific family interaction programs that can help students and families work toward generalizing skills taught in school settings to community or home settings.
- Many related service providers can identify therapeutic, hospital, or community services that emphasize training and education in specific related service areas for families.

TEACHER QUESTION

Another question may concern help afforded to new teachers. A common teacher question is, *If my student requires related services, where can I go for help*? Related service providers can work with new teachers to address how well students respond in all aspects of classroom and home functioning.

Collaborative orientations and responsive practices underscore the necessity of school professionals' strong communication skills in seeking and using each other's assistance. Related service providers can support new teachers on professional skills, dispositions, and development activities necessary in family interactions. Among other areas where related service providers can assist are the following:

- *A collaborative referral group for services.* That is, related service providers can work with new teachers on identifying specific district or state data when a special education referral is first made or as needed by the family.

- *Family education classes.* Related service providers can provide specific information to new teachers on strategies to create family education classes targeting specific areas. Collaborative orientations and responsive practices might focus on such issues as providing joint activities on definition and identification procedures for students with disabilities, specific characteristics of the similarities and differences among the needs of students with and without disabilities, and family stressors and concerns as students age.
- *Skills training.* Many related service providers can help new teachers access specific resources and aids on coping skills, adjustment strategies to various life transitions faced by families, and family coping or problem solving strategies. Skills training can help new teachers to initiate for families members contact with other parents or guardians who face similar issues.
- *Support groups.* Related service providers can offer specific school, home, or community resources for help to new teachers. Lists of therapies, recreation-leisure, and health related experiences can help new teachers to seek support outside their traditional, educational networks as they support families of students they serve.

Family Resources and Services

The following resources and services may be useful to new teachers and related service providers in their work with students and families. We cite specific associations and organizations, government agencies, government-supported organizations, and Internet sites.

ORGANIZATIONS

American Foundation for the Blind
11 Penn Plaza
New York, NY 10001
(800) 232-5463 or (212) 502-7600

Federation of Families for Children's Mental Health
1021 Prince Street
Alexandria, VA 22314
(703) 684-7710

National Association of Developmental Disabilities Councils
1234 Massachusetts Avenue, NW, Suite 103
Washington, DC 20005
(202) 347-1234
e-mail: naddc@igc.apc.org
www.igc.apc.org/NADDC/

National Easter Seal Society
230 W. Monroe, Suite 1800
Chicago, IL 60606
(800) 221-6827 or (312) 726-6200

(312) 726-4258 (TTY)
www.seals.com

National Parent Network on Disabilities (NPND)
1727 King Street, Suite 305
Alexandria, VA 22314
(703) 684-6763 (Voice/TTY)
e-mail: npnd@cs.com

Spina Bifida Association of America (SBAA)
4590 MacArthur Boulevard, NW, Suite 250
Washington, DC 20007-4226
(800) 621-3141 or (202) 944-3285
e-mail: spinabifida@aol.com
www.sbaa.org

United Cerebral Palsy Associations, Inc.
1660 L Street, NW, Suite 700
Washington, DC 20036-5602
(800) 872-5827 or (202) 973-7197 TDD
e-mail: ucnatl@ucpa.org

GOVERNMENT AGENCIES

Clearinghouse on Disability Information
Office of Special Education and
Rehabilitative Services
U.S. Department of Education
Switzer Building, Room 3132
330 C Street, SW
Washington, DC 20202-2524
(202) 205-8241 (Voice/TTY)

National Institute of Child Health and Human Development
P.O. Box 29111
Washington, DC 20040
(301) 496-5133

National Library Service for the Blind and Physically Handicapped
Library of Congress
1291 Taylor Street, NW
Washington, DC 20542
(202) 707-5100
(202) 707-0744 (TTY)

Social Security Administration (Headquarters)
6401 Security Boulevard
Baltimore, MD 21235
(800) 772-1213
(800) 325-0778 (TTY)

GOVERNMENT-SUPPORTED ORGANIZATIONS

Abledata: The National Database of Assistive Technology Information
8455 Colesville Road, Suite 935
Silver Spring, MD 20910-3319
(800) 227-0216 or (301) 608-8998
(301) 608-8912 (TTY)

Research and Training Center on Family Support and Children's Mental Health
Portland State University
P.O. Box 751
Portland, OR 97207
(503) 725-4040
(503) 725-4165 (TTY)
www.rtc.pdx.edu

National Information Center for Children and Youth with Disabilities (NICHCY)
P.O. Box 1492
Washington, DC 20013-1492

(800) 695-0285 or (202) 884-8200
(Voice/TTY)
e-mail: nichcy@aed.org

National Information Center on Deafness
Gallaudet University
800 Florida Avenue, NE
Washington, DC 20002-3695
(202) 651-5051
(202) 651-5054 (TTY)
e-mail: judd103w@wonder.em.cdc.gov

INTERNET SITES

Our Kids
(parenting resource site)
www.rdz.stjohns.edu/lists/our-kids/

Parents Place
(a parenting resource center on the Web)
www.parentsplace.com/index.html

Summary

This chapter's purpose was to examine the roles of related service providers in their collaborative orientations and responsive practices with students, families, and new teachers. Related service providers' relationships must be built on mutual respect and trust. These professionals will collaborate about many school, home, or community issues. Specific chapter themes relate to the following issues:

- Related service providers include school professionals, other than classroom teachers or principals, who offer students, families, and teachers help through specialized services.
- Speech-language pathologists focus on students' problems in receptive or expressive language, including articulation, voice, fluency, and language skills.
- Audiologists are related service providers assisting students with hearing impairments.
- In addition to assessment roles, school psychologists often help to plan classroom-based assessments, behavioral observation systems, data gathering techniques, specially designed instruction, and strategies for facilitating students' maintenance and generalization of skills across home or school settings.
- Social workers assist in planning and providing comprehensive services in life domains that include the family's living situation or community setting. Roles of social workers include involving families in supporting school and community goals.
- Physical therapists help to determine students' gross motor skills. Occupational therapists work on students' fine motor skills.
- Recreational therapists support therapeutic recreation opportunities available to students with disabilities and their families.
- School counselors provide reflection, listening, and counseling expertise and support.
- Orientation and mobility specialists work with students with visual impairments, concentrating on skills to move about freely in environments. Medical services professionals provide diagnostic and evaluation services in students' health areas.
- Collaborative orientations and responsive practices underscore the necessity of school professionals' strong communication skills with, and demonstration of respect and support for, each other.

References

American School Counselor Association (1998). *ASCA position statement.* Author. http:www.cnw.com/ ~wsca/pos-7.html.

Cohen, L. G., & Spenciner, L. J. (1998). *Assessment of children and youth.* New York: Longman.

Downing, J. E. (1999). *Teaching communication skills to students with severe disabilities.* Baltimore, MD: Brookes.

Dunforth, S. (2000). *Cases in behavior management.* New York: Prentice Hall.

Office of Special Education Programs. (1999). *To assure the free appropriate public education of all students with disabilities: Twentieth annual report to Congress on the implementation of the Individuals with Disabilities Education Act.* Washington, DC: Author.

Overton, T. (2000). *Assessment in special education: An applied approach.* New York: Prentice-Hall, Inc.

Rosenfield, S., & Nelson, D. (1995). *The school psychologist's role in school assessment.* College Park, MD: University of Maryland. (ERIC Document Reproductions Service No. ED 391 985).

Tiegerman-Farber, E., & Radziewicz, C. (1998). *Collaborative decision making: The pathway to inclusion.* New York: Prentice-Hall, Inc.

U.S. Department of Education. (1997). *Nineteenth annual report to Congress on the implementation of the Individuals with Disabilities Education Act.* Washington, DC: U.S. Department of Education.

11

Community Professionals' Roles with Families

Diana J. Hammitte

Betty M. Nelson

Chapter Objectives

In this chapter we will

- Identify roles of a range of professionals (medical and social) as they affect family functioning
- Discuss legislative amendments that have increased the participation of families in directing and accessing a range of services from community professionals
- Identify the roles and responsibilities of families in dealing with community professionals
- Provide strategies for developing and maintaining collaborative partnerships among professionals and families
- Identify the role of the classroom teacher in facilitating the process of accessing professional involvement with families of children with disabilities
- Identify resources helpful to families of students with special needs
- Summarize important chapter themes

> *Sarah Smith's parents wanted to place her in an after-school program run by the local department of recreation. Sarah is a nonambulatory, but highly communicative twelve-year-old. She is currently placed in a self-contained classroom for students with moderate intellectual disabilities. She is well known in her school and has numerous successful contacts with students throughout the school. Sarah's father is a teacher at a local high school and her mother works as support staff at a local university. Both of Sarah's older siblings have graduated from college. Despite the level of education evident in the family, when told that the after-school program was not equipped to handle Sarah's level of disability, the family accepted the decision without question.*

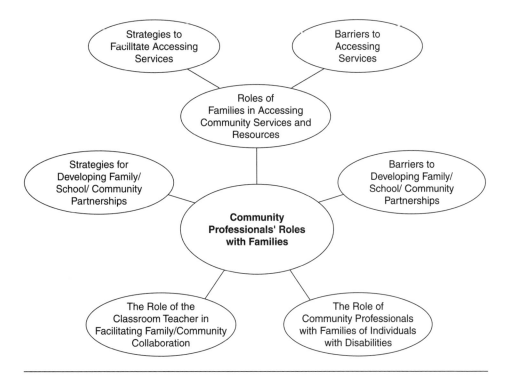

Carlos, an eleven-year-old male with moderate mental retardation, came to the United States with his father, Jose, mother, Maria, and sister, Marquita, when he was nine. Carlos's father died unexpectedly just after the move to this country. Feeling afraid and alone, Maria quickly met, married, and took up residence with another man of Hispanic origin, Antonio. When Carlos was ten, his special education teacher became aware of inappropriate, acting out behaviors exhibited by Carlos. When she discovered bruises on Carlos and reported suspicion of child abuse to the Department of Family and Children's Services (DEFACS), the assigned social worker, Fran, who speaks fluent Spanish, was contacted and immediately went to the apartment where Maria and her children were living. On her arrival she found Maria confused and alarmed because she didn't understand what was wrong, why they had been referred to DEFACS.

Betty Nelson's son, Michael, was born with a limb abnormality. His left hand was missing just below the wrist. Being a special educator, Betty wanted to do all the correct things to ensure Michael's life was as fulfilling as that of any other child. She turned to the medical profession for help.

As our society becomes more aware of the need for community participation in the development of future generations, it is important to understand how such community involvement can be accessed for families of children with disabilities. More than most, such families have areas of need that must be addressed by community professionals, particularly those in the educational, medical, or social fields. When these families are unassisted in their quest to meet these needs, it is the community that will bear the brunt of the family's failure. In this chapter, we examine ways in which families can access the collaborative services of professionals with the assistance of classroom teachers. We discuss barriers to effective collaborative partnerships and strategies for overcoming such barriers.

During the last three decades, professionals in the field of special education have supported the idea of involving families of individuals with special needs in the development of educational programming for such individuals. In reality, however, despite the support of special education professionals and the legislative mandates found in the laws governing the provision of services to individuals with disabilities, families have often remained passive recipients of professionals' judgments about what is best for their child (Turbiville, Turnbull, Garland, & Lee, 1996). This has particularly been the case in dealing with professionals within the community, outside of the schools. With the increased focus on accessing related services as they support educational programming for students with special needs, a concomitant increase in collaborative partnerships between families, teachers, and community professionals will need to develop.

Unfortunately, families have traditionally found related services personnel, for example medical personnel, somewhat intimidating and possessing expertise beyond their understanding (Simons, 1987). The lack of collaborative relationships among families and community professionals can exacerbate the already overwhelming serious concerns of society. The onslaught of AIDS, the random acts of violence in schools, the increase in teen pregnancy, the diversity in family composition, the levels of poverty, and the growing sense of doom that appears to permeate our society can be reduced or increased based on the degree of involvement of families, teachers, and community professionals in the educational decisions regarding its future citizens. The need for such a collaborative partnership is especially important when addressing educational programming for individuals with disabilities.

According to Epstein (1995) partnerships between families, schools, and the community can serve a number of purposes. They can facilitate the timely provision of services and support to families, positively impact school programs, and positively influence the environment of the school. Such collaborative partnerships can provide the vehicle through which families can grow in areas of leadership, and can help teachers in completing the necessary work with the student with disabilities. However, as Epstein so aptly stated, "the main reason to create such partnerships is to help all youngsters succeed in school and in later life. When families, teachers, students, and others view one another as partners in education, a caring community forms around students and begins its work" (p. 701).

The benefits of family and community involvement in the provision of educational services to students with disabilities was supported by Henderson and Berla (1994) in their book, *A New Generation of Evidence: The Family Is Critical to Student Achievement.* They open with a statement indicating that "the evidence is now beyond dispute. When schools work together with families to support learning, children tend to succeed not just in school, but throughout life" (p. 1). Collaborative partnerships that serve to ensure these outcomes will be vital if we are to meet the needs of society today. Table 11.1 provides additional support for such family/school/community partnerships.

TABLE 11.1 *Importance of Family Involvement in Education*

It is generally believed that...

- If families are involved in efforts to improve children's outcomes, those efforts are more effective.

- Involving parents in their child's education facilitates improved performance by the child in school.

- Family involvement in the schools tends to decrease the number of children who are likely to drop out of school.

- Parental involvement in schools creates safer and better schools for their children to attend.

- When parents provide support to the schools and their children, their children perform at higher levels of learning.

- When parents participate in decision making about the educational programming for their children, and when parents assume some teaching responsibilities, their children demonstrate higher levels of performance.

- Partnerships between families and schools foster higher levels of student achievement.

- Positive relationships among families, schools, and community organizations contribute to greater student achievement.

The reauthorization of the Individuals with Disabilities Education Act (IDEA) in 1997 requires documentation of active parent participation throughout the educational process. Such a mandate will necessitate development of collaborative partnerships between families, teachers, and other professionals engaged in the provision of related services. A variety of community agencies such as the Department of Family and Children's Services (DEFACS), the Department of Rehabilitative Services (DRS), Vocational Training Institutes, medical personnel (occupational therapists (OTs), physical therapists (PTs), physicians, nurses), and speech-language pathologists (SLPs) will all be involved. Essential in such involvement is information to assist families, teachers, and community professionals in the inclusion of families in school and community decisions that affect their children.

The Role of the Family in Accessing Community Services and Resources

Turnbull and Turnbull (1997) have identified the 1970s as a time in which parents became political advocates for their children with disabilities. Since that time, such parents have evolved from political advocates to educational decision makers to collaborators in the development of educational programs for their children. In fact, it is unlikely that the changes reflected in the current 1997 reauthorization of IDEA would have occurred had it not been for the political, social, and community influence of families of children with disabilities. Despite the common practice of educators and other professionals to appear to believe that parents are either the source of their child's problems or lack interest in their child's progress, parents of children with disabilities have been the primary catalyst for parental involvement in special education. Parents organized local and national organizations as a result of their frustration with the way professionals were dealing with their children in the first half of the twentieth century. Such organizations were designed to support more appropriate means for achieving the necessary services to meet their child's educational, social, and personal needs.

As families continue to take a more assertive role, legislation such as the Child Protection Act of 1986 (P.L. 99-372), amendments to IDEA (P.L. 99-457, P.L. 101-476, P.L. 105-17), Americans with Disabilities Act (ADA) (P.L. 100-336), and the Family Support Act (FSA) of 1988 (P.L. 100-485) has been enacted which reflects parental assumption of responsibility for protecting the total child, not just addressing their child's educational needs. Of particular interest to families of children with disabilities is the support provided by FSA to strengthen families as part of the reform of the public welfare system. Traditionally, according to the U.S. Department of Education (1996) more families of students in special education are identified as having low socioeconomic status than are families of children in general education. Bucci and Reitzammer (1992) indicated that the FSA recognizes the importance of service partnerships that include educators, work support personnel, medical personnel and social work or other public welfare employees, and support coordination of these services. "FSA recognizes education as central to helping families avoid long-term dependence on public assistance and encourages a relationship between the educational and welfare communities as a key developmental partnership" (Bucci & Reitzammer, 1992, p. 291).

Parents of individuals with disabilities, like all parents, have the responsibility of obtaining appropriate medical, social, and educational services for their own children. Legislative acts have supported the attainment of such services. Despite all the rhetoric of the late 1980s and early 1990s, it is not the responsibility of professionals to "empower" families, but it is the responsibility of the family to assume the power. Professionals should only provide direction and encouragement in achieving this end. Despite best intentions, however, many barriers exist which often preclude families from assuming their time-honored role.

Barriers to Accessing Services

As indicated previously, families have often been intimidated by both the professionals and the process involved in accessing community services and resources. Unfortunately, all too often the process is an unpleasant one, frequently resulting in families being unable to access needed services or available resources. In addition, families often lack knowledge of their rights and responsibilities as provided by law and do not question authorities, but rather accept their word as the final decision (Turnbull & Turnbull, 1997).

Consider the case of Sarah Smith. As indicated earlier, Sarah's family wanted to place her in an after-school program run by the local department of recreation but were told that would not be possible. Program staff indicated that they were not equipped to meet the additional requirements Sarah would impose on the program. Now, consider what might have occurred had the Smiths shared this information with Sarah's teacher, asking about the appropriateness of this decision. Under ADA (1990), Sarah has the right to participate in such a public program or service. In a collaborative partnership, it would be likely that Sarah's teacher would share that information with the Smiths and urge them to continue to pursue the placement. The family, teacher, and professionals in the department of recreation would need to discuss options available for including Sarah in the after-school program. Through the use of a variety of problem solving techniques, this group would work collaboratively to select the most effective option.

According to Simons (1987) several issues are identified by families as barriers to working with professionals in the provision of services to children with disabilities. "Not being treated like an individual—not being listened to—is parents' greatest complaint about professionals" (p. 47). Additionally, parents indicated that professionals often focus on the negative aspects of the child's development rather than focus on what the child can do. A review of current literature (see, for example, Dettmer, Dyck, & Thurston, 1996; Epstein, 1995; Gestwicki, 1996; Kroth & Edge, 1997) identified additional barriers as indicated in Table 11.2. Such barriers may often appear insurmountable to families, however, numerous strategies exist that may be used in tearing down these barriers.

Strategies to Facilitate Accessing Services

Parental responsibilities in accessing services for their children and, in fact, their entire family, are numerous. Joyce Epstein (1992, 1994, 1995), frequently identified as an expert in family/school/professional partnerships, has provided a model for development of effective partnerships which illustrates six types of involvement in which families can participate.

TABLE 11.2 *Barriers for Families in Working with Professionals*

- Schools sometimes undermine parents' own sense of what's best for their child
- Professionals often believe that families, particularly families from low SES situations, are not truly interested in working with the schools and community to enhance their child's development
- Professionals focus on the negative
- Relationships with professionals are often frustrating and combative
- Lack of positive cooperative relationships between and among students, staff, parents, and administrators
- Teachers have not been prepared to work with parents and community professionals
- Cultural competence of professionals
- The responsibilities of parents (work, childcare, financial, etc.)
- The feelings of inadequacy, low self-esteem or self-assurance, and guilt
- Former special education recipients who had unpleasant experiences with professionals
- Feelings of being blamed for their inability to do everything for their child

Viewed from the perspective of parental responsibility, these six types of involvement may be addressed as follows:

- *Type 1: Parenting*—Developing enriching environments within the home to support the academic, social, and personal development of their children. Such an environment might be achieved through participation in parent education courses, workshops, family support programs, and so on.
- *Type 2: Communicating*—Maintaining an open, honest dialogue with school personnel and other professionals. Providing accurate, clear information about family strengths and needs in conferences and responding promptly to communications from teachers and other professionals will assist in keeping the lines of communication open.
- *Type 3: Volunteering*—Demonstrating the willingness to participate in the classroom or school environment or within the community in a voluntary capacity to facilitate program development or maintenance. Parents might achieve such participation by volunteering to put up a bulletin board in the classroom or school, providing support to other parents through agencies such as Parent to Parent, serving in an advisory capacity to organizations involved in providing assistance to children, participating in fund-raising activities from which children will benefit, such as March of Dimes or Special Olympics.
- *Type 4: Learning at home*—Parents might provide their child with the opportunity to generalize learning from the community or school to the home environment. Helping with homework, providing family reading activities, and requesting information from professionals about necessary job skills are all ways in which parents can enhance learning at home.
- *Type 5: Decision making*—Parents can participate as equal partners in the decisions made about their child's academic programming, and advocating for their child's rights to a free appropriate public education. Becoming an active participant in the PTO at school, participating in groups such as Parent to Parent, and being well versed in parental rights and responsibilities under IDEA, particularly with regard to development of the Individualized Education Plan (IEP), are all ways in which parents can assume decision making roles.
- *Type 6: Collaborating with the community*—Parents can assume management of community resources and services that can strengthen their child's learning and social development. In addition to managing related services required by their child's IEP, this can be achieved through accessing information about and participating in community-sponsored programs in education, recreation, health, cultural activities, and other areas of interest to both the child and family.

It is the responsibility of families to recognize both their strengths and areas of need and to address, or seek assistance in addressing the areas of need. Table 11.3 provides some tips to be considered by families in addressing these areas. It should be noted that although these tips are focused on what the families can do, they present keys for successful interactions to professionals as well.

TABLE 11.3   *Tips for Parents in Accessing Services*

- Avoid or overcome roadblocks to effective communication.
- Be assertive—say what you feel and what your goals are.
- Be open to new situations.
- Avoid feelings of defensiveness.
- Explore your own feelings before addressing those of others.
- Keep to the issues at hand—don't dwell on past circumstances or other irrelevancies.
- Remember, your child's future is the focus of your interactions.

The Role of Community Professionals with Families of Individuals with Disabilities

The societal changes cited earlier in this chapter and elsewhere in this text have created numerous changes within the context of the family. More and more frequently families are dealing with issues previously only experienced in isolated instances. In the "land of opportunity" of their ancestors, today's families are dealing with more stress, more isolation as neighborhoods disintegrate, are perhaps at the poverty level, and are likely to need all the help they can get from community professionals, including school personnel.

Today's family is seen as a complex system, with no one pattern prevailing. Single-parent homes, homes in which both parents are present but working, extended family residences, same-sex parents, and residences in which neither parent resides are becoming more typical as society becomes more accepting of diversity. Unfortunately, inadequate parenting skills and a higher level of stress may result from such diversity. According to Gestwicki (1996), "as communities count the cost of inadequate parenting and family stress in the numbers of teenage pregnancies, school drop-out rates, drug addictions and other illnesses, crime rates and other antisocial disruptions, there is powerful motivation for schools, social agencies, legislatures, businesses, and other concerned community organizations to mobilize and combine efforts for family support" (p. 101).

In an effort to combat such costs to society, family resource and support programs are developing across the country. Funding is available for such programs through the Office of Special Education Programs and the U.S. Department of Education. The provision of training and information for families of children with disabilities is the focus of such programs. According to *Exceptional Parent* (1998),

> parent training and information programs can help parents to
> - Understand their children's specific needs
> - Communicate more effectively with professionals
> - Participate in the educational planning process
> - Obtain information about relevant programs, services, and resources (p. 50).

Programs such as the Kentucky Parent Child Education Program, Parents as Teachers Program in Missouri, the Coalition for Students Who Are Medically Fragile and Technologically

Dependent in Alabama, Parent to Parent of Georgia, the Federation for Children with Special Needs in Boston, the Parent Advocacy Coalition for Educational Rights (PACER) Center in Minneapolis, and Sinergia in New York City offer a variety of services and provide linkages to community professionals for parents and families. These programs, run by parents, social workers, teachers, or other professionals, may provide instruction in parenting skills, vocational assessment and training, GED preparation, child care services, lending libraries, resource guides, training in advocacy, training in communication skills, and may provide a major support system for the family. The overarching focus of such programs "is not on intervention as a means of solving a deficit problem, but as a developmental service needed by all families, regardless of socioeconomic or cultural background, to support them to optimum functioning, particularly at key points in the family life cycle when stresses, crises, and change are the norm. The approach is prevention, not treatment. Not all families need exactly the same kinds of support, so family resource and support programs are individualized, flexible, and adaptive. Collaborative efforts between community agencies, offering health, welfare, social services, and education meet the family's comprehensive needs" (Gestwicki, 1996, p. 102).

Mostert (1998) provided the following framework for describing many of the primary duties assumed by caring and competent community professionals when working with parents and families. As indicated, many of these duties may involve interactions with teachers and others in the school systems in supporting interventions for effective changes in educational programming for children with disabilities.

Social Agencies

Providing Information.   Social workers can provide a valuable service to families of children with disabilities in that they possess, or should possess, extensive knowledge regarding services available to the families in areas such as financial aid, child care, transportation, family dynamics, parenting skills, and child-rearing practices. By virtue of their training, social workers have a commitment to help parents of children with disabilities to assume control of the management of their child's educational, social, and emotional development (Fiene & Taylor, 1991). These skills are of particular importance in rural communities where the scarcity of resources is evident. It takes creative solutions to address the environmental barriers and values and belief conflicts that exist in these communities. Providing information doesn't stop with the family. Social workers may find themselves in the job of assisting children with disabilities in being accepted by their nondisabled peers (Greer et al., 1995).

Interpreting Information.   Social workers often work more closely with the families they serve than any other professional. They may be called upon by families to interpret information provided by others. They must be prepared to ensure that their interpretation is accurate and they do not interpret information the way they "think" it should be. They must develop the practice of researching in areas they are not familiar with to be certain to provide accurate information. As the intent of legislation in working with children with disabilities is interpreted, social workers are finding their roles within the schools expanding to include the need to interpret such laws both to meet the needs of families and students with disabilities and to determine their own degree of involvement with these families (Kardon, 1995).

Reporting Evaluation Results.   Although social workers do not traditionally conduct formal evaluations that specifically address areas of disability, they are responsible for gathering intake and ongoing information on family functioning. Additionally, social workers may be called upon by families here again to interpret the information provided by other professionals. It is vital, therefore, that social workers involved with individuals with disabilities and their families become acquainted with the various test instruments and their reporting requirements. For example, social workers could find themselves as the chairpersons of eligibility and placement meetings which might require their interpretation of psychological evaluations in the frequent absence of a psychologist or psychometrist more skilled in such interpretation.

Gathering and Understanding Family Information.   As part of the intake and on-going evaluation it is important for social workers to continue to update their skills in listening and observation to ensure correct interpretation of information. As mentioned previously, social workers are often the individuals with whom families share the most information regarding the day-to-day functioning of the family. Table 11.4 provides a list of skills necessary to become an effective listener and observer.

Understanding Family Diversity.   It is vital that social workers understand the importance of addressing diversity in culture, religion, ability, etc. if they are to provide appropriate services to all individuals. It is crucial that professionals have current knowledge regarding a family's physical, economic, and emotional environment. Without this information families may not receive the services they are entitled to. Because it is the social workers' job to collect information about their clients' background, they are most likely to need to possess cultural competence. Occasionally, success stories are reported.

Carlos represents one of those success stories. Fran, the DEFACS employee identified at the beginning of this chapter, somewhat familiar with the Hispanic culture, chose to proceed slowly with Maria, Carlos's mother. As previously reported, Maria was alarmed by the visit from DEFACS and did not understand what had caused it to occur. Fran told her of the school's concern about possible abuse. Maria indicated that Antonio was only disciplining Carlos in the manner to which they were accustomed in their home country.

Fran informed Maria that while she understood what she was saying, such disciplinary behaviors were not acceptable in the United States and they were left with a couple of choices for how to deal with the situation. DEFACS' policy would dictate two possible courses of action: removal of the children from the abusive situation, or determination that the children were not at undue risk and that intervention and training would be the best approach. Based on Fran's knowledge of the Hispanic culture and completion of the necessary intake information, Fran decided the best course of action for the family would be to recommend the second option.

Fran contacted the school to report the results of her visit and made arrangements for Maria and Antonio to attend some parenting classes offered at the local high school by community counselors and nurses. Throughout the following six months, Fran made frequent

TABLE 11.4 *Active Listening and Observation Skills*

Active listening and observation are learned skills which can be improved with practice. In order to listen and observe you must:

- *Stop talking.* Allow your communication partner to formulate responses to your questions. Show that you want to listen and be helpful. Pay special attention to the feelings behind the facts, and avoid mentally preparing your next statement while the speaker is still talking.

- *Put the speaker at ease.* Relax and make the appropriate amount of eye contact with your communication partner. Remember, some cultures do not engage in direct eye contact.

- *Ask appropriate questions.* Be sure they are open-ended questions which will encourage your partner to answer with more than "yes" or "no" responses. Ask only one question at a time in a clearly phrased manner. Offer a chance for your partner to elaborate on his or her statements.

- *Make appropriate comments.* Be encouraging, demonstrate attending skills such as nodding and making neutral vocalizations such as "yes," "oh."

- *Demonstrate reflection skills.* Use reflective paraphrasing by stating what you believe the speaker has said in your own words. The speaker can then either confirm or deny your understanding and contradictions may be cleared up. Be sure to also reflect on what you perceive to be the speaker's feelings as well. For example, "You sounded distressed when…" or "Were you relieved when…?"

- *Exhibit openness.* Be willing to make statements in which you reveal something that may be personal or private to you. For example, "I was sad when…" or "I was frightened by…"

- *Share topic selection or postponement.* Allow your conversational partner to indicate his or her preference with regard to whether or not to discuss a certain topic. The individual may wish to postpone the topic until a more favorable or comfortable time.

- *Remain objective.* Work to avoid jumping to conclusions in conversations. Be on the look-out for negative feelings you may already have about your conversational partner's point of view or lifestyle. Do not allow your emotions to interfere in your conversation. Accept his or her feelings and do not take ownership of them.

- *Center on your partner's concerns.* Attend to the topics or issues that are important to your conversation partner. Try to listen as if you shared his or her concerns and point of view.

- *Develop attention to detail.* Work on your skills at identifying physical characteristics of feelings. Although we generally associate certain facial expressions with certain feelings, know your partner. They may smile most when they are the most hurt.

- *Focus.* Be sure to focus on your conversational partner and focus out extraneous details. Surveying the room often gives the appearance of lack of interest and attention.

visits with the family and developed a strong, trusting relationship with both Maria and Antonio. This relationship was important when, seven months after the initial contact, Maria decided it was time for her to seek employment outside of the home and Fran was able to guide her into some job skills training and placement services.

One year later, Maria, Antonio, Carlos, and Marquita have developed into a close-knit caring family, one that deals with anger and discipline in more constructive ways. Such changes are reflected in the decrease of inappropriate behaviors exhibited by Carlos in his special education classes. Maria has expressed her gratitude to Fran for giving them the benefit of the doubt and working with them to ensure that her children would continue in her care.

Communicating Effectively: Meetings & Conferences.   As indicated in the previous scenario, effective communication can greatly affect the future of families of children with disabilities and, in fact, all families. Table 11.5 provides a list of necessary skills for professionals to use in developing effective communication with families.

Instruction to Families.   Although professionals may occasionally need to provide specific instruction to families on how to work with their child with a disability, it is often the case that such information is shared with the local school system. Participation in the Individual Education Plan meeting, annual re-evaluations, and other meetings can give social agency personnel the opportunity to provide input into the instructional needs of a family and their child with a disability. Beyond meetings such as these, most instruction provided by social workers and others in the social agency is provided on a one-on-one basis with families in need.

Medical Personnel

Providing Information.   Medical personnel frequently involved with families of children with disabilities include physical therapists, occupational therapists, nurses, and physicians. Each of these professional groups has direct contact with families and responsibilities that can influence the family's abilities to cope with the diagnosis and prognosis concerning their

---

TABLE 11.5 *Tips for Building Communication with Families*

- Establish rapport before the school year or services begin.
- Encourage families to tell you about their culture, hobbies, occupations, experiences.
- Give families the opportunity to tell you what they want for their children as opposed to telling them what you plan to offer.
- Pay attention to families' body language when presenting information.
- Never assume anything when working with families.
- During meetings/conferences, ensure that all parties are introduced and that everyone understands his or her role in each particular setting.
- Consider the use of a bell during meetings where jargon may occur. Assign a person to ring the bell when jargon or acronyms are used so that these terms can be explained.
- Catch the child doing something good and share with the family through a phone call or note home.
- Treat the families as you would a colleague or a work friend.
- Encourage families to volunteer in whatever capacity they can—all families have strengths that can be tapped if properly assessed.

---

child's disability. Medical personnel typically approach things the same way. Fortunately, in today's training centers for medical personnel greater emphasis is being placed on the bed-side manner of personnel involved in providing direct services to individuals.

Interpreting Information.   Medical personnel are in a unique position with regard to in-terpreting information. In fact, frequently they are the only ones who readily understand the information they possess. They must be prepared to ensure that their interpretation is accurate and family friendly, shared in a language that families can understand. Creative approaches to providing and interpreting information to families need to be taken if medi-cal professionals are to work effectively with families. Often medical personnel have lim-ited time to share information and interpret how it can be used in the school or home environment. Videotaping as well as using telemedicine technology can provide an excel-lent means to meet this need. For example, the taping of a physical therapy session with instructions on how to carry out the activity can be invaluable information to a family in carrying out techniques at home. Likewise, telemedicine techniques could facilitate collab-orative diagnosis and intervention within the natural environment. These technologies could be used for conducting or demonstrating a variety of medical procedures (e.g., OT, PT, use of inhalers, catheterizations).

Reporting Evaluation Results.   Medical personnel must be sensitive to the effects the in-formation they may have to share can have on the family of a child with disabilities. Such families are often already overwhelmed with negative information about their child's poten-tial. Medical professionals must be willing and able to soften the blow. In addition, they must be aware of the inability of some individuals to accept or absorb information at given times.

Gathering and Understanding Family Information.   Medical personnel must develop a willingness to listen to families. As indicated previously, a common complaint of families with regard to discussions with medical personnel is their failure to listen to what the family has to say (Simons, 1987). A misdiagnosis or inappropriate treatment can often be avoided if all pieces of the puzzle are presented and heard.

Betty Nelson reported an experience she had with the medical profession that could have had far-reaching repercussions for her youngest son, Michael. As stated earlier, Michael was born missing his left hand. When Michael was two years old, another parent of a child with a limb abnormality urged Betty to get a prosthesis for him. Betty took Michael to a major medical center, had a prosthesis fitted, and participated with him in one week of occupational training in its use. When they returned home, Betty began a daily regime of working with Michael in using the prosthesis with toys and other objects, despite Michael's obvious opposition to the activity. One day after placing the prosthesis on a table and leaving to get toys from another room, Betty returned to find the prosthesis missing. Upon questioning, Michael finally took Betty's hand and showed her that he had placed the prosthesis in the kitchen garbage container. Betty's prior knowledge of special education and strong maternal instincts took over and she made the decision that it was apparently not the time to consider the use of a prosthesis, so discontinued the daily activity.

On a six-month follow-up visit regarding the use of the prosthesis, the resident on duty asked how Michael was adjusting to the prosthesis. Betty responded that Michael had chosen not to wear it. The resident reprimanded Betty, stating it was her responsibility as the parent to ensure that her child wore the prosthesis at all times. When she tried to discuss the issue with him, the resident would not listen and went to get the chief orthopedic surgeon.

Upon his arrival in the examination room, the chief orthopedic surgeon said, "So, I hear Michael doesn't want to wear his prosthesis." When Betty confirmed this and described what had occurred at home, he evidenced no surprise and indicated that it was common for children with this type of limb abnormality to choose not to wear a prosthesis. He indicated that as long as Michael continued to progress and did not evidence great difficulty in fine motor skills, use of a prosthesis was not necessary until such time as Michael should choose to use one.

Had Betty not stated her concerns, or had she just listened to the intern who was unwilling to discuss the issue, she may have continued to force Michael to use a prosthesis which very likely may have damaged their relationship and his development. Seven years later, Michael continues to decline the use of a prosthesis, and it has not affected his development in any apparent way. This year he was selected to be on the local all-star baseball team in his age group. He is actively involved in karate, skates with his peers with no difficulty, and frequently beats his older brother on computer games.

Such success stories are unfortunately not always the case. Hopefully, however, as more current training techniques are integrated into professional curricula, medical personnel and others will be trained in active listening skills which will ensure that they listen to and reflect on all that the families have to say, instead of reacting to bits and pieces.

Understanding Family Diversity.   It is vital that medical personnel understand the importance of addressing diversity in areas such as culture, religion, and ability if they are to provide appropriate services to individuals. Training in multicultural issues should be a major component of professional programs. As indicated in other sections of this book, all families are not alike; in fact, the variability seen in families as we enter the twenty-first century is astounding. If medical personnel are to be effective in providing services to individuals, they must keep abreast of the changing demographics of the communities they serve and provide interventions, diagnoses, and treatments in such a way as to evidence respect for the individual's heritage.

Communicating Effectively: Meetings and Conferences.   Professionals need to develop finely honed communicative skills if they are to effectively support families of children with disabilities and establish open lines of communication. Working on conferencing skills and developing strategies for making meetings and conferences comfortable for all individuals is vital. Paying special attention to the comfort of families will facilitate conversation and willingness on the part of families to discuss issues of importance. Professionals should avoid the use of jargon in meetings with families and professionals outside of their field of expertise, yet avoid "talking down" to these individuals. Seating arrangements can make or break a conference and it is important to seat all parties in an equal manner. For example, do not always assume the chair at the head of the table and avoid putting a desk between you and your communication partners.

Instruction to Families.   Medical personnel all too frequently give hurried, abbreviated directions to individuals who are shocked by information they just received or who haven't absorbed diagnostic information. Consider the allergist who calls in his nurse while providing directions to patients and has her write down in clear, legible handwriting instructions to be followed as opposed to the physician who hurriedly mumbles "take three a day" as the patient is ushered out the door. Here, again, we see a need for medical personnel to place more emphasis on listening to the families, or making every attempt to communicate with them in a manner that can be clearly understood.

Medical and other professionals might consider viewing a 1996 movie, *Doctor,* starring William Hurt. This movie is very effective in demonstrating what often happens to patients when professionals become too busy and removed from their patients, no longer treating them as individuals but as syndromes or diseases. The last scene is cause for hope in changing this trend.

The Role of the Classroom Teacher in Facilitating Family/Community Collaboration

While many teachers are comfortable with, and would prefer to continue in the traditional role of information purveyor, the individual who advises families on the progress and prognosis of their child, that role no longer meets the needs of families of children with disabilities. Nor does it facilitate the integration of the family and their child into the community. Today, the role of the special education classroom teacher has expanded greatly from that traditional model (Thomas, Correa, & Morsink, 1995). Classroom teachers of today may be involved at some level in a variety of roles. In addition to teacher, they may assume the role of advocate, interpreter, case manager, parent educator, or friend. In these roles, teachers may be called on to provide services such as community-based training in survival or job skills, interpretation of professional reports, assistance in meeting financial needs (e.g., welfare payments, food stamps, Social Supplemental Income payments) or transportation for families to attend meetings at school and other events, or simply provide a listening ear. According to Thomas et al., none of these roles should be assumed without careful thought, training, and assistance. (Box 11.1 provides an example of the family taking the lead role in service provision.)

In working together with families to develop family/school/community partnerships, new teachers must first identify where the family is in their readiness to address the needs of their child with a disability. The mirror model of family involvement in education stresses the need to assess families' strengths and needs and to establish guidelines for comprehensive involvement programs (Kroth & Edge, 1997). Chapter 5 in this text, Assessment, provides information regarding needs assessment of families. Nicholas Hobbs (1978) indicated that "parents have to be recognized as the special educators, the true experts on their children; and professional people—teachers, pediatricians, psychologists, and others—have to learn to be consultants to parents."

Unfortunately, in today's climate it is difficult to determine strengths and needs and to assume that families have taken on traditional roles. The 1998 edition of *The State of America's Children* published by the Children's Defense Fund, provides some overwhelming statistics on family/child relationships. The key facts about American children presented in Table 11.6, paint a glum picture for the future of our country. Such facts are particularly disturbing in view of the number of health and social services programs that

BOX 11.1

Family–Teacher–Community Issues

Sophie Langer has been in and out of the hospital for treatment of her diabetes for several years. Ian, her sixteen-year-old grandson, has spent many hours by her bedside. After his last visit, Ian, who is currently enrolled in a self-contained special education class for students with mild/moderate levels of mental retardation, reported to his teacher, Mr. Williams, that he wanted to work in a community hospital. Ian's grandmother also called Mr. Williams and requested that he see if it would be a possibility for Ian to be employed in the hospital. She reported that Ian had been very helpful to the patients on her floor and liked by everyone. Mr. Williams reported that Ian is a neat young man who works hard at anything he attempts. He indicated that Ian was very popular with students at the high school, including students who were not identified as special needs learners, and that he is always willing to help someone out.

Collaborative Orientations and Responsive Practices

Since Ian's IEP must include transition goals, Mr. Williams has decided to begin to train Ian for a possible job in the medical field. He has spoken with Mrs. Langer and together they decided that Mr. Williams would make inquiry with the local hospital staff regarding potential positions. In talking with the hospital director, Mr. Campbell, Mr. Williams found that the hospital did, in fact, hire a small number of individuals with disabilities for patient transfers and cleaning. Mr. Campbell also advised Mr. Williams that they had an on-site job coach who worked with all of the individuals with disabilities on staff to assist with the development of necessary skills. Mr. Williams was able to meet with the job coach, Ms. Lipinski, and schedule time for her to visit with Ian, his grandmother, and Mr. Williams at the school for purposes of developing a training plan for Ian.

---

are provided in today's schools. Today a student can receive substance abuse counseling, participate in before- and after-school care, and receive instruction in parenting skills within the confines of the public school. Child care centers for teen parents, social work services, and health services or clinics are often found. Despite the availability of such services, poverty, hunger, inadequate health care, widespread substance abuse, and homelessness still prevail (Levy & Copple, 1989). A means for coping with such problems may be found in the development of linkages between families, social service agency personnel, and medical personnel in the community.

Today's teachers can facilitate parent/school/community partnerships in a variety of ways. Primarily, however, these facilitative practices fit into three broad categories: providing information, developing partnerships, and providing services.

Providing Information

Classroom teachers should maintain a file of information that can be shared with families of children with disabilities on programs or services available to them covering areas such as recreation, support, health, and cultural activities. Information on summer schools and other learning opportunities in the community (e.g., library summer reading programs, day camps) should also be available. Information on programs or services beyond the local community (e.g., Camp Big Heart, Easter Seals) should also be maintained.

To meet their potential role as interpreter of information provided by medical personnel, classroom teachers should consider keeping a medical reference text such as the *Physicians' Desk Reference,* a medical dictionary, and a general medical guide for childhood illnesses in their classrooms for easy access in responding to parental needs or concerns. Teachers working with culturally diverse, multilingual families may consider purchasing the appropriate language dictionary (e.g., Spanish/English translations) for use as needed. In their role as advocate, classroom teachers should have easy access to a bulleted version of parental rights to give to families.

Developing Partnerships

Classroom teachers can be instrumental in bringing together professionals in the community to work with families in integrated teams. Such teams could include professionals in medical, social, and the business community that could be involved in facilitating a broad based-program for the individual with disabilities to become more integrated into community life. Teachers need to contact professionals within the community to determine their willingness to serve in advisory or other capacities with families of children with disabilities. A list of willing professionals should be maintained and provided to families upon request.

Classroom teachers might consider inviting community professionals to their classrooms to meet with their students and their families to discuss how they might best serve the needs of such individuals. Teachers may also contact the local rotary or chamber of commerce and ask to speak with the membership about the needs of families of children with disabilities and the importance of community partnerships in meeting those needs.

Providing Services

Classroom teachers can develop a system whereby students with disabilities and their families can provide service to the community in areas such as working with senior citizens in

TABLE 11.6   *Disturbing Facts about America's Children*

- Approximately half of today's preschoolers have working mothers and are likely to live in a single-parent family situation during their childhood.
- One-third of newborns have parents who are not married.
- Poverty will affect one-third of today's children, with one in four being born poor.
- One-fourth of mothers have not graduated from high school at the time of birth of their children and are unlikely to have received appropriate prenatal care or to have health insurance.
- Teenage mothers are on the increase.
- One-twelfth of newborns exhibit some type of disability or developmental delay.
- Incidences of violence that affect the lives or development of children is on the rise, and an increasing number of children die before age one.

Source: Adapted from Children's Defense Fund (1998). *The State of America's Children: Yearbook 1998.* Washington, DC: Children's Defense Fund.

retirement facilities, participating in clean-up projects, conducting recycling drives, or assisting in other community campaigns. Teachers can also work with families to develop family support teams that would be available to physicians and others within the community to meet with and encourage other families in situations similar to theirs.

Barriers to Developing Family/School/Community Partnerships

Unfortunately, classroom teachers, like families and community professionals, often face situations that make it difficult to develop effective partnerships. Among such barriers are:

- *Conflict between needs of families and school policies* (Thomas, Correa, & Morsink, 1995)—Unfortunately, school systems may expect teachers to advocate for the school district while families may need their child's teacher to support their requests for better services.
- *Time constraints*—The paperwork requirements for special education teachers have become extremely time consuming. More often than not a teacher's "free" time is spent in assessing students and developing IEPs, or completing a myriad of other reports. Little time is left over for teachers to make the necessary community contacts to ensure successful collaboration with families and other professionals.
- *Lack of support from administrative staff*—It is all too often apparent that school administrators are not adequately informed about legal requirements for special education. Such lack of knowledge often results in failure of the staff to support the special education teacher in his or her quest to provide appropriate services to their students.
- *Limited availability of community resources in some areas*—Many communities, especially rural communities, may lack adequate resources to ensure that individuals with disabilities and their families have a variety of opportunities for learning experiences, job training, recreational activities and social events. In fact, in some of our smaller communities, medical personnel are limited to the local doctor and nurse. Access to occupational and physical therapists and other specialists in medical care or therapy may be nearly impossible to obtain.
- *Limitations in teachers' understanding of other professionals' areas of expertise*—It is difficult to give up ownership of specific areas of expertise, and often equally difficult to understand the specific skills and strategies required by areas of expertise other than our own. When a classroom teacher, or any other professional, is expected to provide information or interpret a professional's information to families, they may feel unequal to the task.
- *Lack of training in strategies for working with families and other professionals*—It has only been within the last decade or so that coursework in working in collaborative relationships with families and other professionals has been included in teacher preparation programs in special education. Many veteran teachers have not had the opportunity to study the research reporting positive results to collaborative relationships and have not been exposed to strategies for their development.

- *Lack of training in communicative skills*—Again, today's teacher training institutes are likely to focus a great deal of attention on the development of effective communication skills for use with other professionals and families.
- *Lack of willingness*—It is unfortunately a reality that many teachers, including those in special education, are unwilling to work with either families or other professionals in collaborative partnerships. Whether this is a result of inadequate training or simply a character trait, lack of willingness to collaborate in providing appropriate services to an individual with disabilities can have a devastating effect on that individual.

Strategies for Developing Family/School/ Community Partnerships

Although numerous barriers exist that make it difficult to develop effective family/school/ community partnerships, so do strategies for overcoming them. Following are strategies that may be effective in facilitating partnerships. Many of these strategies are based on those presented by Thomas, Correa, & Morsink (1995).

- First, and most important, determine the level of involvement desired by the families in your program. It is vital that classroom teachers do not assume a desire for their assistance on the part of all the families of their students. Many families are actively involved in accessing the services of other professionals in the community and are involved in the school to the degree they desire.
- Identify the strengths of the families of students in your classroom and encourage them to use their strengths in your classroom. For example, artistic parents might do bulletin boards, or lead an art activity with the students. Parents who are particularly talented in storytelling might be called in to work with the students to develop a story for use in language arts. Still other parents might lead a cooking class, or work with students on a woodworking project.
- Invite parents and community professionals to participate with the school in an advisory capacity. Such an advisory committee could offer important input in planning for transitioning and in working with families to access community professionals, as well as other areas.
- Provide families with manuals from their local schools. These manuals generally contain policies and procedures, identify the curriculum used by the school, and address other issues endemic to the school. Having families review the manual may help avoid any "conflict of interest" issues for the special education classroom teacher.
- Provide parents with information on medical issues pertinent to their individual child. With today's computer capabilities, this could be a relatively simple task. Once the teacher is aware of a student's specific area of disability, he or she could consult a variety of sources electronically and gather information for a resource file for parents' use.
- Provide parents with a current list of medical personnel and social service agencies within the community. Be sure that the agency and medical professionals you have

listed are willing and qualified to work with individuals with disabilities and their families.

• Establish a resource center for parents within your school. Such a center could contain videotapes, books, articles, or even toys that parents could borrow from the center. The center could also house adaptive, assistive technology for demonstration purposes, together with augmentative communication systems.

• Learn some survival words in the native languages of the families of your students. Also be sure to have an interpreter available at formal meetings. Do not depend on family members, or friends of the family, as interpreters in formal meetings. They may lack sufficient understanding of the school system and the roles of community professionals with regard to students with disabilities.

• Finally, as with families and other professionals, develop effective communication skills. Take particular care to learn of any cultural differences in communication. For example, several cultures refrain from eye contact during conversations, or are uncomfortable with shaking hands as a means of greeting.

Regardless of the strategies employed with families in educational programs, it is important to remember that parental involvement in the education of their child does result in improved performance for the student. Consequently, it is clearly part of a teacher's job to ensure that parental issues are addressed, and that community professionals are made aware of the needs of families of individuals with disabilities beyond immediate medical care or social services.

Family Member Questions

The following represent questions teachers are frequently asked with regard to assisting families in working with community professionals:

• *How do I access related services?* A resource list of available services should be maintained in your classroom. Keeping up-to-date information is important. Understanding the policies of the system in which you are employed is vital to avoid potential problems for families. Failure to know the policies could result in referring families to services for which they are not eligible.

• *What can I do when I am frustrated with the services I'm receiving from community agencies?* As a teacher you may not have input into the provision of related services. To assist the parents you may first ask if they have voiced their concerns to the agency. If not, encourage parents to do so. It may be necessary to remind parents that they have the final decision to accept or reject services.

• *How do I ensure that the services are provided through the school system?* As their child's teacher, it is important for you to advise parents that only those services identified in the Individual Education Plan are the responsibility of the school. If they desire additional services, they must become a part of the plan or they will be responsible for their provision. It is very important for you as a teacher to have access to and understanding of recent revisions to any legislation regarding special education services as well as state and local policies in this regard in order to provide informed information.

Family Resources and Services

The list of resources and services may help new teachers in their work with families and community-based professionals.

Beach Center on Families and Disability
3111 Haworth Hall
University of Kansas
Lawrence, KS 66045
(785) 864-7600

Children's Defense Fund
25 E Street NW
Washington, DC 20001
(800) 233-1200
www.tmn.com/cdf/index.html

Council for Exceptional Children
1920 Association Drive
Reston, VA 20191-1589
(888) 232-7733
www.cec.sped.org

Family Advocacy and Support Association
3700 10th Street NW
Washington, DC 20010
(202) 576-6065

Technical Assistance Alliance for Parent Centers
4826 Chicago Avenue, S.
Minneapolis, MN 55417
(888) 248-0822
www.taalliance.org

National Center for Latinos with Disabilities
1921 S. Blue Island Avenue
Chicago, IL 60608
(800) 532-3393

Alliance for Technology Access
National Office

Technology Access Center
2175 E. Francisco Blvd., Ste L
San Rafael, CA 94901
(415) 445-4575
www.ATAccess.org

National Fathers' Network
The Kindering Center
16120 NE 8th St.
Bellevue, WA 98008-3937
(425) 747-4004
www.fathersnetwork.org

SNAP: Special Needs Advocate for Parents
P.O. Box 641966
Los Angeles, CA 90064
(888) 366-6496

National Health Council
1730 M St NW, Ste 500
Washington, DC 20036-4505
(202) 785-3910
www.healthanswers.com

Parents Alliance Employment Project
Illinois Employment & Training Center
837 S. Westmore Drive
Lombard, IL 60148
(630) 495-4345

Center for Literacy and Disability Studies
P.O. Box 3888
Duke University Medical Center
Durham, NC 27710
(919) 684-3740
www.surgery.mc.duke.edu/hearing/clds/

**National Association of Protection
and Advocacy Systems**
900 2nd St NE, Ste 211
Washington, DC 20002
(202) 408-9514

Exceptional Parent
P.O. Box 3000
Dept. EP
Denville, N.J. 07834
(800) 562-1973
www.eparent.com

**NPSIS (National Parent to Parent
Support and Information Service)**
P.O. Box 907
Blue Ridge, GA 30513
(800) 651-1151
www.npsis.org

Summary

Families of children with disabilities, although often in need of the services of community professionals in the medical and social services fields, have often been intimidated by such individuals. Despite legislative requirements expanding both the need for related services for individuals with disabilities and, concomitantly, collaborative partnerships, we are still faced with barriers to such partnerships.

New teachers may assist in accessing the services of community professionals on behalf of parents of children with disabilities, by working with the families to develop partnerships and open lines of communication. Although barriers still exist, current training for professionals in a variety of medical and social areas has evolved to include training in more appropriate communication skills which can alleviate the traditional concerns of families with regard to feeling inadequate to interact with professionals.

Several strategies for developing communicative interactions are provided, and professionals and families alike are encouraged to develop more appropriate skills in order to establish working partnerships.

References

Bucci, J. A., & Reitzammer, A. F. (1992). Collaboration with health and social service professionals: Preparing teachers for new roles. *Journal of Teacher Education, 43* (4), 290–295.

Children's Defense Fund (1998). *The state of America's children: Yearbook 1998.* Washington, DC: Children's Defense Fund.

Dettmer, P. A., Dyck, N. T., & Thurston, L. P. (1996). *Consultation, collaboration, and teamwork for students with special needs* (2nd ed.). Boston: Allyn and Bacon.

Epstein, J. L. (1992). School and family partnerships. *Encyclopedia of Educational Research* (Vol. 6) (pp. 1139–1151). New York: Macmillan.

Epstein, J. L. (1994). Theory to practice: School and family partnerships lead to school improvement and student success. In C. L. Fagnano & B. Z. Werber (Eds.). *School, family, and community interaction: A view from the firing lines* (pp. 39–52). Boulder, CO: Westview.

Epstein, J. (1995). School/family/community partnerships: Caring for the children we share. *Phi Delta Kappan,* 701–712.

Exceptional Parent. (1998). 1998 Resource Guide. *Exceptional Parent, 28* (1).

Fiene, J. I., & Taylor, P. A. (1991). Serving rural families of developmentally disabled children: A case management model. *Social Work, 36* (4), 323–327.

Gestwicki, C. (1996). *Home, school and community relations: A guide to working with parents* (3rd ed.). Albany, NY: Delmar Publishers.

Greer, B. B., et al. (1995). The inclusion movement and its impact on counselors. *School Counselor, 43* (2), 123–132.

Henderson, A. & Berla, N. (Eds.) (1994). *A new generation of evidence: The family is critical to student achievement.* Columbia, MD: National Committee for Citizens in Education.

Hobbs, N. (1978). Classification options: A conversation with Nicholas Hobbs on exceptional children. *Exceptional Children, 44* (7), 494–497.

Kardon, S. D. (1995). Section 504: Developing a social work perspective in schools. *Social Work in Education, 17,* 48–54.

Kroth, R. L., & Edge, D. (1997). *Strategies for communicating with parents and families of exceptional children* (3rd ed.). Denver: Love Publishing.

Levy, J. E., & Copple, C. (1989). *Joining forces: A report from the first year.* Alexandra, VA: National Association of State Boards of Education.

Mostert, M. P. (1998). *Interprofessional collaboration in schools.* Boston: Allyn and Bacon.

Simons, R. (1987). *After the tears.* San Diego: Harcourt Brace Jovanovich.

Thomas, C. C., Correa, V. I., & Morsink, C. V. (1995). *Interactive teaming: Consultation and collaboration in special programs* (2nd ed.). Englewood Cliffs, NJ: Merrill/Prentice Hall.

Turbiville, V. P., Turnbull, A. P., Garland, C. W., & Lee, I. P. (1996). Development and implementation of IFSPs and IEPs: Opportunities for empowerment. In S. L. Odom & M. E. McLean (Eds.). *Early intervention/early childhood special education: Recommended practices* (pp. 77–100). Austin, TX: Pro-Ed.

Turnbull, A. P., & Turnbull, H. R. III. (1997). *Families, professionals, and exceptionality: A special partnership* (3rd ed.). Upper Saddle River, NJ: Merrill/Prentice Hall.

U.S. Department of Education. (1996). *Reaching all families: Creating family-friendly schools.* Washington, DC: Author.

12

Improving Outcomes and Future Practices: Family-Centered Programs and Services

Sylvia Nassar-McMillan

Bob Algozzine

Chapter Objectives _____

In this chapter we will

- Summarize what is known about working with families in supporting the education of their children
- Describe barriers to family participation in schooling
- Describe perspectives on developing family-oriented teachers
- Summarize important considerations in working collaboratively with families
- Illustrate principles for promoting family-centered programs and services
- List relevant family resources and services
- Summarize important chapter themes

> *Juan is a sixteen-year-old junior at East Lincoln High School. He is enrolled in a life skills program as part of his transition plan prepared in compliance with local special education guidelines. Juan spends part of his day with his peers learning functional academic skills and part of his day working in a community-based job placement. Juan has been working at a local fast-food restaurant for about three months. Recently, his mother came to school to talk to Juan's teachers and counselors. She was very upset because her uncle, who also works at the restaurant with Juan, overheard some coworkers complaining about Juan's job performance. Their concerns were significant: inability to follow directions, limited social skills, lack of motivation, poor attitude, limited organi-*

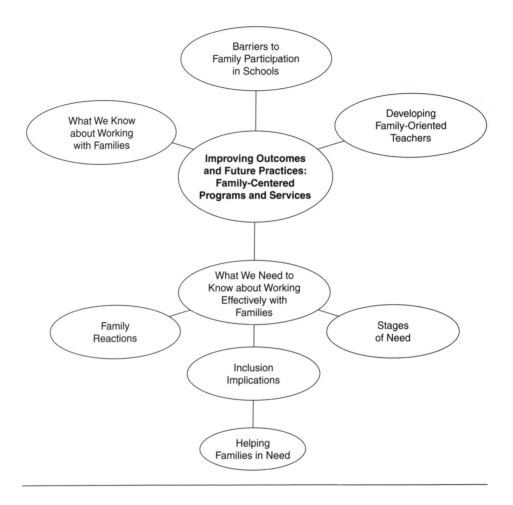

zational skills, and failure to complete tasks. Ms. Martinez is concerned that Juan will lose his job and be unable to find another one; if he finds one, she is very worried that he will be unable to keep it. She wants to know what Juan is being taught in his life skills classes and why he is not better supervised while on the job.

Families play many roles in the educational lives of children. Currently, they are regarded as important collaborators with important needs, responsibilities, and perspectives. Working effectively with families involves flexibility and multiple methods for meeting needs. Barriers to effective family participating in schools include differing perspectives on appropriate treatment within school settings. As we have stressed throughout this text, working effectively with families also requires understanding their reactions to success and failure, recognizing that their needs change over time, and developing strategies for helping them meet their needs.

Although early pioneers of psychotherapy such as Sigmund Freud and Carl Rogers believed that families were responsible for individuals' psychological problems and issues, the family therapy movement beginning in the 1950s countered this notion. Since the emergence of family therapy in the early 1950s, several divergent approaches have developed. Among these are structural, psychoanalytical, experiential, behavioral, Bowenian, and strategic and systemic family therapies (Nichols & Schwartz, 1995; Piercy, Sprenkle, & Associates, 1986). Despite the diversity represented by these perspectives, most approaches to family therapy have noteworthy similarities. These commonalities include focusing on the problem within the context of the familial relationship rather than attributing it to either the family unit or the individual (Nichols & Schwartz, 1995).

The recognition and acknowledgment of these tenets have led to both social and legal movements supporting the premise that in order to effectively address a child's academic or behavioral issues, the individuals playing a prominent role in the child's life must be involved in the intervention. In the context of educational entities, many school-based intervention efforts have begun to include these "key players," including parents, students, and school personnel (Carlson & Hickman, 1992; Peeks, 1993) such as teachers, school counselors, and other school-based mental health professionals (e.g., school psychologists, social workers, and administrators). In working with children with disabilities of all ages, P.L. 94-142, the Education for All Handicapped Children Act of 1975 and its subsequent amendments (i.e., Individuals with Disabilities Education Act) mandate that at the very least, a child's parents or guardians be invited to participate in the intervention throughout its course (Woody, 1994; Ysseldyke & Algozzine, 1994; Ysseldyke, Algozzine, & Thurlow, 2000).

What We Know about Working with Families

Many family theorists advocate working with the entire family system because each member is seen as being either part of the problem or its solution (Nichols & Schwartz, 1995; Fine & Gardner, 1991). Family therapists generally view individuals within the context of their families, whether nuclear or extended (Nichols & Schwartz, 1995). Defining a "normal" family in terms of its developmental process is less common in the family therapy versus individual psychotherapy realm. Most therapists have their own working concepts or perspectives of normalcy in terms of family development (Nichols & Schwartz, 1995). Counter to the traditional concepts of normalcy which may have in the past been discriminatory against or otherwise discounted multicultural or nontraditional family structures, normalcy often is defined in a more contemporary context in terms of overall family functioning (e.g., Cashwell, 1995; Cashwell & Nassar-McMillan, 1997).

The chicken or egg debate has long been present in discussions of dysfunctional families or their children's dyfunctional behavior. While contemporary family theorists differ in terms of focusing on various themes inherent in dysfunctionality of families, they concur that looking at how families cope with the problems encountered is more important than what actually causes them (Nichols & Schwartz, 1995).

Some of the concepts addressed by different family theorists include flexibility of family systems, the function of problematic symptoms, underlying family dynamics, and pathological triangles (Nichols & Schwartz, 1995). Inflexible systems seem to be the most common symptom of family dysfunction. This characteristic is represented by either chronic rigidity or by acute, more reactional rigidity in response to growth or stress. The role and function that symptoms play in the context of individual families can vary depending on the therapist approach or the family itself.

Family theorists' perspectives on symptoms range from postulating that symptoms simply result from failed efforts to change behavior or functioning to pathology of symptoms serving to maintain family instability and pathology. Similarly, approaches to themes of underlying dynamics also vary from focusing on or attempting to uncover the underlying pathology believed to be present, to dealing only with desirable or undesirable surface behaviors through reinforcement. The concept of pathological triangles refers to the following three perspectives: those that occur intrapsychically; those occurring interpersonally in situations in which two individuals in conflict draw in a third for the purpose of creating intergenerational collusion against an individual family member; or those occurring environmentally, in which an unbalanced conflict between two family members results in an imbalance in the overall family structure.

Barriers to Family Participation in Schools

Contemporary family involvement efforts require school personnel to play a variety of roles within a collaborative-consultative framework. Models based on this premise have been proposed for school counselors to provide services to clients. These services include comprehensive parent education efforts such as parent drop-in programs, home visitor programs, and more formalized parent education programs (Fine & Gardner, 1991). This approach counters the more historical view of families being at fault for the problems by being more empowering (Fine, 1991; Nicoll, 1992). Despite the plethora of research substantiating the importance of family dynamics in the academic and behavioral adjustment

BOX 12.1

Family–Teacher Issues
Transition services address important career development and work-related behaviors. Too often, they are provided too late. Martha Orlando realized this was the case with her son, Tony, who was having difficulty adjusting to the work experience provided as part of his IEP transition plan.

Collaborative Orientations and Responsive Practices
Mrs. Orlando, with assistance from one of Tony's job coaches, prepared an article for the local newspaper. She described the importance of early vocational assessment, recognized local businesses that have supported the employment of young people with disabilities, and stressed the need for vocational preparation in elementary and middle school programs.

TABLE 12.1 *Barriers to Home–School Collaboration*

Here are some concerns that parents share when thinking about working with teachers:

- Sometimes parents believe they are not smart enough to talk with teachers.
- Sometimes parents have had bad experiences with teachers.
- Sometimes parents believe they will not be treated fairly at school.
- Often parents believe teachers are better suited to work with their children.
- Often financial pressures override other areas of concern for some parents.
- Sometimes parents see schools as unsafe environments.
- Sometimes parents are unable to come to school because they lack access to transportation.
- Sometimes work prevents parents from participating in school activities.

of children and adolescents, however, school personnel such as teachers and counselors who may be best suited to play this role of liaison between a number of key players comprising a child's world often carry an overall caseload and responsibilities which prohibit them from providing extensive services to any one family (Nicoll, 1992).

Because of the amendments signed into law in June 1997 (Clay, 1998), several changes may pose obstacles to as well as support for this push for parent involvement in their children's education (see Table 12.1). One such mandate is that parents participate as members of the team evaluating the child's eligibility for specific services. Because parents, educators, mental health professionals (e.g., school counselors, school psychologists), and administrators represent such differing views, this potential collaborative may be awkward or difficult in its initial formation.

Second, because the amendments continue to mandate that children receive special education in regular classrooms as much as possible, teachers providing these services will not necessarily have adequate training on how to work with students with special needs. Furthermore, personal barriers those individuals possess must be realized and need to be addressed (Clay, 1998). For example, individuals without specialized training have perhaps not had opportunities to examine their own biases and prejudices against children with special needs.

A final barrier to family participation is that parents often believe that a child's already low self-esteem will suffer more from an evaluation for special services. They also believe that members who are not having problems should not be responsible for correcting the problem of one child, rather, it is viewed as the individual child's problem (Hill, Parker, & Leimbeck, 1988).

Developing Family-Oriented Teachers

The relationship between families' emotional stress and children's school performance has long been established (Widerman & Widerman, 1995). Stress at home can result in peer relational difficulties, conduct disorders, substance abuse, depression, and hyperactivity.

Issues representing home stress include divorce or remarriage of one or more parent, intrafamilial violence or abuse, parental psychopathology, emotional disturbances, or alcoholism (Carlson & Hickman, 1992). While involvement of parents or guardians in the minimal protocol such as traditional parent–teacher associations or student teacher meetings has been shown to be ineffective in isolation, attempts to involve parents in more comprehensive ways must consider the following caveats.

Families are not always consulted at the appropriate time and do not always understand educational or mental health terminology. Second, such involvement is only mandated to occur once per year. Finally, collaborative relationships between educational personnel and parents of special needs children often are restricted to discussion of a specific classroom behavior or adherence to the law in terms of providing appropriate services for a specified disability. These problems in effective communication flow parallel to a medical model in which the institution is the "authority" (Carlson & Hickman, 1992), providing corrective prescriptions and follow-up visits, while parents are viewed as supporters in terms of helping with homework and other school-related activities. Current collaborative models that have proven effective for motivated parents include training parents in their roles as change agents, teachers, advocates, decision makers, and trainers.

Educators, at the same time, are charged with socializing, nurturing, and improving children by providing food, shelter, and safety, and by teaching roles and consequences (Carlson & Hickman, 1992). While traditional educational institutions also parallel families in terms of being open hierarchical systems with males generally representing the authority, and upper levels of decision making trickling down to the lower levels in the hierarchy, the new consultative models focus on a new set of goals. These include focusing on strengths versus pathology, empowering children and families, establishing collaborative partnerships, facilitating brief interventions, focusing on systems versus individuals, and facilitating small changes with the belief that larger changes will result.

Such legislation combats the independently traditional school and family approaches of setting up punishments as power struggles. In effect, childrens' punishment usually is ineffective and does not provide appropriate or accurate corrective action. A second obstacle is that many families view school via its academic function, so school personnel can serve by not only being supportive, but also by recognizing the need for services beyond simply meeting academic needs, and possibly referring families to appropriate family services.

Some practitioners have posed more consultation-based models (e.g., Carlson & Hickman, 1992; Fine, 1991; Nicoll, 1992) in which the teacher, family, and school counselor can meet at any stage of intervention for a learning, behavioral, or academic difficulty. Such models would pose a relatively low time commitment (two or three sessions), often enough to resolve or produce substantial change or to introduce families to a family counseling model, increasing the likelihood that they would pursue a longer-term family intervention in the community.

Such interventions enable teachers and parents to view the child's issues as inextricably related to an adult–child interaction pattern rather than the child's individual problem. Other similar interventions, some of a more extreme nature such as radical decentralization of administratively minded school boards, also have demonstrated an overall improvement of educational quality (e.g., Morrison, Olivos, Dominguez, Gomez, & Lena, 1993).

As a result of this evolution of society "blaming" the family for a child's difficulties to a more systems-focused perspective, several relatively recent sociopolitical movements have resulted in more compatibility between the goals of the key entities in children's worlds. This congruence calls for a definition of such players and the parts they play (Widerman & Widerman, 1995). It is believed that changes in these patterns of behavior, if handled appropriately, will lead to changes in interactions with classroom peers. One obstacle to including all of a child's family members is that siblings usually have other academic time commitments and parents usually have work commitments, but systemic intervention still can be effective when some members are absent, and in fact, sometimes the absences themselves promote discussion on the communication patterns present in the family.

What We Need to Know about Working Effectively with Families

Contemporary models involve school counselors and other school personnel adopting roles of advocate or mediator as well as that of counselor (e.g., Fine, 1991). Solution-focused, or brief therapy, approaches also are commonly adapted to school settings. One such model proposed by Carlson and Hickman (1992) involves the school counselor or other helping professionals facilitating a meeting of student, family, and teacher. Facilitation tasks include eliciting all points of view with active listening, summarizing, and validating, identifying problem and desired behaviors, building into the plan an acknowledgment of small improvements, and clarifying roles and responsibilities including accountability and follow-up.

Nicoll (1992) proposed another model that illustrates a step-by-step brief intervention to be used by counselors or other school personnel in assessment and consultation within the context of a parent–teacher meeting. The steps presented include focusing on the following:

1. Establishing the tone
2. Describing the school problem
3. Sibling constellation and parenting style
4. Typical day
5. Describing the home problem
6. Reframing or referring
7. School recommendation
8. Home recommendation
9. Terminating and scheduling follow-up

Such a comprehensive model can enhance time management of a parent–teacher conference as well as provide a format for including critical facets of students' academic and behavioral adjustment issues that often remain unacknowledged.

Current research on school personnel preparation programs indicates promise for some innovative practices. These include providing trainees with opportunities for cultural immersion, community experiences, family and community research, self-reflection, and interprofessional education. Such experiences also can be facilitated as ongoing or in-service training opportunities for teachers, counselors, and other school personnel.

Implications for Inclusion and New Teachers' Collaboration Practices in Schools and Classrooms

Having a child or relative with a disability can have a profound impact on a family (Batshaw, Perret, & Tractenberg, 1992). Positive, negative, and neutral effects are likely depending on the nature of the nuclear family. Successful families are supported by a reasonable mix of affection, financial independence, care, recreation, and education (Turnbull & Turnbull, 1997).

Studies of successful families consistently illustrate the value of caring, affection, and unconditional love while bringing up children (Turnbull & Turnbull, 1997). Although some siblings may express resentment, guilt, and embarrassment, many experience positive rewards from living with a brother or sister with a disability. These outcomes are clearly controlled by the relationships developed within the family and the household in which the child lives.

Similarly, raising a child with a disability adds financial costs to the family. Managing specialized diets, dealing with mobility concerns, providing medical care, addressing architectural needs, and providing specialized services are some factors creating potential monetary problems. Parents also sometimes have to consider the potential effects of lost income as a result of having to care for a child with a disability. Sometimes family members create concerns in other areas by taking second and third jobs to provide finances to support raising a child with a disability.

In many families, the care needs of all children are the same; however, assistance with daily living and the increased possibility of an occasional crisis may create conditions that impact families of children with disabilities (Turnbull & Turnbull, 1997). Simple activities like finding a babysitter or getting ready for school become significant events in the lives of families living with a child with a severe disability, and creating a circle of friends or participating in social relations can become very difficult.

Sometimes families are forced to create special recreation times to accommodate the special needs of a child with a disability. Alternatively, they may seek out and participate in specially organized activities unavailable to other families, but this may limit opportunities for getting to know their neighbors without disabilities.

Families of children with disabilities also often feel more responsible for teaching their children, for making sure their children receive appropriate services, and for working toward creating as normal a life as possible. These added educational concerns create stresses that are often not experienced by families of children without disabilities. Regardless of the mix of factors associated with positive, negative, and neutral outcomes, most families experience similar stages of reactions and adaptations in living with children with disabilities.

Family Reactions and Adaptations

It is natural for parents to want their children to be the best and the brightest. When they first learn that a child has a disability, they often see their hopes and dreams crash. The most common reaction is a combination of shock, disbelief, guilt, and a profound feeling of loss (Singer & Irvin, 1989). With time, however, most families proceed through a series of stages of grieving similar to those described by Kubler-Ross (1969), including denial, depression, anger, guilt, bargaining, and acceptance.

Denial and Depression.   Typically, parents of a child with a disability deny the diagnosis. They often think the doctor has made a mistake and, consequently, they may engage in varying levels of "doctor shopping" in attempts to find opinions that they believe are more optimistic. This can lead parents to a better understanding of their child's disability and needs; however, it can also lead to confusion and delays in obtaining needed assistance. Once disbelief and denial have worn off, some family members experience a period of extreme fatigue, loss of appetite, restlessness, and irritability commonly associated with depression. Social isolation during this time can also be a problem; at a time when needs for support are heightened, extended family members and friends may be least likely to provide it. Typically, such depression improves over time, but it may become chronic when the passage of life events creates increasing pressures and problems for particular children with disabilities. In working with families, it helps to understand their need for assurance in any disability diagnosis.

Anger and Guilt.   At some point, many of these parents are angry and they search for someone or something to blame. Sometimes they blame themselves and other times they blame others (e.g., professionals who don't provide answers). Parents of children with disabilities may experience problems with their own self-esteem if they believe their genetic makeup or behavior caused the disability. When poverty or other social and cultural challenges are part of family life, resentment and fault can be even stronger issues for parents to address. Being responsive to a family's need to express and deal with anger and guilt is an important step in developing a supportive and collaborative relationship.

Bargaining and Acceptance.   Frustration and failure are sometimes evident when families go through a stage of searching for alternative treatments as a result of their need for social bargaining. They acknowledge their child's disability, but are not willing to accept it without first trying to make it go away. Ultimately, however, families and their children are better served by accepting the disability and going about the business of redirecting energies toward successfully handling its natural needs and consequences.

Stages of Need

Family needs change over time. For most families, the early childhood years are full of opportunities for learning and developing. Early school years add additional adventures and adolescence creates a world of its own. Achieving independence can provide families and adult children with a strong sense of accomplishment. These stages also represent challenges for families of children with disabilities.

Preschool Years.   After a disability diagnosis, most parents' first concern is finding treatment as soon as possible. Public law (i.e., the Individuals with Disabilities Education Act) provides a structure for making special education services available for preschool age children. Early intervention typically focuses on promoting language and motor skills for children and supporting positive interactions within families.

Early School Years.   Entering organized school programs creates a whole new set of challenges. Families of students with disabilities often are faced with issues related to expectations and appropriateness of schooling. Negative attitudes from professionals and other families represent obstacles that make difficult times tougher. Similarly, making decisions about where and under what conditions education will be provided is not a simple task for families of children with disabilities. Turnbull and Turnbull (1997) offer a perspective supported by many parents:

- Schools should value all children and include them in all experiences of schooling.
- Life involves interacting with individuals of different backgrounds, abilities, and experiences. Schools are an excellent environment for preparing for life.
- Students with disabilities belong in age-appropriate classrooms with their natural neighbors and peers.
- Students with disabilities have a right to free, appropriate education designed to meet their individual needs.

Adolescent Years.   Adolescence can be difficult for any child, and for children with disabilities the challenges are often severe. Peer group pressures, needs for independence, and heightened social interactions create opportunities for growth and development. Self-image and self-control are often a reflection of the impressions of others. Fragile personality characteristics sometimes common in individuals with disabilities are particularly susceptible and vulnerable to sometimes brutal honesty and deviance offered by teenagers and young adults. Adolescence is also a critical time for developing abilities to function independently as an adult. Adolescents with disabilities who have difficulties with independent behavior are likely to remain dependent as adults. Because of limitations imposed by disabilities, some adolescents have difficulties in social interactions and may have less-developed social skills than their peers. Families should be encouraged to give their children needed freedom while carefully monitoring and managing their needs for age-appropriate social interaction.

Adult Years.   The transition to adulthood has traditionally been difficult for families and individuals with disabilities. Achieving a quality life with opportunities for living, working, and playing in communities with neighbors and peers without disabilities has been encouraged by efforts to teach competitive and supported employment and living skills as part of high school special education programs. Of course, continuing issues related to competence and residence face families of children with disabilities with more salience and immediacy than they do for other families. This is a time when support is most needed and often least accessible.

The nature of a disability can influence a family's reaction to it. Children with complex medical conditions have higher illness-specific needs that require more adaptations in family routines. Other disabilities create concerns that relate more to social and behavioral challenges. Each disability creates different needs to connect and collaborate with specialists, teachers, and other families to muster support and foster success in overcoming life's challenges.

Helping Families in Need

As stated throughout this text, increasing parental involvement in the education of their children is a fundamental goal of the Individuals with Disabilities Education Act (IDEA), extant federal legislation (P.L. 105-17) signed by the president on June 4, 1997, and designed to help children with disabilities achieve a free, appropriate education. Families are viewed and supported as increasingly important partners in this process. There are many ways new teachers and other school personnel can help families better cope with a child's disability: first, by helping to change perceptions; second, by collaborating in planning individualized educational programs; third, by encouraging and supporting family-centered practices; and, fourth, by monitoring progress of family-centered practices.

Changing Perceptions.   Perceptions are the ways people view their lives and the lives of those around them. Changing perceptions can have very positive effects on people's experiences. According to the Beach Center on Families and Disabilities (1997d), families buying into several of the following four perceptions tend to function better and to benefit from higher levels of functioning:

1. *The view that special needs exist because of specific causes or reasons*—When parents attribute a disability to something they (or some professional) did or did not do, they feel more in control of the situation. Helping them identify a cause often gives them strength to deal with the disability.
2. *The view that some things that happen can be controlled*—If parents think they can do something, they are more likely to do it. Information provides support and with support comes mastery and power. Joining advocacy and support groups, keeping up-to-date, being involved in their children's lives, and taking direct action make all parents, especially those of children with disabilities, feel better about their lives.
3. *The view that others are living comparable lives*—Some parents compare themselves to others who seem to be doing well; this provides a positive model. Others compare themselves to others doing about the same as they are; this offers affiliation and additional positive social comparison. Comparing themselves with people whose lives are more difficult can also provide perception-changing information and support.
4. *The view that a child with special needs contributes positively to family life*—Changing perceptions from viewing a child with a disability as a burden to viewing the child as a contribution can significantly improve the overall outlook in a family. Helping parents identify positive contributions is the first step in helping children with disabilities to be viewed favorably in any family.

Collaborating in Education Planning.   The Individualized Education Program (IEP) sets out a plan for meeting the needs of students with disabilities (Beach Center on Families and Disabilities, 1997a, b; Ysseldyke & Algozzine, 1994). Typically, a service coordinator is responsible for matters related to planning the IEP. IDEA directs that parents actively participate in IEP planning, and meetings are typically organized to facilitate this participation. Before the meeting, parents should be contacted for input on their time preferences and other needs. The meeting should take place at a convenient time and place for them. If necessary, they should be offered assistance with transportation, child care, or other needs. A letter should be sent to them informing of the date, time, place, participants, and meeting agenda. The goal is for parents to feel welcome in a collaborative educational meeting with direct and important consequences for their child. At the meeting, all participants should be greeted and introduced. Name tags should be provided to facilitate communication. The purpose of the meeting should be explained by the service coordinator and input from participants should be controlled to encourage collaboration and active joining in by parents.

Encouraging Family-Centered Practices.   In traditional health care, the child with a disability, not the family, was the focus of professional practice. Recently, family-centered practices have become more popular (cf. Friesen & Koroloff, 1997; Koroloff & Friesen, 1997; Turnbull & Turnbull, 1997). After reviewing extensive literature, Beach Center researchers came up with the following definition (Allen & Petr, 1995; Beach Center on Families and Disability, 1997c, p. 2):

> Family-centered service delivery, across disciplines and settings, recognizes the centrality of the family in the lives of individuals. It is guided by fully informed choices made by the family and focuses upon the strengths and capabilities of these families.

When families are given what they want and need, their power is enhanced. Family-centered practices and policies are not restricted to the health care or disability fields. Counseling, social work, education, psychology, sociology, occupational therapy, and related disciplines also are focusing on this form of service delivery.

The key components of family-centered practice include (Beach Center on Families and Disability, 1997c, p. 1):

- Focusing on the family as the unit of attention
- Organizing assistance collaboratively (e.g., ensuring mutual respect and teamwork between team workers and clients)
- Organizing assistance in accordance with each individual family's wishes so that the family ultimately directs decision making
- Considering family strengths (versus dwelling on family deficiencies)
- Addressing family needs holistically (rather than focusing on a member with a "problem")
- Individualizing family services
- Giving families information in a supportive manner
- Normalizing perspectives (i.e., recognizing that much of what those receiving services are experiencing is typical)
- Structuring service delivery to ensure accessibility, minimal disruption of family integrity and routine

Family-centered care providers acknowledge that each family member influences the family as a whole. The behavior, characteristics, and resources of one member influence other family members as well. Family-centered professionals look hard for the strengths—the talents, resources, attributes, and aspirations—of each family member. Service providers become consultants who provide families with information that empowers them to make their own decisions. Information is actively shared and everyone involved with the child collaborates in final decisions. Benefits of this approach include improvements in the following areas (Beach Center on Families and Disability, 1997c, p. 2–3):

- Child functioning
- Parent skills and emotional well-being
- Parents' view of service effectiveness and sense of control over their child's care
- Problem solving
- Ability of families to care for their child at home
- Service delivery
- Cost-effectiveness
- Family empowerment

Promoting Change and Promising Outcomes

The following case study follows Nicoll's (1992) Family Counseling and Consultation Model for School Counselors, representing one of the most comprehensive approaches in the field, and illustrates some fundamental principles for working effectively with parents. The model, presented earlier in this chapter, includes establishing the tone, describing the school problems, identifying sibling constellation and parenting style, describing a typical day, describing the home problem, reframing or relabeling, making school recommendations, making home recommendations, termination, and follow-up.

Timmy Jones has just entered the sixth grade in a neighborhood middle school. Prior to enrolling in the middle school, Timmy's grades were in the A-to-B range. His grades started out in the same range in the beginning of this academic year but have fallen dramatically within the first several months. His father, with whom Timmy lives, became concerned when he received the midsemester report and noted that the grades were almost all in the D-to-F range. He has requested a parent–teacher meeting with the three teachers in whose classes Timmy is receiving F grades. The school counselor, Ms. Nelson, was asked to facilitate the meeting between Mr. Jones and Teachers A, B, and C, Timmy, and herself. In addition, Ms. Nelson requested the attendance of Ms. Jones, with whom Timmy lives every other weekend.

In establishing the tone of the meeting, Ms. Nelson reminds herself that the outcome of the meeting is not a reflection on her personal skills as a counselor, but rather, that the focus should remain on Timmy's difficulties in school. Next, she establishes contact with each parent to find a meeting time that is convenient for all involved. In making this contact, she asks Mr. and Ms. Jones to become involved as consultants to help the school work with Timmy on his academic difficulty issues more effectively, rather than talk to them about what they are doing wrong. Finally, because Ms. Jones chose not to be involved in the meeting, Ms. Nelson decided to include only one of the teachers involved, so that Mr. Jones would not be drastically outnumbered in the meeting, and planned to consult with each of the other teachers after the meeting. She ensures that comfortable seating is available for each member of the consultation team and that the seats are not separated by desks or tables. At the meeting, she suggests that first names be used in order to promote equality and collegiality. Along the same lines, she reiterates that while no one is responsible for Timmy's problems, all are responsible for helping him within their respective roles.

Ms. Nelson begins the meeting by asking the teacher to explain the classroom problems that she sees occurring in Timmy's case. In preparing for the meeting, she had asked the teacher to think about the issues in behavioral terms, so that he would describe the child's *behavior* rather than the *child*. For example, the teacher might explain the situation as follows: "I asked Timmy why he wasn't paying attention. Timmy responded by shrugging his shoulders. I then reprimanded him for not being more enthusiastic. After it all, I felt frustrated about the incident." Ideally, in describing the situation in these terms, teachers are aided in realizing how their own behavior might serve to reinforce a child's behavior.

Next, Ms. Nelson asked Mr. Jones to describe Timmy's respective living situations. To help them get started, she asked them to describe a typical day, including the activities of all members in the household. Mr. Jones began by explaining that Timmy and his sister, who is two years younger than he, both wake up about 6 A.M. Timmy often has trouble getting out of bed and is prodded by his father or his sister. He generally chooses not to eat breakfast, although his sister does. Mr. Jones has only three living relatives; his sister and her two five-year-old twin daughters, who live in a nearby city and are involved in most holiday and vacation activities. All of Timmy's grandparents and Timmy's uncle have died in the past five years, including his maternal grandmother, who just died several months ago. Mr. Jones drives his children to and from school because although their schools are local, the bus rides are long. After the children come home from school, they play in the neighborhood, then they go out for dinner, and then they come home in time for Mr. Jones to help them with their homework. Mr. Jones does explain that on alternating weekends, both children live with their mother, who has three other younger children from a subsequent marriage. His impression is that both Timmy and his sister are asked to help with the household management there.

Ms. Nelson then asks Mr. Jones whether he perceives Timmy as having any similar issues at home as those described by the teacher. Mr. Jones described Timmy's behavior at home to be "unfocused" and "fidgety," especially during homework sessions, and shares that he becomes easily frustrated with his son under those circumstances.

During the course of the teacher's and Mr. Jones's description of the classroom and home situations, Ms. Nelson formulates her hypotheses. She believes that, from the classroom account, Timmy does not take responsibility for his work. This is reinforced by the attention he receives from the teacher. At home, the same situation seems to be occurring. Possibly because Mr. Jones has no other close family, he tends to overprotect Timmy, even to the extent of doing his homework projects for him, thereby not holding Timmy accountable for his own work and rewarding his lack of involvement with additional attention. This lack of responsibility, while representing a behavior *chosen* by Timmy, may simultaneously be frustrating for him. While at his mother's home, he is given and accepts considerably more responsibility. The attention he receives in response to his maladaptive behaviors also helps him to feel more secure with his very small (and becoming smaller) family network.

Ms. Nelson helps to relabel and reframe the presenting problem in practical terms. For example, rather than labeling Timmy as irresponsible or unmotivated, she describes him as being frustrated by the reinforcement he receives for his under-functioning behavior in the settings in which he spends the most time (i.e., his primary home and his school).

In developing an alternative view, teachers and parents can begin to focus on series' of small behavior changes that ultimately should result in larger, more long-term ones. In this situation, because the issue seems to overlap both school and home, Ms. Nelson asks each key player to address a different part of the problem, but is careful not to recommend more than one primary and concise recommendation for each. In addition, the goal of effective interventions is to increase positive behaviors versus focusing on problematic ones. For example, she asks the teacher to reinforce Timmy when he is actively involved in classroom activities by soliciting his input. She asks Mr. Jones to praise Timmy's active homework behavior rather than to offer to do it for him.

Ms. Nelson then summarizes the session, asking all team members to participate by sharing their insights or perspectives gained from the consultation. She then writes out the intervention and gives each member a copy. A follow-up meeting is scheduled for two weeks later.

Tips for New Teachers' Work with Parents

Parents are increasingly viewed as important partners in successful education programs. In writing P.L. 94-142 and subsequently renaming and amending it in the Individuals with Disabilities Education Act (IDEA), members of Congress created safeguards for students with disabilities and their parents (cf. Ysseldyke, Algozzine, and Thurlow, 2000). Strengthening the role of parents and ensuring that families of children with disabilities have meaningful opportunities to participate in their education at school and at home has always been a part of special education legislation and practice. The most recent IDEA amendments (P.L. 105-17) and reauthorization have substantially increased the intent and directives for parent involvement (Yell, 1998). The following suggestions are based on best practices for working effectively with parents.

1. *Maintain a supportive role in all interactions.* Help families identify specific school problems and appropriate interventions. Avoid placing blame unless doing so leads to a corrective action that will be immediate and positive. Focus on identifying solutions rather than admiring or enjoying the problem.
2. *Focus on the child's behavior, not the child.* Changing behavior is evidence of learning and parents expect teachers and school personnel to help children learn. Help parents understand that behavior is an important aspect of schooling, just as important as reading, mathematics, or other academic content.
3. *Families are more likely to be involved when interventions are manageable and easy to monitor.* When formulating behavior change plans, start with several specific activities rather than a global one designed to bring about dramatic change.
4. *Focus on family strengths.* Develop interventions that increase the capacity of all family members to solve problems in partnerships with school personnel. Avoid situations in which primary responsibility for change is placed on a single individual.

5. *Monitor frequently and share information with the child and his family.* When providing feedback, focus on positive changes rather than continuing deficiencies.

Family Member Questions

The following questions may be addressed to new teachers during school-based conferences.

• *We have been told that parents are often the best advocates for their children. What can we do to identify, initiate, and implement positive changes in our child's education?* The Coordinated Campaign for Learning Disabilities (CCLD) provides the following tips to help parents develop advocacy skills:

  • **Know the rules.** All public schools abide by specific laws and regulations, which provide special services for children with learning disabilities who qualify for such services. The criteria for eligibility varies from state to state, but all schools must adhere to a minimum federal standard. To find out the laws in your state and your rights as a parent, contact your local school district office, or state Department of Education.

  • **Get to know the people who make decisions about your child's education.** Connect with educators and administrators in both casual and formal settings. Talk with your child's teacher on a regular basis. If possible, volunteer in the classroom and help out with school functions. If you have concerns or problems that a teacher cannot or will not address, be willing to follow the chain of command through the school, and if necessary, to the district office. Remember that you as a parent have the right to request that the school evaluate your child if you think he or she may have a learning disability. Be sure that your request is in writing.

  • **Keep records.** Parents should maintain an organized file of educational records and assessment information. Take notes during telephone and face-to-face meetings, and ask for people's full names and contact information when communicating by phone or by e-mail. In addition, keeping less-formal examples of children's academic progress, such as homework papers, artwork, and writings, may be useful in establishing patterns and documenting both abilities and challenges.

  • **Gather information.** Read books and articles on learning, attend conferences, and join a parent support group or affiliate organization in your area. Get comfortable with education acronyms and jargon. Ask professionals lots of questions, and don't be afraid to ask for clarification if their answers are confusing or complicated.

  • **Communicate effectively.** Come to meetings prepared, and know the specific outcomes you want. Be clear, calm, and direct when speaking and put things in writing whenever possible. Listen, and take time to think about pertinent information. Consider when documentation or data might help your case, and present it in an orderly and readable format. While assertiveness and persistence are crucial, anger and aggressiveness can work against you and can damage important relationships.

  • **Know your child's strengths and interests and share them with educators.** By highlighting a struggling child's capabilities and talents, you not only help professionals know your child as a whole person, you can also assist in identifying learning accommodations.

- **Emphasize solutions.** Although there are no miracle cures or magic bullets for learning disabilities, it's important to stress the positive, and to help identify ways to improve your child's experience. Once appropriate programs have been identified and agreed on, make every effort to encourage follow-through.
- **Focus on the big picture.** Simply put, don't sweat the small stuff. Knowing the specifics of a law may be important on one level, but constantly arguing technicalities can ultimately waste time and inhibit rapport. Try not to take things personally, and always consider both sides of the story. Details are important, but don't let them get in the way of negotiating the best educational experience for your child.
- **Involve your child in decision making as early as you can.** Learning disabilities are a life-long issue. Mastering self-advocacy skills is one of the keys to becoming a successful adult. Resist the natural urge to pave every road for your child, and respect and support your child's need to take informed academic risks. [Available online at www.ldonline. org/ld_indepth/parenting/ccld_advocacy.html]

- *As our daughter gets older, her medical needs are becoming more complex. We want to find a doctor who can help us. What should we do?* Check your local Parent Information Center for a list of physicians with experience and expertise in working with young people with disabilities. Make some direct contacts with doctors before actually bringing your child for a visit. In "A Parent's Guide To Doctors, Disabilities, and the Family," Suzanne Ripley offers the following questions to ask on the phone when interviewing doctors:

1. Do you see children with disabilities in your practice?
2. Do you have experience with children who have (describe your child's disability)?
3. Would you be comfortable working in a medical team situation with other doctors who will be seeing my child?
4. Can you schedule extra-long appointments?
5. Who sees your patients when you are not available?
6. Which hospital do you use for patients who require hospitalization or hospital tests?
7. What are the facilities of this hospital for children and families like mine? If my child were hospitalized, would I be allowed to stay with her?
8. After you've examined my child, can you arrange for one of your staff to watch him for a few minutes so we can talk alone?
9. Would there be any additional charges for any of these arrangements?
   [Available from National Information Center for Children and Youth with Disabilities (NICHCY), P.O. Box 1492, Washington, DC 20013, 1-800-695-0285]

Family Resources and Services

Important family resources and services are summarized here.

Children and Adults with Attention Deficit Disorder (CH.A.D.D.)
499 N.W. 70th Avenue, Suite 101
Plantation, Florida, USA, 33317
(305) 587-3700

(800) 233-4050
(305) 587-4599 (FAX)

CH.A.D.D. is a national organization working toward helping children and adults with ADD achieve success. CH.A.D.D. publishes a regular newsletter, and an expanded magazine-style publication covering the latest developments in ADD research, diagnosis, and treatment. There is also a Fact Sheet series and regular updates on breaking news. On the state level CH.A.D.D. is developing ADD councils to help local and state school systems implement the U.S. Department of Education Federal Policy on ADD, which tells schools how to serve students with attention deficit disorders through IDEA and section 504 of the Rehabilitation Act.

Beach Center on Families and Disability
311 Haworth
University of Kansas
Lawrence, KS, 66045
(913) 864-7600
www.Isi.uknas.edu/beach/beachhp.htm

Funded by the National Institute on Disability and Rehabilitation Research (NIDRR) of the U.S. Department of Education, the Center offers newsletters, advocacy how-to publications, opportunities for parents to make connections with other parents of children with disabilities, and information on coping strategies for a disability diagnosis and laws that affect families.

Parent to Parent Program
Beach Center
(913) 864-7600

Using mutual support, veteran parents of children with disabilities offer emotional and informational support to rookie parents in one-to-one matches. Beach Center provides information about local programs.

PEAK Parent Center
6055 Lehman Drive, # 101
Colorado Springs, CO 80910
(719) 531-9400

Provides information and support regarding inclusion of students with disabilities.

National Information Center for Children and Youth with Disabilities
(800) 695-0285

Provides publications, such as fact sheets on specific disabilities, state resource listings, and booklets.

Educational Resources Information Center Clearinghouse on Disabilities and Gifted Education
(800) 601-4868

An excellent source of information including free publications that summarize research findings.

Exceptional Parent
(800) 247-8080

Excellent magazine covering families and disabilities. Has the section "Parent Search and Parent Respond" for parents to contact each other for information and other needs.

A Guide to Thoughtful Friendships: Facilitation for Education and Families
by C. Beth Schaffner and Barbara Buswell
Available from the PEAK Parent Center
6055 Lehman Drive
Suite 101
Colorado Springs, CO 80918

Summary

Families are playing prominent roles in the educational lives of children. From providing information about current levels of functioning to cooperating with teachers and other school personnel in implementing interventions, parents and other family members are active collaborators. Teachers have found that focusing on strengths rather than weakness, empowering children and families to be active partners, and facilitating small, meaningful changes rather than large, difficult-to-manage ones facilitates successful school–family collaboration.

Studies of successful families consistently illustrate the importance of appropriate care, affection, and unconditional love in bringing up children. Sometimes reactions to a child with a disability work against a family's positive qualities. School personnel understanding these responses and the different stages of need these families go through are better able to provide continuing support.

Information is power and in the future it will be controlled by technology. New teachers and other professionals need access to the massive amounts of information available. The Beach Center on Families and Disability (913-864-7600) provides several methods for accessing information; other similar clearinghouse resources are available as well (e.g., ERIC Clearinghouse on Disabilities and Gifted Education, 800-328-0272; National Information Center for Children and Youth with Disabilities, 800-695-0285).

References

Allen, R. I., & Petr, C. G. (1995). *Family-centered service delivery: A cross-disciplinary literature review and conceptualization.* Lawrence, KS: University of Kansas, Beach Center on Families and Disability.

Batshaw, M. L., Perret, Y. M., & Tractenberg, S. W. (1992). Caring and coping: The family of a child with disabilities. In M. L. Batshaw & Y. M. Perret, *Children with disabilities: A medical primer (pp. 563–578).* Baltimore: Paul M. Brookes Publishing Company.

Beach Center on Families and Disabilities. (1997a). *Collaborate with the family in individualized education planning.* www.lsi.ukans.edu/beach/html.6i.htm.

Beach Center on Families and Disabilities. (1997b). Family-centered service delivery. *Families and Disability Newsletter, 8* (2), 1–3.

Beach Center on Families and Disabilities. (1997c). *Get a family-friendly IFSP.* www.lsi.ukans.edu/beach/html.1i.htm.

Beach Center on Families and Disabilities. (1997d). *How to better cope with a family member's disability.* www.lsi.ukans.edu/beach/html.1c.htm.

Carlson, C., & Hickman, J. (1992). Family consultation in schools in special services. *Special Services in the Schools, 6* (¾), 83–112.

Cashwell, C. S. (1995). Family functioning and self-esteem of middle-school students: A matter of perspective? *Journal of Humanistic Education and Development, 34,* 83–91.

Cashwell, C. S., & Nassar-McMillan, S. C. (1997). Family functioning and peer relationships: Influences on adolescent drug use. *Journal of At-Risk Issues,* 30–35.

Clay, R. A. (1998). New laws aid children with disabilities. *APA Monitor, 29* (1), 19.

Fine, M. J., & Gardner, T. R. (1991). Facilitating home-school relationships: A family-oriented approach to collaborative consultation. *Journal of Educational and Psycholgical Consultation, 1,* 169–187.

Friesen, B. J., & Koroloff, N. M. (1997). Family-centered mental health services research: Introduction to part II. *Journal of Emotional and Behavioral Disorders, 5* (4), 194–195.

Gonzalez, V., Brusca-Vega, R., & Yawkey, T. (1997). *Assessment and instruction of culturally and linguistically diverse students with or at-risk of learning problems.* Boston, MA: Allyn and Bacon.

Hill, J. W., Parker, T., & Leimbeck, J. (1988). Family self-esteem at the crisis apex before one family member's special education evaluation and the family's therapy assessment. *Family Therapy, 15* (2), 175–184.

Koroloff, N. M., & Friesen, B. J. (1997). Challenges in conducting family-centered mental health services research. *Journal of Emotional and Behavioral Disorders, 5* (3), 130–137.

Kubler-Ross, E. (1969). *On death and dying.* New York: Macmillan.

Morrison, J. A., Olivos, K., Dominguez, G., Gomez, D., & Lena, D. (1993). The application of family systems approaches to school behavior problems on a school-level discipline board: An outcome study. *Elementary School Guidance and Counseling, 27,* 258–272.

Nicoll, W. G. (1992). A family counseling and consultation model for school counselors. *School Counselor, 39,* 351–361.

Nichols, M. P., & Schwartz, R. C. (1995). *Family therapy: Concepts and methods* (3rd ed.). Needham Heights, MA: Allyn and Bacon.

Peeks, B. (1993). Revolutions in counseling and education: A systems perspective in the schools. *Elementary School Guidance and Counseling, 27,* 245–251.

Piercy, F. P., Sprenkle, D. H., & Associates. (1986). *Family therapy sourcebook.* NY: Guilford Press.

Singer, G. H. S., & Irvin, L. K. (1989). *Support for caregiving families: Enabling positive adaptation to disability.* Baltimore: Paul M. Brookes.

Turnbull, A. P., & Turnbull, H. R. III. (1997). *Families, professionals, and exceptionalities: A special partnership.* Columbus, OH: Merrill/Prentice Hall.

Widerman, J. L., & Widerman, E. (1995). Family systems-oriented school counseling. *School Counselor, 43,* 67–72.

Woody, R. H. (1994). Legislation for children with disabilities: Family therapy under Public Law 101-467. *American Journal of Family Therapy, 22* (1), 77–82.

Yell, M. L. (1998). *The law and special education.* Upper Saddle River, NJ: Prentice Hall.

Ysseldyke, J. E., & Algozzine, B. (1994). *Special education: A practical approach for teachers.* Boston, MA: Houghton Mifflin.

Ysseldyke, J. E., Algozzine, B., & Thurlow, M. L. (2000). *Critical issues in special education* (3rd ed.). Boston: Houghton Mifflin.

Index